Table of Contents

Other Books by the Author

Afterlife – What Will It Be Like?
Answer the Call – Finding Life's Purpose
Be Holy and Come Near– A Devotional Study of Leviticus
Behold the Saviour
Be Angry and Sin Not
Conquest and the Life of Rest – A Devotional Study of Joshua
Door of Hope – A Devotional Study of the Minor Prophets
Exploring the Pauline Epistles
Forsaken, Forgotten, and Forgiven – A Devotional Study of Jeremiah
Glories Seen & Unseen
Hallowed Be Thy Name – Revering Christ in a Casual World
Hiding God – The Ambition of World Religion
In Search of God – A Quest for Truth
Infidelity and Loyalty – A Devotional Study of Ezekiel and Daniel
Knowing the All-Knowing
Managing Anger God's Way
Mind Frames – Where Life's Battle Is Won or Lost
Out of Egypt – A Devotional Study of Exodus
Overcoming Your Bully
Passing the Torch – Mentoring the Next Generation For Christ
Relativity and Redemption – A Devotional Study of Judges and Ruth
Revive Us Again – A Devotional Study of Ezra, Nehemiah, and Esther
Seeds of Destiny – A Devotional Study of Genesis
Sorrow and Comfort – A Devotional Study of Isaiah
The Beginning of Wisdom – A Devotional Study of Job, Psalms, Proverbs,
    Ecclesiastes, and Song of Solomon
The Bible: Myth or Divine Truth?
The Evil Nexus – Are You Aiding the Enemy?
The Fruitful Bough – Affirming Biblical Manhood
The Fruitful Vine – Celebrating Biblical Womanhood
The Hope of Glory – A Preview of Things to Come
The Kings – A Devotional Study of Kings and Chronicles
The Olive Plants – Raising Spiritual Children
Your Home the Birthing Place of Heaven

A Heart for God

A DEVOTIONAL STUDY
OF 1 AND 2 SAMUEL

WARREN HENDERSON

All Scripture quotations are from the New King James Version of the Bible, unless otherwise noted. Copyright © 1982 by Thomas Nelson, Inc. Nashville, TN

A Heart for God – A Devotional Study of 1 and 2 Samuel

By Warren Henderson
Copyright © 2019

Cover Design by Benjamin Bredeweg

Published by Warren A. Henderson
3769 Indiana Road
Pomona, KS 66076

Editing/Proofreading: Keith Keyser,
    Marilyn MacMullen, Dan Macy,
    and David Lindstrom

Perfect Bound ISBN: 978-1-939770-52-3
eBook ISBN: 978-1-939770-53-0

ORDERING INFORMATION:
Copies of *A Heart for God* are available through www.amazon.com/shops/hendersonpublishing or www.order@gospelfolio.com (1-800-952-2382), and many online retailers.

Preface

First and Second Samuel trace the lives of three Jewish men residing in Israel during the eleventh century B.C.: Samuel, the last of the judges and the first of the prophets; Saul, the first of the kings, but rejected by God; and David, the beloved shepherd-king. Hannah, whose name means *grace*, "asked of the Lord" (the meaning of Samuel's name) and received a male child who would greatly bless the Jewish nation. Samuel was a Nazarite from birth and consecrated his entire life to selflessly serving the Lord's people.

Saul's name means "asked for," but he was not given in grace, but rather in God's anger to teach His wayward people the ills of trusting a human ruler instead of Himself. Saul was a man after the flesh who permitted his carnal passions to guide his behavior, rather than submitting to God's word and control. Thankfully, God's solution for what Israel really needed in a king was answered in *the beloved*, the meaning of David's name. Our solution to all life's difficulties is also found in God's Beloved – the Greater David, the Lord Jesus Christ:

And suddenly a voice came from heaven, saying, "This is My beloved Son, in whom I am well pleased" (Matt. 3:17).

Having predestined us to adoption as sons by Jesus Christ to Himself, according to the good pleasure of His will, to the praise of the glory of His grace, by which He made us accepted in the Beloved (Eph. 1:5-6).

Through Saul's forty-year reign, God taught His people the painful consequences of living in the flesh instead of relying on His grace provided in His beloved. They should have desired a "man of God" who delighted in the Lord and His Law to lead them, rather than an unproven, "choice young man." The Lord had just such a man in mind, a faithful shepherd boy from Bethlehem in Judah. Spiritually speaking, David is everything that Saul is not, and more. In a coming day,

1

David's greater Son, the incarnate Son of God, will exercise through His own death and resurrection a greater kingship than David's because all who trust in Him will also reign through and with Him forever!

A Heart for God is a "commentary style" devotional which upholds the glories of Christ while exploring the books of 1 and 2 Samuel within the context of the whole of Scripture. I have endeavored to include in this book some of the principal gleanings from other writers. *A Heart for God* contains dozens of brief devotions. This format allows the reader to use the book either as a daily devotional or as a reference source for deeper study.

— Warren Henderson

Overview of 1 and 2 Samuel

The Author

The two books of Samuel are one in the Jewish Talmud and the Hebrew manuscripts. The book was first divided in Alexandria in the third century B.C. to maintain a conventional scroll size for the Septuagint version of the Old Testament. Samuel may have penned the portion of the book occurring before his death (1 Sam. 25:1). It is unknown who either completed the work or perhaps authored the entire book with input from Samuel directly or from his writings later.

The fifteenth-century Jewish historian Abarbanel has suggested that either Nathan or Gad performed this service, while Goldman insists that Jeremiah compiled the writings of all three prophets (Samuel, Nathan, and Gad) centuries later.[1] The author may have been one of the young prophets studying under Samuel, who later included the writings of his teacher into his work. Another possible author is Abiathar, who was with David during the majority of the events recorded in the book and, as a priest, would have been well trained in accurate documentation.

Date

The books of Samuel cover approximately 130 years beginning at about 1100 B.C. when Samuel was born to the time of David's death in 970 B.C. The references to Israel and Judah as separate entities throughout the book (11:8, 15:4, 17:52, 18:16) may indicate that it was not written until after the nation divided in 931 B.C. (after Solomon's death). Phrases like "to this day" (e.g., 5:5, 6:18, 27:6) and "formerly in Israel" (9:9) convey the parenthetical tone of a historical explanation, rather than an autobiographic narrative. As the Assyrian captivity of the northern tribes is not mentioned, the book undoubtedly was written before 722 B.C.

Theme

First and Second Samuel record Israel's transition from a theocracy administered by Jehovah's judges to a monarchal system of government. Israel's repetitive cycle of declension, distress, and deliverance recorded in Judges continues throughout the life of Samuel, Israel's fifteenth and final judge. Samuel and Israel's first king, Saul, shared a coregency of sorts for about 18 years, but no lasting spiritual change occurred in Israel until God's beloved David, a man after His own heart, was seated on Israel's throne. He united the nation under Jehovah's rule, ushered in an era of economic prosperity, brought Israel's enemies into subjection, and excited the nation to build a temple to testify of Jehovah's greatness among the nations.

Outline

The Era of the Judges Ends (1 Sam. 1-12)
The Era of the Kings Begins (1 Sam. 13-31)
The Best King Is Crowned (2 Sam. 1-24)

Summary of David's Life

After David, about fifteen years old, slew Goliath, he lived in Saul's palace at Gibeah for about seven years (1 Sam. 17:45-18:2). From the age of 22 to 30, David was either on the run from King Saul or was dwelling among the Philistines in Ziklag (1 Sam. 27:7). In his fugitive years during Saul's reign, David wrote several psalms, ten of which address this crisis directly; the likely order of these poems is: 7, 59, 56, 34, 52, 63, 54, 18, 57, and 142. In all, Saul made fourteen recorded attempts on David's life.

Unfortunately, while dwelling at Ziklag, David lapsed spiritually and engaged in gruesome covert raids on villages; there is no evidence that David composed any psalms during this time. At the age of thirty (after Saul's death) he began to reign over Judah in Hebron. Seven years later he captured Jerusalem from the Jebusites and was subsequently anointed king over all the tribes of Israel (2 Sam. 5:1-3). He ruled over God's people for a total of forty years before dying at the age of seventy (2 Sam. 5:4).

It is evident from David's writings that the man after God's own heart (1 Sam. 13:14) frequently suffered a broken heart. He was often despised, plotted against, slandered, and persecuted for doing the will

4

of God. Many sought to kill David; yet, through each challenging situation he found the Lord to be a faithful Refuge of peace, an unmovable Rock of strength, and a mighty Fortress of protection. David proves that those who suffer patiently with the Lord in righteousness know more about God's true nature than those who do not.

Key Events in 1 and 2 Samuel

The following table summarizes in chronological order the main events in the lives of Samuel, Saul and David – dates are approximate and represent a best fit with the biblical record.

Date (B.C.)	Key Events in 1 and 2 Samuel
1100	Birth of Samuel (1 Sam. 1:19-28)
1076	Birth of Saul
1070	Death of Eli (1 Sam. 4:15-18)
1050	Saul becomes Israel's first king (1 Sam. 13:1)
1040	Birth of David
1027	David anointed by Samuel (1 Sam. 16:13)
1025	David kills Goliath (1 Sam. 17:33)
1025	David dwells with Saul in Gibeah (1 Sam. 18:2)
1018	David's fugitive years begin (1 Sam. 21)
1012	Samuel dies (1 Sam. 25:1)
1010	Saul dies; David, at 30, rules from Hebron (2 Sam. 5:4)
1003	David is made king at Jerusalem (2 Sam. 2; 5:1-3)
990	Solomon is born (2 Sam. 12:24)
979	Absalom's rebellion and death (2 Sam. 15-18)
970	David dies at 70; Solomon is king at 19 (1 Kgs. 2:10-12)

1 Samuel

1 Samuel

Devotions in 1 Samuel

Legitimate Lineage
1 Samuel 1

The Family of Elkanah (vv. 1-7)

The book of Judges identifies thirteen individuals who judged Israel during a time in which everyone did what was right in their own eyes. Samson judged Israel during the first twenty years of Philistia's forty-year oppression of the Jewish nation. Eli followed Samson during the latter years of Philistia's cruelty. First Samuel records the names of Israel's final two judges, Eli and Samuel, before identifying Israel's first two kings, Saul and David.

We are introduced to Samuel's parents in this chapter and to the dramatic circumstances that led to his conception and birth.

Samuel's father was Elkanah and he resided within the mountainous region of Ephraim in the town of Ramathaim Zophim, also called Ramah (v. 1). Ramah was about five miles northwest of Jerusalem. Elkanah's genealogy indicates that he was the son of Jeroham, a descendant of the Levite Korah (1 Chron. 6:22-37) who rebelled with others against the Aaronic priesthood in Numbers 16. Elkanah's existence verifies Moses' statement after Korah was judged: *"Nevertheless the children of Korah did not die"* (Num. 26:11). Though a Levite by birth, Elkanah was disengaged from active religious service.

We are informed that Elkanah had two wives, Hannah, who was barren, and Peninnah, who had at least four children (v. 2). Because the Jews considered children as evidence of God's favor (Deut. 7:13-14; Ps. 127:3), barren women bore the extra hardship of being socially scorned in addition to being childless.

It was not unusual for a Jewish man to take a second wife if his first wife could not bear him children. This practice was to ensure that there was an heir to maintain the family inheritance and to manage the family's affairs when parents were no longer able to do so because of age or death. Elkanah likely took Peninnah as a second wife because Hannah was unable to bear him children.

God never endorses polygamy in Scripture, nor does Scripture portray it in a positive light, but like divorce, it was permitted under the Law with limitations (Deut. 21:15). In contrast to polygamy, God's best pattern for marriage is beautifully displayed in Genesis 2 and affirmed by Christ in Matthew 19 – one man and one woman until death separates them. Married apostles, elders, and deacons in the New Testament maintained monogamous relationships to exemplify God's best design for biblical companionship (1 Cor. 9:5). In fact, the criterion for church elders and deacons demanded that they be the husband of one wife (1 Tim. 3:2, 12).

During this period of Israel's history, the tabernacle of the Lord was erected at Shiloh; David later brought the tabernacle to Jerusalem. Shiloh was situated within Ephraim's territory about nine miles northeast of Bethel, twelve miles south of Shechem, and fifteen miles north of Ramah. The high priest at Shiloh was Eli; he judged Israel for about forty years (v. 3, 4:18). His two wicked sons, Hophni and Phinehas, served as the priests with him at Shiloh. J. N. Darby comments on Eli's character and leadership in Israel at this time:

> Eli, pious himself, and fearing God, maintained no order in the priestly family. The priesthood, instead of binding the people to God, morally separated them. Hophni and Phinehas, the sons of Eli, were at Shiloh; but their conduct made the offering of the Lord to be abhorred of the people. Such was the state of things in Israel. At the same time, in the family of Elkanah, Hannah, chosen of Jehovah for blessing, was in trial.[2]

Elkanah was a religious man who honored *"the Lord of Hosts"* or *Yahweh-Sabbaoth* by annually visiting Shiloh (a day's journey north of his hometown) to offer a sacrifice (vv. 3, 11). Whether he was traveling to Shiloh three times a year to observe the feasts, which the Law required of every Jewish man, is unknown (Ex. 23:14-17). The narrative mentions only a single annual journey to Shiloh (see 2:19 also). During the era of the Judges, the Jewish nation suffered much declension and, generally speaking, did not observe the Law precisely, including the Feasts of Jehovah.

Yahweh-Sabbaoth is first found in verse 3, but then occurs over two hundred and sixty times afterwards in the Old Testament. *Yahweh-Sabbaoth*, rendered "the Lord of hosts," is one of eight compound names, or descriptions, of God in Scripture which invoke His personal name *Yahweh*. Others include:

Yahweh-Jireh, "The Lord Will Provide" (Gen. 22:14)
Yahweh-Rapha, "The Lord Who Heals" (Ex. 15:26)
Yahweh-Nissi, "The Lord Our Banner" (Ex. 17:15)
Yahweh-Maccaddeshcem, "The Lord Your Sanctifier" (Ex. 31:13)
Yahweh-Shalom, "The Lord Is Peace" (Judg. 6:24)
Yahweh-Tsidkenu, "The Lord Our Righteousness" (Jer. 23:6)
Yahweh-Shammah, "The Lord Is Present" (Ezek. 48:35)

At Shiloh, Elkanah's family enjoyed a fellowship feast and partook of some of the meat from the sacrifice. This meant that the priests had offered a Peace Offering to the Lord on his behalf. On this festive occasion, Elkanah gave portions of the meat to Peninnah and to her sons and daughters, but to his beloved Hannah, he gave a double portion (vv. 4-5). Nevertheless, being exceedingly sorrowful, she did not eat or drink wine at the feast. We then learn why Hannah was suffering in her soul; her rival, Peninnah, made her life miserable by continually ridiculing her barren condition (vv. 6-7).

Hannah's Vow (vv. 8-18)

Seeing the dismal countenance of his wife, Elkanah tried to encourage his cherished wife: *"Hannah, why do you weep? Why do you not eat? And why is your heart grieved? Am I not better to you than ten sons?"* (v. 8). But *"she was in bitterness of soul"* and could not be comforted (v. 10). Indeed, *"bitterness of soul"* and helplessly fruitless is what the barren woman spiritually symbolizes in Scripture. C. H. Mackintosh further expounds on the typology:

> The barren woman is in Scripture the type of nature's ruined and helpless condition. There is no ability to do anything for God – not power to bring forth any fruit to Him; all is death and barrenness.

11

Such is the real condition of every child of Adam. He can neither do anything for God nor for himself, as regards his eternal destiny.[3]

After the family finished feasting, Hannah quietly departed and made her way to the entrance of the tabernacle (v. 9). This was as close as she was permitted to come to the Ark of the Covenant in the most holy place of the tabernacle. With eyes swollen with tears, she prayed inaudibly to the Lord of Hosts to remove her affliction and then vowed what she would do if He did (v. 12):

> *O Lord of hosts, if You will indeed look on the affliction of Your maidservant and remember me, and not forget Your maidservant, but will give Your maidservant a male child, then I will give him to the Lord all the days of his life, and no razor shall come upon his head (v. 11).*

Apparently, Hannah was unaware that Eli was sitting by one of the entryway posts of the tabernacle and was observing her. The post represents the seat of priestly authority, but, sadly, Eli was resting in his official dignity instead of serving the Lord and ministering to His people. He observed that her lips were moving as she silently prayed and he concluded that she was intoxicated from too much feasting. Eli then unjustly rebuked Hannah, *"How long will you be drunk? Put your wine away from you!"* (v. 14). Though upright and loyal to the Lord, Eli's spiritual vitality and discernment had waned (as we will see more clearly in the next chapter).

Being far from the Lord, Eli could not discern Hannah's burden. Eli unfortunately mistook the activity of the Spirit of God for the activity of the flesh – he believed Hannah to be drunk, when in fact she was in anguish of soul! Poor Hannah, not only had she suffered years of barrenness and jeering from her rival, but now she was misjudged by the chief spiritual leader of her people. She had been led by painful years of desolation (which God permitted) to this very juncture time.

Hannah quickly responded to Eli's charge:

> *No, my lord, I am a woman of sorrowful spirit. I have drunk neither wine nor intoxicating drink, but have poured out my soul before the Lord. Do not consider your maidservant a wicked woman, for out of the abundance of my complaint and grief I have spoken until now (vv. 15-16).*

Clearly, Hannah understood better than Eli that the spiritual need of the nation for godly leadership could be met only in one who was a perpetual Nazarite – a leader fully devoted to the Lord. She was willing to be the vessel used of the Lord to provide through such "a male child" to deliver the nation. Perhaps she had been pondering her circumstances while considering the last great judge of Israel – Samson, who was born a Nazarite and also from the womb of a barren woman.

After understanding the true nature of Hannah's behavior, Eli promised Hannah that God would attend to her urgent request: *"Go in peace, and the God of Israel grant your petition which you have asked of Him"* (v. 18). Hannah concluded the dialogue by saying, *"Let your maidservant find favor in your sight."* This meant that she was affirming her delight in Eli's brief intercession on her behalf. By faith, Hannah left her burden with the Lord at that moment and she departed from the tabernacle with renewed joy and vigor. She came to the Lord in bitterness, but departed with His peace! Now she could enjoy eating and rejoicing with her husband before the Lord. Peter J. Pell suggests that God will always turn barrenness into fruitfulness when His people act in genuine faith as Hannah did:

> Where saints are going on carelessly, the form of godliness continues but the power is lacking; if there is general insensibility the individual may take the place of confession and importunity and find God does not fail in meeting the need of His people. What might not be done for God's glory today if someone were in the secret of the Lord as to the need of His own and would pray as did Hannah? There is so much that answers to the "sitting by the post on the seat," and so little exercise before God. "Men of God" would be seen in His saints if there were more who would follow Hannah and lay hold on God as she did.[4]

Hannah had promised the Lord that if He gave her a male child, she would dedicate him to the Lord as a Nazarite, meaning "a separated one." Those voluntarily entering into the Nazarite vow were placing themselves in the most holy and separated position that a non-Levitical Jew could enter. Samson and Samuel are examples of those chosen for such a life-long consecration. Numbers 6:1-21 informs us that there were three main constraints for a Nazarite: eating or drinking anything from the grapevine was prohibited, as was cutting one's hair, and touching a corpse.

Those dedicated to the Lord would not want to touch anything dead to avoid becoming ceremonially unclean and unfit for service. Figuratively speaking, wine symbolizes earthly joy (i.e., what is derived from nature that cheers the heart). Such enjoyments are not wrong or evil in themselves (though drunkenness is prohibited in Scripture), but represent what the human heart often clings to – a Nazarite was to cling to the Lord alone.

We might wonder why God required the Nazarite to let his hair grow. John J. Stubbs suggests this requirement should be linked with Paul's explanation in 1 Corinthians 11:14: *"Does not even nature itself teach you that if a man has long hair, it is a dishonor to him?"* The uncut hair of the Nazarite represents separation from the rights and dignity of manhood. Long hair is a sign of subjection to another, and that is not God's order for the man who represents the image and glory of God.[5] Hannah's coming son was to be both fully consecrated to the Lord and fully satisfied in Him alone. He was to be a humble servant of the Lord who shunned worldliness and yearned for God his entire life.

Samuel Dedicated (vv. 19-28)

Early the next morning the family arose, worshiped before the Lord and returned to Ramah (v. 19). As Eli had promised, Hannah did conceive by her husband and gave birth to a son. She called his name Samuel, *"because I have asked for him from the Lord"* (v. 20). Samuel's name means "heard of God" and was heaven's answer to what *"she asked of God"* in faith. As Hannah's name means "grace," there is a lovely truth displayed in the narrative: what is asked of God in faith is furnished in His grace, thus Hannah gave birth to the son that she had prayed for!

Elkanah returned to Shiloh the following year to sacrifice and to pay his vow (v. 21). Under the Law, Elkanah could have revoked Hannah's vow within one day of becoming aware of it, but he did not (Num. 30:8). This meant that he too was bound to keep the vow despite the personal cost to himself. (Let us not forget that he had waited many years for his beloved Hannah to have a baby also.) The vow to be paid was Samuel, but after further consideration, he agreed with Hannah that Samuel was too young to be to be placed in Eli's care. It was decided that the family would fulfill their vow after Hannah had weaned Samuel (vv. 22-23).

There is some evidence to suggest that Jewish women in ancient times nursed their children longer than our Western culture deems necessary; this practice would allow natural spacing of their children. According to section 1:31 of the Shemmot Rabbah (a rabbinic commentary of Exodus), Moses was nursed by his mother for approximately two years. Second Maccabees 7:27 refers to a Jewish mother who nursed her son for three years. The text seems to favor this timing as Hannah will eventually deliver Samuel to Eli as a young child, not an infant (e.g., 15:3). This would mean that Hannah did not return to Shiloh for at least three years, perhaps four. Hence, Samuel was two or three years of age when he was taken to Shiloh and dedicated to the Lord.

We pause to consider the timing of the events in this chapter. Of special consideration is how long Hannah suffered the mental anguish of her barrenness. Hannah was probably in her late teens when she married, and Elkanah perhaps waited five or six years before taking a second wife to have children. His second wife, Peninnah, had already given birth to at least four children (i.e., she had sons and daughters) and was apparently not nursing a child when Hannah uttered her vow at Shiloh. In Hannah's song in the next chapter, she refers to Peninnah's many sons (i.e., three or more sons; 2:5). Furthermore, Elkanah says to Hannah that he was better to her than "ten sons" (v. 8). All of these statements indicate that Peninnah had been abundantly fruitful after becoming Elkanah's wife, probably ten to fifteen years earlier.

Assuming that another year passed before Samuel's birth, Hannah probably became a mother in her mid-thirties, thus ending her distressing barrenness of some fifteen to twenty years. In the next chapter we read that the Lord blessed Hannah's diligence by granting her three sons and two daughters (2:21). If all these assumptions are correct, this would mean Hannah was having babies into her mid-forties.

In summary, it took years of anguish for Hannah to come to the point of desperation in which she cast herself upon the Lord in such a way to surrender to Him that which she wanted most – a son. There is nothing wrong with a woman desiring what God created her for – motherhood, unless she wants it too much. John Calvin put it this way, "The evil in our desire typically does not lie in what we want, but in

15

that we want it too much." If what we long for becomes so preeminent in our thoughts that it displaces our joy in the Lord and our desire to adore Him, are we not guilty of mental idolatry?

As is so often the case for God's people, Hannah met her greatest trial in the place of God's calling for her – the home. Abraham encountered a great famine in the place of his calling, but chose to venture down to Egypt to alleviate his difficulty rather than being sustained by God through it, and we all know the costliness of such fleshly endeavors. H. L. Rossier overviews the journey Hannah traveled to obtain God's blessing and to come to the place of rejoicing in Him:

> Hannah has a remarkable trait: her character is that of the believer in all ages. Hannah means *"grace,"* but before answering to her name, she represents the flesh incapable of bearing fruit for God. We must always begin there. The Word of God teaches us that the natural man has two characteristics: wickedness and incapacity, and the Law has no other purpose than to convince us of this. But it is easier to confess that we are guilty than to admit our incapacity, for to admit the powerlessness of our flesh is deeply humiliating. Hannah felt this. ... [she] was full of bitterness and wept abundantly. One resource remained to her: to present her affliction before the Lord. Only God's heart could give her an answer in grace, for she had no resource within herself.[6]

As Hannah shows us, it is best to remain in the place of our calling and to suffer through (by God's grace) whatever He deems is best to strengthen our faith, mature our character, and bring glory to His own name. The result of doing so is witnessed in the next chapter, a blessed and joyful Hannah praising God!

The day that she knew would come, finally came. Samuel was weaned and it was time to dedicate him to the Lord at Shiloh. Willingly choosing to part from her young son must have been traumatic for Hannah, but her prayer magnifying God (in the next chapter) confirms that it was not a bitter experience for her. Hannah's resolve to fulfill her vow proved that her devotion to the Lord was above her yearnings for motherhood. The Lord had heard the prayer of a contrite, barren woman willing to make the greatest sacrifice to be healed. Her sacrifice also served His sovereign plan to raise up a godly prophet and priest to judge His people. Consequently, both the Lord and Hannah received what each wanted and Hannah, in the place of her calling, is able to rejoice in the Lord again – God had granted her request and ended her trial.

Hannah (Elkanah was also with her, 2:11) brought Samuel to Eli. Hannah identified herself as the woman sorrowful in spirit that he had spoken with earlier. It is likely that at least three years had elapsed since their previous meeting. Besides young Samuel, they also brought three bulls, one ephah of flour, and a skin of wine to Eli at the house of the Lord in Shiloh (v. 24). One of the bulls was slaughtered and sacrificed in association with Samuel's consecration per Hannah's vow.

Hannah acknowledged to Eli that the Lord had heard her prayer and granted her a son, whom she now was dedicating to the Lord as she had vowed to do: *"Therefore I also have lent him to the Lord; as long as he lives he shall be lent to the Lord"* (v. 28). This meant that she was fully surrendering and returning to the Lord what He had graciously given her in response to her prayer. Hannah reminds us that there is nothing that we have that was not first received from God (1 Cor. 4:7). Therefore, all we give Him were first His gifts to us.

In the Church Age, we do not dedicate our children to serve God at the tabernacle as Hannah did, but the prophet Ezekiel reminds us that children are born unto the Lord – they are for Him (Ezek. 16:20). The psalmist states that parents are merely stewards, not owners, of the children God entrusts to their care: *"Children are a heritage from the Lord"* (Ps. 127:3). If reared in the ways of the Lord, children become a rich blessing to all and further the kingdom of God. May we count on the Lord and His Word alone to build up our homes!

The chapter ends with Elkannah's family worshiping before the Lord at Shiloh; this would include Samuel too. Because Hannah was willing to dedicate the firstfruit of her womb to the Lord, her son's formative years were spent serving and learning of the Lord at Shiloh. Years later, God used Samuel as an honorable prophet and judge to wonderfully bless the Jewish nation. Seeing all the good that God was able to accomplish through her son must have further affirmed what Hannah already knew – there is no genuine personal sacrifice that outweighs God's response to it. This was the solution to Hannah's physical barrenness and indeed it is the remedy for the Church's spiritual lethargy today also.

Meditation

People talk of the sacrifice I have made in spending so much of my life in Africa. It is emphatically no sacrifice. Say rather it is a privilege.

— David Livingstone

For God no cost is too high. Anything can be sacrificed if only we may please Him. Let us daily learn to be obedient children.

— Watchman Nee

God Praised and Eli Warned
1 Samuel 2

Hannah's Song (vv. 1-11)

Hannah's prayer of desperation and consecration in chapter 1 is wonderfully contrasted with her song of joyful thanksgiving and praise in this chapter. So inspiring is Hannah's poetic prayer that Mary includes portions of it in her Magnificat of praise to God for selecting her to be the human mother of Jesus, the Jewish Messiah (Luke 1:46-55).

Hannah commences her song by celebrating that her Deliverer is a Rock of strength (v. 1). She then extols God's holy character and attributes (vv. 2-3) before describing His wondrous works (vv. 3-10). Hannah's God is clearly sovereign over all human affairs and the only source of salvation:

God's Attributes
All-holy (v. 2)
Unique – God alone (v. 2)
All-powerful – the unmovable Rock (v. 2)
All-knowing (v. 3)

God's Actions
Judges man's doings (v. 3)
Brings low the mighty and proud, but sustains the humble (v. 4)
Delivers those who hunger (v. 5)
Blesses the barren with children (v. 5)
Controls the lives of the living (v. 6)
Brings down the influential, lifts up the poor (v. 7)
Exalts and rewards the lowly (v. 8)
Created the earth (v. 8)
Protects His saints (v. 9)
Judges all men on the earth, especially His adversaries (v. 10)

Gives strength to His king and anointed (v. 10).

Hannah acknowledges God's sovereignty in her own life by referring to a barren woman as being blessed with seven children (v. 5). Being the more cherished wife of Elkanah, Hannah's fruitfulness ended Peninnah's opportunities to demean her. Given that God would later bless Hannah with two more sons and two daughters (v. 21), we understand Hannah's reference to the number seven to be metaphoric. That is, her barren years had ended and God had granted her maternal completeness (which anticipated more children to follow after Samuel). Her prophetic reference to God raising up His anointed may refer to Israel's coming kings like David, whom God would raise up to lead His people, or, even more likely, to Israel's future Messiah (v. 10). Though God may seem silent now in judging wickedness, there is a coming day when His Anointed will come and thunder judgment on all His adversaries.

Hannah demonstrates a good pattern for us to follow in our own prayers. She first acknowledged who God is before rejoicing in what He had done. Worship looks beyond our received blessings to understand the heart of God and His ability to do what is good (Jas. 1:17). Because Jehovah is the only all-knowing and all-powerful God, He is able to overcome all His people's trials and calamities in such a way to best honor His own name. He alone is able to completely deliver the suffering and exalt the contrite! Hannah knew this by faith and from personal experience; hence she greatly rejoiced in her God.

Immediately after recording Hannah's song, the writer informs us that Elkanah was with Hannah when Samuel was dedicated to the Lord at Shiloh (v. 11). Samuel's service to Eli the priest at the tabernacle of the Lord began at an early age. He was probably about four years old.

Eli's Wicked Sons (vv. 12-17)
We sense that Eli was a sincerely consecrated servant to the Lord, but he utterly failed in rearing his two sons, Hophni and Phinehas to be the same (vv. 34, 1:3). Eli's sons were perverse men who did not know the Lord and therefore abused the priesthood (vv. 12-13). The writer first notes their corrupt treatment of the peace offering, and then alludes to their carnal sexual appetites (v. 22).

Their sins were twofold – against the Lord and against His people. Eli's sons stole, forcefully if necessary, the portion of the peace offering that by Levitical Law was to be given to the people (vv. 13-14). They also demanded raw meat from the people for roasting instead of waiting until it was cooked by boiling (vv. 15-17). Their corruption dishonored the Lord's name and discouraged those who genuinely desired to worship Jehovah at the central sanctuary at Shiloh. Barnes suggests that *"the women who assembled at the door of the tabernacle of meeting"* (v. 22) were sincere women who had come to serve the Lord by doing fabric work (e.g., spinning, knitting, embroidering, mending, washing, etc.) and yet were sexually abused or persuaded to do evil by Eli's sons.[7]

Eli himself was a man of piety, but as H. L. Rossier surmises, he lacked a critical component of consecration, which crippled his testimony:

> What was this man of God lacking? Just this: *He judged the evil, but he did not separate himself from it.* It is a sad and humiliating thing to state: this is the situation of the majority of God's children in Christendom. Their bonds, their relationships, their affections, and their customs, which they are more attached to than the Lord's glory, prevent them from recognizing that *one is liable for an evil which one judges but from which one does not separate oneself.* This is what the man of God is charged to declare to Eli. In no way was Eli personally following the ungodly and disorderly behavior of his sons, but nevertheless these solemn words are addressed to him: *"Wherefore do ye trample upon My sacrifice"* … *"Thou honorest thy sons above Me!"* Poor Eli! Despite all his piety, he was honoring men (his sons) more than the Lord. God had been patient with him, but now he was about to reap the bitter fruit of the lack of *holiness* in his walk, for holiness is nothing other than separation from evil in view of God's service.[8]

The Lord does not have one word of commendation for Eli's past faithfulness or personal virtue; rather, he is branded as one who despised the Lord. May the Church learn an important lesson from God's rebuke of Eli: It is possible to know much about the Lord and say much that is right, but if our conduct is estranged from Christ's character, we cause more contempt for His name than blaspheming sinners do. Hence, *"Let everyone who names the name of Christ depart from iniquity"* (2 Tim. 2:19).

Although the carelessness of Eli and the perverseness of his sons will demand the most tragic consequences – their deaths – Samuel Ridout highlights the bright contrast of the faithful remnant (Elkanah and Hannah) against the dark backdrop of Israel's corruption at this time:

> God has always had a remnant among His people, even in darkest days, and it is most refreshing to see in Hannah a faith and a desire in lovely contrast with Eli's feebleness and his sons' wickedness. She lays hold of God, and spite of nature's impotence and the discouragement of a reproof from Eli, she holds fast. What a reproach to Eli! He has no energy to control his wicked house, and therefore has no discernment in administering reproof outside.[9]

Numbers 25:7-13 informs us that God instituted a covenant with Aaron's grandson Phinehas because of his zeal for the Lord. The Lord commended Phinehas' actions of judging a leader from the tribe of Simeon who was defiling himself with a pagan Midianite woman. As a result, Israel's future high priests were to be descendants of Phinehas, and not from the line of Aaron's fourth son, Ithamar. Aaron's first two sons were struck down by the Lord for intruding into His presence with strange fire (Lev. 10). Phinehas' father, Eleazar, was recognized as Israel's high priest after Aaron's death (Num. 20:23-28) and Phinehas became high priest after Eleazar died (Judg. 20:28).

Yet, comparing 1 Kings 2:27 with 1 Chronicles 24:3, we can deduce that Eli and his wicked sons were descendants of Ithamar. How Eli became high priest without being a descendant of Phinehas, per God's covenant, is unknown. However, the Lord will act (chp. 4) to remove Eli from being high priest and to ensure that neither of his wicked sons wears the holy ephod. The Lord sent a prophet to Eli to inform him of the coming judgment on his house (vv. 27-36).

Samuel's Childhood (vv. 18-21)

The Law did not permit a priest to begin service in the tabernacle until he was thirty years of age, but God had uniquely brought Samuel into the world as a Nazarite from birth; thus he wore a priestly ephod and served before the Lord as a child (v. 18). Remember that Aaron's two youngest sons, Eleazar and Ithamar, were both under twenty years of age, but also were permitted to serve in the sanctuary as priests (Num. 3:4). Young Samuel is in the process of gaining what elderly Eli will soon lose – the priesthood. In times of spiritual declension, God often resorts to unconventional means to restore order to His people, such as using a juvenile or a woman (e.g., Deborah) because no man is willing to properly represent Him in leadership.

Hannah made a coat for her son and brought it to him year by year (v. 19). Eli said that God would bless Hannah for loaning Samuel to Him; afterwards she bore two more sons and two daughters (vv. 20-21). Although Eli lacked discernment, he did know God's word. He taught young Samuel the way he should walk and Samuel grew in wisdom and stature. The narrative specifically states that *"the child Samuel grew before the Lord"* while he was serving the Lord in the tabernacle (v. 21). This shows that personal intimacy with God cannot be separated from effectively serving Him. As a result, Samuel's service and character were pleasing to God and also to all who observed him (v. 26). Luke similarly commends the Lord Jesus in His youth (Luke 2:52).

Judgment Pronounced Against Eli's Household (vv. 22-36)

After hearing of the evil deeds of his sons (even their immorality with women at the entrance of the tabernacle), the elderly Eli warned Hophni and Phinehas to cease from their corruption (vv. 22-23). He told them that they were causing God's people to sin and that there was no one who could make intercession for priests who engaged in such conduct (vv. 24-25). Commenting on Eli's poor parenting, Matthew Henry writes:

> Eli shunned trouble and action. This led him to indulge his children, without using parental authority to restrain and correct them when young. He winked at the abuses in the service of the sanctuary till they became customs, and led to abominations; and his sons, who should have taught those that engaged in the service of the sanctuary what was good, solicited them to wickedness. Their offence was committed even in offering the sacrifices for sins, which typified the atonement of the Savior! Sins against the remedy, the atonement itself, are most dangerous; they tread underfoot the blood of the covenant. Eli's reproof was far too mild and gentle.[10]

Eli's sons ignored their father's toothless warning. Though objecting to their wickedness, Hophni and Phinehas knew their father would not act against them, hence, in the practical sense, Eli condoned their sin. God, however, was determined to execute Eli's sons for their crimes against Him, since Eli would not judge them. Eli, being the high priest, was accountable to the Lord and should have, at a minimum, put his sons out of the priesthood. But because he did not, God would judge him also.

The Lord sent an unnamed prophet to Eli to foretell God's judgment of Eli's household. The prophet began by recalling the great privilege Jehovah had extended to Aaron's descendants who were to serve before Him as priests on behalf of the Jewish nation (vv. 27-28). God rewarded their service by providing food for them from the Altar, His table. Yet, Eli had permitted his sons to violate God's law for the offerings and to demean their importance (v. 29).

Speaking for the Lord, the prophet then pointedly asks Eli: *"Why do you kick at My sacrifice and My offering which I have commanded in My dwelling place, and honor your sons more than Me, to make yourselves fat with the best of all the offerings of Israel My people?"* (v. 29). The prophet identified three separate offenses that Eli had committed against the Lord. First, by ignoring God's regulations, Eli had made God's sacrifices a thing of contempt. Second, by not punishing his sons, Eli had shown that he valued them over the Lord. Third, the priests had gorged themselves and become fat on the best that Israel had brought to His altar. As a result of these offenses, the Lord had a stern message for Eli:

> *"I said indeed that your house and the house of your father would walk before Me forever." But now the Lord says: "Far be it from Me; for those who honor Me I will honor, and those who despise Me shall be lightly esteemed. Behold, the days are coming that I will cut off your arm and the arm of your father's house, so that there will not be an old man in your house"* (vv. 30-31).

The expression *"far be it from Me"* (rendered *"God forbid"* in the KJV) is derived from the Hebrew word *chaliylah* and is found eleven times in 1 and 2 Samuel. It literally means, "be it an abomination to me" and is used here to preface the announcement of judgment on Eli and his sons.

Metaphorically speaking, an "arm" is used in Scripture to speak of strength. The meaning of God's promise to cut off Eli's arm was that he would have no male descendants to continue his name. Not only would Eli's sons die, but if they had sons, they also would perish; some would die at early age to ensure that they would not father children (vv. 32-33). The prophet then provided a sign to Eli to confirm this prophecy – both his sons would die on the same day (v. 34). The Lord promised to render to Eli's household what was deserved for the dishonor caused to His name: *"Do not be deceived, God is not mocked; for whatever a man sows, that he will also reap"* (Gal. 6:7).

Although the Lord promised to bring Eli's house to an end, He would not terminate the office of priest altogether. Instead the Lord would raise up unto Himself a faithful priest (v. 35). The family line of this priest would be firmly established and would serve before God's anointed (i.e., His appointed king) forever. The prophecy closes by stating that, after the Lord removed Eli's house from the priesthood, there would be surviving family members who would desire the priesthood back, not to serve the Lord, but for something to eat (v. 36).

This prophecy was fulfilled when Solomon took the priesthood from Abiathar, a descendent of Aaron through his son Ithamar, and assigned it to Zadok, a descendant of Aaron's son Eleazar through Phinehas (1 Kgs. 2:27-35). Zadok was a faithful priest and loyal to both King David and then to King Solomon (1 Chron. 29:33). He was the first high priest to oversee Solomon's temple and his descendants would have an honored position of authority in God's Millennial Temple. Ezekiel affirms that only the priests in the lineage of Zadok will be able to enter the sanctuary of the Millennial Temple to serve the Lord (Ezek. 44:15-16). The Lord indeed rewards faithfulness.

While much of the verse 35 prophecy was fulfilled long ago, it continues to foreshadow a day when God's "faithful priest" and God's "anointed one" will be fulfilled in the same person, the Jewish Messiah. This aspect of the prediction is brought out by the word "forever" which promises permanency of the offices of both priest and king. This will occur during the Kingdom Age when distant sons of Zadok will be serving the Lord Jesus Christ, who will be both Israel's Great High Priest and King forever.

Meditation

Praise Him! Praise Him! Jesus, our blessed Redeemer,
For our sins He suffered and bled and died;
He, our Rock, our Hope of eternal salvation,
Hail Him! Hail Him! Jesus, the Crucified.

Praise Him! Praise Him! Jesus, our blessed Redeemer,
Heavenly portals, loud with Hosannahs ring!
Jesus, Savior, reigneth forever and ever;
Crown Him! Crown Him! Prophet and Priest and King!

— Fanny Crosby

The Call of Samuel
1 Samuel 3

A few years have transpired since the previous chapter. The Jewish historian Josephus suggests that Samuel was twelve years of age when this incident occurred. Traditionally speaking, this is the age that Jewish males are obliged to honor the time-bound commands as celebrated in the *bar mitzvah.* It is the age at which the young Jesus Christ baffled the scribes in the temple by His questions (Luke 2:31-50). Although there is no scriptural evidence that Samuel was twelve, his activities in this chapter suggest that he is not a small boy, but an able lad. The fact that Samuel was responsible for opening the doors of the tabernacle each morning, that God determined he was mature enough to be His prophet, and that Eli put him under an oath seem to validate this conclusion.

The type of service Samuel rendered at Shiloh is noteworthy, *"Samuel ministered to the Lord before Eli"* (v. 1). The text does not say, "Samuel ministered to Eli before the Lord." The opposite was true, the young Levite ministered to the Lord in the presence of Eli. He was not merely Eli's boy-servant, but was in training for his life's ministry among God's people even at an early age. The opportunity to serve the Lord in a consecrated environment benefitted Samuel much during his childhood, suggests C. Knapp:

Samuel was serving diligently; his young mind developing, and his intelligence in the holy things enlarging, under the Spirit's influence, for he was, according to his mother's vow, a Nazarite from his birth, and for life. No razor came upon his head, no wine or strong drink touched his lips, nor was he even to eat any fruit of the vine. The symbols of natural joys and dignity were denied him, that his heart might be the more occupied with Him to whom he had been dedicated.[11]

Samuel's selfless service to the Lord was in stark contrast to the self-serving behavior of Eli's sons. There can be little doubt that Samuel suffered Hophni's and Phinehas' ridicule and hostility for doing what was expected, but God preserved young Samuel from their corruption. And despite their taunting and disgust, Samuel behaved himself appropriately. He learned early in life that doing what pleases the Lord is more important than what one may suffer for doing so.

Because of the moral and spiritual declension of Israel, fresh revelation from the Lord was rare during the latter era of the judges (v. 1). This meant that there was nearly no expression of God's mind to His people through dreams, visions, prophets, or even through the high priest's Urim and Thummim. But, as we soon shall see, the Lord finally had someone to whom He could entrust His messages – Samuel. Although young, Samuel was called by God not only to be a faithful priest, but also an authentic prophet to the Jewish nation.

The burning wicks of the Golden Lampstand in the tabernacle were to be attended to throughout the night and extinguished in the morning (Ex 27:20-21; Lev 24:2-3). The narrative begins as a nearly-blind Eli and young Samuel were sleeping in the wee hours before dawn (v. 2). Apparently, at this time, it was acceptable not to trim lamps on the lampstand during the night, which meant that their light would slowly diminish throughout the night, eventually burning out sometime before dawn (v. 3). The entire scene pictures the condition of Israel at that time: evil darkness and spiritual blindness blanketed the land – the light of truth was nearly quenched. It is interesting that the book of Samuel begins by referencing God's lampstand going out, but concludes with David's final words foretelling the divine Light which will never fade:

The God of Israel said, the Rock of Israel spoke to me: "He who rules over men must be just, ruling in the fear of God. And he shall be like the light of the morning when the sun rises, a morning without clouds" (2 Sam. 23:3-4).

The Lord calls to Samuel, but Samuel mistakenly believes that his elderly mentor has summoned him, probably from an adjoining room or tent compartment (v. 4). Samuel hurries to where Eli was sleeping and replies, *"Here I am, for you called me."* A startled Eli replied, *"I did not call; lie down again,"* which Samuel did (v. 5). The Lord called Samuel two more times and again the lad, thinking that Eli had

28

beckoned him, aroused the slumbering priest (v. 6). But Eli had not called Samuel's name, so he told Samuel to go back to bed. However, on the third occasion, Eli perceived that the Lord may be calling the boy, so he instructed Samuel: *"Go, lie down; and it shall be, if He calls you, that you must say, 'Speak, Lord, for Your servant hears'"* (vv. 7-8).

The writer (perhaps Samuel himself) provides a helpful insight in verse 7: *"Now Samuel did not yet know the Lord, nor was the word of the Lord yet revealed to him."* Samuel had been a faithful servant at the tabernacle since his early childhood. Thus, this statement does not mean that Samuel did not have faith in Jehovah, but as of yet he did not know Him in a personal way. That is, Samuel had not experienced direct communication with the Lord up to that time.

Samuel returned to his bed for the third time as instructed and waited. On the fourth time, *"the Lord came and stood"* by Samuel before calling his name, *"Samuel! Samuel!"* This suggests that God did more than speak to Samuel; He actually visited him. We refer to this as a theophany (i.e., a pre-incarnate visit of the Son of God, Christ to the earth). In the dark, Samuel was probably able to see only the form of a person, but regardless, he answered, *"Speak, for Your servant hears"* (v. 10). This might explain why Samuel omitted the word "Lord" from his response (as Eli had directed in verse 8); he was not completely sure to whom he was speaking.

If the Lord called his name twice when addressing him previously, that would explain why Samuel ran to Eli, for the double-name address conveys the idea of urgency (e.g. Gen. 22:11). There are only ten such divine addresses in Scripture, and "Samuel, Samuel" is one of them. The entire scene pictures Israel's crucial need to be immediately awakened from the slumber of spiritual darkness and to be revived by a fresh revelation from God.

H. L. Rossier suggests that, at this juncture, Samuel's spiritual development lacked two things without which there can be no public testimony for the Lord:

First: *"Samuel did not yet know Jehovah."* The point here is *personal* knowledge of the Lord, for Samuel belonged to Him, served Him, and worshiped Him from his infancy, but he had not yet met the Lord face to face. It may happen in our Christian career that we joy in the finished work of the cross on our behalf without knowing the Lord personally. Knowing salvation and knowing the Author of salvation are two different things. Now, there is no power for testimony in one who does not know the person of Christ.

Second: "Neither had the word of Jehovah yet been revealed to him." Often in times of ruin the revelation of the mind of God is hindered by the enemy. Just so it is said in verse 1: "The word of Jehovah was *rare* in those days; a vision was not *frequent*." But although hindered, the word had not been stopped, for grace provides for the needs of each era, and most consolingly, it is often in the darkest days of decline that God gives the most new light in order to guide and encourage His own. ... God could not leave His people without help and without a means of communicating with Himself. He gives Samuel, that is to say prophecy, through which in sovereign grace He approaches man and communicates His mind.[12]

Indeed, for a servant of the Lord to have an effective ministry, he or she must first personally know the Lord, and then know and yield to God's revealed Word. Whatever we pursue outside the will of God is meaningless to Him and usually results in the disdain of His name. Because a true servant of God knows and loves the Lord, he or she is determined to abide in His word. The Lord Jesus put the matter this way to His disciples: *"If you abide in My word, you are My disciples indeed"* (John 8:31).

The Lord Jesus also promised that those who keep His commandments will bask in His love and be entrusted with more illumination: *"He who has My commandments and keeps them, it is he who loves Me. And he who loves Me will be loved by My Father, and I will love him and manifest Myself to him"* (John 14:21). Those demonstrating their love for the Lord through obedience will be blessed with an enhanced understanding of God and of things important to Him. Hence, the obedient servant is continually drawn into deeper communion with God and is permitted to increasingly experience God's security, peace, power, and love.

It is, therefore, no surprise that young Samuel is not long without a message from the Lord. It was not just the dim eyes of an elderly priest that noticed young Samuel's faithfulness in the solitude of the tabernacle – the eye of heaven was upon him also. Though dedicated, he was still young in his faith, and accordingly there was much running back and forth on his part until he learned to rest quietly before the

Lord and to wait for Him to speak. It is easy for those older in the faith to repeat Samuel's two mistakes while learning the same lesson. First, we may get so busy serving the Lord that we forget to wait on Him, to rest in Him, and to be led by Him in ministry. Second, many in Christendom today waste time running to the religious and fruitless Elis of the world for what they can receive only from the Lord.

The Lord began by confirming the decree of judgment against Eli and his house announced previously by the unnamed prophet. The Lord informed Samuel that He was going to accomplish this in such a way that the ears of everyone in Israel would tingle (v. 11), a poetic way of saying that the Jewish nation would be stunned. This is a reference to Israel's great defeat by the Philistines and their capture of the Ark of the Covenant in 1 Samuel 4. Because Eli had not restrained his wicked sons from sinning, nor punished them for their offenses, he was as guilty as Hophni and Phinehas and would perish with his sons (v. 13).

At a minimum, Eli should have put them out of the priesthood, but the Law demanded that they be put to death for their sacrilege and immorality. If God struck down Aaron's two older sons for bringing strange fire before the Lord (Lev. 10:1-6), Eli's sons deserved immediate death even more. The Lord told Samuel that because of the nature of their sin as priests, there was no sacrifice that could atone for their sin – their imminent judgment could not be avoided (v. 14). Because Eli was the high priest, God had confirmed His judgment against his household by two witnesses: an unnamed prophet in chapter 2 and Samuel in chapter 3.

Samuel had apparently stood up to answer the Lord's call and to receive his message, and then had laid back down again until morning. Evidently during this era in Israel's history, the tabernacle had become more than just a tent with curtains for an entryway. The tabernacle here had doors, which would require some type of framed structure to encase and support them. Samuel was about his morning duties of opening the doors of the tabernacle when Eli inquired of Samuel what the Lord had told him (vv. 15-16).

The lad was afraid to tell Eli what the Lord had revealed to him earlier that morning, but after Eli put Samuel under a solemn oath, he told the aged priest everything (vv. 17-18). It was a mercy of the Lord for Eli to hear such a grave indictment against him from a tender, blameless lad like Samuel. Eli received this sobering news with a submissive heart and did not murmur against the Lord or plead for

31

mercy: *"It is the Lord. Let Him do what seems good to Him."* Matthew Henry suggests that Eli's response is that of a repentant man who knows he has done wrong and accepts his punishment:

> Those who do not restrain the sins of others, when it is in their power to do it, make themselves partakers of the guilt, and will be charged as joining in it. In his remarkable answer to this awful sentence, Eli acknowledged that the Lord had a right to do as He saw good, being assured that He would do nothing wrong. The meekness, patience, and humility contained in those words show that he was truly repentant; he accepted the punishment of his sin.[13]

Eli humbly acknowledges that the forthcoming judgment against him was deserved and he accepts it from the hand of God without complaint. Surely the Lord knows best how to honor His own name when His people sin against Him. Although he failed to honor the Lord in his priestly post, Eli's personal piety and devotion for God remained strong to the end.

It will require almost a century for the Lord to completely fulfill His promised judgment against the house of Eli. Eli and his two sons will perish in the next chapter. Doeg the Edomite, as commanded by Saul, will slay eighty-five priests at Nob for supposedly aiding David (1 Sam. 22). Only one priest, Abiathar, escaped this slaughter and fled to join David who was hiding in the cave of Adullam. Abiathar stayed with David during his years of wandering and ministered as a priest during David's reign. However, Solomon later deposed Abiathar from the priesthood and banished him to the town of Anathoth because of his part in Adonijah's conspiracy (1 Kgs. 2:27). Solomon's action against Abiathar completed God's judgment against the house of Eli as spoken at Shiloh.

Young Samuel continued to quietly minister to the Lord in the purity demanded by the priestly office and, in return, the Lord revealed His secrets to Samuel. The chapter closes with his growing fame throughout Israel as being a true prophet of the Lord (vv. 19-20). The Lord appeared to Samuel at Shiloh and Samuel faithfully shared God's word with His covenant people (v. 21). Jamieson, Fausset, and Brown explain the meaning of the phrase, "[The Lord] *let none of his words fall to the ground."* "This is a metaphor derived from water being spilt on the ground (e.g., Josh. 21:45; Est. 6:10), and signifying that none of

Samuel's judgments were falsified by the event, but that all his predictions were fulfilled."[14] God was with and for Samuel!

Luke tells us that Samuel was the first among the prophets in Israel (Acts 3:24), John the baptizer being the last (Matt. 11:7-13). Obviously, Moses and Joshua prophesied for the Lord, as did Jesus Christ, but Samuel and John mark the beginning and the end of the era in which God sent Jewish prophets to guide and warn Israel after they were settled in Canaan. John was the forerunner of Christ and heralded His "kingdom" message, and Samuel announced God's chosen shepherd to rule Israel, King David. It took several years for David to assume his rightful place on the throne of Israel as prophesied. Likewise, it will require many centuries before his descendant, Jesus Christ, will rule as King of kings on the throne of Israel forever.

After years of darkness and despair, God had raised up a true prophet to rebuke and instruct His people. Samuel's integrity, faithfulness, and discretion were appreciated by everyone – it was evident that the Lord was with Samuel!

Meditation

Integrity is keeping a commitment even after circumstances have changed.

— David Jeremiah

Spiritual advancement is measured by faithful obedience.

— Watchman Nee

"The Glory Has Departed"
1 Samuel 4

A few years have passed since the previous chapter; Samuel is now a young man. The Lord has wonderful plans for Samuel, but He cannot put him into a place of prominence in Israel until He has rid Himself of Eli and his sons, which happens in this chapter.

Israel encamped near Ebenezer, while the Philistines gathered their forces at Aphek, which was only two miles northwest of Ebenezer. The outcome of the first battle was devastating for Israel; four thousand cold and lifeless bodies were scattered across the battlefield (vv. 1-2). Apparently, the opposing forces were so lopsided in power that the elders of Israel wondered, *"Why has the Lord defeated us today before the Philistines?"* (v. 3). This question seems more about expressing disgust for their failed religious cause than an actual heart-searching. They had been soundly defeated by the Philistines, but were not yet smitten in their hearts before God. If the elders had humbled themselves before the Lord and had asked the Lord to show them their sin, perhaps the lives of thirty thousand Jews would have been spared in the next confrontation. As Joshua learned at Ai, when there is sin in the camp, God does not go out with His people into battle.

But the Jewish elders had forgotten this important lesson. They were self-focused and not aware that the Lord was not with them. They had been soundly defeated because they were far from the Lord and He likewise was far from them. The Lord never pursues His people into darkness, but rather works to draw them back into the light (1 Jn. 1:5-7). In an effort to rally the troops and to hopefully turn the tide of the battle, the elders requested that the Ark of the Covenant be brought into the camp. *"Let us bring the ark of the covenant of the Lord from Shiloh to us, that when it comes among us it may save us from the hand of our enemies"* (v. 3).

Interestingly, the Ark has not been mentioned in Scripture for over two hundred years, which is another indication of how far Israel had drifted from their God. Their first step of spiritual declension was to disassociate the truth from the form which made it valuable (i.e., the Ark represented Jehovah's presence among His people). The next step was to place their confidence in the form which was separate from God (i.e., the Ark, not God, would defend them). The final step of their apostasy was to revere the Ark as being gloriously powerful, *"it may save us"* (i.e., to commit idolatry). The Church should learn from Israel's sin – religious formality is as cold and powerless today as it was in Samuel's day. Any form which contradicts the scriptural truth imputing its value, especially if it is adored instead of God, is to be flatly rejected as idolatry.

Shiloh was situated about 25 miles east of Israel's encampment, which meant it would require at least four days to travel there and to return with the Ark of the Covenant. Eli's sons Hophni and Phinehas accompanied the Ark (v. 4). Whether the Ark was carried on the shoulders of the Levites as commanded seems doubtful at this time, but, regardless, the Lord did not judge Israel for their negligence on the matter. In fact, the Lord had already determined to accomplish something greater through the Ark in the coming months.

The sight of the Ark invigorated the Israelites, who *"shouted so loudly that the earth shook"* (v. 5). During the days of Moses and Joshua the Ark accompanied God's people into battle to acknowledge His presence with them (Num. 10:35; Josh. 6:6). However, at this juncture, the Lord was not with His people because of their spiritual negligence and outright wickedness. Hence, all the shouting in the world could not win the battle. C. Knapp and Peter J. Pell, respectively, derive the following practical applications from the text:

> It was much easier to shout than it was to fight; just as today, it is easier to grow enthusiastic under the influence of big meetings and stirring addresses with exhilarating music, than it is to live devotedly to God, in separation from the world, crucifying the flesh, and courageously resisting the devil.[15]

> The words of the lukewarm Church of our day are like the shout of Israel. Though confusion of face becomes us and confession of heart, though anathemas are hurled at one another, hardly a tear is shed, hardly a heart is broken. *"They that sow in tears shall reap in joy."* In the state of confusion in which the Church is now we will find that the place of humiliation, with our faces in the dust, is the place of blessing.[16]

35

Although Israel's loud shouts did not equate to real power, it did have a stimulating effect on the enemy. The thundering noise from Israel's camp terrified the Philistines, who rightly surmised that the Ark of the Lord was with the Hebrew army (v. 6). They spoke among themselves:

> *"God has come into the camp!" ... "Woe to us! For such a thing has never happened before. Woe to us! Who will deliver us from the hand of these mighty gods? These are the gods who struck the Egyptians with all the plagues in the wilderness"* (vv. 7-8).

The Philistines supposed that Israel was shouting because their God was actually with them and ready to fight for them. They saw the outward expression of matchless power, but it was not the reality of the matter. The Philistines did not know that Jehovah had already abandoned His people because of their carnality and the corrupt priesthood. Therefore, the Jews were completely on their own against their enemies and it was more likely that God would actually side against Israel in battle.

So while having possession of the Ark caused shouts of jubilation in Israel's camp, it also had an inspiring effect among the Philistines, who assumed that to fight Israel and Israel's gods they must give their all in battle: *"Be strong and conduct yourselves like men, you Philistines, that you do not become servants of the Hebrews, as they have been to you. Conduct yourselves like men, and fight!"* (v. 9). And that is what they did. The result was the slaughter of 30,000 Jewish soldiers, the capture of the Ark, and the deaths of Hophni and Phinehas (vv. 10-11). Eli's sons perished on the same day, as was previously prophesied.

This defeat was the worst loss of life in Israel's history to this juncture. Sadly, the Jews engaged with a powerful enemy that feared God more than they did! The Jews believed that the Ark of the Covenant would protect them from defeat, instead of trusting in the One who gave them the Ark as a testimony of His covenant. The spiritually fickle Jews in Jeremiah's day thought similarly that they were invincible against the Babylonians because they had Solomon's temple (Jer. 7:4).The temple was viewed as a good luck charm because it had weathered centuries of military campaigns against Israel. Strangely, the building now disassociated from Jehovah was itself regarded as a bastion of safety (i.e., the people trusted in a man-made structure to protect them rather than trusting the One it honored). In 586 B.C., after a long siege, the Babylonians destroyed Jerusalem and Solomon's temple, proving the foolishness of their religiosity.

In this chapter, Israel put their trust in a well-decorated gold box instead of in the God of the universe, and they were soundly beaten. Superstition and religiosity will always replace the Lord with broken cisterns and empty wells. There are no good luck charms for believers to trust in today. We are at war with a fierce enemy – the spiritual hosts of wickedness in the heavenly places (Eph. 6:12). By standing on the triumphant ground of Calvary with the Lord Jesus, we can do all things (Phil. 4:13), and without Him we can do nothing (John 15:5).

Most of Israel's remaining soldiers fled to their own tents after this devastating defeat, but one Benjamite survivor with dirt on his head and his clothes torn brought the tragic report to Shiloh (v. 12). Jewish men customarily covered their heads (e.g., 2 Sam. 15:30) or put dirt on their heads (v. 12; 2 Sam. 1:2) to indicate shame, disgrace, and mourning, as seen here over the loss of the Ark.

Eli, nearly blind, was sitting in chair by the roadside waiting for news, for he had been fretting over the Ark not being in the tabernacle (v. 13). After hearing the alarming tumult in the town, he inquired as to what it was about (v. 14). The Benjamite responded by coming to Eli and reporting all the details of Israel's appalling loss, including the death of both his sons (vv. 15-17). The news was so crushing that the overweight, ninety-eight-year-old priest fell backwards off his chair and broke his neck (v. 18). Eli had judged Israel for forty years.

All these traumatic events caused Phinehas' very pregnant wife to go into hard labor (v. 19). Her deep grief over the loss of the Ark and the deaths of her father-in-law and husband were so overwhelming that she refused to be consoled by the news that she had given birth to a son (v. 20). Rather, she named her son Ichabod because *"the glory has departed from Israel!"* (v. 21). And then, with her dying breath, she uttered what had broken her heart, *"The glory has departed from Israel, for the ark of God has been captured"* (v. 22).

Her glory and her desires centered in the Ark, and that had been lost! But in reality the Philistines had captured only a gold box that symbolized Jehovah's presence among His people. And since God had not dwelt among His people for some time, nothing of spiritual consequence was really lost through Israel's defeat. Yet, it would be hard to imagine a crisis more humiliating for the Jewish nation. The Ark had been snatched out of their hands, they had been crushingly defeated in battle, and all the nations would learn of their utter failure as Jehovah's representatives to the nations. God, who is above all, will show in the next chapter that He is quite capable of honoring His own name when His people fail to do so.

Although God, who is omnipresent, cannot be captured and removed from Israel, Phinehas' unnamed wife does surpass her husband in spiritual discernment. She felt the scorn against Jehovah's name caused by Israel's foolishness. The incident marks Israel's lowest point of despair during Samuel's lifetime. The Jews had suffered their greatest loss of life in any battle in biblical history! Their high priest was dead! All the high priest's sons were dead! And the Ark of the Covenant was in the hands of their enemies!

However, as we soon shall see, God is able, through one faithful prophet and priest (Samuel) and one king after His own heart (David), to rebuild the ruined testimony of His people among the nations. This reminds us that it takes only a few committed men and women, zealous for God, to change the overall spiritual despondency of His people in times of declension. It is a reality true today also!

Meditation

I hope some of you will agree with me that it is of far greater importance that we have better Christians than that we have more of them! If we have any spiritual concerns, our most pressing obligation is to do all in our power to obtain a revival that will result in a reformed, revitalized, purified church. Each generation of Christians is the seed of the next, and degenerate seed is sure to produce a degenerate harvest – not a little better than but worse than the seed from which it sprang. Thus the direction will be down until vigorous, effective means are taken to improve the seed. Why is it easier to talk about revival than to experience it? Because followers of Christ must become personally and vitally involved in the death and resurrection of Christ. And this requires repentance, prayer, watchfulness, self-denial, detachment from the world, humility, obedience and cross carrying!

— A. W. Tozer

Philistia in Despair
1 Samuel 5

The Ark of the Covenant is now in the hands of the Philistines, who brought it from "the stone of help" (Ebenezer) to Dagon's temple in Ashdod. Ashdod, one of five chief cities in Philistia, was located about fifty miles southwest of Shiloh (v. 1). William MacDonald observes that chapters 4 through 6 follow the Ark of the Covenant on a journey into and back out of enemy territory: "God would defend His honor in the midst of the Philistines (chp. 5), but He would not defend the Israelites when He was in their midst because they had ceased to honor Him (chp. 4)."[17]

The Philistines thought that because they had the Ark they could prevent Israel's gods from helping the Jews. The reference to plural deities probably meant that the Philistines assumed that the two cherubim over the Ark represented Israel's gods. Pagan nations usually did not exchange their gods, as foolish Israel often did, but they were not opposed to adding to their deity collection – the more gods on their side the better. The Philistines will soon learn that having the Ark did not hinder Israel's God from acting against them; in fact, just the opposite was true.

The Philistines brought their new trophy into the temple of Dagon and set it next to Dagon's image (v. 2). Dagon, the fish god, was widely revered in Mesopotamia and along the eastern Mediterranean coast (vv. 1-7; Judg. 16:23-24). Archeologists have actually unearthed several images of Dagon as far east as Nineveh.

When the people of Ashdod entered Dagon's temple the next morning, they found the huge image of their god face down on the ground before Jehovah's Ark. Not willing for Dagon to remain in such a humiliating position, they labored to reset its image on its pedestal.

It should have occurred to the Philistines that, if Dagon were a real god, the Ark of the Covenant would have toppled over before Dagon's image, not vice versa. Ironically, only a corrupt pagan heart can revere an image incapable of standing up on its own. The Dagon worshipers did not comprehend God's first demonstration for them, so He prepared another. (One can only imagine the amusing scene in heaven if the Lord had asked for a volunteer to go down and knock over Dagon's image – what angel would not have enjoyed such a delightful task?)

The very next morning they again found Dagon face down before the Ark, but this time its head and its hands had broken off when it struck the threshold before its pedestal (v. 4). Now all that was left of poor Dagon was the fishy-part (its tail-torso). C. H. Mackintosh highlights the spiritual application from the religious scene before us:

> The effort of the Philistines to keep the ark of God among them proved a complete failure. They could not make Dagon and Jehovah dwell together – how blasphemous the attempt! *"What accord has Christ with Belial?"* None! The standard of God can never be lowered so as to accommodate itself to the principles which govern the men of this world, and the attempt to hold Christ with one hand and the world with the other must issue in shame and confusion of face. Yet, how many are making the effort! How many are there who seem to make it the great question, how much of the world they can retain without sacrificing the name and privileges of Christians! This is a deadly evil, a dreadful snare of Satan, and it may with strict propriety be identified as the most refined selfishness. It is bad enough for men to walk in the lawlessness and corruption of their own heart, but to connect evil with the holy name of Christ is the climax of guilt.[18]

Indeed, Dagon and Jehovah could not dwell together as equals. By removing Dagon's head and hands, Jehovah was showing that idols had neither the wisdom nor the power to move against Him. The Ashdodites now knew that Jehovah was able to protect His own glory, even when His people had ceased to care for it. Additionally, they were forced to realize, that if Dagon could not protect itself against Israel's God, they could not expect Dagon to safeguard them.

Instead of fearing Jehovah, the superstitious Philistines responded to this mishap with a new tradition to honor Dagon: *"Neither the priests of Dagon nor any who come into Dagon's house tread on the threshold of Dagon in Ashdod to this day"* (v. 5). Apparently over time, this pagan practice developed into a tradition of not stepping on any threshold even when entering one's house. The prophet Zephaniah will later condemn this practice, promising all who engage in such pagan superstitions will be judged by Babylonian invaders (Zeph. 1:9).

Jehovah had symbolically demonstrated His superiority over Dagon in its own temple, but the Philistines had rejected God's warning. Therefore, He would use increasingly drastic measures to get their attention. He ravaged the people of Ashdod and its territory with plagues, even smiting them with tumors (v. 6). The inhabitants of Ashdod recognized that the God of Israel was against them and decided the Ark could not remain among them (v. 7). The lords of the Philistines were gathered to consider the matter and it was decided that the Ark should be carried from Ashdod to Gath, and so it was (v. 8).

However, the citizens of Gath also experienced the wrath of Jehovah and many of the people, both young and old, suffered from tumors (v. 9). Accordingly, the people in Gath took the Ark to Ekron; however, the Ekronites were already aware of what had happened in Ashdod and Gath and cried out, *"They have brought the ark of the God of Israel to us, to kill us and our people!"* (v. 10).

The Ekronites also experienced terrible death and destruction in their city and demanded that the lords of the Philistines *"send away the ark of the God of Israel, and let it go back to its own place, so that it does not kill us and our people"* (v. 11). Apparently, the death toll was especially high in Ekron (v. 12). Those in that city who did not die were stricken with painful tumors. Peter J. Pell offers this application from this incident for those in the Church Age:

> The final verdict is, *"Send away the ark of the God of Israel, and let it go again to his own place."* As long as Christianity is one religion amongst many, the world will tolerate it. Christians who serve God and money get on well in the world, but let the power of God be manifested in grace or judgment and the world tries to rid itself of His presence.[19]

The groaning of the sick and the wailing of mourners made such a din as to be heard in the heights of heaven. Unfortunately, the Philistines were concerned only about being healed from the diseases Jehovah had inflicted on them; they had no regard for God's remedy for their sin-sickened souls. Israel knew what the Philistines did not; Jehovah was not merely a God who punishes evil, but One who delights in delivering and blessing the humble and the righteous.

41

Because of our first parents' separation from God through sin, we all were born as condemned creatures into a cursed world full of sorrows (John 3:18; Rom. 5:12; 8:20-22). If God had not intervened with the death and resurrection of His Son to extend the offer of forgiveness and eternal life, man would have suffered a most miserable and meaningless existence. Having been reconciled to God through Christ means that all the events in our lives have been permitted or designed as opportunities to better us and to honor God's name (Rom. 8:28; Eph. 2:10; Phil. 1:20-21). In Christ, suffering has purpose and is beneficial. Calamity therefore clarifies our condition, persecution purifies our convictions, and suffering determines our glory in Christ (Rom. 8:18)! As we will see in the next chapter, the pestilence and death experienced in Philistia enlightened the Philistines as to their position before Israel's God – they had offended Him and were suffering His wrath!

Meditation

> We all know people who have been made much meaner and more irritable and more intolerable to live with by suffering: it is not right to say that all suffering perfects. It only perfects one type of person – the one who accepts the call of God in Christ Jesus.

> — Oswald Chambers

> God will not permit any troubles to come upon us, unless He has a specific plan by which great blessing can come out of the difficulty.

> — Peter Marshall

The Ark Is Returned
1 Samuel 6

All the devastation in the previous chapter occurred in the space of seven months while the Ark was in Philistia (v. 1). The Philistines now understood that the Ark of the Lord was not some victor's trophy that they could gloat over. It was not a spoil of war, but rather had spoiled their warfare. The people sought counsel from the pagan priests and diviners how to properly send the Ark back to where it belonged – Israel (v. 2).

Their instructions were: *"If you send away the ark of the God of Israel, do not send it empty; but by all means return it to Him with a trespass offering. Then you will be healed, and it will be known to you why His hand is not removed from you"* (v. 3). The people then asked the diviners what type of trespass offering should accompany the Ark. The pagan priests answered, *"five golden tumors and five golden rats"* and then they explained their reasoning, *"for the same plague was on all of you and on your lords"* (v. 4). Their idea was that, since Jehovah had ravaged the Philistines with tumors and Philistia with rats, they should acknowledge that fact by returning the Ark with a trespass offering (v. 5). This was to be ten gold images (five of rats and five of tumors). Some believe that God used the rats to spread the plague among the people (e.g., the bubonic plaque is carried by fleas on rats). The Philistines hoped that God would accept their offering and cease plaguing them.

The pagan priests devised a way of determining whether or not Jehovah had accepted this trespass offering. The plan was to put the Ark and a chest containing their gold images on a newly constructed cart to be pulled by two milk cows that had never been yoked (vv. 7-8). If the cows, separated from their calves, were led, with no human intervention, to carry the Ark to Beth-Shemesh in Israelite territory, then they would know all was well. Since the gold tumors and rat images were with the Ark, this would mean that Jehovah had accepted their trespass offering (v. 9).

The Philistines did exactly what was suggested and then Philistia's leaders followed the lowing cows that were pulling the cart loaded with the Ark and with their chest of gold images (vv. 10-11). The cows did not veer off the road to Beth-Shemesh even once but pulled the cart to a place near a large stone in the field of Joshua of Beth-Shemesh (v. 14). The inhabitants of Beth-Shemesh were reaping wheat in the valley when the Ark of the Covenant suddenly appeared before them (v. 13). This was an occasion for great rejoicing – the Ark was back in Israel!

The Ark and the chest of gold images were unloaded by the Levites (and apparently some priests). They set both on the large stone and the wood of the cart was split and the cows offered as burnt offerings to the Lord (v. 15). The Philistine lords who followed the cart were watching from a distance. After witnessing what had occurred, they returned to Ekron confident that Israel's God had accepted their offering of restitution (v. 16). We learn, in verses 17-18, that there were five lords from Philistia present, one from each of the five cities that had been plagued (Ashdod, Gaza, Ashkelon, Gath, and Ekron).

Sadly, this festive occasion in Israel was marred by disobedience; some of the men from Beth-Shemesh did not treat the Ark as a profound symbol of God's holy presence. They removed the mercy seat over the Ark to look inside, perhaps to see if the stone tablets containing the Law were still there (v. 19). God did not strike down the pagan Philistines for desecrating the Ark because they did not know better, but the Jewish men of Beth-Shemesh did, and thus they perished for the blatant offense.

The Mosaic Law permitted only the Levites to handle (carry) the ark (Num. 4). The priests assigned to cover the Ark with a veil to prepare it for transport during the wilderness wanderings could not even look upon it. Why the Levities permitted the common people to touch the holy Ark is unknown. There would have been many Levites present at the scene, for Beth-Shemesh was one of the forty-eight Levitical cities established by Joshua (Josh. 21:16).

The KJV and NKJV versions of the Bible indicate that 50,070 men perished in this divine judgment; however, some older Hebrew manuscripts have the correct number – 70 men. The accurate recording of numbers in Hebrew text has proven to be particularly challenging for Jewish scribes (copiers). The Hebrew numerical system was somewhat like that of the Romans in that they used a series of letters for numbers. Some of the Hebrew letters were quite similar to one another, making the job of copying numbers even more difficult. However, these types of errors are often obvious when comparing parallel Bible passages or by using common sense. So how many men would be living in the small rural town of Beth-Shemesh? Not 50,000; perhaps, at most, a few hundred.

This discrepancy is best explained as a scribal error in copying the Hebrew number accurately. The original writings of Scripture were inspired, but the copyists were not inspired, and they made errors. Through textual criticism, we can affirm that the Hebrew manuscript is very close to the original autograph with a very high degree of confidence. In fact, ninety percent of the existing Old Testament manuscripts are without variance and nearly all the remaining ten percent variance can be attributed to stylistic, spelling, or word order differences. The Jews took great care in copying the manuscripts accurately, but no amount of carefulness is going to prevent mistakes when a text is hand-copied dozens of times.

God's judgment had a sobering effect on those living in Beth-Shemesh: *"Who is able to stand before this holy Lord God?"* (v. 20). They did not want the Ark to stay in their community lest more of them die, so they sent messengers to the inhabitants of Kirjath-Jearim, saying: *"The Philistines have brought back the ark of the Lord; come down and take it up with you"* (v. 21). They probably did not mention that many of their men had died because of the Ark, as that detail may have discouraged those at Kirjath-Jearim from receiving it.

How often man, being overzealous in religious matters, is punished by God for some self-willed offense, but then, after being corrected, they fly off to the opposite extreme in utter defiance of God. Such was the case with the men of Beth-Shemesh; they had been eager to handle the Ark, but then did not want anything to do with it after God's judgment fell on them. We will see in the next chapter that the men of Kirjath-Jearim were not afraid to have the symbol of God's holy presence with them. They will come to Beth-Shemesh and, handling the Ark with proper care, will take it to the house of Abinadab located on a hill (6:1). The men of Kirjath-Jearim show us the proper balance of holy reverence and emotional fanfare while serving the Lord.

Meditation

O God, most holy are Thy ways,
And who like Thee deserves my praise?
Thou only doest wondrous things,
The whole wide world Thy glory sings;
Thine outstretched arm Thy people saved,
Though sore distressed and long enslaved.

— The Psalter

The Ark Remains at Kirjath-Jearim
1 Samuel 7

The Ark in Abinadab's Home (vv. 1-2)

Over the previous eight months the Ark had covered about 120 miles as it was transported from Shiloh to Ebenezer, to Aphek, to Ashdod, to Gath, to Ekron, to Beth-Shemesh, and then finally to the house of Abinadab at Kirjath-Jearim (v. 1).

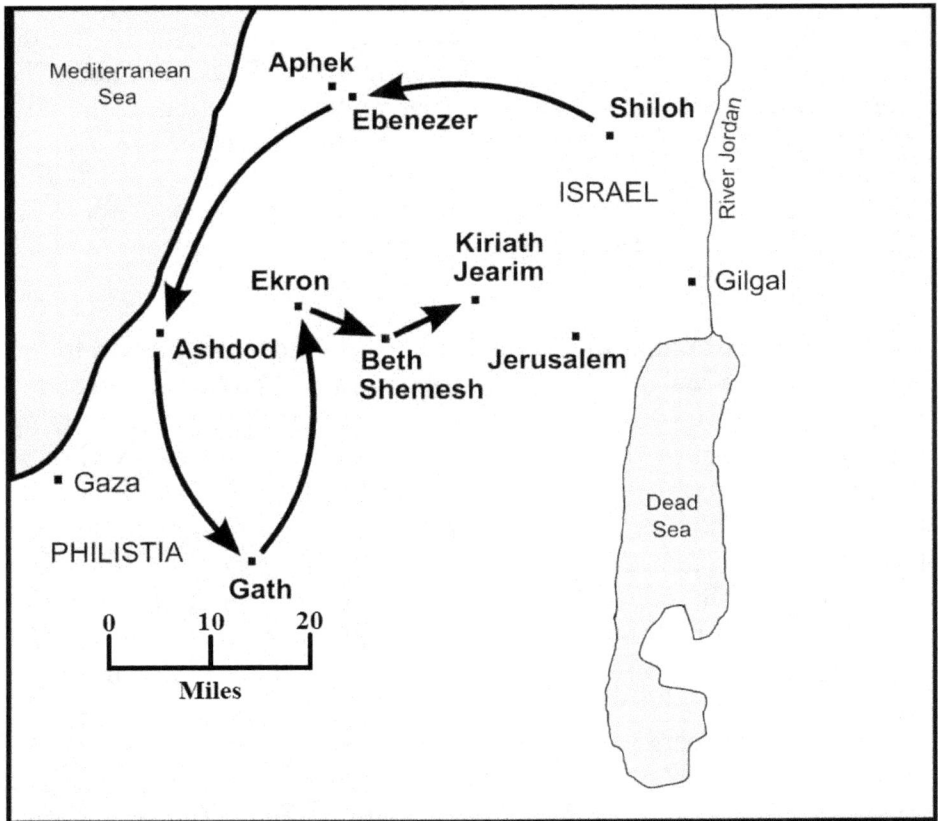

Interestingly, Kirjath-Jearim was one of four towns belonging to the Gibeonites who were not of Jewish descent (Josh. 9:17). The congregational prayer of Psalm 132 recounts how the Ark of the Covenant was joyfully found by David in Ephrathah, after it had been returned by the Philistines years earlier (Ps. 132:6-8).

Abinadab opened the door of his home and his heart to sanctify a proper resting place for the Ark. Many would be coming and going from his home for decades to see the Ark and, during that time, he and his household guarded God's testimony among His people. His example should prompt believers today to maintain a proper testimony of Christ in our hearts, homes, and church gatherings so others who come and go may see Him also.

Abinadab put the care of the Ark of the Lord into the hands of his son Eleazar. Albert Barnes suggests that, given the edicts of the Law, Abinadab must have been a Levite to be entrusted with the Ark's care.[20] Other than a passing reference to the Ark in chapter 14, we do not hear of it again until King David brought it to Jerusalem, about 70 years later (2 Sam. 6). The twenty-year reference relating to the Ark being at Kirjath-Jearim has been the focus of much debate:

> So it was that the ark remained in Kirjath-Jearim a long time; it was there twenty years. And all the house of Israel lamented after the Lord (v. 2).

Textually speaking, the twenty-year period does not pertain to the Ark's arrival to and departure from Abinadab's house, but rather the interim between its arrival and the revival under Samuel's leadership (see the latter part of verse 2). Israel languished twenty years while the Ark was at Abinadab's home until the Jews gathered to lament before the Lord. At this time, Samuel is approximately forty years of age. He has been long esteemed by Israel for his high character and faithfulness as a priest, but he does not enter into the duties of a civil magistrate until this chapter. The most likely explanation for this delay is that Samuel simply lacked the respect and wisdom that naturally accompanies age.

The twenty years cannot possibly be linked to David moving the Ark from Abinadab's house to Jerusalem after taking the city from the Jebusites in his eighth year as king (2 Sam. 5:6-7). We learn from 2 Samuel 5:4-5 that David was thirty years old when he began to reign and that he ruled in Hebron over Judah seven years and six months, and then in Jerusalem for thirty-three years over all Israel and Judah. We also know that Saul ruled for forty years (Acts 12:21), that the Ark was at Abinadab's house long before Saul was recognized as Israel's king (10:24), and that the revival in this chapter occurred several years before Saul was king.

Some scholars suggest that the awkwardness of *the twenty-year* reference in the text suggests that a scribe added it much later in an attempt to provide chronology with David's moving of the Ark. While this may be possible, there is nothing in Scripture to suggest that the reference is out of place. If we assume that twenty years did elapse from the Ark's arrival at Kirjath-Jearim to the beginning of the revival, that would mean that the Ark would have been at Abinadab's house for 70 years, if Saul was recognized as king two years after the arrival. Josephus suggests this gap was twelve years, which would mean that the Ark was at Abinadab's house a total of 80 years. Seventy years better fits the chronology in the book.

Regardless of the position one takes about the twenty-year reference, the household of Abinadab faithfully protected the Ark for a long time until David took it to Jerusalem. Would-be thieves were probably discouraged from trying to steal the gold Ark after hearing how the Philistines had been severely judged for wrongly possessing it.

For about four centuries, the Ark had resided in the most holy place of the tabernacle pitched at Shiloh. The high priest resided at Shiloh also. Those Jews loyal to Jehovah, like Elkanah, went to Shiloh to worship the Lord throughout this period. However, that all changed after the Ark was captured by the Philistines and then returned to Kirjath-Jearim in Israel. Instead, the Jews started offering their sacrifices on high places throughout Israel rather than at the central sanctuary (1 Kgs. 3:2-4), which the priests subsequently moved from Shiloh to Nob (21:1-4). Obviously, without the Ark, some ceremonies, such as the Day of Atonement, could not be performed at all. Other ceremonies, such as maintaining a lighted Lampstand and presenting weekly show bread in the tabernacle, were continued.

Revival Comes to Israel (vv. 3-17)

After the Ark had been in Kirjath-Jearim for twenty long years, Samuel senses the time for revival has come. He does not mince words about his countrymen's sin, but rather rebukes their idolatry directly. He then challenges the people to prove their loyalty to Jehovah by ridding themselves of their images. They must stop honoring Baal and Ashtoreth, and worship only Jehovah:

> *Then Samuel spoke to all the house of Israel, saying, "If you return to the Lord with all your hearts, then put away the foreign gods and the Ashtoreths from among you, and prepare your hearts for the Lord, and serve Him only; and He will deliver you from the hand of the Philistines." So the children of Israel put away the Baals and the Ashtoreths, and served the Lord only* (vv. 3-4).

The reference to plural "Baals" and "Ashtoreths" indicates the widespread practice of worshiping these false gods at Canaanite shrines scattered across the hillsides of Israel. Eugene H. Merrill explains the identity of these pagan deities:

> Baal, variously identified as son of El (Chief of the Canaanite pantheon) or as son of Dagan (the Mesopotamian deity), was particularly recognized as the god of thunder and rain whose task was to make the earth fertile annually. Ashtoreth (or Astarte) was goddess of both love and war, as were her Babylonian and Greek counterparts Ishtar and Aphrodite respectively. She apparently functioned with Baal as a fertility deity and by their sexual union in some magical way the earth and all its life supposedly experience annual rejuvenation and fruitfulness.[21]

We are reminded of two important truths in verses 3-4. First, the lost cannot be delivered without first becoming aware of how much their sin grieves the Lord. Second, the Lord will not tolerated a divided heart in those who worship Him; they must "serve the Lord only." The Lord Jesus warned His disciples that having more than one master would keep them from committing to live their lives for Him: *"No one can serve two masters; for either he will hate the one and love the other, or else he will be loyal to the one and despise the other. You cannot serve God and mammon"* (Matt. 6:24). Divided allegiance is not possible, for ultimately a slave can be devoted to only one master. The Lord states that there can be no middle ground; He is either the believer's first love or He is not the believer's Master at all.

The Lord Jesus demands that He have first place in our hearts: *"He that loves father or mother more than Me, is not worthy of Me; and he that loves son or daughter more than Me, is not worthy of Me"* (Matt. 10:37). The church at Ephesus was solemnly warned by the Lord Himself concerning their diminishing love for Him – He was no longer their first love (Rev. 2:4). Twice He tells them to repent of that offense. Dear reader, examine your own heart today. Is the Lord Jesus your first love?

Verse 4 informs us that the people responded well to Samuel's challenge for they put away their idols. Israel's first step to being restored to God was agreeing with Him about the abomination of paganism, and then turning from it.

After observing this step of consecration, Samuel summoned the nation to Mizpah so that he might pray for them there (v. 5). Mizpah was located about seven miles north of Jerusalem on the western boundary of Benjamin's territory (Josh. 18:26). Much of the nation responded to this charge and met at Mizpah to fast and to weep before the Lord to confess their sins (v. 6). The water poured out on the ground symbolized their utter weakness and unworthiness before the Lord. Jeremiah will later apply the same metaphor: *"Pour out your heart like water before the face of the Lord. Lift your hands toward Him"* (Lam. 2:19). Water on the ground is completely lost – it cannot refresh a thirsty soul.

This gesture confirmed that a real work of God was taking place among His people. Their confession of sin together with this symbol indicated that they no longer had confidence in a lifeless form (i.e., the Ark), but rather in His means of restoring them through the atoning blood of the lamb. It is when God's people so humble themselves in His presence and rely solely on the blood of His Lamb, the Lord Jesus Christ, that *"He who is able to do exceedingly abundantly above all that we ask or think"* (Eph. 3:20) – does so!

Their bitter enemy, the Philistines, were alarmed by this large assembly and assumed that Israel was preparing to attack them. In response to the perceived threat, they gathered their own forces to preempt Israel's supposed attack (v. 7). But the Philistines were mistaken; Israel had gathered at Mizpah to confess their sins and to get right with the Lord.

The town of Mizpah had served previously as a place for the Jewish nation to assemble when important matters needed to be decided (Judg.

19-21). Later, Samuel will present Saul as Israel's first king at Mizpah (10:17). Mizpah became the capital of Judah after the Babylonians destroyed Jerusalem in 586 B.C. (2 Kgs. 25:23-25).

After learning that the Philistines were amassing against them, the Jews, being totally unprepared for battle, were much afraid. They begged Samuel, *"Do not cease to cry out to the Lord our God for us, that He may save us from the hand of the Philistines"* (v. 8). Samuel responded by offering a sucking lamb for a burnt offering to the Lord, and then cried out to Him on Israel's behalf (v. 9).

We observe in Scripture that repentance is the first step a sinner must take and that without it there can be no salvation (e.g., vv. 3-6). The Lord Jesus said, *"Unless you repent you will all likewise perish"* (Luke 13:3). Repentance means, firstly, that we agree with God that we are sinners deserving His judgment and then that we turn away from all we ever thought would earn us heaven; such repentance indicates a deep grief over personal sin and a desire to turn from wickedness (Jer. 8:6). Secondly, we must turn to something – that is, we must believe in God's way of salvation, which is the gospel of Jesus Christ in the Church Age. The Thessalonians, for example, faithfully turned from paganism to God through the sacrifice of God's Lamb (Christ; 1 Thess. 1:5-9).

Samuel shows us that proper intercession to God to deliver the guilty is possible through the blood of an unblemished innocent lamb. Here the suckling lamb represents the tender, perfect, sinless Lamb of God who was wholly consumed in judgment (as symbolized in the burnt offering) for sins that were not His own. By Calvary's Lamb (which Samuel's lamb typifies), God's forgiveness and victory are assured for all who want deliverance from sin and the power and peace of His communion!

The Lord, therefore, accepted Samuel's offering and heard his prayers for Israel. In response, the Lord "thundered" on the Philistines to confuse them (v. 10). The Lord may have used bolts of lightning to strike down some of the Philistines, but clearly the loud peals of thunder caused by the lightning disoriented them. Josephus suggests that in addition to the lightning and thunder, a violent earthquake also struck the Philistines. Israel then pursued and smote their stunned and beleaguered attackers all the way to Beth Car (v. 11). Beth Car is an unknown location, likely west of Mizpah and towards Philistia. To acknowledge God's intervention and deliverance, *"Samuel took a stone and set it up between Mizpah and Shen, and called its name Ebenezer, saying, 'Thus far the Lord has helped us'"* (v. 12). The stone pillar symbolized a new era of hope for the Jews – God was with them and was helping them again!

Peter J. Pell summarizes why Israel was victorious:

> The battle was the Lord's; the victory was theirs. Israel follows in the path of a beaten foe pursuing them as far as Beth Car, literally "the house of the lamb." Thus the path of victory led from the lamb sacrificed to the lamb "housed and happy." Our trail of triumph leads from the cross to the throne, for in His triumphant story is the record of our own.[22]

The "Stone of Help" would remind Israel that when they were armed and numerous, they had been soundly defeated by the Philistines, but now, years later at the same location, being few and unarmed, God had fought for them and had defeated the Philistines. Dear believer, despite our trials and oppression, life is simply much easier when we walk with the Lord, for He is able!

God's victory at Mizpah brought to an end the long, brutal years of oppression at the hands of the Philistines that Israel had suffered while languishing in spiritual declension. Not only did the Philistines not venture into Israel's territory again during the years of Samuel's judgeship of Israel, but the Lord's people actually regained the land that the Philistines had taken from them (vv. 13-14). How was this possible? Because the Jews were honoring Jehovah again and His hand *"was against the Philistines all the days of Samuel."* Furthermore, the fame of this spectacular victory over the Philistines spread throughout the region, thus discouraging other people groups from intruding into their affairs. For example, the writer notes that there was peace between Israel and the Amorites also.

There are similar revivals and spectacular deliverances by God of His people throughout Israel's history (e.g., the building of the temple in the days of Zerubbabel, and of the wall during Nehemiah's day). May the Church too repent of her sins, humbly reach up to heaven with clean hands, and may God visit His people again with revitalizing power! As in Samuel's day, our enemy, the devil, fears God's people when they humble themselves, repent of their sins, and become desperate for God.

53

The Itinerant Judge (vv. 15-17)

Samuel judged Israel all the remaining days of his life. During the latter years of his judgeship, he shared authority over the people with King Saul. Samuel was a shepherd burdened with the care and protection of God's flock. He annually visited cities such as Bethel, Gilgal, and Mizpah as an itinerant judge (v. 16). We learn in verse 17 that Samuel made Ramah (the place of his birth) his home. This is where his family resided and also where he built an altar to the Lord. Undeniably, Samuel was busy serving others, but not too busy that he neglected his relationship with the Lord. Samuel's altar at Ramah shows us that he remained a loyal worshiper of Jehovah while he served others.

With that said, it is natural for us to wonder why Samuel did not return to the Lord's altar which was now at Nob or why he did not remove the Ark from Abinadab's home? William MacDonald suggests that such quandaries are best answered by realizing that "these were days of irregularities, many things being practiced which God allowed even though they weren't according to His original design."[23]

Samuel was a lifelong Nazarite who served the Lord by representing the people to God as a priest and representing God to the people as a prophet. He judged the people with justice so that they would not lose the benefit of either office.

Both the work of intercession on behalf of others and the ministry of God's word to others are important ministries, but notice that Samuel put the work of prayer (v. 5) before ministry (v. 15). This was the example of the apostles in the early Church: *"we will give ourselves continually to prayer and to the ministry of the word"* (Acts 6:4). We also would do well to seek the Lord first to obtain guidance and grace for the coming day, before recklessly charging ahead on our own.

Meditation

Lord, we confess our numerous faults, how great our guilt has been!
Foolish and vain were all our thoughts, and all our lives were sin.
But, O my soul, forever praise, forever love, His name
Who turns thy feet from dangerous ways of folly, sin, and shame.

— Isaac Watts

Israel Demands a King
1 Samuel 8

Josephus places the birth of Samuel in 1064 B.C. and his death in 1012 B.C.[24] While the year of Samuel's death is well-placed, the date of his birth does not coordinate well with the biblical narrative. (Samuel must be older at this juncture than Josephus assumed.) Eli's death may have occurred about the time Samuel turned thirty so that he could legitimately replace Eli as the high priest and comply with the minimum age requirement of thirty to enter the sanctuary (Num. 4:3). Special circumstances granted Samuel access to the sanctuary at an early age, but he only assisted the priests; there is no evidence that he performed sacrifices himself. We do know that Samuel judged Israel for twenty years after Eli's death and before the revival occurred (7:2), and then an additional period of time elapsed before Saul's anointing (7:14).

This suggests that Samuel would be in his late forties as chapter 8 commences. If this age is correct, Samuel could have had two sons in their mid-twenties, whom he could have then appointed as judges in Beersheba over Israel (v. 1). The name of Samuel's firstborn son was Joel, and the name of his second, Abijah (v. 2). Sadly, Samuel's sons did not possess the integrity of their father in upholding their duties; rather, they sought *"dishonest gain, took bribes, and perverted justice"* (v. 3). Apparently, Samuel's many years of itinerant ministry came at a personal cost to his family – his sons were not the godly seed the Lord desired (Mal. 2:14-15).

Moses learned, while en route to Egypt, that God's word must be obeyed in the home before greater feats for God can be accomplished outside the home. He had become complacent about obeying God's command of circumcision, likely to avoid a family altercation with his wife Zipporah who, as a Midianite, opposed the rite. How serious a matter is obedience to the Lord? The Lord was ready to slay His chosen deliverer, if the rite were not immediately carried out on Gershom (Ex.

4:24-26). As head of the home, Moses was responsible to God for his family, and until things were right with God in his own house, there could be no God-honoring ministry outside the home. Zipporah was forced to immediately circumcise her young son to save the life of her husband. James Vernon McGee suggests that Moses obviously thought he could get away with this area of disobedience:

> He just let it slide like many Christian workers do who neglect their own families while trying to fix up other people's families. God intervened in Moses' life. He waylaid him on the way to Egypt and revealed to him the seriousness of the situation.[25]

May Moses' and Samuel's family situations be a warning to all God's servants not to neglect their primary responsibility to honor the Lord in their homes. Spouses should not be neglected and children should be nurtured in the admonition of the Lord – lest God's word be blasphemed by onlookers (Tit. 2:5).

Samuel's only mistake recorded in Scripture was stepping ahead of the Lord in appointing his sons as judges over Israel. Their duplicitous behavior prompted the elders to visit Samuel at his home in Ramah (v. 4). Their message was painfully blunt: *"Look, you are old, and your sons do not walk in your ways. Now make us a king to judge us like all the nations"* (v. 5). Although the years had not yet diminished Samuel's ability to judge Israel, the elders knew that he was almost fifty years of age, the appointed time for priests to retire from the rigors of their office (Num. 8:25). Scripture does not record any sign of senility or decay in Samuel's faculties even to the very end of his full and eventful life. For example, in about twenty-five years from now he will powerfully rebuke Saul for his folly and will personally hew Agag into pieces with a sword (15:33).

If Samuel had not appointed his sons as judges, the elders would probably not have confronted him at this time. Because he had relinquished some of his judicial responsibility to unfit men, these leaders assumed that Samuel would be retiring soon. Certainly, no one wants to suffer injustice at the hands of perverse judges, but the elders' excuse really revealed a deeper problem – their dissatisfaction with God's administration over them. Realistically, it is doubtful Samuel's sons would be more prone to take bribes than ordinary Gentile judges would be, meaning that the complaint enabled the deeper issue to surface – Israel wanted to be like the Gentile nations with a king ruling over them (v. 6). The motivation of the request was not to pursue greater holiness with God, but for greater freedom to pursue personal gratification and political vanity.

The fact that the elders had rejected his sons, and even called him "old," did not upset Samuel, but he was greatly displeased that they wanted a king to judge them. Their request was a flat rejection of God's form of government, which Samuel knew must result in stern discipline. It seems evident that Samuel also felt slighted by the request because the Lord consoled him over the offense (v. 6).

Samuel then sought guidance from the Lord, who promptly answered his request:

> *Heed the voice of the people in all that they say to you;* ***for they have not rejected you, but they have rejected Me, that I should not reign over them.*** *According to all the works which they have done since the day that I brought them up out of Egypt, even to this day – with which they have forsaken Me and served other gods – so they are doing to you also. Now therefore, heed their voice. However, you shall solemnly forewarn them, and show them the behavior of the king who will reign over them* (vv. 7-9).

First, the Lord told Samuel not to take the offense personally; Israel was rejecting Him, not His prophet, as their ruler. The Lord consoled Samuel by telling him that He too had felt dejected and abandoned by Israel's previously idolatry. Now Israel was rejecting Him as their King. The Lord did not want Israel to be ruled by a king because He would oversee them better than any human ruler could. Additionally, the Lord desired that His people remain unique among the nations and consecrated to His holy purposes; they were not to adopt secular notions of government.

Obviously, none of this caught the Lord by surprise. Moses had foretold centuries earlier that Israel would eventually want a king, instead of the Lord, to rule over them. Moses also warned his countrymen of the dangers of anointing a king. Anticipating their future request, he also laid down rules for the kings to follow, lest they stray from the Lord (Deut. 17), for if the king drifted from the Lord, the people would forsake Him also. In God's grand plan of redemption, He always intended to anoint a righteous king to rule over Israel – David –

who typified a descendant of his who would be the King of kings and would rule over the whole earth in righteousness. This plan is clearly seen in the promise God made to Abraham and Sarah that some of their descendants would be kings (Gen. 17:16).

The Lord instructed Samuel to forewarn the people of the cost of choosing a human king to rule them (vv. 11-17). C. Knapp suggests that God's response to be given by Samuel to Israel's insistent elders must have been a great relief to God's prophet:

> Samuel's position was a trying one; for if he flatly refused to grant them their request for a king, it might appear to them that he was unwilling to resign his authority, or he wished for his sons to succeed him in office; and if he had acceded to their demand, he might become an accessory to their sin, as did Aaron with this stiff-necked people, when they said, *"Up, make us gods, which shall go before us,"* and like him, bring wrath upon himself and them for yielding to their sinful desire.[26]

So Samuel told the people that a king would demand many of their sons, daughters, and servants to create an army, to make weapons, to till and to reap his fields, and to cook and to bake for him. Furthermore, the king would take for himself and his servants the best of their fields, vineyards, and olive groves. He would also seize their donkeys for labor and a tenth of their sheep for food (i.e., alluding to a general ten percent income tax). Speaking of the kings, Samuel says six times that *"he will take"* from the people, and twice that he will "give" what is taken to his servants and officers. His point was that the livelihood of the common people would suffer by having a king.

Lastly, Samuel sarcastically warned the people not to cry out to the Lord if they were oppressed by a tyrannical monarch in the future; God would not heed their prayers (v. 18). They had been forewarned as to what would happen if they sought a king and therefore would have no business complaining to God about him later. Before we look down our noses at Israel, we must confess our own propensity to hero-worship when we also are out of touch with God. While we may not create a golden calf to worship, we still long for a visible captain to lead, protect, and comfort us. But we must realize that our flesh is oblivious to the administration of the Holy Spirit. His presence within remains secret until true faith acts to overrule our natural impulses of carnal rule – then the communion and power of God are emphatically enjoyed.

Despite Samuel's forthrightness, the people would not relent; they wanted to be like the nations and to have a visible ruler over them: *"No, but we will have a king over us, that we also may be like all the nations, and that our king may judge us and go out before us and fight our battles"* (vv. 19-20). The reference to *"go out before us and fight our battles"* suggests that Israel's elders were anxious about a growing threat or threats against the Jewish nation. We later learn that they did fear an imminent attack by Nahash the Ammonite (11:1, 12:12). Under Samuel's leadership the Philistines had been suppressed, but they were growing stronger and a breach of Israel's existing peace treaty with Philistia seemed probable. Chapter 13 indicates that this was a valid concern, though it was actually Saul who broke the treaty.

We pause to consider three applications for the Church today as drawn from what Israel said to Samuel. First, are we willing to be fully identified as Christ-ones among the mass of unregenerate souls in the world today? Our speech, behavior, character, and the message that we preach should all identify us as Christ's ambassadors – are we His peculiar people on the earth? Second, are we content with God's government and order for the family and the home as decreed in Scripture? Third, is the Lord truly our Rock and Shield or do we trust in the devices of men or our own resources to deliver us out of hardships and calamities? Israel did not want to be different than the nations, nor did they want to submit to God's government, or trust in the Lord to defeat their enemies. Rather, they wanted a king. But before we look down our noses at Israel, let us remember that, in practice, we can have the same attitudes that angered the Lord in Samuel's day!

An annoyed Samuel again took the entire matter to the Lord, who instructed Samuel to *"heed their voice, and make them a king"* (vv. 21-22). As Israel had already learned in the wilderness (when they whined for meat and then God inundated them with quail), sometimes God corrects His people by giving them what they want, rather than what they need. We all must learn that the soul will never be satisfied with that which lacks God's approval and blessing. The psalmist puts the matter this way: *"He gave them their request, but sent leanness into their soul"* (Ps. 106:15). Since the Lord had granted the elders' request, Samuel dismissed them and each man returned to his home (v. 23).

The rebellion of His wayward people angered the Lord – His people did not want Him to reign over them! Israel had rejected His sovereign rule; they had forgotten His past goodness. Instead the Jewish nation wanted a selfish, fallible human leader. But in reality, nothing could have been worse for them than to get what they craved. They would soon learn that seeking to gratify one's lusts leaves a bitter taste in one's mouth. Israel was still suffering from the same delusion three centuries later. At that time, Hosea reminded Israel that God in His anger had appointed Saul as their king to teach them the repercussions of rejecting Him (12:12; Hos. 13:11).

Praise God for His providential care of His people, but woe to those who needlessly choose to stir up His righteous indignation. No God-appointed judge of Israel was ever slain in battle. Additionally, under Samuel's leadership, Israel had enjoyed both deliverance from the Philistines and economic prosperity. In contrast to God's proven administration, the king of their choice would be a fleshly man, who would attempt to kill God's man (David) and who would ultimately perish in battle against the Philistines because God was not with him.

God always accomplishes His predetermined purposes – may we choose to walk with God in them! How we respond to what He reveals will determine if we are swept away against our will by punitive waves of judgment or are joyfully carried along in currents of His sovereign grace and peace.

Meditation

Come, Thou Fount of every blessing,
Tune my heart to sing Thy grace;
Streams of mercy, never ceasing,
Call for songs of loudest praise.

Prone to wander, Lord, I feel it;
Prone to leave the God I love:
Take my heart, oh, take and seal it
With Thy Spirit from above.

Rescued thus from sin and danger,
Purchased by the Savior's blood,
May I walk on earth a stranger,
As a son and heir of God.

— Robert Robinson

Saul Chosen
1 Samuel 9

In this chapter, the Lord chooses a king for Israel – one who is well-suited to the carnal palates of His people. His name is Saul, the son of Kish, a Benjamite of prominence residing in Gibeah (v. 1, 10:26, 11:4). Not only did Saul stand head and shoulders above everyone else, we also read that *"there was not a more handsome person than he among the children of Israel"* (v. 2). Because Israel had asked for a king, God chose Saul knowing that His fleshly people would approve of Saul's features. In time, the Jews would learn the fallacy of appraising a leader by his appearance, instead of by his integrity and passion for God.

Throughout Saul's forty-year reign, God would teach His people the painful consequences of living in the flesh instead of relying on His grace. They should have desired a "man of God" who delighted in the Lord and in His Law to lead them, rather than an unproven, "choice young man." The Lord had just such a man in mind, a faithful shepherd boy from Bethlehem in Judah. Spiritually speaking, David is everything that Saul is not, and more.

Kish sent his son Saul with a servant to find some lost donkeys (v. 3). Commenting on the lost donkeys, Jamieson, Fausset, and Brown explain the grazing scenario of that day:

> The probability is that the family of Kish, according to the immemorial usage of Oriental shepherds in the purely pastoral regions, had let the animals roam at large during the grazing season, at the close of which messengers were dispatched in search of them. Such traveling searches are common, and as each owner has his own stamp marked on his cattle, the mention of it to the shepherds he meets gradually leads to the discovery of the strayed animals.[27]

Over the next three days, Saul and Kish's servant will journey southeast from Gibeah through the mountains of Ephraim, then northeast to Shalisha (probably near Gilgal), then west to Shaalim, before turning back south to the land of Zuph, but they did not find the donkeys (v. 4). Since Zuph was Samuel's great-great-great-grandfather (1:1), their location after three days would have been near Samuel's hometown of Ramah (perhaps Gibeon just two miles west of Ramah or Mizpah about the same distance to the north). The two men had traveled 25 to 30 miles in a wide-sweeping counterclockwise loop. They were now likely less than five miles from their starting point, but unfortunately, still donkey-less.

Like Balaam in Numbers 22, Saul's association with a donkey seems to correlate with his fleshly, obstinate disposition. The donkey was an unclean animal, not fit for sacrifice (Lev. 11:3), and, as we all know, the donkey is a proverbial symbol of stubbornness.

Saul wanted to return home so that his father would not be worried over his absence (v. 5). However, the servant suggested something quite different: *"Look now, there is in this city a man of God, and he is an honorable man; all that he says surely comes to pass. So let us go there; perhaps he can show us the way that we should go"* (v. 6). Apparently, the servant did not personally know Samuel, but was aware of his good reputation. Saul was skeptical of the idea, because their supplies had been consumed during their three-day journey, which meant they had no gift to offer the man of God (v. 7). It was the normal custom to present a gift to a seer when seeking counsel from him. However, the servant has what Saul does not, currency, and he is willing to give what he has (one-fourth of a shekel of silver) to receive direction from God as to how to proceed (v. 8).

The writer inserts an explanatory note at verse 9 to assist us in understanding the cultural thinking at that time: *"(Formerly in Israel, when a man went to inquire of God, he spoke thus: 'Come, let us go to the seer'; for he who is now called a prophet was formerly called a seer.)"* Samuel Ridout clarifies the meaning of this statement:

In former times it was the custom to speak of the man of God as a "seer" – one who sees the future, or that which is not visible to the eyes of sense. In other words, the people were more occupied with the result of the prophet's ministry than with its Source. The later word "prophet" suggests the Source from which he received all his inspiration, which then flowed forth from him. This explanation in itself is in keeping with all the circumstances at which we have arrived, both in Saul himself (who surely was not troubled about his relation with God, or how the man of God would gain his information, but rather with the benefit which he might receive from this divine insight) and in the nation at large, of which he was the fitting representative.[28]

Samuel should not be considered as some fortune-telling seer to be paid for advice, but rather as a representative of God who delivered His word to the people.

Saul's lackluster introduction underscores his deficient leadership ability as already shown in a variety of affairs. First, Saul is tasked with finding lost donkeys and he fails. Second, he lacks initiative to finish what he has been tasked to do. Third, he does not consider seeking the Lord's help to find the missing animals, though his servant does (v. 9). Fourth, he has no resources to bless those serving God; again, it is the servant who supplies what Saul lacks. It is evident from the narrative that it is the servant who is leading Saul, not otherwise. Saul seeks what he cannot find, follows when he should lead, and benefits from what others possess, but has nothing to give in return.

While Samuel's narrative does highlight Saul's meager spiritual and leadership qualities, H. L. Rossier notes that he did possess several positive characteristics which are desirable in a good leader:

He is strong and valiant, handsome, tall, a choice man (vv. 1-2). ... He is subject to and affectionate toward his father (v. 5), disposed to listen to the counsel of his inferiors (v. 10), and little in his own eyes, whether it be in his tribe or in his family (v. 21). If the trial that God is about to make does not succeed with such a man, it is definitely because man's condition in general leaves no hope. Let us add that without this trial of the king according to the flesh, the ways of God toward David, His anointed, would not have been complete. What would have become of David's sufferings and affliction, the necessary prelude to his glory, if Saul had not been raised up?[29]

It is becoming evident that the Lord's selection of Saul as Israel's first king will have multiple benefits. The Lord will better prepare His people to receive their next king and also better David to serve His people. Saul's reign will teach the Jews what not to esteem in a king, and David's eight-year trial with Saul will teach him to humbly depend on the Lord to overcome his difficulties. Of course, we all benefit from

witnessing the consequences of living in the flesh while trying to serve
God, as exemplified in Saul's behavior.

Saul agrees with his servant's counsel, *"Well said; come, let us go"*
(v. 10). So the two men travel to a particular city where they believe
God's prophet will be. The city is not named, but did have one specific
high place associated with it (i.e., *bamah* is singular, thus "the high
place"). Ramah, Samuel's hometown seems likely, as it is in the area
that we find Saul, and Samuel had earlier erected an altar at Ramah.
Furthermore, Kish's servant from Gibeah specifically knows that a man
of God resides in that city. With that said, there were other high places
of worship throughout Israel at this time. Hence, it is possible that
Samuel might be in another city near Ramah; some suggest a city
further south in the vicinity of Bethlehem (7:17).[30] Samuel had just
arrived at the city in question (v. 12), which meant that he either had
just returned to Ramah from completing one of his judicial circuits, or
that he was still engaged in the iterant work.

As the two men neared the city, they inquired from some young
women drawing water where they might find God's prophet (v. 11).
They learned that Samuel was in the city and would be coming out
shortly to offer peace offerings on a hilltop altar just outside the city
(vv. 12-13). Some sort of religious festival was in progress, as the
general populace was all aware of it. Just as Saul and the servant
entered the city gate, they met Samuel coming out (v. 14).

The Lord had informed Samuel the previous day that Saul would be
visiting him:

> *Tomorrow about this time I will send you a man from the land of
> Benjamin, and you shall anoint him commander over My people
> Israel, that he may save My people from the hand of the Philistines;
> for I have looked upon My people, because their cry has come to Me*
> (vv. 15-16).

We pause to consider the sovereign ways of a merciful God with
His wayward people. First, notice that the Lord continues to identify
with those who had just rejected His rule in the previous chapter, twice
referring to them as *"My people."* Second, the Lord will not leave
Israel as a body without a head – He sends them "a captain" to deliver
them from the Philistines. As C. Knapp explains, our amazing God is

able to correct His people for their defiance while delivering them from their misery:

> Though God had told the people in the plainest terms, through Samuel, that when groaning under the oppression of their distress, He would not hear them (8:18), yet here He says, *"Their cry is come unto Me."* The first was in government, and they most bitterly reap what they had willfully sown: this is in grace, and He looks upon His people's misery, and purposes to deliver them. Their sufferings under His government were caused by a scourge from *within* – from Saul their king; their groanings that called for the compassion of His grace came from *without* – from the uncircumcised Philistines, and He is quick to hear and is ready to relieve. Behold, Christian reader, in this an example of the working out of His grace and government, *"the goodness and severity of God,"* always evenly balanced in Scripture. Let us take heart, and be encouraged by the grace, and be warned and put on our guard by the government.[31]

As soon as Samuel met Saul, God whispered into Samuel's ear that this was the Benjamite that He had spoken of the day before, the man who was to be anointed king of Israel (vv. 17-18). An ignorant, but polite, Saul then asked Samuel where he might find the house of God's prophet (v. 19). Actually, Saul did not want to find the prophet's house, but the prophet himself. This highlights man's carnal efforts to gain heaven without actually knowing the only One who can grant access there.

Samuel lived only three miles from Saul's hometown, and yet Saul is both unfamiliar with whom Samuel is and unable to discern who in the group of people departing the city was God's prophet. This would suggest that Saul was disinterested in civil affairs and in the welfare of the Jewish nation whose livelihood depended on knowing and obeying God's word. Despite his imprudence, Samuel spoke kindly to Saul:

> *I am the seer. Go up before me to the high place, for you shall eat with me today; and tomorrow I will let you go and will tell you all that is in your heart. But as for your donkeys that were lost three days ago, do not be anxious about them, for they have been found. And on whom is all the desire of Israel? Is it not on you and on all your father's house?* (vv. 19-20).

No doubt, Saul was glad to have found Samuel, to learn that the donkeys were found, and to eat at the prophet's table, but Samuel's latter statement perplexed him. How could he and his father's house be what was precious or worth desiring in Israel (i.e., how could he fulfill their yearning for a king)? Saul then issues a modest rebuff to Samuel's bizarre statement: *"Am I not a Benjamite, of the smallest of the tribes of Israel, and my family the least of all the families of the tribe of Benjamin? Why then do you speak like this to me?"* (v. 21). Saul was suggesting that Samuel must not be aware of his family's lineage and though he knew all about the donkeys, the prophet was dead wrong on this matter – he did not consider himself fit to be Israel's king. On the latter point Saul was correct.

Like Gideon before him (Judg. 6:5), Saul humbly deemed his family unworthy of such an honor, for the house of Kish was the least in Benjamin, the smallest tribe in Israel. During the days of Joshua, the tribe of Benjamin received as their inheritance a modest portion of land (about 14 by 28 miles) in Canaan's interior. At that time, the tribes of Levi, Gad, Simeon, Reuben, and Ephraim were fewer in number than Benjamin, according to the second census (Num. 26). However, the tribe was nearly wiped out by the civil war which ensued because of the lewdness of Benjamin's brethren in Gibeah, ironically Saul's hometown (Judg. 20).

After the civil war, there were only 600 surviving Benjamites to settle the entire tribal possession. This meant that each survivor obtained a substantial portion of land as an inheritance. So while it was true that the tribe of Benjamin was small in size, most Benjamites, like Saul's father Kish, were well-to-do. In other words, Saul was using facts to fog over the truth in an attempt to bolster his objection to Samuel's decree.

Samuel did not respond to Saul's statement; he had succeeded in opening Saul's mind to an inconceivable possibility and that was sufficient for their first discourse. The brief discussion ended and Saul and the servant joined the entourage en route to sacrifice at the high place.

Samuel's meekness throughout this unfolding drama is praiseworthy. Clearly, the advancement of Saul would diminish Samuel's authority and responsibilities in Israel; yet, he is far from envying Saul or contriving any ill-will against him. Instead, Samuel will be the first to honor him. Though Samuel knew what kind of man

Saul was, he still respected him in compliance with God's will for Israel. We do well to follow Samuel's example, for those who resist God's governing authorities oppose Him and will be judged (Rom. 13:1-2). Sometimes it is not possible to respect a particular person in authority, but we still should salute that individual's rank (i.e., honor the position of authority that the person holds). God is using human government to teach us submission to His authority and no human supervision will be perfect until the Kingdom Age!

After worshiping the Lord, Samuel invited Saul and his servant to join him and thirty others (respected men of the city) in eating a fellowship meal of what remained of the sacrifice (v. 22). Saul and his servant were seated in the place of honor at the table. Samuel had previously instructed the cook to set aside the best portion of the thigh (i.e., the best roast) and put it before Saul (v. 23). Samuel then told Saul that this portion of meat had been purposely set aside for him, as Samuel foreknew that Saul would be joining them for this meal (v. 24). Through honoring Saul before all the feast attendees, Samuel had begun the process of publicly installing Saul as Israel's king.

It is interesting that the breast and thigh (probably the right thigh; Lev. 7:32-33; Num. 18:18) of a peace offering were to be given to the offering priest, in this case Samuel. The breast speaks of *affections*, while the thigh symbolizes *strength*. Saul's stature indicated that he was indeed a strong man, but his affections were selfish and not God-focused. While all this must have been baffling to Saul, he is content to eat the sumptuous fare before him, remaining ignorant of what was meant by it all. A carnal man is gratified by temporal things, and Saul was such a man.

After returning from the high place, Samuel spoke with Saul privately on the rooftop of the same house in which he was residing; perhaps it was his own home (v. 25). Saul and the servant then lodged on the rooftop that night. These flat and railed housetops were ideal for sleeping comfortably during the summer months. Probably to avoid the attention of others, Samuel woke his guests just before daybreak to send them on their way (v. 26). Just as the three men were coming to the outskirts of the city, Samuel requested that Saul send his servant ahead, so that he could talk with him privately (v. 27). In the next chapter we learn that Samuel will quickly and privately anoint Saul as Israel's king (10:1).

Before leaving this chapter, let us revisit Samuel's instruction to Saul concerning the donkeys (v. 20): *"set not thy mind on them; for they are found"* (KJV). Samuel told Saul that it is possible to focus or set the mind on a particular thing by an act of the will. He was to no longer be worried about his donkeys, but rather to focus his mind on the Lord and exercising piety. Isaiah informs us that this is ultimately how we maintain peace in our minds. *"You will keep him in perfect peace, whose mind is stayed on You, because he trusts in You"* (Isa. 26:3). Nearness to God is the greatest defense against depression and the best means of promoting a stable mind. True peace is found in God alone.

William Kelly reminds us that "strength depends upon what passes between our own souls and God, who in His gracious and vigilant care watches over His saints individually."[32] Each saint must personally appreciate and rest in Him to do what is appropriate and right each day. May we then heed Paul's exhortation, *"Set your affection on things above, not on things on the earth"* (Col. 3:2). Samuel was turning Saul's attention from unclean earthly things to honoring the Lord through selfless worship.

Meditation

Peace, perfect peace, in this dark world of sin?
The blood of Jesus whispers peace within.
Peace, perfect peace, with sorrows surging round?
On Jesus' bosom naught but calm is found.

Peace, perfect peace, death shadowing us and ours?
Jesus has vanquished death and all its powers.
It is enough: earth's struggles soon shall cease,
And Jesus call us to Heaven's perfect peace.

— Edward H. Bickersteth, Jr.

Saul Anointed
1 Samuel 10

Signs for Saul's Anointing (vv. 1-16)

After Saul's servant was sent ahead, the prophet privately anoints Saul as king and then expresses his devotion to and allegiance to Israel's new leader with a kiss (v. 1). Jamieson, Fausset, and Brown suggest the kiss was a proper salutation, as explained by the words that accompanied it; this respectful homage was a token of congratulation to the new king (see Ps. 2:12).[33]

It is quite lovely to see how freely and fully Samuel relinquishes his authority as Israel's leader to Saul. The anointing oil is poured over Saul's head without restraint or resentfulness. Samuel knew that it was God's expressed will for Saul to rule Israel instead of himself; therefore he performed the sacred rite without hesitation. True, Samuel foreknew the consequences to Israel of Saul's leadership, but in faith Samuel also knew that God would be able to work the matter for a greater good. God was quite able to honor His own name and to correct His wayward people no matter who was Israel's king.

Being anointed with oil by a prophet marked God's man for a task whether as a prophet, priest, or king (Ex. 30:30; 1 Kgs. 19:16). A new king was anointed with oil when a new royal dynasty began, as we will soon see with David (16:13) and later with Jehu (2 Kgs. 9:1). Solomon, who was anointed with oil, would be an exception to this observation.

Ironically, Saul left Gibeah looking for donkeys and found a crown instead. Indeed, as T. Wilson observes, chapters 9 and 10 are largely about seeking and finding: "Saul seeking asses and another finding them; Israel seeking a king and Samuel finding him; Saul finding two men by a sepulcher, then when the lot identified Saul, the people seeking and finding him."[34]

Samuel then gives Saul three prophetic signs to assure him that he was God's chosen man to be Israel's king, and also specific instructions he must obey to witness these signs (v. 7).

First, after leaving Samuel, Saul was to travel about ten miles south (if he was in Ramah) to Rachel's tomb at Zelzah. According to Genesis 35:16, her sepulcher was located a short distance north of Bethlehem. There two men would specifically say to him: *"The donkeys which you went to look for have been found. And now your father has ceased caring about the donkeys and is worrying about you, saying, 'What shall I do about my son?'"* (v. 2). Why did Samuel send Saul to the tomb of his own ancestor who died in childbearing as she delivered his forefather Benjamin? Perhaps this revered site was to teach Saul about his own mortality; though an anointed king, the grave was still waiting to claim all of his honor. Jacob had already foretold that the rightful heir to the throne of Israel would be from the tribe of Judah (Gen. 49:10); therefore no royal dynasty from Benjamin could sit for long on the throne of Israel. Sooner or later, Saul or one of his descendants was destined to fall.

Second, Saul was to journey to a notable landmark, a huge terebinth tree at Tabor somewhere between Zelzah and Gibeah (probably about six miles north-northwest of Rachel's tomb). At that location he would meet three men traveling to Bethel. Samuel then told Saul what each of the three men would be carrying, so there would be no mistaking their identity: *"one carrying three young goats, another carrying three loaves of bread, and another carrying a skin of wine"* (v. 3). These men would greet Saul kindly and give to him two loaves of bread which he was to receive (v. 4).

Third, Saul was then to travel to a specific city near the *"hill of God where the Philistine garrison"* was located. The Hebrew word for "hill" is also the word for Gibeah, so this location was likely associated with Saul's hometown. If he did start his journey from Ramah, Saul and the servant would need to walk about eighteen miles to experience all three signs. Twenty miles was generally considered a day's journey in ancient Israel.

As Saul approached the city, he would meet *"a group of prophets coming down from the high place with a stringed instrument, a tambourine, a flute, and a harp before them; and they will be prophesying"* (v. 5). Notice that the prophets were not merely speaking by the power of God, but also were accompanied by instruments to praise God as they spoke with others. *"In Your presence is fullness of joy"* David rightly says, meaning that worship in the Lord's presence should be marked by joyful praise and accompanied by sound prophecy (i.e., the revelation of God's own mind). These same characteristics were to mark the singing of believers in the Church Age (Eph. 5:19; Col. 3:16).

After seeing the prophets, Saul was told that the Spirit of the Lord would come upon him and he would be a changed man and would prophesy with the prophets (v. 6). Throughout the Old Testament we see individual Jews being filled by the Holy Spirit in order to speak for the Lord or to serve Him effectively (v. 10; Ex. 35:30-35), but the nation as a whole has never been indwelt by the Spirit of God (Zech. 4:4-7). This will not happen until Christ's second coming to the earth (Isa. 59:21).

This national event of receiving the Holy Spirit is widely foretold in Scripture (Isa. 11:1-16; Hos. 3; Zech. 14:1-21; Rom. 11:7-25). Afterwards, the Lord will gather all surviving Jews from among the Gentiles back to Israel where they will have God's protection (Ezek. 39:28-29). Indeed, God has issued many wonderful promises of Israel's future spiritual renewal and restoration to Jehovah, which is all accomplished by the pouring out of the Holy Spirit. As we see here, the Holy Spirit is able to transform even a carnal man like Saul into something that he could not be naturally. But, as William MacDonald notes, this does not mean he was a converted man:

> It should not be concluded from verse 9 that Saul was genuinely converted. Actually, he was a man after the flesh, as his later history so evidently demonstrates. He was equipped for his official position as ruler of God's people by the Spirit even though he did not know God in a personal, saving way. In other words, he was God's man *officially* even though we believe he was not a true believer.[35]

Under the influence of the Holy Spirit, Saul received *"another heart,"* was *"turned into another man,"* and "he prophesied." In the next chapter he will be empowered by the Spirit to overcome the Ammonites. Yet, God's Spirit, acting in power, does not save a man when his conscience is dull to what is important to God. Later, Saul will be sternly rebuked when what was in his carnal heart comes out – disobedience, lying, blame shifting, etc. So, even the gift of prophecy, conferred by the Spirit of God, did not make Saul a man of God!

Besides being encouraged by these confirming signs, Samuel also told him that God's Spirit would come upon him (v. 6) and that God was with Him (v. 7). This meant that Saul was without excuse for failure; if he obeyed the Lord, he would succeed in whatever the Lord had for him to do – the Lord would be with him. However, flesh is flesh, and although the outlook is promising at this juncture, flesh can go only so far in imitating the things of God before failure proves that it is not of God at all. Time always proves out what God is in and not in. This is why Paul exhorted believers in Galatia:

> *I say then: Walk in the Spirit, and you shall not fulfill the lust of the flesh. For the flesh lusts against the Spirit, and the Spirit against the flesh; and these are contrary to one another, so that you do not do the things that you wish* (Gal. 5:16-17).

Saul, being a man of the flesh, will naturally resist the working of the Holy Spirit and hence he is destined to fail. We, too, will experience failure every time if we live according to the flesh. Paul summarizes the manner of our lives as weighed in the balances of eternity: *"For if you live according to the flesh you will die; but if by the Spirit you put to death the deeds of the body, you will live"* (Rom. 8:13). The flesh always leads us into sin, and, consequently, severs communion with God and separates us from His goodness.

Sometime after Saul's public installment, he was to journey to Gilgal and wait for Samuel to offer burnt offerings to the Lord (v. 8). This first meeting at Gilgal related to confronting the Ammonites (13:7-15). This procedure, according to Josephus, was to be a standing rule for Saul to observe during times of crisis (such as a hostile incursion): Saul should sound the alarm, return to Gilgal, and wait seven days which would afford sufficient time for the tribes on both sides of the Jordan River to assemble, and for Samuel to reach Gilgal. [36] Gilgal, besides its historical role as an Israelite stronghold, was along the eastern border of Israel, which meant it was far away from Israel's most formidable enemy at that time, the Philistines. This would be the best gathering place for forming an army.

All three prophetic events occurred just as Samuel had said, and, after Saul prophesied and had gone up to the high place (perhaps to worship), he returned to his nearby home (vv. 9-13). Several witnesses were startled to see Saul, the son of Kish, prophesying among the prophets. This led to a proverb among the locals for someone acting out of character: *"Is Saul also among the prophets?"*

After arriving back home, Saul's uncle quizzed him about his whereabouts during the previous days (v. 14). Saul told his uncle that he went to look for his father's lost donkeys, and sought Samuel's help when they could not be located. Saul's uncle was then curious to know what Samuel had told Saul (v. 15). Saul informed him what Samuel had said about the donkeys being found, but he said nothing about the kingdom he was to rule (v. 16).

Saul Proclaimed King (vv. 17-27)

The time had come for Samuel to publicly inaugurate Israel's king (the year is estimated to be 1050 B.C.). Accordingly, he summoned the nation to gather at Mizpah (v. 17). Before the proceedings began, Samuel reminded the nation as to why their first king was being recognized. Despite God's past faithfulness in delivering the nation from slavery in Egypt and from their formidable enemies inside and outside Canaan so they could inherit the land He promised them, they had rejected His authority (v. 18). They yearned to be like other nations having a human king over them. So Samuel instructed each of the tribes to present themselves before the Lord and God would choose a king for them (v. 19). The casting of lots was likely used here instead of God speaking through Samuel so that the evidence of God's decision could be witnessed by all, for *"the lot is cast into the lap, but the whole disposing is of the Lord"* (Prov. 16:33). Joshua used this same method to divide the Promised Land among nine and a half tribes (Josh. 14:2).

As the tribes came near the altar where Samuel was standing, the tribe of Benjamin was chosen. This must have been troubling to many, because there is nothing in Scripture to suggest that Benjamin ever repented of the moral corruption and rebellion that marked them during the civil war recorded in Judges 20. Then the clan of Matri was selected, and finally Saul, the son of Kish, was chosen. But he could not be found (vv. 20-21). Then the Lord answered through Samuel, *"There he is, hidden among the equipment"* (v. 22). We are left to our own conclusions on this matter, as Scripture does not tell us why Saul was hiding with the equipment (wagons, carts, etc.).

Was Saul hiding to avoid being selected, or did he want to see if his anointing would be again confirmed by the lot, or was he expressing genuine humility for the role he was being entrusted with? But God had already informed him of his royal appointment and had validated it through signs. As Samuel Ridout suggests, true humility does not ignore the expressed will of God:

> Flesh-like, Saul hides himself when he ought to be present, and obtrudes himself when he should be out of sight. Self-depreciation is a very different thing from true lowliness of spirit. As the poet says, Satan's "darling sin is the pride which apes humility." He had already spoken to Samuel of his tribe being the smallest in Israel and his family the least in that tribe. All this had been overruled by the prophet who had anointed him. He had already received the assurance that he was the appointed king. God Himself had spoken to him through the signs that we have been looking at, and in the spirit of prophecy which had indeed also fallen upon himself. Why, then, this feigned modesty, this shrinking from the gaze of his subjects? Does it not indicate one who is not truly in the presence of God? For when in His presence, man is rightly accounted of. The fear of man indicates the lack of the fear of God and "brings a snare." In God's presence, the lowliest can face the mightiest unflinchingly.[37]

To this we say, Amen. When God's servants are walking in the Spirit as they perform their divine callings, they are immortal and invincible until God's mission for them is complete. Matthew Henry suggests that Saul hid because he did not want to yield to God's calling for his life. He gives four reasons why Saul was averse to governing Israel:

1. Because he was conscious to himself of unfitness for so great a trust. He had not been bred up to books, or arms, or courts, and feared he should be guilty of some fatal blunder.

2. Because it would expose him to the envy of his neighbors that were ill-affected towards him.

3. Because he understood, by what Samuel had said, that the people sinned in asking a king, and it was in anger that God granted their request.

4. Because the affairs of Israel were at this time in a bad posture; the Philistines were strong, the Ammonites threatening: and he must be bold indeed that will set sail in a storm.[38]

Regardless of the reason, may we learn from Saul's example what not to do when called to the Lord's work – we should never think that the Lord asks more from us than He deserves (Luke 17:10).

Despite why Saul chose to hide during the selection process, two things are evident. First, Saul is preoccupied with self, which is incompatible with genuine yieldedness to God. Second, Saul could not escape God's calling for him, so the Lord pointed him out to the crowd (probably through Samuel). We always lose when playing the game of "hide and seek" with the Lord! No matter how hard we try, we cannot hide our sin and fleshy attitudes from an omniscient God – He knows all about it, all the time.

The sight of the older prophet raising his arm and pointing at Saul in hiding is comical. The people then found their hiding king and were enthralled with Saul's features – he was tall, strong and handsome. The people approved of God's selection – truly this man is every inch the king we have been waiting for (v. 23)!

Samuel then speaks patronizingly of them to highlight their carnality, *"Do you see him whom the Lord has chosen, that there is no one like him among all the people?"* (v. 24). Entrapped by their own folly, the people agreed and shouted, *"Long live the king!"* There was much excitement in Israel that day, but Samuel knew it would be a day that Israel would eventually live to regret.

Samuel had previously told them that the king would tax them and take their sons, daughters, and servants to labor for him and to build up his army (chp. 8). He now affirms *"the manner of the kingdom."* Barnes suggests that this was the law, or bill of rights, by which the king's power was limited as well as secured (perhaps even referring to Moses' instructions in Deut. 17:14-17). To close the formalities, Samuel puts them on notice and records the entire matter on a scroll so that none would forget what had transpired that day.

The public record of the "law of the kingdom" was necessary to limit the abuse of power. The strong are prone to take from the weak whatever they desire. Whatever was pertinent to remember was put down in writing, so later, when the people pulled down calamity upon their heads, they would be reminded that it was of their own doing. This scroll was then *"laid up before the Lord"* (i. e., placed by the side of the Ark of the Covenant with the copy of the Law; v. 25; Deut. 31:26). It would then be available for reference if either king or people violated the "law of the kingdom." The Ark was still residing at Kirjath-Jearim at this time.

Samuel then sent the people back to their homes. Saul returned to Gibeah with valiant men stirred up by the Lord and full of holy zeal (v. 26). But the chapter concludes on a sour note. Apparently, some of the locals (probably those who knew Saul) rejected his appointment, saying, *"How can this man save us?"* (v. 27). Although these men despised Saul and did not bring him any celebratory gifts, he endured their hostility with a spirit of meekness and said nothing against them. This humble tolerance might well be Saul's most noble achievement of his royal career!

Saul has now been privately anointed and publicly installed as Israel's first king. In the next chapter he will be afforded the opportunity to serve the people in an official capacity as decreed on this day.

Meditation

It is no great thing to be humble when you are brought low, but to be humble when you are praised is a great and rare attainment.

— Bernard of Clairvaux

Do you wish people to think well of you? Don't speak well of yourself.

— Blaise Pascal

Saul Defeats Ammon
1 Samuel 11

Apparently, the Jewish elders came to Samuel demanding a king (chp. 8) because they perceived a growing threat and wanted a king to fight their battles for them (8:20). We learn in this chapter that they feared primarily Nahash the Ammonite (12:12). The people of Ammon descended from Lot through his youngest daughter and therefore were kin to the Moabites. They dwelled just north of Moab on the eastern side of the Jordan River. Ammon threatened Israel about seventy years earlier, but God raised up Jephthah to deliver His people from their oppressors (Judg. 10:6-11:33). The Ammonites had been suppressed since that time but now had become strong enough to threaten God's people again.

There is a valuable lesson in all of this. Nahash means "serpent." The first serpent, the devil (Rev. 12:9), though defeated at Calvary by our Lord Jesus, still raises his ugly, bruised head again and again to strike fear into God's people and to deceive them from the path they should tread. He continually revives past heresies and blasphemous doctrines to be taught as Christian truth. This shows a perpetual activity of evil, which must be constantly countered in faith by the power of His Spirit. There is a day coming when the Serpent of Old will be cast into the Lake of Fire, but until then, believers must be vigilant to battle against both the Amalekites (speaking of our flesh disposition; Ex. 17:16) and the demonic deception of the Nahashes in this world.

Scarcely had Saul been crowned as Israel's king when Nahash moved his army west into Gad's territory and encamped near Jabesh Gilead, just a few miles east of the Jordan River. Rather than enter a conflict they could not win, the elders of Jabesh Gilead sought to make a peace treaty with Nahash, promising their servitude (v. 1). Nahash sardonically agreed to do so if he was permitted to literally "scoop out" all their right eyes (v. 2). Of course, if the desperate inhabitants of Jabesh Gilead had agreed to this, it would have been a long-lasting insult to the Jewish nation. The loss of an eye would permit the Jews to labor for Nahash and yet would ensure that the men would never be able to take up arms to resist him. Nahash knew that this hideous demand would not be agreed to, so in retrospect, his ploy was nothing more than a melodramatic way of telling the inhabitants of Jabesh Gilead to prepare to die, or to be tortured and enslaved.

These Jews preferred to die rather than to live in shame for the remainder of their days. Agreeing to labor for the Ammonites to preserve their lives was an entirely different matter than being painfully brutalized and mutilated. So the elders petitioned Nahash to give them seven days before meeting him in open battle, as this would be adequate time to seek assistance from their countrymen in Canaan proper (v. 3). Notice that they had no thought towards God on the matter, but rather thought their countrymen to be their only viable option for help. The seven-day truce was agreeable to the overconfident Nahash who was not prepared to storm a walled city, did not want a long and costly siege, and who also knew that Israel did not have a standing army to rescue Jabesh Gilead in any case.

Messengers from Jabesh Gilead were then sent throughout Israel to rally support. This action shows that there was no central government in Israel to appeal to at that time. When the people of Gibeah heard the sad news, they wept loudly (v. 4). Saul was attending livestock in a field and did not hear the initial report; however, later, when he neared the city, he saw the people weeping and inquired about the matter (v. 5).

Notice that despite Saul's anointing, he was content to return to his agricultural duties, taking no action to formalize the government that he has been entrusted with. It reminds us of Peter and six other disciples temporarily returning to their fishing profession after being entrusted with the affairs of Christ's kingdom (John 21). After the risen Savior admonished Peter publicly three times, we never read of him fishing again. In this case, it took an appalling affront to Israel before Saul was moved to take action. Sometimes the Lord permits terrible things to happen in our lives to awaken us to the importance of doing His will.

We learn next how Saul responded to the plea of those at Jabesh Gilead:

Then the Spirit of God came upon Saul when he heard this news, and his anger was greatly aroused. So he took a yoke of oxen and cut

them in pieces, and sent them throughout all the territory of Israel by
the hands of messengers, saying, "Whoever does not go out with Saul
and Samuel to battle, so it shall be done to his oxen" (vv. 6-7).

It would be appropriate for Israel's king to be enraged against those
threating his subjects, but even more inflammatory was the fact that
those at Jabesh Gilead were his distant kin. After the civil war which
nearly wiped out the tribe of Benjamin, the elders of Israel took 400
virgins from Jabesh Gilead to be wives for some of the surviving 600
Benjamites who were held up in a stronghold (Judg. 19-21). These
wives were needed because, in their holy zeal to cleanse the land from
wickedness, the eleven tribes also slaughtered the women and children
of Benjamin. Not wanting Israel to lose a tribe, they devised this
scheme to right their mistake; however, they did not seek counsel from
the Lord on the matter. Jabesh Gilead was selected because none of its
inhabitants had gathered to attack Benjamin when Israel gathered to
punish that tribe's debauchery and rebellion.

Saul was angry over the matter and took steps to assemble an army
to fight the Ammonites. Anger is an emotion that can produce selfish
behavior with devastating consequences, or it can accomplish God's
righteous indignation. This is a good example of man's righteous anger
being brought under the Spirit's control to promptly serve others and to
glorify God. Saul's anger prompted a positive response that led to a
great victory.

Later, however, his jealousy over David impelled him to be unjust
with his son Jonathan: *"Saul's anger was aroused against Jonathan,*
and he said to him, 'You son of a perverse, rebellious woman!'"
(20:30). Saul's anger was so intensely reckless that he actually
attempted to thrust a javelin through his own son. This is nothing less
than manic rage. Resentment and rage are destructive anger-motivated
behaviors, but releasing our offenses to the Lord to deal with and
pursuing righteous God-honoring responses are constructive outcomes
of our anger. May we strive to put all our emotions under the Spirit's
control, so that all that we do will honor the Lord.

The summons, accompanied by pieces of hewn oxen, carried a
terrible threat if ignored. This symbolic act, like the cutting up of the
Levite's concubine in Judges 19:29, made a profound impression on the
recipients. Saul also added Samuel's name to the subpoena to give it
more clout, as he knew that some rejected his appointment, but still

respected the aging prophet. However, it was not Saul's efforts to solicit a response that caused the people to heed his bloody summons. Rather, the fear of the Lord fell on the people and much of Israel gathered to Saul (v. 8). The Jews assembled at Bezek and were numbered off. Incredibly, three hundred thousand soldiers from Israel and thirty thousand from Judah had volunteered for duty (v. 9). The relatively small contingent from Judah suggests that discontent over Saul's appointment ran strong in that tribe. The most likely reason for this, as previously mentioned, is that Jacob had foretold that a long-reigning king would come from their tribe (Gen. 49:10).

Saul then sent messengers to Jabesh Gilead informing them that they would receive assistance on the following morning. Based on Saul's promise to help, the elders from Jabesh Gilead sent word to Nahash, *"Tomorrow we will come out to you, and you may do with us whatever seems good to you"* (v. 10). Obviously, there was no mention of Saul's army advancing on their position, so Nahash likely felt that his military campaign would terminate the following day with a complete victory over Jabesh Gilead.

Bezek was situated about twelve miles west of Jabesh Gilead and about nine miles west of the Jordan River. After dividing his army into three companies, Saul marched his troops eastward and probably rested that evening near the upper fords of the Jordan River. Saul then took his army the final leg of the journey in the early morning hours. Saul's tactics enabled Israel to engage the Ammonites in a surprise attack just before dawn. Israel's preemptive strike so demolished the enemy's ranks that by that afternoon no two Ammonite soldiers could be found together (v. 11).

Under Saul's leadership, God had granted an incredible victory to His people. This was Saul's first accomplishment in office, and, sadly, it would be the high-water mark of his forty-year reign. Elated by their victory and with enthusiastic admiration for Saul, the Israelites sought to vindicate Saul by killing his previous critics (10:27). However, Saul wisely said, *"Not a man shall be put to death this day, for today the Lord has accomplished salvation in Israel"* (v. 12). It was not a time for mourning in Israel, but for joyful thanksgiving.

But God's man goes farther than what the natural man can; Samuel prompts the people to worship God and to reaffirm their allegiance to His choice of king – Saul. The prophet therefore instructs the people, *"Come, let us go to Gilgal and renew the kingdom there"* (v. 15). The people obeyed Samuel's directive and Saul is recognized as Israel's king for a third time (the first time being at or near Ramah and the second at Mizpeh).

Gilgal was where the Israelites obeyed the law of circumcision after thirty-eight years of neglect. And God responded by "rolling away" (the meaning of Gilgal) their shame and reproach and beginning again with them after forty years of wandering (Josh. 5:9). Hence, Gilgal became a symbol of spiritual renewal and is probably why Samuel wanted to gather the nation there. Samuel presented peace offerings to the Lord at Gilgal, which also provided meat for their celebratory feasting (v. 16).

Technically, peace offerings could be offered before the Lord only at the central sanctuary (Lev. 3), but with the Ark of the Covenant in Kirjath-Jearim and the tabernacle at Nob, that was not possible. Many abnormalities of Levitical Law were tolerated during this era of the Judges, which was generally marked by national declension. Thankfully, God was determined to put a king after His own heart on the throne; then all that was amiss in Israel would be corrected. As we soon shall see, this man would be David. But David is a mere shadow of the One who will one day rule the nations with a rod of iron, restore Israel to greatness, and fill the earth with God's glory. He is the Lord Jesus Christ, the King of kings, and Lord of lords!

Meditation

Come, Thou Almighty King, help us Thy name to sing, help us to praise:
Father, all glorious, over all victorious, come and reign over us, Ancient of Days.

Come, Thou Incarnate Word, gird on Thy mighty sword, our prayer attend;
Come, and Thy people bless, and give Thy Word success: Spirit of holiness, on us descend.

Come, Holy Comforter, Thy sacred witness bear in this glad hour:
Thou who almighty art, now rule in every heart, and never from us depart, Spirit of power.

To the great One in Three, eternal praises be hence evermore.
His sovereign majesty may we in glory see and to eternity love and adore.

— Anonymous

Samuel's Final Address
1 Samuel 12

While Israel was gathered at Gilgal, Samuel seizes the opportunity to address those he has faithfully served. He began by asserting that he had appointed them a king as requested (v. 1). This meant that Samuel would no longer bear the weight of leading the nation. Regrettably, the unfolding chapters prove that whenever a natural man (like Saul) leads, there will always need to be a diligent prophet alongside. When God's shepherds are complacent and carnal, they must be rebuked by the One who placed them in authority (e.g., Ezek. 34:1-10).

Samuel, now a gray-headed prophet, appeals to his audience, for he may not have another opportunity to speak to them collectively; therefore, they should lend him their ears. As Samuel is about fifty years old at this time and will not die until his late-eighties, this seems to be a melodramatic attempt to prompt their attention than a speech by a near-to-death Samuel.

The man of God then spreads out his entire life before them. He speaks of his childhood when he obeyed God's calling for his life to be a prophet. From his early years to that present day he had walked before them in integrity (v. 2). Like Joseph before him and Daniel after him, Samuel lived a faithful and blameless life, which permitted God to wonderfully bless His people and honor His own name.

He then says, *"my sons are with you."* They were likely present that day in the assembly, but if not, they resided in Israel. Matthew Henry suggests that Samuel was inviting the nation to "call them to an account for anything they have done amiss. ... They are on the same level as you, subjects to the new king as well as you; if you can prove them guilty of any wrong, you may prosecute them now by a due course of law, punish them, and oblige them to make restitution."[39] Samuel cannot commend his sons, for they were not upright and faithful men. Rather, his contempt for their behavior further contrasted and emphasized Samuel's own veracity.

Samuel then challenges them to witness against him if covetousness, self-interest or injustice had ever clouded his judgments (v. 3). If wrongs had been committed, this was their opportunity to have them righted, if indeed there were any. Only a righteous man walking in holiness could throw out such a taunt to every Jew in the commonwealth of Israel and before the king. Samuel was such a man. His only blemish was rearing sons who were not as upright as himself.

The people admitted that he had been an honest judge and a selfless leader. He had neither defrauded, nor oppressed them in any way, nor had he taken anything from them (v. 4). As honorable servants of the Lord, Nehemiah and Paul also proved, centuries later, that a blameless life quells the power of accusations, even from fellow brethren (Neh. 5:15; Acts 20:33-34). The autumn years of life are most enjoyable for those who can look back and see that their steps did not stray from the path of righteousness.

Based on their affirmation of his integrity, Samuel says, *"The Lord is witness against you, and His anointed is witness this day, that you have not found anything in my hand"* (v. 5). The people answered, *"He is witness."* Having heard from their own mouths a full exoneration of his character, Samuel would have had the perfect platform to upbraid them for their ingratitude for his lifetime of selfless service, but he does not. Rather, he uses the opportunity to uphold God's honor, not his own.

The faithful prophet wanted his countrymen to glean an important principle from their history (vv. 6-11) and from their recent victory over Nahash (v. 12) in how to live for God. They must obey the Lord and learn to wait on Him for all their needs, rather than ignoring His Law and trusting in themselves. C. Knapp further comments to what Samuel wanted them to learn:

He shows them that God is sovereign; He is able to care for His interests on earth, as vested in His people, and can save by any, and by whom He will, by many or with few. *"It was the Lord that advanced Moses and Aaron;"* it was He that brought them safely out of Egypt, through the Red Sea, and preserved them forty years in *"that great and terrible wilderness,"* in the midst of dangers and enemies innumerable.

Samuel bids them *"stand still,"* as Moses told the people, when hedged in at Pi-hahiroth, between the hosts of Pharaoh and the sea: *"Stand still,"* he said, *"and see the salvation of the Lord, which He will show you today"* (Ex. 14:13). This is never an agreeable attitude to the flesh, but a very necessary one to the spirit, if we are to hear to profit what God the Lord would say to us....This attitude of quiet waiting becomes the soul that would know the power and resources of the Almighty, "swift to hear and strong to save" (Isa. 30:7).[40]

Samuel begins by bidding them to look back to Egypt where God first appeared to deliver them. Jehovah used Moses and Aaron to rescue the Israelites from the hardship and cruelty of Egyptian slavery and then to safely conduct them to the Promised Land. The prophet reminds them of the suffering and calamities which their fathers brought on themselves for forgetting the Lord and for bowing down to Canaan's false deities, such as Baal and Ashtoreth. So the Lord, at various times, gave them over to tormenters such as Sisera from Hazor (including the Canaanite king Jabin of Hazor; Judg. 4:2), the Philistines, and the Moabites to teach them the cost of rebellion and to cause them to long for His deliverance.

Samuel then reminds them of their forefathers' humiliation before God when they cried out to the Lord and repented of their idolatries, saying *"We have sinned."* Afterwards, God helped them by lifting up judges, such as Jerubbaal (Gideon), Bedan (probably Barak, as in the Septuagint), Jephthah, and Samuel to liberate them. There is no reason to think any less of Samuel for including himself in the list of God's mighty deliverers, as he was the final judge over Israel before the era of the monarchs began.

Even though God had been faithful to deliver His people from their oppressors when they repented, Israel now had affronted God by wanting a king to rule over them. This implied that a human agent in authority would take better care of them than God had. So Samuel comes to the main point of his speech: you desired a king and God has set him over you as requested – here he is; now obey the Lord, or having a king over you will avail you nothing (v. 13):

If you fear the Lord and serve Him and obey His voice, and do not rebel against the commandment of the Lord, then both you and the king who reigns over you will continue following the Lord your God. However, if you do not obey the voice of the Lord, but rebel against the commandment of the Lord, then the hand of the Lord will be against you, as it was against your fathers (vv. 14-15).

Verses 14-15 summarize Moses' central message to Israel centuries earlier recorded in the book of Deuteronomy, but they did not heed. Samuel puts the same promise and threat before them once more. God was beginning with them again under a different form of government to show Israel that it was not authority that was causing their repeated failures and suffering, but rather their own depraved hearts.

To ask for a king was not only a rejection of God's authority over them, but it ultimately put blame on God because things were not better than they were. Samuel then called their attention to the standing wheat ready to be harvested (which meant that it was mid-May – normally their dry season). To prove his assertion, He called on the Lord to immediately send a thunderstorm. Because it rarely rained during that time of year, they would know that such an impromptu storm would not be a naturally-occurring phenomenon (vv. 16-17). The Lord honored Samuel's prayer. The immediate torrential rain and pounding thunder caused the people *"to greatly fear the Lord and Samuel"* (v. 18).

The people then begged Samuel: *"Pray for your servants to the Lord your God, that we may not die; for we have added to all our sins the evil of asking a king for ourselves"* (v. 19). Two things are noted in their petition to Samuel. First, that the people did not beg Saul to pray for them, but rather the man they knew had God's ear. When the human conscience is exercised, as in this situation, the guilty seek the prayers of those whom they know intimately know God. The ornamental prayers of non-believers, no matter how influential they are, count for nothing. Saul, being a man of the flesh, could pray only if in duress. In fact, Scripture never records Saul praying to the Lord even once in his forty-year reign as king. In contrast, godly kings like David and Hezekiah were moved to pray often for the people and then relied on the Lord for deliverance. Obedience and dependence always characterize those engaged in effective praying. Saul lacked both qualities.

Second, they requested that Samuel pray to *"the Lord your* [his] *God,"* not "their God." This acknowledges that the prophet enjoyed a special communion and privilege with the Lord that they did not. This highlights that willing, holy consecration to the Lord places the believer on a higher plane of experiencing God than carnality can ever obtain. In any dispensation, a holy walk is characterized by spiritual power and joyful fellowship with God.

Effective praying requires a genuine pursuit of God in righteousness and humility. So, Samuel's response to his countrymen is one that all sincerely repentant, forgiven, and God-seeking believers should heed:

> *Do not fear. You have done all this wickedness; yet do not turn aside from following the Lord, but serve the Lord with all your heart. And do not turn aside; for then you would go after empty things which cannot profit or deliver, for they are nothing* (vv. 20-21).

The Lord loved His covenant people despite all their past unfaithfulness. They were His people and, though He must chasten them for their wickedness, He could not forsake them (v. 22). They could not change their past, but their future could be bright and blessed if they remained devoted to the Lord. Samuel promised to faithfully pray that they would cling to the Lord and to teach them *"the good and the right way"* to tread before Him (v. 23).

Indeed, Samuel was quite willing to pray for them; he even felt that it would be sin not to pray for them. Samuel epitomizes what James would later write: *The effective, fervent prayer of a righteous man avails much* (Jas. 5:16). In this chapter Samuel has been shown to be a man of integrity, in tune with God's heart, and burdened for his countrymen to wholly follow the Lord. Because he was a righteous man and knew the will of God, he had great confidence that his prayers would be answered. *"Now this is the confidence that we have in Him, that if we ask anything according to His will, He hears us* (1 Jn. 5:14). Believers today can have this same assurance in the Lord.

We probably will not call down a thunderstorm as a sign to God's wayward people to consider, but, we should be willing to pray that God will do whatever it takes to show the Church her sin and complacency. Like Samuel, we should also consider it a sin not to pray for other believers to know the truth, and then to fearfully and to faithfully walk in it: *"fear the Lord, and serve Him in truth with all your heart; for consider what great things He has done for you"* (v. 24). If the Church fervently focused on these two aspects of prayer, might we also see a revival of God's people, as Samuel did at Gilgal?

Fear the Lord Only

The prophet closes his address with a final warning: fear the Lord only, serve Him in truth with all your heart, and do not forget all the great things He has done for you; if you return to wickedness, He will sweep you and your king away in judgment (vv. 24-25). The Lord's people often forget God's past faithfulness and *"the great things He has done"* during seasons of distress. However, like Israel, we are indebted to the Lord's goodness and should serve Him with a spirit of gratitude at all times. This is why Paul exhorted newly saved believers, *"In everything give thanks; for this is the will of God in Christ Jesus for you"* (1 Thess. 5:18).

Samuel mentions the word "fear" three times in this chapter and comes full circle in instructing the people how to behave: *"Fear the Lord"* (v. 14), *"Do not fear"* (v. 20), and *"Only fear the Lord"* (v. 24). After the thunderstorm, the people feared God and Samuel, but the prophet, being zealous for the Lord's glory, corrects them – they should "only fear the Lord." They were to fully honor their holy and righteous God above all else. It was He who had promised to severely chasten them if they departed from Him and His Law. They should fear His chastisement, but if they revered God as they should, then they did not need to be anxious about His wrath upon them.

Jehovah is not an angry God poised to instantly crush those who stray from righteousness. Rather, He is a longsuffering, merciful, gracious, loving God who is slow to anger and quick to forgive. The more we know of God, the more we will reverently fear Him and appreciate Him, but there is no reason for His children walking with Him to fear anything else but Him. From God's perspective, any fear other than towards Him, indicates faithlessness. That is why believers are to *"be anxious for nothing, but in everything by prayer and supplication, with thanksgiving, let your requests be made known to God; and the peace of God, which surpasses all understanding, will guard your hearts and minds through Christ Jesus"* (Phil. 4:6-7). One day the Lord Jesus spoke plainly to a large crowd about what, or better whom, they should fear:

> *My friends, do not be afraid of those who kill the body, and after that have no more that they can do. But I will show you whom you should fear: Fear Him who, after He has killed, has power to cast into hell; yes, I say to you, fear Him!* (Luke 12:4-5).

Indeed, the enemy can harass believers during their lives, and if permitted by God, end their natural lives, but the devil has no hold on the hereafter and does not possess eternal life as God does. For those who have trusted Christ as Savior, and have been forgiven and placed in God's family, there is no reason to fear God's judicial wrath over sin. We are to realize that God's anger against us fell on Christ at Calvary once for all and, because that judgment is past, we are liberated to wholly love God. John puts the matter this way:

> *There is no fear in love; but perfect love casts out fear, because fear involves torment. But he who fears has not been made perfect in love. We love Him because He first loved us* (1 Jn. 4:18-19).

Believers should not be distracted by needless worry, such as whether they are heaven-bound or not. Knowing the claims of God's Word, we realize by faith that the entire matter is eternally settled: *"Most assuredly, I say to you, he who hears My word and believes in Him who sent Me has everlasting life, and shall not come into judgment, but has passed from death into life"* (John 5:24). Oh that we might all have God's holy fear before us and the infinite love of Christ flowing through us.

Meditation

God incarnate is the end of fear, and the heart that realizes that He is in the midst... will be quiet in the middle of alarm.

— A. W. Tozer

If we cannot believe God when circumstances seem to be against us, we do not believe Him at all.

— Charles H. Spurgeon

Saul to Lose the Kingdom
1 Samuel 13

The awkward reading of verse 1 has been the source of much debate: *"Saul reigned one year; and when he had reigned two years over Israel."* There are two general opinions on the meaning of this verse, which nearly all scholars agree contains a scribal error (dropped letters on one or both the numbers). First, chapters 11 and 12 occurred during Saul's first year as king, and the events in this chapter occurred in the following year (as in NKJV and KJV). Second, Saul's age is indicated in the first missing number and there are also some missing letters associated with the second number "two," which refers to the total number of years that Saul reigned.

The latter position opens the door for much speculation as to what the original autograph actually stated, as shown by varying numbers in different Bible versions. This is probably why the Septuagint omits the verse altogether. The NASB and NIV assume Saul's age to be 30 at this time and that he ruled for 42 years. While 30 years is possibly Saul's age, 42 years disagrees with Acts 13:21, which states that Saul ruled Israel for 40 years. The ASV assumes that Saul was 40 years old when he was crowned, and that this chapter occurred in his second year as king. Darby's translation of the Bible recognizes that the first number is missing, and leaves it missing, and assumes that this story occurs in Saul's second year.

While this is the safe approach to translating the verse (i.e., to assume that it was Saul's second year as king), Jonathan's obvious age poses an unresolved difficulty with that approach. We do know that Saul was a young man at the time he was anointed (9:2), yet, at this juncture, his son Jonathan is old enough to be an able soldier and a leader of men (v. 3). This means that more than one year has passed between chapters 10 and 13. Furthermore, if it was only Saul's second year of rule, that would mean David would not be born for another eight years, but the narrative refers to him as someone already having a heart for God. It is perhaps best to leave the first missing number missing as Darby does.

The following seems to best explain the meaning of verse 1. If Saul was about 26 years of age when he was anointed king, he would have been 66 at the time of his death forty years later (Acts 13:21). At the time of his death, Saul was old enough to have a five-year-old grandson named Mephibosheth through Jonathan (2 Sam. 4:4). This would mean that about twenty years has passed between this chapter and chapter 12. If the second number in verse 1 was twenty-two years, this would better explain the deteriorating situation in Israel identified in this chapter (i.e., why there were no blacksmiths and no weapons in Israel; vv. 19-21). While Samuel governed Israel, the Philistines withdrew from the land, but under Saul's inactive rule, successive Philistine raiding parties had ensured that the Jews did not have weapons to retaliate against them. If this assumption is correct, David would be twelve years old at this time and would be anointed king of Israel the following year. This also means that Jonathan would be in his mid-twenties.

After years of inactivity, Saul sounds the shofar to summon men to serve as soldiers in a standing army. After selecting 2,000 soldiers to abide with him at Michmash in the mountains of Bethel and 1,000 soldiers to remain with Jonathan at his hometown of Gibeah, he sent the rest home.

Apparently, Saul commanded Jonathan to attack the Philistine garrison at Geba and then later attributed Jonathan's victory to himself (v. 4). H. L. Rossier observes:

> When God acts through His instruments at the beginning of a revival and gains the victory over the enemy, all those who profit by this victory not belonging to the family of faith do not fail to attribute the victory to their own merit and vaunt themselves in it. Never does the flesh seek to gather souls around Christ: it makes itself the center.[41]

Under Samuel's leadership, the Philistines did not dare invade Israel. However, Saul's slothfulness had permitted Philistine raiding parties to pillage Israel for many years, though technically Samuel's peace treaty between Philistia and Israel was still in effect. Jonathan's seemingly unprovoked attack was viewed as a violation of that accord and caused the Philistines to loathe Israel (although they were not guiltless in the matter).

Why Saul sought this occasion to provoke a much larger and better-equipped army to move against Israel is unknown. Perhaps he knew that the Philistines were strengthening themselves and thought a preemptive strike was necessary to quell a more organized advance into Israel. As agreed previously during times of distress, Saul blew the trumpet to summon the Jews throughout the land to Gilgal within seven days.

Jonathan's attack on their garrison became a rallying cry throughout Philistia, raising an enormous army to avenge the insult. They gathered together *"thirty thousand chariots and six thousand horsemen, and people as the sand which is on the seashore in multitude. And they came up and encamped in Michmash, to the east of Beth Aven"* (v. 5). Some translations following the Syriac and some manuscripts of the Septuagint place the number of chariots at 3,000, which seems to fit better with the number of 6,000 horsemen.[42] Barnes even suggests the number should be 300, which is even more reasonable. Regardless, this was a massive, well-provisioned army in comparison to Israel's much smaller number of soldiers, in which only Saul and Jonathan had swords and no one had spears (v. 22). Saul's strategy against the Ammonites was brilliant, but his military tactics against the Philistines were foolish. The first blunder was that one should raise and equip one's army prior to attacking and provoking the enemy to battle.

In previous years, the Philistines had successfully removed the blacksmiths from Israel to prevent the Jews from forging weapons (vv. 19-21). That limitation forced the Jews to pay the Philistines to sharpen their farm implements, such as plows and sickles. Consequently, Israel did not have proper weapons for their soldiers. Accordingly, Saul's men would be equipped with axes, sickles, goads, slings, and forks against the well-armed Philistines.

A number of Hebrews did respond to Saul's summons to gather at Gilgal. However, when the reconnaissance report revealed how hopelessly outnumbered they were, some soldiers began deserting Saul's ranks. These cowards hid in caves, thickets, rocky crevasses, and pits; some even crossed the Jordan to escape into Gad's territory. The latter hoped to find safety from the Philistines where they had previously defeated the Ammonites (vv. 6-7). This was an agonizing situation for Saul, who had to wait seven days for Samuel to arrive to offer sacrifices to the Lord. Each day that passed, Saul's army diminished, while the Philistines became better prepared (v. 8). Notice that Saul's waiting indicates that he fully understood what God expected of him.

Even the loyal soldiers who remained with Saul at Gilgal *"followed him trembling."* This disconcerting situation climaxed on the seventh day (probably the morning of) when Saul observed that Samuel still had not arrived. Feeling the pressure of time lest he lose any more men, Saul decided he could wait no longer for Samuel. It seems likely that Saul intruded himself on the priesthood himself by sacrificing a burnt offering to the Lord, but it is possible that he may have ordered the priests to make the sacrifice. However, the latter action was still contrary to the prophet's command (v. 9) and the former a direct violation of God's expressed Law, for only a Levitical priest could present a burnt offering to Him (Lev. 1:8).

To Saul's credit he did wait seven days, but not seven full days, for Samuel to arrive. Saul apparently did not consult Samuel before ordering Jonathan's assault and now again we see the self-sufficient king proceeding with his plans without the counsel and blessing of God's prophet. Flesh is impulsive; its impatience stops where faith begins – when all natural solutions are gone! The sacrifice had hardly been laid on the altar when the elderly Samuel arrived (his age being about 72). Saul boldly went out to greet him (even warmly blessing him). Clearly, the king did not understand the gravity of the sin he had just committed (v. 10).

Samuel has no pleasantries for Saul; rather, he abruptly rebukes the king with a pointed question, *"What have you done?"* (v. 11). Saul explained to Samuel the dire situation he was in and that, because his army was scattering, he *"felt compelled, and offered a burnt offering"* (v. 12). The king interjects a motive of piety to justify his disobedience; in effect he was saying, "I had to restrain myself from obeying your orders and to force myself to offer a burnt offering." But true faith is never forced; it rests on God's expressed will and then patiently waits for Him to act on what He has promised to do. From Saul's conduct we observe that the flesh nature is impatient, and will infer piety to justify its actions or compromise the truth to get its way.

Additionally, Saul shows us that it is our nature to shun legitimate guilt and blame others for our failures. For example, Saul blamed Samuel for his own infraction because the prophet had not arrived when he said he would. But Samuel had arrived as prescribed, just not as early in the day as Saul deemed appropriate. Samuel had learned to rest in the Lord during arduous times, and therefore did not feel the same pressure of time as the impatient king did. Impulsiveness, irritability, anxiety, fear, and restlessness are all symptoms of being controlled by carnal impulses, rather than by the Spirit of God. Samuel minces no words in responding to Saul's pitiful excuses for violating God's Law:

> *You have done foolishly. You have not kept the commandment of the Lord your God, which He commanded you. For now the Lord would have established your kingdom over Israel forever. But now your kingdom shall not continue. The Lord has sought for Himself a man after His own heart, and the Lord has commanded him to be commander over His people, because you have not kept what the Lord commanded you* (vv. 13-14).

Saul's actions had invoked God's wrath and hence Samuel informed him that his kingdom would not continue. Only a true prophet of God could get away with telling the king of Israel that he was a foolish transgressor, and live! God is not a respecter of persons; disobedience is sin and must be judged, even when the king is the one playing the fool. Samuel says nothing more and Saul does not offer an apology or further rebuttal either. The king has shown that he does not need a priest or prophet, so as suddenly as Samuel arrived at Gilgal he turns and departs for Gibeah (v. 15).

Sadly, the spiritual significance of Gilgal as the place of circumcision (i.e., having no confidence in the flesh) and the rolling away of reproach and shame had been lost. Revival cannot occur where carnal flesh is at work and Samuel will have no part of it – he immediately leaves Gilgal. This meant that Samuel probably had arrived at Gilgal late morning or early afternoon, leaving plenty of daylight for traveling back the direction he had just come.

We might have thought that Saul would have been devastated by Samuel's decree that he would spawn no lasting royal dynasty. But in his self-centeredness, Saul neither weeps over nor bemoans the edict. Rather, being fully absorbed in the urgent matter at hand – confronting the Philistines – the king is completely untouched by a sense of guilt. Permitting busyness to soothe or even numb the conscience from doing its intended work is a dangerous state of mind to be most feared.

William MacDonald observes that offering the sacrifice was the first of several offenses against God which would eventually cost Saul the throne. The others are:

> His rash vow (chp. 14); sparing Agag and the best of the spoil in the battle with the Amalekites (chp. 15); the murder of Ahimelech and the eighty-four other priests (chp. 22); his repeated attempts on David's life (chps. 18-26); and consulting the witch at En Dor (chp. 28).[43]

Saul's failure in this chapter, in type, is one that all believers will be tempted to repeat (i.e., surrendering truth to fix stressful circumstances). During difficult times, the proper response is to hold to the truth and to rejoice in the Lord, no matter how bad things seem to be. Paul exhorts the Christians at Thessalonica to *"rejoice evermore"* (1 Thess. 5:16). Joy removes the burden. God's family should be a happy family, meaning we all must contribute to the atmosphere of joy. As a believer chooses to rejoice in the Lord while in the midst of a dire situation, God often glorifies Himself by working a miraculous solution to end the trial. It may be that our rejoicing does not specifically or immediately bring relief or conclusion to our difficulty, but God has promised to work a greater good, and to glorify Himself, through every situation (Rom. 8:28). The Lord was quite able to protect Israel from the Philistines and to honor His own name in the process, without Saul rushing ahead of His schedule in folly. If the Lord is not in what we do, then we are acting in the flesh, just like Saul.

Because Saul trespassed on the priesthood (or at least disobeyed the seven-day directive), the Lord promised to take the kingdom from him and to give it to a man who valued Him more highly. We have not been introduced to David as of yet, but Scripture will have much to convey about him. David was *"the sweet psalmist of Israel"* (2 Sam. 23:1) and arguably the nation's mightiest king, but the most significant thing about him was that he was a man after God's own heart (v. 14; Acts 13:22).

In this chapter, Saul, God's anointed, was tall, strong, and well-known, but he failed to honor the Lord. Chapter 16 emphasizes just how ordinary and unnoticed David was as a young shepherd, yet the Lord knew all about David's strong affection towards Him. In the Lord's timing, God would cause others to notice and approve of him also. The unimportant lad tending sheep in a remote location would soon be God's anointed over Israel for one reason only – he had a heart for God.

When Saul numbered the people, he found that he now had only six hundred soldiers (v. 15). Interestingly, Saul takes his men to the same city to which Samuel is journeying, Gibeah (14:2), but the two men do not travel together because of Saul's offense. Saul could not return to Michmash, because the Philistines were there, so he decides to join forces with Jonathan at Gibeah. Much is in motion now, Saul is heading to Gibeah with a small battalion of troops, the Philistines are positioning themselves in the pass of Michmash, and the Lord is preparing to summon a devout, young man named David into action.

Meditation

Take my life, and let it be consecrated, Lord, to Thee.
Take my moments and my days; let them flow in ceaseless praise.
Take my hands, and let them move at the impulse of Thy love.
Take my feet, and let them be swift and beautiful for Thee.

Take my will, and make it Thine; it shall be no longer mine.
Take my heart, it is Thine own; it shall be Thy royal throne.
Take my love, my Lord; I pour at Thy feet its treasure store.
Take myself, and I will be ever, only, all for Thee.

— Frances R. Havergal

The Philistines Are Defeated
1 Samuel 14

Jonathan Is Victorious (vv. 1-23)

Saul and his 600 men join Jonathan at Gibeah (v. 2). We learned, in the last chapter, that the Philistines had gathered an enormous army at Michmash, located about five miles northeast of Gibeah, and perhaps three miles northeast of Migron where Saul was encamped with his much smaller army. There was a narrow ravine with steep, rocky cliffs situated southwest of Michmash and northeast of Migron and Gibeah. The cliff on the north side was called Bozez and on the south side, Seneh (vv. 4-5). This constricted corridor (now called Wadi Suweinit) running west-northwest to east-southeast prevented a large number of troops from passing through it, thus a defensible position for either side. The Philistines had a garrison situated on the northern side of this ravine.

Inactivity was unacceptable to Jonathan, who was ready, if the Lord be with him, to attempt a great feat – to walk boldly to the enemy's stronghold and challenge them in hand-to-hand combat. Obviously, complacent Saul would have never approved of such a seemingly harebrained plan, especially if he knew his son was going to be the Jewish combatant. So Jonathan spoke to his armorbearer secretly: *"Come, let us go over to the Philistines' garrison that is on the other side"* (v. 1). *"It may be that the Lord will work for us. For nothing restrains the Lord from saving by many or by few"* (v. 6). Jonathan was not trusting in his own sword, but knew if God was for them, it did not matter how many soldiers they might face.

> If we desire our faith to be strengthened, we should not shrink from opportunities where our faith may be tried, and therefore, through trial, be strengthened.
>
> — George Mueller

96

This is not the first time that Jonathan has shown courage in confronting the Philistines, but his heroic victory of the last chapter was mostly nullified because of his father's poor leadership. He now places the lives of his armorbearer and himself in the hands of God and apart from Saul's direct control. His armorbearer was of the same mind, *"Do all that is in your heart. Go then; here I am with you, according to your heart"* (v. 7). Saul, sitting beneath a pomegranate tree, displays the empty pomp of fleshly stature, while Jonathan, energized by sincere faith and humility, becomes a mighty instrument in the hand of God. Saul is a man of the flesh, not of faith and, when the flesh intrudes into the things of God, it hinders the work of God (a fact borne out later in this chapter).

Jonathan refers to the Philistines as "the uncircumcised" (v. 6). This was not meant as a slur, but to acknowledge that they, being Jews, were under a special covenant with Jehovah that afforded them His blessing; the Philistines were not protected by such a pledge. Male circumcision was the outward sign of loyalty to this Jewish covenant from generation to generation. Commenting on Jonathan's thinking, J. N. Darby writes:

> It is hard for faith to endure the oppression of God's people by the enemy, and the dishonor thus done to God Himself. Jonathan endures it not. Where does he seek for strength? His thoughts are simple. The Philistines are uncircumcised; they have not the help of the God of Israel. *"There is no restraint to Jehovah to save by many or by few,"* and this is the thought of Jonathan's faith, that fair flower which God caused to blossom in the wilderness of Israel at this sorrowful moment.[44]

Jonathan was probably in his mid- to late-twenties at this time and his armorbearer was younger still. The plan was for the two men to climb down into the narrow ravine and to show themselves openly to the Philistines positioned up on the opposite (northern) cliff (v. 8). If the Philistines said wait until we come down to you, then the two of them would stand still and wait (v. 9). But if their enemy invited them to climb up to their protected position, then they knew that this was a sign from the Lord that He had delivered the Philistines into their hands (v. 10). Jonathan shows us that though true faith is gallant, it is not hasty; it waits on the Lord to confirm His way.

This plan was executed and indeed the Philistines invited the two Jews to come up into their fortification (vv. 11-12). No doubt they were planning to have some amusement, some playful sport, with such a reckless morsel of opposition. Having received God's endorsement of his plan, Jonathan told his armorbearer, *"Come up after me, for the Lord has delivered them into the hand of Israel"* (v. 12). Clearly, this bold assault was not for personal fame; rather, Jonathan identifies with his countrymen, though many were far from the Lord, and he longs for the entire nation to prevail through his efforts.

The two men climbed up Bozez, the northern cliff, and Jonathan engaged the Philistines in hand-to-hand combat in a small field of only a half-acre. Jonathan defeated Philistine after Philistine and his armorbearer finished off those Jonathan had wounded but not slain (v. 13). In all, twenty enemy soldiers fell in the conflict (v. 14). When confronting the enemy, Jonathan proves that it is not having God's Ark (as a good-luck charm) that matters, but having God Himself fighting for you that makes the difference. The following map illustrates Jonathan's approach to the Philistines and the subsequent victory.[45]

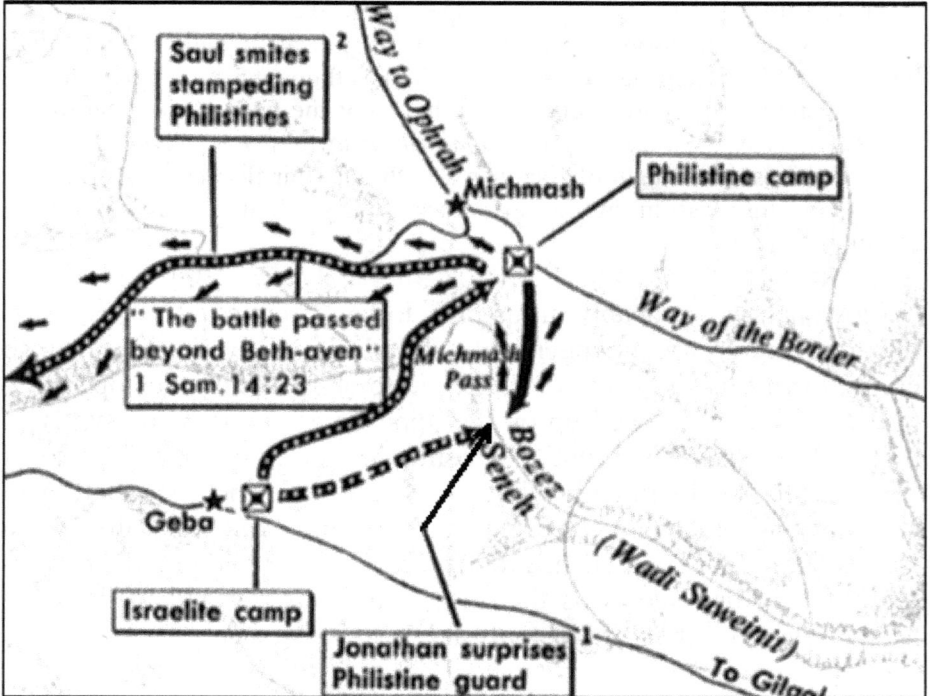

The Lord used Jonathan's victory and a well-timed earthquake to create panic in the Philistines who broke ranks and began fleeing (v. 15). One of Saul's watchmen observed the commotion and the disorder of the enemy camp and reported it to Saul (v. 16). Realizing that such a ruckus meant that someone was engaging the Philistines, Saul did a quick roll call of his troops and found that Jonathan and his armorbearer were missing (v. 17). It is ironic that, while Jonathan's faith is in action and counting on God alone, fleshly Saul is numbering his men. In the last chapter, Saul appeals to "the Hebrews" (13:3) for assistance, but did not call on the Lord – actually there is no record in Scripture of Saul ever requesting the Lord's help to overcome "his enemies."

A priest from Shiloh named Ahijah was with Saul (v. 3). He, being a descendant of Eli through Phinehas, was destined to come under God's announced judgment against Eli. Ahijah was wearing the holy ephod of the high priest. Saul may have requested that Ahijah bring the Ark of the Covenant from Kirjath-Jearim to the Jewish encampment to signify God's presence was with them and perhaps to protect it from being captured by the Philistines (v. 18). However, there is no evidence in the narrative that the Ark was ever actually moved. The Septuagint states that only the priestly ephod was present. It is likely that only the high priest's ephod, which was with the Ark, was requested to be brought to the battlefield so that the king could obtain God's counsel at any moment if desired. Regardless of exactly what was meant in reference to the Ark, instead of jumping into action, Saul rightly pauses to seek counsel from the Lord through Ahijah.

The Lord had used various forms of communication to direct His covenant people through the centuries. Besides dreams and visions, He had sent prophets to deliver specific messages. The Lord also provided the Urim and the Thummim, two stones in the high priest's breastplate, to answer questions asked of Him by the high priest (Ex. 27:21). Additionally, the casting of lots by the hands of a priest or recognized prophet had also been used to discern the mind of the Lord, as in the distribution of tribal inheritances in Canaan (Josh. 14:2; Prov. 16:33).

But, seeing that the opportunity to advance against the fleeing Philistines would soon be lost, Saul told Ahijah *"withdraw your hand."* This command could mean one of two things: That there was no need for the priest to finish building an altar for sacrifice, a formality that usually preceded the use of the Urim and Thummim, or that he was to lower his hands that were lifted and spread out to the Lord while praying. Saul knew what had to be done and therefore did not need to wait to receive the Lord's counsel on the matter (v. 19). Furthermore, he spoke of avenging himself on his enemies, as if the Philistines were not the Lord's enemy (v. 24). His thoughts were not towards God at all, but rather toward the pursuit of selfish gain and vain praise.

Clearly the Lord was with Jonathan and directing his brave assault while his sedentary father rested under a pomegranate tree in Migron (just north of Gibeah). Saul is a man of the flesh, as shown by his propensity not to act when God's interests are paramount and then to jump into action in his own strength without waiting on the Lord's direction and blessing. Convinced in his own mind as to what should be done, the king feels no confirmation from the Lord is needed.

Because of the challenging circumstances he faced at Gilgal, Saul compromised the truth by presenting a burnt offering to the Lord. Despite knowing what God wanted, Saul felt disobedience was an appropriate response to prevent more of his soldiers from abandoning him. A carnal person cannot wait on the Lord, does not need the Lord, and dismisses God's Word for the sake of his or her own agenda. Saul was such a man, but he will be shown in this chapter that his strength is not in the number of his men, but in the great God of Israel.

When Saul arrived to confront the Philistines, the scene was chaotic. Their enemy was so confused and disoriented with fear that they were actually killing each other (v. 20). Commenting on this scene, Matthew Henry writes:

> When they fled for fear, instead of turning back upon those that chased them, they reckoned those only their enemies that stood in their way, and treated them accordingly. The Philistines were very secure, because all the swords and spears were in their hands. Israel had none except what Saul and Jonathan had. But now God showed them the folly of that confidence, by making their own swords and spears the instruments of their own destruction, and more fatal in their own hands than if they had been in the hands of Israel.[46]

As the word of their pandemonium spread, Jews from the surrounding countryside joined Saul and Jonathan in pursuing and slaughtering the Philistines who first retreated northwestward towards

Beth Aven and then later southwestward into the Aijalon Valley (vv. 21-22).

The writer summarizes what happened that day: *"the Lord saved Israel"* (v. 22). The catalyst for the miracle was the bravery of Jonathan, who put his trust solely in the Lord. His faith then inspired his loyal armorbearer to do the same. As a result, the complacent followed the Lord also, which then prompted even the fearful to join in the slaughter of the Philistines. *"But without faith it is impossible to please Him, for he who comes to God must believe that He is, and that He is a rewarder of those who diligently seek Him"* (Heb. 11:6). This story shows us how much God delights in working great wonders to honor Himself and to benefit His people, when even just one person is willing to trust Him wholeheartedly! Jonathan was willing to put his life into God's hands to accomplish the spectacular for Him. Many will join the work when it is nearly complete, but oh that there would be more believers like Jonathan who can see clearly through the eyes of faith what could be.

Saul's Rash Oath (vv. 24-46)

Unfortunately, though God miraculously saved Israel that day, Saul diminished God's blessing to Israel by uttering a rash oath: *"Cursed is the man who eats any food until evening, before I have taken vengeance on my enemies"* (v. 24). Saul placed a curse on any man who ate anything before evening so he could more fully avenge himself of his enemies. However, the hasty vow was not well thought out and ignored the principle that Moses had taught the people, *"You shall not muzzle an ox while it treads out the grain"* (Deut. 25:4). The soldiers deserved and required sustenance while they were vigorously laboring in battle. Saul's foolish edict stands in sharp contrast to the compassion shown by the Good Shepherd towards the hungry and weary people who were with Him: *"I have compassion on the multitude, because they have now continued with Me three days and have nothing to eat. And I do not want to send them away hungry, lest they faint on the way"* (Matt. 15:32).

Additionally, notice that Saul wanted to vindicate himself on *his* enemies to preserve *his* own honor in Israel. However, Jonathan adopts a more noble view of oneness with his countrymen and that the Lord should be the one honored in the victory: *"the Lord has delivered them into the hand of Israel"* (v. 12). The distinguishing marks of both the carnal man working to benefit himself in God's name and the man of faith seeking to benefit others for the glory of God abound in this chapter. This contrast reaches its apex in a few verses when the man of the flesh desires to sacrifice the man of faith to save face.

While cutting through the forests of Ephraim, the Jewish soldiers found several wild beehives saturated with honey that had fallen to the ground. The earthquake in verse 15 may have caused a tree holding a hive to topple over, or a limb with a heavy swarm to snap and fall to the ground. Although Saul's men were faint, none tasted it because of their king's oath (vv. 25-26). Jonathan, who had not heard his father's charge, dipped his rod into the honey and put some of it into his mouth and was immediately refreshed (v. 27). Having plunged from their peaceful abode aloft, the bees would not have been too friendly, so using a rod to reach the broken honeycomb would have been the safest way to get the honey. Afterwards when one of the soldiers informed Jonathan of his father's curse (v. 28), Jonathan said:

> *My father has troubled the land. Look now, how my countenance has brightened because I tasted a little of this honey. How much better if the people had eaten freely today of the spoil of their enemies which they found! For now would there not have been a much greater slaughter among the Philistines?* (vv. 29-30).

Hand-to-hand combat is physically exhausting and requires proper nourishment to sustain it. Jonathan's point was that if Saul had permitted his famished men to eat properly as they pursued the Philistines, they would have had more strength to achieve an even greater victory. But because of the foolish oath, the Jews became fainter as they chased their enemy throughout the day into the Aijalon Valley (v. 31). Apparently, the Philistines fled westward, passing between the two Bethhorons to enter into the Aijalon Valley which then opened up into the western plain of Philistia. Aijalon would be 15 to 20 miles from Michmash.

Saul's command expired at the end of the day and the Jewish soldiers were so hungry that they quickly slaughtered sheep, oxen, and calves taken as spoil right on the ground and were eating the raw meat with its blood (v. 32). This was strictly forbidden by Levitical Law (Lev. 17:10-14). They had been careful all day to observe Saul's impromptu charge, but, in their weakened state, they ignored God's long-standing command. Even carnal Saul was shocked by his men's behavior, *"Look, the people are sinning against the Lord by eating with the blood!"* (v. 33). The entire scene illustrates what we know to be true today also – the traditions of man-made religion eventually lead God's people into sin!

Self-righteous Saul then exclaimed: *"You have dealt treacherously."* He commanded that a large stone be rolled to him so that animals could be properly slaughtered (i.e., with the animal on the stone and its head hanging down, the animal's blood would drain from its slit throat). The people obeyed Saul, and brought the animals to him for slaughter. Then portions of the animals were offered to the Lord (presumably by Ahijah the priest) on an altar that Saul had built to atone for the offense (v. 34). We learn in verse 35 that this was the first altar Saul had erected to the Lord. This altar was built in haste in reaction to his soldiers' sin, not for the purpose of personal worship or in response to his own sin.

With his men fed, Saul suggested that they go down after the Philistines by night, and plunder and slaughter them until the morning light, lest they lose the opportunity to do so (v. 36). The men were agreeable to this, but the priest (probably Ahijah) thought it would be good first to seek counsel from the Lord. Notice that this was not Saul's idea, but he agreed to the suggestion and asked the Lord: *"Shall I go down after the Philistines? Will You deliver them into the hand of Israel?"* (v. 37). Since Ahijah was wearing the priestly ephod, the means of discerning the Lord's will was likely through the Urim and the Thummim. But the Lord did not answer Saul's question.

Saul rightly assumed that the silence meant that there was sin in the camp and that someone had defied his oath and was thus cursed. Although Saul's decree was imprudent, God honored his authority as the one who ruled Israel and had invoked His name. This was who Israel had wanted to be their king and now they would begin to suffer because of their folly. Albert Barnes notes, "Saul's rashness becomes more and more apparent. He now adds an additional oath, to bring down yet further guilt in taking God's name in vain, so that none dared to resist his will."[47] Some of the people knew what Jonathan had innocently done, but since Saul threatened to kill the perpetrator, even if it was his own son, everyone kept silent. Nobody wanted the king to kill their valiant hero in a foolish rage. Jonathan was the brave victor of Israel that day and his father Saul, *the troubler of Israel.*

The king was determined to identify the guilty person, and asked the priest to cast a lot. Whether the Urim and Thummim or a common lot was used is unknown. The king started by putting himself and Jonathan on one side and all the people on the other (v. 40). This was probably done to show the people that those in authority were innocent of the offense. Saul then asked the Lord to *"give a perfect lot"* (v. 41). To his surprise, the lot indicated himself and Jonathan, so he separated himself from his son and the lost was cast again, and Jonathan was taken (v. 42). Saul demanded that Jonathan tell him what he had done (v. 43). Jonathan humbly confessed what he had done in ignorance, *"I only tasted a little honey with the end of the rod that was in my hand. So now I must die!"* (v. 43).

Saul was infuriated that his own son would defy his command. Now the Lord has put His finger upon the utter folly of Saul's oath and everyone knew it. Will the king realize the absurdity of his vow and confess it as such. No! Instead, without consulting the Lord, Saul immediately passed sentence on his own son to save face: *"God do so and more also; for you shall surely die, Jonathan"* (v. 44). Jonathan's high character shone brilliantly through Saul's self-centered cloud of wretchedness looming over them all. He does not accuse his father of erring, nor does he defend himself, but rather he acknowledges what he did (though not confessing it as sin) and what he deserves as a consequence.

Thankfully, the people would not allow the young, courageous hero to be put to death. They boldly challenged the king, *"Shall Jonathan die, who has accomplished this great deliverance in Israel? Certainly not! As the Lord lives, not one hair of his head shall fall to the ground, for he has worked with God this day"* (v. 45). So the people rescued Jonathan, and, thankfully, the sanity of the people overruled the folly of the king that glorious day. Enough was enough, and, in an instant of time, respect for Saul's authority all but vanishes. As a result, the Jews ceased from pursuing the Philistines and everyone returned to their homes – the greater victory being forfeited because of Saul's self-centeredness (v. 46).

There are a number of lessons to be learned about the flesh in this chapter, as depicted in Saul's behavior. There are always consequences when fleshly men lord themselves and their rules over God's people.

First, a loss of God's blessing occurs as seen in the reduced agility of famished soldiers engaging the enemy, and, while Saul was wasting time casting lots, the Philistines were able to retreat further. The flesh always turns spiritual victories into defeat.

Second, man-made rules eventually displace the importance of observing God's Law, thus leading God's people into sin. Saul's men killing the animals so they could eat, instead of properly letting them bleed out first, is a good example.

Third, human pride judges those acting in the liberty and power of the Holy Spirit. Those who enforce their own foolish rules will do whatever it takes to save face, even to wallowing in utter stupidity, rather than humbly acknowledging their error. This is why the holy books of world religions are so large: what is not of God must be continually augmented through developing traditions to reinforce what was flawed to begin with. Real truth does not contradict itself, and therefore needs no such supporting fanfare to be observed and accepted.

Fourth, because these human traditions are void of God's endorsement, they ultimately put divinely-given authority to public shame. Accordingly, we should not be surprised when "the people" rise up and speak out against their carnal leaders, and rightly so (1 Tim. 5:20)!

Saul's Warring (vv. 47-52)

Saul established his sovereignty over Israel by defending Israel against all her enemies (v. 47). The Moabites, Ammonites, Edomites, the Philistines and the Zobahites (Arameans) are specifically mentioned. According to verse 52, the Philistines were Israel's fiercest nemesis during Saul's reign. To ensure that his army remained resilient, Saul took the strong and valiant men in Israel for himself. Some of Saul's successes are then summarized: he defeated *"the Amalekites, and delivered Israel from the hands of those who plundered them"* (v. 48). Saul's war against the Amalekites is recorded in the next chapter.

The writer pauses to tell us more about Saul's family in verses 49-51. Saul sons were Jonathan, Jishui, and Malchishua. Jishui is elsewhere called Abinadab; and Saul's fourth son, Eshbaal or Ishbosheth, is not mentioned here. Saul had two daughters; the name of the oldest was Merab and her younger sister was Michal. The name of

Saul's wife was Ahinoam the daughter of Ahimaaz, but he later took a second wife named Rizpah and had children by her (2 Sam. 21:8). Sadly, most of Israel's kings disregarded God's design for monogamous marriage and took multiple wives to ensure plenty of sons who could succeed them to the throne. His uncle Abner was the commander of his army. Kish was Saul's father. Kish and Abner were sons of Ner.

Meditation

"We go" in faith, our own great weakness feeling,
And needing more each day Thy grace to know.
Yet from our hearts a song of triumph pealing,
"We rest on Thee, and in Thy name we go."

— Edith G. Cherry

Obliterate the Amalekites
1 Samuel 15:1-9

The strength of Saul's kingdom is at its apex; the longtime oppressors to the west, the Philistines, have been vanquished, as have the aggressive Ammonites to the east. Saul has bolstered his army with the sturdiest men in Israel. The time is now come for the Lord to settle a four-century-old score with the Amalekites. These nomadic raiders were never fully punished for their unprovoked attack on the weary Israelites being led by Moses from Egypt to Mount Sinai.

Amalekite Symbolism

The children of Israel had hardly quenched their thirst from the water flowing from the rock Moses struck at Horeb when they were attacked by the Amalekites (Ex. 17). Amalek was the grandson of profane Esau, *"who for one morsel of food sold his birthright"* (Heb 12:16). Consequently, both Esau and Amalek are used in Scripture to picture the lusts of the flesh which continue to war against God's people.

This battle will continue until God removes all that is evil from the earth. Today, the new nature the believer receives at regeneration, which cannot sin (1 Jn. 3:9), continues to war against our flesh nature within: *"For the flesh lusts against the Spirit, and the Spirit against the flesh; and these are contrary to one another, so that you do not do the things that you wish"* (Gal. 5:17). There is nothing in the old nature that can please God (Rom. 8:8) – only when our vessels are under God's control do we have the capacity to please Him.

To lay hold of our spiritual possessions in heavenly places believers must travel along the unencumbered path of righteousness, but our flesh will always be blocking the way of such a journey; it must therefore be fought, beaten, and driven out of the way again and again. There are no other paths leading to spiritual blessings in Christ – the enemy must be engaged and defeated in His strength. The Israelites learned this lesson the hard way at Kadesh-barnea about a year after they approached Mount Sinai. The Amalekites would again block their way into the Promised Land (Num. 14:25), but this time the flesh was victorious because the Israelites believed the evil report of the ten spies who said they were not able to take the land, instead of the favorable report by Caleb and Joshua.

Despite all God's demonstrated goodness and power, the Israelites doubted God's ability to keep His promises to them – just the threat of the Amalekites and giants in the land was enough to detour them off the path of blessing. The flesh magnifies the believer's opposition, whereas the Holy Spirit enables us to overcome it and to seize our spiritual blessings in Christ. This is why the Lord promised to *"have war with Amalek from generation to generation"* until the day that He *"will utterly blot out the remembrance of Amalek from under heaven"* (Ex. 17:14, 16).

About forty years later, Moses, just before his death, again affirmed God's resolve to wipe out the Amalekites (Deut. 25:17-19). The idea was that whoever truly valued God's glory and cherished His people, when the opportunity availed itself, would aggressively attack the Amalekites. Thankfully, there is a day coming when sinful flesh will be eradicated and all that has done so much harm to humanity and caused much disdain of God's name will come to an end.

God's Command (vv. 1-3)

For the first time since the days of Joshua, Israel has a significant standing army. Saul is back in Gilgal, the place where he was *"made king before the Lord"* (11:15); it will also be the place where God announces that He is stripping the kingdom from him. While the nation was still savoring its astonishing victory over the Philistines, Samuel brings a command to Saul from the Lord:

> *The Lord sent me to anoint you king over His people, over Israel. Now therefore, heed the voice of the words of the Lord. Thus says the Lord of hosts: "I will punish Amalek for what he did to Israel, how he ambushed him on the way when he came up from Egypt. Now go and attack Amalek, and utterly destroy all that they have, and do not spare them. But kill both man and woman, infant and nursing child, ox and sheep, camel and donkey"* (vv. 1-3).

For the first time in centuries there was an opportunity for the Lord to honor His word spoken through Moses. The Amalekites were to be attacked and nothing that breathed was to be spared – it all was to be devoted to the Lord and to be destroyed!

Saul's Disobedience (vv. 4-9)

The powerful Amalekites inhabited a vast area, northeast of the Cushites, which extended over the eastern portion of the Sinai desert all the way westward to Rephidim. After receiving his divine marching orders, Saul led Israel's army of 210,000 soldiers south against the Amalekites (vv. 4-5). This scene shows us that the flesh (pictured in Saul) will pretend to act on God's behalf if it can gain something in the process. Yet, Paul affirms that God will not tolerate such mock piety: *"No flesh should glory in His [God's] presence ... as it is written, 'He who glories, let him glory in the Lord'"* (1 Cor. 1:29, 31). Sadly, Saul, a man of the flesh, will use God's favor to exalt himself and to diminish God's glory in the eyes of others.

Because of their past kindness to Israel while en route to the Promised Land, Saul warned the Kenites (descendants of Moses' father-in-law), who were dwelling among the Amalekites, to flee (v. 6; Num. 10:29-31; Judg. 4:11). After the Kenites departed, Saul attacked the Amalekites' capital city and successfully smote Amalekites from Havilah all the way to Shur (just east of Egypt; vv. 6-7). But Saul spared Agag, their king. The writer also identifies other Amalekites who survived Saul's assault (30:1-17; 2 Sam 8.12). For example, years later, when David retaliated against the Amalekites for attacking Ziklag (his place of residence), four hundred Amalekite men escaped on camels (30:17).

Saul brought the Amalekite king and the best of Amalekite livestock back into Israel (vv. 8-9). Agag is a royal title for the Amalekite king and not a proper name. Saul did not spare Agag because he was compassionate, but for personal glory. In the preceding chapter, Saul was willing to kill his own son for unknowingly defying his foolish command to fast. Later, Saul will have the entire priestly community of Nob slaughtered for innocently aiding David's escape. Saul was not a man marked by decency or compassion. He kept Agag alive for one reason – to gloat.

Saul, acting in the flesh against another who, like him, represented the flesh, failed God's test – his carnal heart was exposed. If Saul had been right with God, he would have executed God's justice swiftly and fully. A believer truly consecrated to God understands that the flesh must be given no provision or say in one's life; otherwise one's lusts become further inflamed (Rom. 13:14). Amalek was the first great obstacle to the redeemed coming into God's presence at Mount Sinai and today it still attempts to keep us from communion with God. Our flesh knows that it cannot have its way while we are walking in the Spirit with the Lord: *"Walk in the Spirit, and you shall not fulfill the lust of the flesh. For the flesh lusts against the Spirit, and the Spirit against the flesh; and these are contrary to one another, so that you do not do the things that you wish"* (Gal. 5:16-17).

The flesh measures success differently than God does. Saul thought he had performed his task spectacularly and so, while en route to Gilgal (for celebratory feasting and sacrifices), he stopped to erect a monument at Carmel to testify to his achievement (v. 12). Carmel was located southeast of Hebron in Judah (25:2; Josh. 15:55). Years earlier, while Moses interceded on Mount Sinai, Joshua victoriously battled the Amalekites below. After Israel's sweeping victory, Moses erected an altar to Jehovah-Nissi, or "Jehovah my banner" to honor and to thank the Lord (Ex. 17:8-16). Saul's monument, to immortalize his own achievement, was in stark contrast to the altar Moses had built. However, despite his egotistical efforts to exalt himself among the people (just as a Gentile king would do), the king of Israel was about to learn that partial obedience is disobedience and disobedience always has consequences.

Additionally, such consequences often have an ironic twist, for the Lord frequently uses the thing we failed in as a rod of chastening. Saul would experience this satirical displeasure: for sparing a king – he would lose his kingdom, and for sparing an Amalekite – an Amalekite would later claim to have slain him (2 Sam. 1:1-10). The repercussions of Saul's sin would again be felt six centuries later. Esther chapter 3 introduces us to Haman, who persuaded King Xerxes to approve a law that would exterminate Jews throughout the Persian Empire. He was an Agagite, a royal descendant of Hammedatha of the Amalekites. Because Saul failed to obey God's command to wipe out the Amalekites, they lived on to war against God's covenant people centuries later.

Believers today must desire to be controlled by the Holy Spirit, and not by their lusting flesh (the Amalekite within) – only then are the deeds of the flesh mortified and fellowship with God maintained: *"If by the Spirit you put to death the deeds of the body, you will live"* (Rom. 8:13). Positionally speaking, co-crucifixion took place at the cross and became effectual for a believer at his or her conversion (Rom. 6:6). The Greek verb translated "put to death" or "mortify" is in the present tense and active voice, meaning that believers are to be on active duty to mortify the deeds of the flesh. If your flesh nature raises its ugly head – you are to inflict a mortal blow against it. The only way to deal with lusting flesh is to put it to death; no pity, no mercy, and no procrastination.

Death and dying are not pleasant topics of conversation. There is a certain finality associated with death that our flesh loathes, because it ceases to function. But from God's standpoint, as Paul reminds the Galatians, Christians have already died positionally with Christ, and should therefore live out this truth: *"Those who are Christ's have crucified the flesh with its passions and desires"* (Gal. 5:24). The purpose of crucifixion was to end a life, though death would occur sometime after the victim was crucified. Accordingly, the cross ensures that as time moves on, there will be less of the believer's flesh and more of Christ apparent in his life.

Ultimately, complete freedom from the pull of sin within will be achieved at glorification. Until then, consistent mortification, as Paul explains to the believers at Rome, is to be an ongoing exercise of all believers:

> *Likewise you also, reckon yourselves to be dead indeed to sin, but alive to God in Christ Jesus our Lord. Therefore do not let sin reign in your mortal body, that you should obey it in its lusts* (Rom. 6:11-12).

> *But put on the Lord Jesus Christ, and make no provision for the flesh, to fulfill its lusts* (Rom. 13:14).

Gratification and mortification are the only two things the flesh understands. The danger is that if we choose to gratify the flesh, even a little, it will want more the next day because the flesh is never satisfied – *"The eye is not satisfied with seeing, nor the ear filled with hearing"* (Eccl. 1:8; KJV). The only spiritual recourse to deal with the lusting of the flesh is to extend it a deadly blow and to keep on mortifying it day after day – this is God's will for every believer.

The only motivation for engaging in such a long-lasting conflict is love for the Lord Jesus Christ. Love for the Lord is the noble conqueror of lust. Saul did not love the Lord and therefore he chose not to fully destroy the Amalekites so that he might glory in Agag (also picturing the flesh). Metaphorically speaking, Saul and Agag being together represent the flesh glorying in the flesh. However, the foolish king did not realize that by allowing an Amalekite to live, he was also permitting an Amalekite to strike him dead later (supposedly – though it was likely a false claim). James tells us that this is always the end of unchecked lust – death or, spiritually speaking, separation from God (Jas. 1:14-15)!

Meditation

> While Moses stood with arms spread wide,
> Success was found on Israel's side;
> But when through weariness they failed,
> That moment Amalek prevailed.
>
> Restraining prayer, we cease to fight;
> Prayer makes the Christian's armor bright;
> And Satan trembles, when he sees
> The weakest saint upon his knees.

> — William Cowper

Saul's Kingdom Torn Away
1 Samuel 15:10-35

Samuel's Rebuke (vv. 10-21)

Samuel, now in his mid-seventies, was in his hometown of Ramah when the word of the Lord came to him: *"I greatly regret that I have set up Saul as king, for he has turned back from following Me, and has not performed My commandments"* (vv. 10-11). Being deeply moved by the severity of this statement, Samuel wept before the Lord in intercessory prayer. Matthew Henry extols Samuel's behavior as a pattern that we should follow:

> It grieved Samuel that Saul had forfeited God's favor, and that God had resolved to cast him off; and he cried unto the Lord all night, spent a whole night in interceding for him, that this decree might not go forth against him. When others were in their beds sleeping, he was upon his knees praying and wrestling with God. He did not thus deprecate his own exclusion from the government; nor was he secretly pleased, as many a one would have been, that Saul, who succeeded him, was so soon laid aside, but on the contrary prayed earnestly for his establishment, so far was he from desiring that woeful day. The rejection of sinners is the grief of good people; God delights not in their death, nor should we.[48]

Indeed, given how Samuel had earlier been rejected by the people, he would have had just cause to rejoice in the downfall of the man that they had preferred over him. But those in communion with the Lord will not stoop to such envying. What will best benefit God's people and honor His name must remain paramount in our thinking. Accordingly, Samuel genuinely grieved over Saul and earnestly pleaded with the Lord all night on his behalf.

Early the next morning the faithful prophet began his heartbreaking journey to rebuke Israel's king, who was back in Gilgal (v. 12). Saul was not expecting Samuel and the suddenness of his arrival probably signaled trouble for him. Saul pretentiously greeted Samuel with an air of religious piety: *"Blessed are you of the Lord! I have performed the commandment of the Lord"* (v. 13). This is the first time we have heard Saul recognize anyone as being blessed of the Lord. Years later he will use similar speech to commend the Ziphites for betraying David (23:21).

Instead of patiently waiting to hear whether the Lord had a message for him, Saul hastens to justify his action. Samuel, however, will have nothing to do with this pitiable attempt to gloss over his sin. With Saul's hollow words still ringing in Samuel's ears, the prophet hears a more convincing testimony than what the king has just told him: *"What then is this bleating of the sheep in my ears, and the lowing of the oxen which I hear?"* (v. 14). Samuel wasted no time in calling the king's attention to his disobedience. T. Wilson suggests that believers should consider the evidence of one's profession, rather than accepting testimonies that promote oneself under the guise of Christianity.

> Samuel's ears could also hear the bleating of sheep and the lowing of cattle (v. 14), as clearly as Joshua could hear what initially he thought was "the noise of war," but soon realized was *"the noise of them that sing"* (Ex. 32:17-18). Sadly there are times when saints draw near with their lips but other extraneous noises betray that in heart they are far from Him, noises that tell that they have espoused double standards and sing the world's songs.[49]

Seeing that there was no means of refuting the evidence against him, Saul then shifts from being the guilty defendant to the scornful accuser: *"the people spared the best of the sheep and the oxen, to sacrifice to the Lord your God"* (v. 15). Even if this were true, Saul is the king and bears the responsiblity for the actions of those under his authority. Samuel promptly rejects Saul's attempt to deflect guilt and tells him, *"Be quiet! And I will tell you what the Lord said to me last night"* (v. 16). Rebuked and anxious, Saul agrees to listen to God's message.

Samuel relays the three-part message given him the previous night while he was praying to the Lord (vv. 17-19). First, the prophet reminds Saul of his former insignificance and that he was indebted to God for his present high position. Second, Samuel reviews the command given to Saul, to sweep away any lies the king might try to hide behind.

Third, the man of God indicts the king with a piercing question: *"Why then did you not obey the voice of the Lord? Why did you swoop down on the spoil, and do evil in the sight of the Lord?"* (v. 19).

Rather than trembling at God's charge, Saul tries to duck under the prophetic blow by justifying his sin (vv. 20-21). In effect Saul says, "I did obey the Lord, but I kept Agag as a prisoner to testify of our victory and permitted the people to spare the best animals for a higher cause – to honor the Lord through sacrifices. The king's conscience was apparently undisturbed by God's rebuke. This is the most dreadful spiritual condition a person can reach – to be so controlled by the flesh that sin can be justified no matter the cost, including the rejection of God's word. Paul later tells us that, when God withdraws from such people, the worst carnality within them becomes apparent (Rom. 1:18-32). Obedience is the true test of loyalty – the foundation of all true worship!

Saul's Rejection (vv. 22-35)

So far, Samuel has been unsuccessful in reaching Saul's conscience through probing questions. Saul initially lied about what he had done, then blamed the people for his failure, and then tried to justify his sin by smug religiosity. Samuel now assumes an unequivocal tone to pass sentencing on the king:

> *Has the Lord as great delight in burnt offerings and sacrifices, as in obeying the voice of the Lord? Behold, to obey is better than sacrifice, and to heed than the fat of rams. For rebellion is as the sin of witchcraft, and stubbornness is as iniquity and idolatry. Because you have rejected the word of the Lord, He also has rejected you from being king* (vv. 22-23).

Because Saul thought that sacrifice was greater than obedience, an irreversible curse from heaven descended upon him. The prophet affirmed that God desired obedience more than anything that could be offered to Him. There was nothing valuable enough that Saul could place on the altar to compensate for his rebellion. Likewise, there was nothing more valuable to God than devoted obedience! As C. H. Mackintosh suggests, sacrifices offered to God which ignore His expressed will are but self-willed forms of idolatry:

115

> *"To obey is better than sacrifice."* It is far better to have the will in subjection to God than to load His altar with the costliest sacrifices. When the will is in subjection, everything else will take its due place, but for one whose will is in rebellion against God to talk of sacrificing to Him is nothing but deadly delusion. God looks not at the amount of the sacrifice, but at the spirit from which it springs. Moreover, it will be found that all who, in Saul's spirit, speak of sacrificing unto the Lord have concealed beneath some selfish object – some Agag or other – the best of the sheep – or something attractive to the flesh, which is more influential than service or worship of the blessed God.[50]

Such things are putrid to Him. What God values trumps what we think He should want more!

Interestingly, the Bible reveals seven things that God values more than burnt offerings: obedience to His word (v. 22), a broken heart (Ps. 51:17), genuine praise and thanksgiving (Ps. 69:30-31), the knowledge of God (Hos. 6:6), walking humbly with God in justice, love and mercy (Micah 6:8), loving God with your whole heart (Mark 12:33), and doing the will of God (Heb. 10:9-10). These are the things that please the Lord and cause His face to shine on His people in every dispensation, including the Church Age.

Previously, Samuel had told Saul that he would have no lasting royal dynasty. Now God's messenger informs the king that God had fully rejected him. If Saul had completely obeyed the Lord in destroying all that pertained to the Amalekites, no doubt some measure of mercy would have been extended to him. Even if he had just humbly admitted his sin instead of justifying it and had pleaded for mercy, God would have shown some kindness to Saul. But it was not to be, and God's departure from Saul was permanent. As God's anointed, he would be permitted to sit on a phantom throne until his death, but God already had another in mind to replace him, and we will be introduced to him in the next chapter.

On one particular Sabbath day the Lord Jesus was eating bread in the house of a renowned Pharisee. After healing a man of dropsy, the Lord told a parable about a wealthy man who was determined to have his house full of guests to celebrate a great feast (Luke 14:25-35). Many excuses were offered by those declining his personal invitation. A general invitation was heralded through the streets and byways.

Many poor and disabled people responded so that the host's house was packed full of guests.

Many swarmed in to follow Christ after hearing this appealing parable. However, the Lord did not desire a throng of followers, but rather disciples who would learn of Him and be committed to Him. Our Lord later affirmed in John 14:15 that a true disciple demonstrates love for Him by willingly obeying His Word: *"If you love Me, keep My commandments."* Is there any greater way to show the Lord you love Him than by doing what He says to do?

This is why Samuel told Saul *"to obey* [God] *is better than sacrifice"* (v. 22). Obedience can be forced, but submission is a heart issue, a matter of the will. The Christian experience is not a matter of Christ being in your heart, but of Christ having your heart. Remaining in fellowship with God is dependent on giving Him your will.

Samuel's words expressing God's judgment against him overwhelmed Saul who finally admitted his sin:

I have sinned, for I have transgressed the commandment of the Lord and your words, because I feared the people and obeyed their voice. Now therefore, please pardon my sin, and return with me, that I may worship the Lord (vv. 24-25).

If Saul had uttered those words in all honesty when Samuel first arrived at Gilgal, the outcome of his failure would have been different, though Saul, a man of the flesh, was never destined to sit on Israel's throne for long. Saul not only admits his guilt, but then explains why he disobeyed the Lord – because he feared the people. What kind of king fears the people he rules more than the God who rules him? What kind of king worships a God that he fears less than his people? The answer is a carnal man who does not truly know or fear God. The king's conscience is briefly awakened, but his confession was not one of sincere repentance. Despite God's word against him, Saul still wants to avert the sentence against him or, at least, to maintain a favorable public impression.

Although Saul has admitted wrongdoing, his subsequent request reveals his lack of brokenness in the matter. His request that Samuel offer sacrifices for him and that they worship the Lord together indicates Saul's refusal to accept God's judgment against him. Thus, the prophet says, *"I will not return with you, for you have rejected the word of the Lord, and the Lord has rejected you from being king over Israel"* (v. 26). There was nothing more to say. The prophet was prepared to let Saul go his own way and fall prey to his own devices. However, when Samuel turned to depart, the desperate king seized the prophet's robe and tore it (v. 27). Saul further compounds his sin by again rejecting God's Word, so Samuel uses his torn garment to utter one last prophecy against Saul:

> *The Lord has torn the kingdom of Israel from you today, and has given it to a neighbor of yours, who is better than you. And also the Strength of Israel will not lie nor relent. For He is not a man, that He should relent* (vv. 28-29).

After learning that the kingdom had been torn from him that very day, Saul finally seems to grasp the gravity of his offenses. He pleaded with Samuel: *"I have sinned; yet honor me now, please, before the elders of my people and before Israel, and return with me, that I may worship the Lord your God"* (v. 30). Saul apparently accepts the judgment against him, but still desires Samuel to accompany him to worship the Lord so that he will retain the honor of the people. Commenting on Saul's request, C. Knapp writes:

> Saul cares little for what Samuel, or even God, may think of him, so long as he may be honored before the elders and the people, and thus continue with the semblance of authority and approbation from their former judge and leader, the prophet, whom he seems to have feared above God himself. He still would be accounted before the multitude as a religious man, and reckoned among the worshipers of Jehovah. Samuel, in grace and condescension, yields to the king's entreaty.[51]

Through Samuel, God had completely denounced the king; all was to be stripped from him, and yet Saul is so full of himself that he pleaded with Samuel, *"Honor me now."* Samuel obliges Saul's request because his office deserved respect, although he could not honor the man in that office. So, Samuel did not depart from the king, but neither did he worship the Lord with Saul – *"Saul worshiped the Lord."* H. L. Rossier observes:

> To the end Saul has himself and his own reputation in view. Samuel does, in fact, honor him, but then leaves him. As long as God has not

executed His sentence on the powers established by Himself, we are to acknowledge them.[52]

What a laughable sight, the carnal man that has been rejected by the Lord is publicly revering Samuel's God; yet, Samuel and the Lord are absent. Indeed, many today have some knowledge of God and even identify with Him in name, but sadly serve Him in profession only (Matt. 7:21-23).

Saul's behavior in this chapter highlights the unproductive rudiments of the fallen nature in all of us:

- The flesh justifies incomplete obedience (vv. 8-9).
- The flesh boasts itself against the truth (v. 13).
- The flesh defends itself when confronted (v. 20).
- The flesh fears man more than God (v. 24).
- The flesh values the honor of man more than God's (v. 30).
- The flesh has two ends, gratification or mortification (v. 33).

We should also consider and learn from the consequences of Saul's recent carnal decisions. We should not forsake the truth to alleviate difficult circumstances (chp. 13). We should not permit the pressure of time to cause us to act before we know God's mind (chp. 14). We should not fear man more than God (chp. 15).

As previously mentioned, both Saul and the Amalekites are types of the flesh. Saul represents the flesh's best attempts to puff up self through religious fanfare. The Amalekites reflect its outright rebellion against God, His people, and His plans and inheritance for them (Ex. 17:7-8). C. H. Mackintosh rightly concludes, then, that it was impossible for Saul to do what only the Holy Spirit could accomplish – the execution of Agag (i.e., mortification of the flesh).

Saul's entire course was one of hostility to the principles of God. How, then, could he destroy Amalek? Impossible. *"He spared Agag."* Saul and Agag suited each other too well, nor did Saul have power to execute the judgment of God on the great enemy of His people. And mark the ignorance and self-complacency of this unhappy man.[53]

Saul a man of the flesh could never mortify another form of the flesh represented in the chief Amalekite. Only a servant of God empowered by the Spirit of God can overcome the impulses of the flesh and land the death blow (Rom. 8:1-13). Samuel is such a man. Those under the Spirit's control never hesitate to mortify the flesh (Rom. 13:14). So, before Samuel, God's appointed judge in Israel, departs from Gilgal, he will render judgment against Agag.

Samuel commanded Agag to be brought to him (v. 32). Apparently the Amalekite king believed the time of death was past and he had nothing to fear, especially from the elderly prophet. He was wrong. The flesh is most vulnerable to defeat when a mature, spirit-filled saint steps forward to confront it. Samuel took a sword and hacked Agag in pieces after affirming his sentencing: *"As your sword has made women childless, so shall your mother be childless among women"* (v. 33). Likewise, it is *"the sword of the Spirit, which is the word of God"* (Eph. 6:17) which defeats the seductive impulses of our flesh that are outside God's will. Full submission to God's Word provides no opportunity for the flesh to escape its deadly blow. The prophet's actions then demonstrate God's hatred of the carnal impulses lurking within His people. On this point Samuel Ridout writes:

> Samuel also hews Agag in pieces, as though he would illustrate God's abhorrence of the lusts of the flesh, the controlling principle of which is represented by its king. Good would it be for us if we allowed the keen sword of the word of God to do its complete work, and if we, as Samuel, would mortify our members which are upon the earth.[54]

Samuel returned to Ramah, and Saul went to his house at Gibeah (v. 35). Samuel did not speak to Saul again until the day of his death, when he returned from Sheol to announce one final decree against Saul – his impending death. The prophet felt constrained to take up a position of separation from the one God had completely set aside. Saul, the people's "choice young man," had proven that he was not God's man.

Not only did Saul lose God's blessing at Gilgal, he also lost a trusted friend and counselor. Notwithstanding, Samuel mourned for Saul, and likewise the Lord grieved for His people too – because He had chosen to punish them by placing a man like Saul over Israel (v. 36). William MacDonald clarifies what seems to be an apparent contradiction between God not changing His mind in verse 29 and God regretting that He had made Saul king in verse 35:

> Verse 29 describes God in His essential character. He is unchanging and unchangeable, the immutable One. Verse 35 means that a change in Saul's conduct required a corresponding change in God's plans and purposes for him. To be consistent with His attributes, God must bless obedience and punish disobedience.[55]

Indeed, *"the Strength of Israel"* is a title for God in association with His covenant people (v. 29). Samuel affirms that God cannot *"lie nor relent,"* neither can He forget to recompense wicked deeds, such as Saul's swollen pride and blatant rebellion.

Truth is a prominent moral and personal attribute of God: He is *"the God of truth"* (Isa. 65:16), thus all that God says and commands is founded in truth (Ps. 119:142, 151). The Psalmist declares, *"the entirety of Your word is truth"* (119:160). God's perfect nature ensures that nothing less than absolute truth will be evident in all His words and deeds; He cannot lie or act contrary to His holy character (v. 29; Heb. 6:18). Therefore, if man truly desires to lay hold of deep truth (i.e. those unfathomable mysteries beyond natural explanation), he must venture beyond humanism, religiosity, and pride to humbly beseech Him who is the embodiment of all truth. Being a man of flesh, Saul had no desire to do so!

Meditation

> An affection which is not inspired by the Lord will soon be transformed into lust. Samson is not alone in the history of man in failing in this regard. Delilah is still cutting the hair of man today!

> — Watchman Nee

Look at the Heart
1 Samuel 16

The book of Samuel (in its two parts) covers the lives of Samuel, Saul, and David. Samuel and Saul we have been following for some time, but David, one of the most beloved characters in the Bible, is introduced to us in this chapter. He is likely thirteen or fourteen years old at this time. Against the dark backdrop of Saul's carnal leadership appears a young man who is honorable, brave, and tender-spirited and who loves the Lord above all else.

Unfit Saul had to grow into the office that he had been called to (i.e., he had to prove himself), but David's fitness was gained through his unobserved conflicts while caring for his sheep before he ever contemplated ruling Israel. David had a heart for God and His people, which Saul did not; that alone would make him a better king than Saul ever could be.

An Introduction of David

David is the main author of Psalms and many of his poems were composed during distressing circumstances. A greater understanding of these arduous experiences in the unfolding chapters will enable us to better appreciate how David lived a blessed life amidst them. After David, around the age of fifteen, slew Goliath, he dwelt in Saul's palace at Gibeah for about seven years (17:45-18:2). From the age of twenty-two to thirty, David was either on the run from King Saul or was dwelling among the Philistines in Ziklag (27:7).

During his years of fleeing from Saul, David wrote several psalms, ten of which address this crisis directly; the likely order of these poems would be: 7, 59, 56, 34, 52, 63, 54, 18, 57, and 142. In all, Saul made fourteen recorded attempts on David's life. Unfortunately, while dwelling at Ziklag, David lapsed spiritually and engaged in gruesome covert raids on villages; there is no evidence that David composed any psalms during this time. At the age of thirty (after Saul's death) David began to reign over Judah in Hebron. Seven years later he captured Jerusalem from the Jebusites and was subsequently anointed king over all the tribes of Israel (2 Sam. 5:1-3). He ruled over God's people for a total of forty years before dying at the age of seventy (2 Sam. 5:4).

It is evident from David's writings that the man after God's own heart (13:14) frequently suffered a broken heart. He was often despised, plotted against, slandered, and persecuted for doing the will of God. Many sought to kill David; yet, through each challenging situation, he found the Lord to be a faithful Refuge of peace, an unmovable Rock of strength, and a mighty Fortress of protection. David proves that those who suffer patiently with the Lord in righteousness know more about God's true nature than those who do not.

David Anointed King (vv. 1-13)

The Lord admonishes Samuel for continuing to mourn for Saul because He had rejected Saul from reigning over Israel (v. 1). As many years had passed since their last exchange, it was not likely that Samuel was grieving for Saul personally, but rather for the man on whom all the hopes of Israel rested at that time. God's rejection of Israel's king could mean only shame and sorrow for the nation he ruled over. So, the Lord's next words concerning Israel's new king must have encouraged Samuel's doleful heart. This meant that Israel's shame would not continue for much longer.

Dear believer, there is a valuable lesson for us to glean from Samuel's disposition. It is quite possible for a faithful servant of God to be emotionally out of sorts because his or her thoughts are not aligned with God's mind. Note the ways that Samuel demonstrates that he is out of step with God in this chapter: First, he mourned for the king that God had flatly rejected. Second, he hesitated to go to Bethlehem to anoint Israel's new king after being told to. Third, Samuel approved of Eliab based on sight, but God reminded his prophet that integrity and devotion in a man was what He valued. The solution to Samuel's melancholy demeanor was to enter into the thoughts of God, advocates C. H. Mackintosh:

> Communion with God will ever lead us to acquiesce in His ways. Sentimentalism may weep over fallen greatness, but faith grasps the great truth that God's unerring counsel shall stand, and He will do all His pleasure. Faith could not shed a tear over Agag, when hewed in

pieces before the Lord, neither would it continue over a rejected Saul, because it ever flows in harmony with God, in His ways. But there is a wide difference between nature and faith; while the former sits down to weep, the latter arises and fills the horn with oil.[56]

Indeed, human sorrow will ever flow until the human heart finds tranquility in the immense resources of our most blessed, sovereign God. The Lord offered Samuel the solution to his apprehension – he was to align his mind with God's thoughts. This would require him to fill a horn with oil and to journey to Bethlehem to anoint one of Jesse's sons as Israel's new king.

The Lord then announced, *"For I have provided Myself a king."* Hannah had asked for Samuel, and the people had demanded Saul, but David was God's own provision of grace for Israel. The progressive expressions in Scripture of God's joy in exalting David to the throne of Israel are quite lovely and picture the future day when God will place His own Son over all principalities and powers.

The Lord has sought for Himself a man after His own heart (13:14).

I have found My servant David; with My holy oil I have anointed him (Ps. 89:20).

He chose David His servant, and took him from the sheepfolds (Ps. 78:70).

I have provided Myself a king (16:1).

Given all that the Lord intended to accomplish through David, to anoint him king over Israel was likely the most honorable task of Samuel's prophetic ministry.

As just mentioned, Samuel's initial response to his charge is uncharacteristic of the selfless prophet who has exercised strong faith throughout his tenure: *"How can I go? If Saul hears it, he will kill me"* (v. 2). Samuel probably recorded this detail to indicate how despicable Saul had become since his rejection. Of course, the Lord fully understood the political ramifications of what He was commanding Samuel to do and had already devised a plan to disguise Samuel's mission to Bethlehem to protect His prophet and also to keep His plans concerning David secret. This is not deception, but rather *"the wisdom of God in a mystery."* God followed the same pattern of progressive revelation concerning the true purpose of His incarnate Son's first advent (1 Cor. 2:8-9).

Samuel was to take a heifer and to invite Jesse and his family to worship with him and then to enjoy a feast together after the animal had been sacrificed (v. 3). The Lord promised to point out then which of Jesse's sons was to be anointed. The elders of Bethlehem trembled when they saw the distinguished prophet enter their town, and accordingly asked him if he had come in peace (v. 4). Samuel had anointed Saul king, and during this era of Saul's rule there was no security or rest for those in Israel – there was good reason to be anxious about Samuel's arrival. The prophet eased their anxiety by confirming that he had come to worship the Lord there and then invited them, with Jesse's household, to join him (vv. 4-5).

After Jesse's family arrived, Samuel observed the eldest son of Jesse, Eliab, and said, *"Surely the Lord's anointed is before Him!"* (v. 6). But the Lord immediately corrected His prophet from a Saul-like evaluation of Eliab, which esteemed outward appearance and physical stature above what God appreciated, the heart of the man (v. 7). Indeed, the Lord rejected Eliab, then Abinadab, then Shammah, and then four more unnamed sons of Jesse (vv. 8-9). It is likely that only Jesse was present with Samuel when each of his sons was privately presented to the prophet.

The perplexed prophet then told Jesse, *"The Lord has not chosen these."* He then asked, *"Are all the young men here?"* Jesse answered, *"There remains yet the youngest, and there he is, keeping the sheep"* (v. 10). Samuel requested that Jesse's youngest son be brought to him, for he would not sit down to eat until he had performed the Lord's bidding (v. 11). The situation shows just how insignificant Jesse thought David to be; he was not even called to the banquet hosted by the most distinguished prophet in Israel. Of course, David is a wonderful type of the Lord Jesus Christ, who, though first being rejected by His brethren (John 7:5), would later be anointed king in the midst of them (Isa. 61:1; Luke 3:21-22, 4:18).

Jesse sent for David and brought him before Samuel. *"He was ruddy, with bright eyes, and good-looking. And the Lord said, 'Arise, anoint him; for this is the one!'"* (v. 12). So Samuel took the horn of oil and anointed David king of Israel in the midst of his brothers and the

Spirit of the Lord came upon him that day forward (v. 13). But as J. N. Darby writes, the Lord did not set David immediately into the height of power, as He did with Saul, for various reasons:

> David must make his way by grace and faith through all kinds of difficulties, and, although filled with the Holy Spirit, he must act in the presence of a power devoid of the Spirit, and which God has not yet set aside. He must be subject and be humbled, he must feel his entire dependence on God, and that God is sufficient in all circumstances, and his faith must be developed by trial in which God is felt to be all. Beautiful type of One who, without sin, journeyed through far more painful circumstances! Not only a type, but at the same time a vessel prepared by God for the Holy Spirit, who could fill him with sentiments which, while describing so touchingly the sufferings of Christ Himself and His sympathy with His people, exhibit, to those who were to tread in weakness the same path as Himself, their resource in God. For one cannot doubt that the trials of David gave rise to the greater part of those beautiful psalms, which, depicting the circumstances, the trials, and the complaints of the remnant of Israel in the last days, as well as of Christ Himself ... have thus furnished so many other burdened souls with the expression and the relief of their sorrows.[57]

After the feast concluded, Samuel returned to Ramah. We will hear from the aged prophet only twice more – during a brief visit by David and then after his death when he rebukes Saul.

David is first introduced to us as a faithful young shepherd attending his sheep. Scripture refers to him seven times in this way to show us that God chose a proven, selfless shepherd to care for His sheep. Attending sheep was not a glamorous job, but an important one, and the youth that was obscure and unnoticed by others was just the kind of man God was looking for to lead His people! C. H. Mackintosh observes that there is something in the shepherd's character which is in harmony with the mind of the triune God:

> The Father, the Son, and the Spirit all act in the character of a shepherd. Psalm 23 may be primarily viewed as the experience of Christ delighting in the assurance of His Father's shepherd-care. Then, in John 10, we find the Son presented as the Good Shepherd [who willingly lays His life down for the sheep]. Lastly, in Acts 20 and 1 Peter 5, we find the Holy Spirit acting in that blessed capacity,

by raising up and gifting for the work the subordinate shepherds. It is edifying to mark this. It is like our God to present Himself in the most endearing relationship, and the most calculated to win our confidence and draw out our affections. Blessed be His name forever! His ways are all perfect; there is none like Him.[58]

The Lord knows the secrets of the heart (Ps. 44:21) and is able to discern the thoughts and intents of the heart (Heb. 4:12). The Lord chose David, a shepherd, to be Israel's new king because He appreciated David's zeal for righteousness and his dedication to Him. David desired what God desired (Acts 13:22), and therefore, unlike Saul, would do what God wanted. David had a heart for God! As we will see, David was not a perfect man, but he was humble before the Lord, faithful and obedient to the Lord, and dependent on the Lord. As witnessed in Scripture, God frequently uses people who nurture these same qualities to do the unimaginable.

The Righteous Branch From the Stem of Jesse

We pause to consider the prophetic ramification of David's anointing. Isaiah would later prophesy that the coming Jewish Messiah would be both a "stem" ("shoot") and the "Root of Jesse": *"There shall come forth a Rod from the stem of Jesse, and a Branch shall grow out of his roots"* (Isa. 11:1). J. A. Motyer explains the striking features of the dual titles relating to Christ in this verse:

> The reference to Jesse indicates that the *shoot* is not just another king in David's line but rather another David. In the books of Kings, successive kings were assessed by comparison with "their father David" (e.g., 2 Kgs. 18:3) but no king is called "David" or "son of Jesse." Among the kings, David alone was "the son of Jesse" (e.g., 1 Sam. 20:27-33; 1 Kgs. 12:16), and the unexpected reference to Jesse here has tremendous force: when Jesse produces a shoot, it must be David. But to call the expected king *the Root of Jesse* is altogether another matter, for this means that Jesse sprang from him; he is the root support and origin of the Messianic family in which he would be born. ... In the same way, here, the Messiah is the root cause of his own family tree pending the day when, within that family, he will shoot forth.[59]

The house of David would be in spiritual decline, but suddenly, out of this decaying branch, a fresh shoot of promise springs out. Hence, the Messiah, the *Rod* or *Branch* of David, will spring up from the *stem of Jesse*, but He will also be the *root cause* of this new life.

The prophet Samuel anointed David, the eighth son of Jesse, as the king of Israel (17:12). In David's autumn years the Lord promised him, through the prophet Nathan, that a new and everlasting dynasty would be established and one of David's descendants would sit on his throne forever (2 Sam. 7:12-16).

Although the Messiah must be in the royal line of David, we also know that He could not be a descendant of evil King Jeconiah, on whom Jeremiah pronounced a curse (Jer. 22:30). Jeremiah's prophecy then magnifies the incarnation of the Lord Jesus Christ as Messiah. Joseph, the husband of Mary (the mother of the Lord Jesus), was a descendant of Shealtiel who was the son of Jehoiachin or Jeconiah (Matt. 1:12; 1 Chron. 3:17). Therefore, no son of Joseph could sit upon David's throne. Mary, however, was also a descendant of David through Nathan (Luke 3:24-38). Thus, the son of Mary could fulfill both prophecies if she conceived supernaturally through the power of the Holy Spirit and not by Joseph her husband.

In summary, a David-like Jewish Messiah would originate His own birth as a descendant of David in such a remarkable way that He would avoid the curse of Jeconiah. Therefore, He would not be corrupted by the fallen nature inherited from Adam, but would be the rightful heir to the throne of David forever. All this explains why there are fifty-eight references to David in the New Testament; he was an esteemed patriarch greatly respected by the Jewish nation and a wonderful type of the coming Messiah, who was both David's Lord and his Son! (Luke 20:41-44).

A Troubled Saul (vv. 14-23)

The Holy Spirit had already departed from the rejected king, but He came upon David powerfully (v. 14). The absence of light is darkness (Isa. 45:7); the absence of God's abiding presence permits the darkness of the human mind to be harassed and controlled by demonic forces. This is what is meant by the reference to *"a distressing spirit from the Lord"* that was troubling Saul (vv. 15-16).

Saul's spirit was suffering from the absence of divine light, leaving only the darkness of his depraved mind. His distressing situation may have been caused by some form of mental illness or by direct demonic harassment. Dr. Rendle Short suggests that Saul was likely suffering from a manic-depressive insanity. This condition is characterized by "periods of intense gloom with occasional outbreaks of homicidal violence for no particular reason than the delusion that people were plotting against him."[60] Matthew Henry says that through willful sin, the Good Spirit had been forced to depart from him, which had made him prey to an evil spirit:

> If God and His grace do not rule us, sin and Satan will have possession of us. The devil, by the divine permission, troubled and terrified Saul, by means of the corrupt humors of his body and passions of his mind. He grew fretful, and peevish, and discontented, nervous and suspicious, ever and rapidly starting and trembling; he was sometimes, says Josephus, as if he had been choked or strangled, and a perfect demoniac by fits. This made him unfit for business, precipitate in his counsels, the contempt of his enemies, and a burden to all about him.[61]

Saul may have been suffering from some form of mental illness, meaning his agitation and distress would be further heightened when harassed by satanic forces. With the absence of the Holy Spirit, demonic foes would have been permitted to attack Saul in at least three ways: possession, oppression, and obsession.

Possession occurs when an unbeliever is indwelt by a demon, or demons. These demons gain direct control of the body and the mind, much the same way commandos would forcibly gain control over a weak military installation. The believer may witness demon possession, but he cannot be possessed himself. If the Holy Spirit has sealed (Eph. 1:13) and taken up residence in an individual (1 Cor. 6:19), He will in no way relinquish that vessel for Satan's inhabitation. Therefore, a believer cannot be indwelt by demons, but the oppression that demons can inflict upon a vulnerable or carnal believer may indeed lead to behavior that seems to an observer much like that of a possessed individual.

Oppression can speak of a wide range of internal and external influences that Satan may bring to bear on humanity. In respect to the believer, these are external influences that try the patience of our faith. Job is a classic example in the Bible of obvious physical and mental oppression. Satan not only afflicted Paul's body (2 Cor. 12:7), but also hindered him from visiting the Christians at Thessalonica (1 Thess. 2:18). Thank the Lord, Christ came to deliver those oppressed by Satan (Acts 10:38).

Obsession is the direct injection of evil thoughts into the human mind. Paul acknowledges that there is *a "spirit that is now at work in the sons of disobedience"* (Eph. 2:2). This is not possession or external oppression. Obsession is a tool used by Satan to mentally torment believers. The enemy may plant tempting thoughts so he can establish a stronghold in the flesh (such as pornography), or he may observe a self-erected stronghold in the heart, such as bitterness, and seek to stir up unforgiving thoughts. Satan, or his cohorts in crime, then stimulates these strongholds with ungodly thoughts to inflict anxiety, distress, and depression. If there were no strongholds (i.e. bitterness, anger, envy, etc.), Satan's efforts to obsess the believer's mind would be ineffective, and would soon cause him to terminate the mental attack (Jas. 4:7). Ananias is an excellent example of satanic obsession targeting the mind. Apparently, a stronghold of greed and envy existed in the heart of this believer and he became susceptible to attack (Acts 5:3).

The importance of holy living, renewing the mind, and the power of prayer to combat the offensive engagements of the enemy bring victory over such demonic attacks. Unfortunately, Saul was not holy, his thoughts were self-focused, and the Lord did not heed his prayers because he had been rejected. In application, believers in the Church Age who do not walk in the Spirit, but choose to live "carnally," will be easy prey for the devil's devices.

Seeing Saul's wretched mental state, his servants asked if they could search for a skilled harp player to ease his distress (v. 16). But as we all know, drowning one's cares by overwhelming one's senses does not alleviate the deep burdens of the soul for long. Whether it be substance abuse, gluttony, entertainment, sexual encounters, or intellectual exercises, such things cannot but temporarily numb the mind that is suffering from the persistent spiritual unrest of a guilty conscience. Nevertheless, Saul agreed to the request and one of his servants suggested that Jesse from Bethlehem had a son, *"who was skillful in playing, a mighty man of valor, a man of war, prudent in speech, and a handsome person; and the Lord is with him"* (vv. 17-18).

Evidently, even as a teenager, David's devotion to the Lord and his reputation as a brave shepherd (as Saul mentions this in the next verse) was already being circulated. Plus, David was a skilled harpist!

Saul, unaware that David had already been anointed as Israel's next king, sent a message to Jesse: *"Send me your son David, who is with the sheep"* (v. 19). Jesse agreed to the king's request and, as a kind expression of his allegiance to Saul, *"took a donkey loaded with bread, a skin of wine, and a young goat, and sent them by his son David to Saul"* (v. 20). David traveled north to Gibeah and stood before Saul, who immediately loved David and made him his armor bearer (i.e., one of Saul's personal body guards; v. 21).

Interestingly, Scripture records three people in Saul's household who specifically loved David: Saul (v. 21), his son Jonathan (18:1), and his daughter Michal (18:20). There can be little doubt that the qualities Saul admires in David were what he wished he had himself: youthful zeal, the respect of the people, prudent speech, and the presence of the Lord. Saul may have been head and shoulders above the people, but David's inner qualities of grace and loveliness easily captivated the hearts of all those who observed him. Such will be the reality of heaven, for the One whom David typifies, the Lord Jesus Christ, will completely enthrall every saint with His charming character and the radiance of His presence.

From his introduction in Scripture, David is a selfless and faithful servant. It did not matter if he was tasked with protecting his father's sheep from bears and lions or dispelling Saul's contrary spirit, he would do what was required of him and to the best of his ability. This is a wonderful example for all believers to follow – until the Lord redirects His servants, they should remain in their calling (1 Cor. 7:20), be submissive to authority (Col. 3:22-24), and do everything for the glory of God (1 Cor. 10:31). Wherever you are – be all there, and whatever you are doing – be faithful to the Lord.

David so pleased Saul that he sent a messenger to Jesse requesting that David remain with him (v. 22). Thus David would be available to play his harp to soothe Saul's soul whenever he became disturbed (v. 23). Although only his instrumental music is mentioned in the biblical record, Josephus suggests that David sang hymns and songs of praise while playing his harp. This seems likely, given David's prolific songwriting ability that is later exhibited in the book of Psalms. Although most of us would not understand ancient Hebrew, a skillful harpist strumming notes of praise to God and accompanied by the voice of someone fully devoted to the Lord would be a thrill to hear. David shows us that we can enjoy true rest only in the Lord's intimate presence.

Meditation

He is able to deliver thee, though by sin oppressed,
Go to Him for rest, our God is able to deliver thee.

— William A. Ogden

David and Goliath
1 Samuel 17

Although the forty-year Philistine oppression, that began before Samuel's judgeship, had concluded, its aftereffects continued into David's reign. At this particular juncture, the Philistines had restrengthened themselves and were threatening Israel again. Most of the weapons that Israel's army possessed were probably confiscated from the Philistines after the battles at Ebenezer and Michmash.

During this long struggle, the battle lines of Philistia and Israel often formed where the Plain of Philistia succumbed to the Judean foothills in the Shephelah. The Jews would dig in on the high ground and the Philistines were wise enough not to assault them in that fortified position. The Philistines had war-chariots, so they had a huge tactical advantage on level ground; Israel had no such weapons of war. The Philistine chariots were useless in the hill country where Israel usually positioned its army. All of this is to say that a standoff situation between Israel and the Philistines along the western edge of the Judean highlands was commonplace.

The narrative begins by describing the ongoing deadlock between the two armies about fifteen miles west of Bethlehem. The Philistines were encamped on the north and south sides of the Valley of Elah (Wadi es-Sant) between Sochoh and Azekah, and the Jews were dug in on the opposite crest north and east of the valley (vv. 1-3). The Philistines wanted Israel to come down into the valley to fight them, but Saul knew better than to give up their defensive stronghold.

To further complicate matters, the Philistines had a giant named Goliath for a champion (v. 4). He was nearly ten feet tall, and wore a bronze helmet and coat of armor that weighed 126 pounds (some estimate it to be as much as 220 pounds; v. 5). His legs were clad with bronze greaves and he carried a brass javelin between his shoulders (v. 6). The staff of his spear was like a weaver's beam and boasted a

133

fifteen pound iron-tipped head. His armor bearer carried Goliath's bronze shield until his master needed it in battle (v. 7).

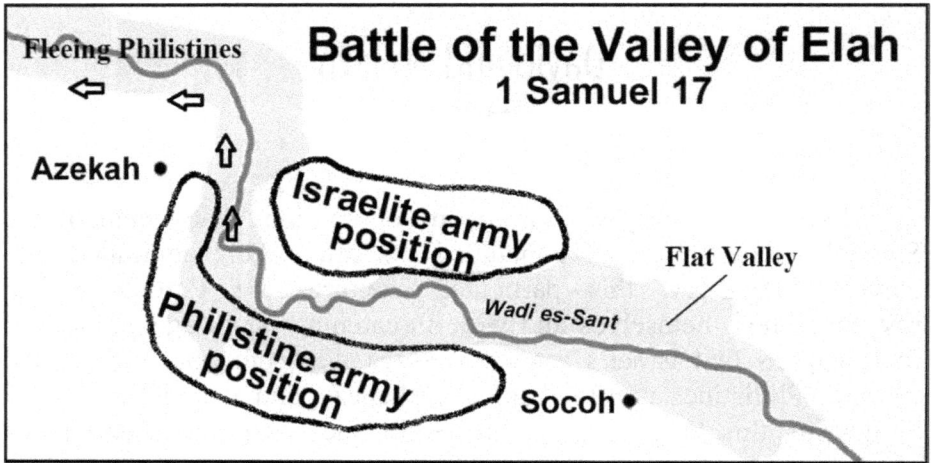

Battle of the Valley of Elah
1 Samuel 17

Fleeing Philistines

Azekah •

Israelite army position

Flat Valley

Philistine army position

Wadi es-Sant

Socoh •

Goliath's solution to the ongoing stalemate was for Saul to provide his best challenger to represent Israel in hand-to-hand combat with him. Then the army of the losing combatant would serve the winner's king; his scheme would avoid unnecessary bloodshed (vv. 8-10). Goliath taunted Israel daily with this offer in an attempt to lure the Jews away from their high-ground position. Goliath was winning the psychological war; forty days of threats and taunts had struck fear in Israel's army (vv. 11, 16). *Forty* is the number representing probationary testing in Scripture. Israel had been tested and their shallow spirituality had been revealed; they were merely frightened *"servants of Saul,"* not faithful "servants of Jehovah."

The God of Israel, whom Goliath continually blasphemed, had an entirely different solution to the impasse and he appears in verse 12 – David, the eighth son of Jesse. The number eight symbolizes new beginnings in Scripture, in the same way that every eighth note in a scale starts a new octave and every eighth day begins a new week. In Noah's day, eight souls entered an ark (a picture of Christ), to escape God's judgment upon the wicked through a flood (1 Pet. 3:20). The ark protected its occupants from God's wrath, lifted them off the earth to be alone with God, and safely carried them to a new life in a new world. The prophet Samuel has anointed a new king of Israel, a man after God's own heart, who is the eighth son of Jesse. Through David a new and everlasting dynasty would be established: the Lord Jesus Christ will rule from the throne of David forever.

David occasionally returned from serving Saul to attend to his father's sheep in Bethlehem (v. 15). On one particular visit home, Jesse tasked David with taking supplies to his three oldest brothers and their captain who were all with Saul at the Valley of Elah battling the Philistines (vv. 13-14, 17-19). The elderly Jesse was anxious for David to return with a report on how his brethren fared. After delivering the cheese, grain, and bread to a supply keeper, David ran to greet his brothers where the army was dug in (vv. 20-23). He arrived just in time to hear Goliath's challenge and blasphemous words.

The men of Israel scattered and hid when Goliath appeared to taunt them (v. 24). However, David keenly felt the insult against his God. Swelling with holy zeal, David inquired of the men standing by him: *"What shall be done for the man who kills this Philistine and takes away the reproach from Israel? For who is this uncircumcised Philistine, that he should defy the armies of the living God?"* (v. 26). David knew that the uncircumcised giant was not protected by God's covenant with Israel and therefore desired to engage and defeat the giant on that basis. Saul's soldiers affirmed that the king had promised great riches, his daughter's hand in marriage, and a tax-exempt status to the man who defeated Goliath (vv. 25, 27). Despite this reward, no one wanted to face the colossal Philistine.

Overhearing this conversation, David's oldest brother Eliab had enough of his baby brother's meddling in affairs that did not pertain to him. Eliab insulted David by calling him a proud and insolent youth who should be home attending the few sheep placed in his charge (v. 28). David, however, felt that he had not done anything wrong and that there was a holy cause which demanded that the giant be confronted (v. 29). What a test for David! Not only was he alone in this time of difficulty, but he had to endure taunts from the flesh (through Eliab) contrary to what he knew was required to uphold Jehovah's honor.

It was not long before David's words among the fighting men reached the king who sent for him (vv. 30-31). David answered the king's inquiry: *"Let no man's heart fail because of him; your servant will go and fight with this Philistine"* (v. 32). Saul appreciated David's zeal, but he rejected the entire idea because David was but a youth and not a man of war (v. 33). Without hesitation David then asserted his qualifications as a proven shepherd who (with the Lord's help) had slain both lion and bear to protect his sheep (vv. 34-35). With complete confidence in the Lord, David settled the matter:

> *"Your servant has killed both lion and bear; and this uncircumcised Philistine will be like one of them, seeing he has defied the armies of the living God." Moreover David said, "The Lord, who delivered me from the paw of the lion and from the paw of the bear, He will deliver me from the hand of this Philistine"* (vv. 36-37).

David asserts an argument of faith – God had delivered him from past difficulties and would again – there was no difference to Him in the matter. It seems likely that David had not spoken of this achievement previously, as no one seems to know about a shepherd boy successfully slaying lion and bear to save his sheep. There was no "if" in David's statement, as there had been in Jonathan's previously conflict (14:9). In fact, there was nothing to do but for him to go! Many will talk about what should be done, to exalt themselves in the presence of their hearers, while others think much about what should be done, but then take no action. Both pride and complacency have their origins in the flesh and thus are tools of the devil against a true work of God. But David, being a man of faith, neither promotes himself nor scurries away from the crucial task at hand; rather, his boast and confidence is in his God.

No doubt Saul was dumbfounded by young David's determination. All he could say was *"Go, and the Lord be with you!"* Saul made David put on his armor, mail, and helmet, and then he fastened his sword to the armor, but David was greatly encumbered by the size and weight of it all (v. 38). He could hardly walk with Saul's armor on, much less fight someone while wearing it. David, a man of faith, chose to remove all of the provisions that the man of the flesh had offered him. The young defender of sheep then departed from the king's presence, without armor, to face Goliath, the great blasphemer of Israel's God (v. 39). C. H. Mackintosh suggests that Saul's armor posed a greater challenge to David than the giant did:

> David's trial was not when he met the giant, in actual conflict, but when he was tempted to use Saul's armor. Had the enemy succeeded in inducing him to go with that, all was gone; but, through grace, he rejected it, and thus left himself entirely in the Lord's hands, and we

know what security he found there. This is faith. It leaves itself in God's hand.[62]

David chose to confront the giant with the armor that God had enabled him to overcome bears and lions with: his shepherd's staff and his sling. He paused at a brook to choose five smooth stones, which he placed in a pouch in his shepherd's bag (v. 40). David was not thinking that he might miss the huge Philistine with his first stone, but rather, being led of the Spirit, depicted a prophetic message in the stones. A brief review of Jewish history is necessary to understand the significance of the five stones.

While the Anakim in Hebron were defeated by Caleb during the Canaan Conquest, Joshua notes that some of the giants escaped to Gaza, Gath, and Ashdod (Josh. 11:22, 15:14). Now, centuries later, Goliath, a descendant of those giants living in Gath, is defying Israel's army and, more importantly, Israel's God. The Lord will use young David to take down Goliath with a stone from his sling. A few years later, David's mighty men will also finish off Goliath's four oversized brothers in battle. David, selecting five specific smooth stones before confronting and defeating Goliath in battle, was a prophetic sign that all five brothers would be defeated by David and his men. This outcome proves that when God's people become desperate for Him and are willing to fully trust Him, mountains are moved and giants are toppled (Matt. 17:20).

Goliath came out with his armor bearer to battle Israel's challenger, but when the giant saw David, *"he disdained him; for he was only a youth, ruddy and good-looking"* (vv. 41-42). Infuriated that Saul would send such a feeble combatant out to engage him, Goliath addressed the young shepherd with contempt:

"Am I a dog, that you come to me with sticks?" And the Philistine cursed David by his gods. And the Philistine said to David, "Come to me, and I will give your flesh to the birds of the air and the beasts of the field!" (vv. 43-44).

Seeing his attire and sling, Goliath mocked David, "Do you think you can best me, as easily as you would beat a shepherd's dog with a stick?" David's bold response to Goliath's slander was fostered in righteous indignation and framed in faith:

You come to me with a sword, with a spear, and with a javelin. But I come to you in the name of the Lord of Hosts, the God of the armies of Israel, whom you have defied. This day the Lord will deliver you into my hand, and I will strike you and take your head from you. And this day I will give the carcasses of the camp of the Philistines to the birds of the air and the wild beasts of the earth, that all the earth may know that there is a God in Israel. Then all this assembly shall know that the Lord does not save with sword and spear; for the battle is the Lord's, and He will give you into our hands (vv. 45-47).

The Philistine said nothing more. If he must fight such a morsel of a man, he will do so with all the pomp and grandeur demanded of a magnificent bronze-clad giant. As the towering bronze warrior moved towards David, David responded by running towards the great blasphemer (v. 48). Why could David charge a heavily armed giant in battle? The honor of his God's name was at stake! The Jewish soldiers were unconcerned that the name of their God was brought into disrepute, but David felt the matter keenly. He courageously defended the Lord's name because he understood that *"the name of the Lord is a strong tower; the righteous run to it and are safe"* (Prov. 18:10). Likewise, our conduct must consider Christ and His name first in all things, for we are His saints. Believers compose the household of God, His living temple on earth to shine forth His virtue; God forbid that we disdain His name before the nations through corrupt or cowardly conduct.

David took one of the five stones from his shepherd's bag, placed it in his sling, and hurled it at Goliath. The stone sunk deep into Goliath's forehead, causing the Philistine to collapse to the ground with a crashing thud (v. 49). Whether Goliath lifted his helmet to mock David and his sling, or if the stone struck an unprotected area of his forehead to penetrate his skull (such as the top of the nose or eye) is unknown.

The brave shepherd then seized the stunned giant's sword and chopped off his head with it, just as he had said he would do in the name of Jehovah (vv. 50-51). Genuine faith honors God, and God honors such faith. David had put himself into the hands of God and God had moved against the giant, while protecting His servant.

After seeing their champion defeated by a mere youth, the enemy quickly fled westward to Philistia. Israel's army rallied to pursue the Philistines to the gates of Gath and Ekron (v. 52). After routing the

Philistines, the Jews returned to plunder their camp (v. 53). David had his own battle souvenirs; Goliath's head which he took to Jerusalem and the giant's armor which he put in his own tent (which may have been Goliath's tent – the prize of the victor; v. 54).

David's victory over Goliath typifies the ultimate victory that the future Son of David would have over Satan and all the evil powers of darkness. Just as David bore the head of Goliath as a testimony of his achievement, the Lord Jesus Christ spoiled the devil and his servants and made an open showing of them. Hence, in Him, believers are more than conquerors and are enabled by faith to triumph over the prince and power of this world in the daily confrontations against evil (Col. 2:15).

Additionally, we will see that David's selfless love demonstrated in conquering Goliath also drew Israel to his person – the Jewish nation fell in love with David. C. H. Mackintosh highlights the same outcome for those who have been delivered from the power of death and sin through Christ's redemptive work:

> Who that has felt the real depth of his need, and groaned beneath the burden of his sins, can fail to love and adore that gracious One who has satisfied the one and removed the other? The work of the Lord Jesus is infinitely precious; it meets the sinner's need, and introduces the soul into a position in which it can contemplate the Person of Christ. In a word, then, the work of the Savior is for the sinner; the Person of the Savior is for the saint: what He has done, is for the former; what He is, is for the latter.[63]

The final dialogue of the chapter is puzzling as Saul seems to be unfamiliar with David, but in the previous chapter David regularly played his harp in Saul's court and was his armor bearer (16:21). While David was facing down Goliath, Saul asked Abner, *"Whose son is this?"* and Saul's general responded that he did not know (v. 55). The king told Abner to find out (v. 56). How tragic that someone would defeat a man's greatest foe and yet that benefactor would be a stranger to him. Yet, this typifies the coming ministry of the Lord Jesus Christ who overcame the prince of the world at Calvary, yet most of those benefiting from His victory did not know Him.

However, the issue before us was not that the king was completely unfamiliar with David, but that he was unaware, or had forgotten, David's family background. Given the king's promise of tax exemption and his daughter's hand in marriage to the victor (a promise honored in the next chapter), it was important for him to understand David's lineage and his father's position in society.

Abner later found David, still clutching Goliath's head in his hand, and brought him before the king (v. 57). Saul then asked David whose son he was and David answered, *"I am the son of your servant Jesse the Bethlehemite"* (v. 58). The approximately fifteen-year-old young man had defended the honor of Jehovah's name and delivered Israel from the Philistines in the process. There are no limits to what genuine faith can accomplish for a righteous cause that God endorses.

Meditation

> Encamped along the hills of light ye Christian soldiers rise,
> And press the battle ere the night shall veil the glowing skies.
> Against the foe in vales below, let all our strength be hurled;
> Faith is the victory we know that overcomes the world.

> — John H. Yates

Jealousy and Envy
1 Samuel 18

Saul Resents David (vv. 1-16)

Saul decided that David should reside with him in Gibeah and not return to Bethlehem (v. 2). The soul of his son Jonathan quickly bonded with David and a deep admiration developed between the two men, Jonathan being David's senior by twelve to fifteen years (v. 1). This deep friendship was so strong that *"Jonathan and David made a covenant, because he* [Jonathan] *loved him* [David] *as his own soul"* (v. 3). As a sign of his unfailing loyalty to David, Jonathan gave David the robe he was wearing, his armor, sword, bow, and belt.

Jonathan's surrender of his royal robe, which marked him as heir to the throne of Israel, was a poetic way for Jonathan to lay his own claims to honor and glory at David's feet. Jonathan watched David descend into the valley to face a giant and return again with the spoils of victory. David had earned his esteem and devotion. This gesture was to show David that he was yielding to what he already knew was to be God's plan – David, not himself, would be Israel's next king!

Seeing that David behaved wisely on whatever errand he sent him, Saul set him over some of his men of war (v. 5). Saul probably hoped that David being a young man and an untrained warrior would fail in leading veteran soldiers or better yet, fall in battle. However, it was not to be. David conducted himself favorably before everyone. In time, Saul's soldiers, the people, and even Saul's servants all accepted and approved of David's leadership in Saul's court. David went in and out among the people in a manner suggestive of a true selfless shepherd, and they all cherished him for it.

However, David's troubles began soon after he returned home from slaughtering the Philistines one particular day. Women came out of the city to welcome David home. They danced joyfully in the king's presence with tambourines and other musical instruments while singing: *"Saul has slain his thousands and David his ten thousands"*

141

(vv. 6-7). The lyrics infuriated Saul, for David had obviously won the hearts of the people, and the only thing remaining for him to take would be the kingdom (v. 8). From that day forward, Saul observed David with suspicion and apprehension (v. 9). Verses 5-9 cover a lengthy period of time, perhaps even two or three years.

It did not take long for Saul's jealousy to get the best of him. The very next day his spirit was vexed. So David played his harp as he had done on previous occasions to ease the king's turmoil (v. 10). The contrast in the king's court is alarming; the king raves violently (apparently under the control of an evil spirit), while David plays softly on his harp while singing praises to God.

The king can take no more. Controlled by unchecked jealousy and seeing a nearby spear, he picked it up and tried to pin David to the wall with it (v. 11). Thankfully, David escaped without injury, even after a second effort by Saul with the spear. Saul may have merely swung the spear at David the first time and then haphazardly thrown it at him on the second attempt. Notice that the text does not say the spear stuck in the wall, as was the case in the next chapter when the king again tried to kill David (19:10). This indicates that Saul's jealousy is swelling with time and will eventually lead him into a murderous fit and obsession that will usher him into his grave. *"Jealousy as cruel as the grave; its flames are flames of fire, a most vehement flame"* (Song 8:6). Peter Pell warns believers to quickly extinguish such conflagrant passions lest carnal savagery be permitted to rage in our own hearts.

> Let us beware of the beginnings of jealousy in our own hearts. Envy is one of Satan's most subtle poisons, blinding the eyes and hardening the hearts, withering all the blossoms of the fruit of the Spirit in the soul and working death in the garden of the Lord.[64]

Saul was terrified of David because he knew the Lord was with David, but had abandoned him (v. 12). Rather than having that constant reminder, Saul discharged David by promoting him as a captain over a thousand soldiers (v. 13).

No doubt Saul was hoping the Philistines would take care of David for him, but this honorable exile proved to be a twofold mistake by the king. First, Saul dismissed the only person who was able to soothe his troubled soul and to serve as a bulwark against satanic attacks on his mind. Second, the battlefield became David's proving ground, and every time the wise victor returned home, his reputation as Israel's champion only increased (v. 14). Because David was a model of humility and grace, his popularity swelled throughout Israel and Judah – everyone loved David (v. 16). But his budding fame and astute character only caused Saul to fear David even more (v. 15).

David Marries Michal (vv. 17-30)

Saul had already pledged to give his daughter in marriage to the man who slew Goliath, and David's growing popularity probably prompted the king to make good on his promise. However, the monarch conveniently forgot that David was already due one of his daughters and he offered David another arrangement that better suited his agenda.

Saul told David (who was now probably 18 or 19 years of age) that he could have his oldest daughter Merab in marriage, but he expected something in return for her (v. 17). David, being of common social status, could not pay the expensive dowry customary for a king's daughter, so he brushed aside the idea (v. 18). But Saul was not concerned about receiving gold or silver from David. He wanted David to fight the Philistines, thus hoping to rid himself of David by the hand of his enemy. The king even promoted the proposal under the guise of a holy war to prompt David to accept it– certainly a brave servant of the Lord like David would want to *"fight the Lord's battles"* anyway!

The arrangement was agreeable to David who then engaged the Philistines. However, while David was earning Saul's daughter's hand in marriage on the battlefield, the king reneged on his pledge and gave Merab to Adriel the Meholathite as a wife (v. 19). This was an unethical move by Saul, who had already promised Merab to David. Matthew Henry suggests Saul did this to arouse David's resentment and to cause him to act foolishly:

> He did what he could to provoke him to discontent and mutiny, by breaking his promise with him, and giving his daughter to another when the time came that she should have been given to him (v. 19). This was as great an affront as he could possibly put upon him, and touched him both in his honor and in his love. He therefore thought David's resentment of it would break out in some indecency or other, in word or deed, which might give him an advantage against him to take him off by the course of law. Thus evil men seek mischief.[65]

Undeniably, Saul's offense was malicious, but the injustice would be righteously judged later, for all five sons from the union of Merab and Adriel would later perish at the hands of the Gibeonites. This judicial decree was issued by David for Saul's attempted genocide of the innocent Gibeonites (2 Sam. 21:1-10).

David committed himself to the Lord and did not retaliate in any way for the injustice Saul had committed against him. The Holy Spirit moved David to act in the same way Paul later exhorts all believers to behave: *"If it is possible, as much as depends on you, live peaceably with all men. Beloved, do not avenge yourselves, but rather give place to wrath; for it is written, 'Vengeance is Mine, I will repay,' says the Lord"* (Rom. 12:18-19). To avenge ourselves usually requires us to rob time and resources from the Lord's work to do so. Furthermore, saints defending themselves to redeem their reputations normally cause further harm to the body of Christ. David demonstrates how exercising patience and restraint can be used by the Lord to further honor the honorable and, in God's timing, humble the proud. Samuel Ridout concludes that unrelenting pride always ends with the loss of God's blessings and peace:

> Poor Saul, we cannot but pity him. He stands in the way of his own peace, and his pride robs him of all blessing. It is ever thus when pride asserts itself. We see it in full measure in the world, but even in the children of God, if pride is harbored in the heart, it thrusts out the enjoyment of the Lord, and He is, for the time, in a place of distance.[66]

Saul then learned that his daughter Michal loved David; apparently Merab did not, which may have prompted Saul's treachery (v. 20). The matter pleased the king because he thought he could use Michal to ensnare David in such a way to cause his death; *"therefore Saul said to David a second time, 'You shall be my son-in-law today'"* (v. 21). Having suffered Saul's fickleness twice, David answers the king nothing. Saul then asked his servants to pursue David with the idea of marrying Michal and becoming the king's son-in-law (v. 22).

David again rejected the notion because he would not be able to afford the dowry for the king's daughter (v. 23). After hearing David's response, Saul devised a dowry that David could afford: a hundred foreskins of the Philistines (vv. 24-25). This payment was more than what was requested for Merab, and apparently needed to be paid during the original time allotted for Merab. If David agreed, Saul believed that David would likely perish while battling the king's enemies, for the time constraint would require David to behave recklessly. Saul believed this to be an ethical means of ridding himself of his rival without prompting the derision of the people.

The king's proposal pleased David who quickly led his men into battle and killed two hundred Philistines (v. 26). Albert Barnes explains David's expediency, "David was so rapid in his attack upon the Philistines that he was able to bring the required dowry within the time, and to receive his wife (Michal), before the time had expired within which he was to receive Merab."[67] To show his respect for the princess, David doubled the number of foreskins required to earn Michal's hand.

The full count of foreskins was verified and Saul gave Michal to David as his wife (v. 27). In effect, David had actually earned Michal's hand in marriage three times before receiving her. Unfortunately, though Michal loved David, she was nonetheless her father's daughter and what is of the flesh remains the flesh. The Holy Spirit resided in David, and a child of God and a child of the devil will never have a happy marriage because of the controlling influence of the in-laws, so to speak. This is one reason why Paul implores believers not to be unequally yoked with children of the devil (2 Cor. 6:14).

David's military success again affirmed in Saul's mind that God was with David, which only fueled his own anxiety and dread of David (v. 28). David had now won over the hearts of some in his own family, namely his son Jonathan and his daughter Michal. David, not the Philistines, had become Saul's number one enemy! With every battle against the Philistines, the king's jealousy and trepidation became worse because the astute and daring David triumphed again and again. All that the king had done to covertly cause David's death had only served to increase his esteem in Israel (v. 30).

The darkness of Saul's hatred and his self-focus poses a stark backdrop to David's bright, charming, humble, and prudent personality. No wonder everyone was drawn to him like iron to a magnet. In this chapter we learned that David was loved by Jonathan, Michal, Saul's servants, and all Judah and Israel. No other Old Testament character attracted so many, and so quickly, to his person as David. He foreshadows the Lord Jesus Christ whose excellent character and perfections draw out of our own hearts deep and deserved affections.

Meditation

Submission, when properly understood and applied, replaces the pain and strife of rebellion and greatly increases human happiness.

— James MacDonald

Saul Pursues David

1 Samuel 19

The Son's Voice of Reason (vv. 1-7)

Saul commanded his servants and Jonathan to slay David, if given the opportunity (v. 1). Because Jonathan delighted in David, he informed his younger friend of his father's plot against him:

My father Saul seeks to kill you. Therefore please be on your guard until morning, and stay in a secret place and hide. And I will go out and stand beside my father in the field where you are, and I will speak with my father about you. Then what I observe, I will tell you (vv. 2-3).

Jonathan quickly followed through with his promise to David. The phrase "my father" occurs twice and "his father" once in verses 3-4. This implies that Jonathan approached the king from the tender perspective of a loving son concerned for his father's good. Exhortations and warnings are best received when a transparent relationship of love exists between the parties involved. Noble love calms the agitation of exhortation because the motives of the exhorter are not in doubt. For this reason, Jonathan gained his father's ear and a favorable outcome resulted.

Jonathan reminded his father about David's triumphs in the king's name against the Philistines, that David had behaved wisely before everyone, and that he had not sinned against the king (v. 4). Saul had previously rejoiced in David's accomplishments, hence, there was no just reason to execute David; he was innocent before God and the king (v. 5). The reference to the shedding of "innocent blood" would remind the king of the severe consequences promised to those who slay people gratuitously in Israel; God's land was to remain unpolluted by such deadly injustice (Deut. 19:10-21).

Jonathan's intercession on David's behalf is one of his longest discourses in Scripture (vv. 4-5). He was a man of few words, but when he did speak, his speech was marked by grace and truth, and is therefore worthy of attention. Such were the words of the Lord Jesus (John 1:14), who set the perfect example of communication that all believers should aspire to (Col. 4:6).

The king heeded his son's words and swore, *"As the Lord lives, he shall not be killed"* (v. 6). Although this was a heartfelt declaration, H. L. Rossier suggests that nothing had really changed in Saul's heart:

> By presenting grace to the heart of the natural man, God allows his wickedness to be momentarily arrested in its development, but this is not conversion. Saul's murderous intention is changed, yet nevertheless he does not repent. He retracts his decision, makes a new resolution when faced with the exhortations of a man of faith, but hardly is this resolution made than he shows himself to be in no way free from his impulses and by his behavior proves that he is a miserable slave of Satan.[68]

Sometimes a prudent presentation of the truth may convict a person's conscience to take a particular moral action but without repentance of their evil intentions. As illustrated in the shallow soil of the first kingdom parable of Matthew 13, the Word of God can prompt a guilty conscience to self-reformation without coming to true repentance and experiencing rebirth. The plant we see above the ground may look genuine for a time, but eventually trials (exposure to the hot sun) proves what is actually in the human heart (i.e., what is below the ground and we do not see). Only God knows if there is really a root of faith there or not, which means what we see above ground may be misleading. Time will eventually prove the reality of a true believer, for a real plant cannot exist long without a true root. "No root" means that there never was true faith resulting in regeneration. God's truth had an effect on the person, but repentance resulting in spiritual rejuvenation, as evidenced by spiritual fruitfulness, never happened. Saul demonstrates to us the shallow soil of hearing the truth, but not fully acting on it to obtain the long-lasting benefit of true conversion.

Jonathan informed David of his father's vow of goodwill and then brought the innocent fugitive to the king. David then played music in the king's presence as he had previously done (v. 7).

Deception and Escape (vv. 8-18)

There was another Philistine uprising, which David decisively put down (v. 8). His victory, however, aroused another episode in Saul's jealous heart. Saul sat with a spear in his hand while David played sweet strains on his harp (v. 9). The king's evil spirit eventually overcame sound reason and he thrust his spear at the young harpist. The agile David quickly slipped away, leaving the empty spear shuddering in the wall (v. 10).

David escaped to his own home that evening. Anticipating that this might be David's place of flight, Saul sent men to watch his house (v. 11). After learning that David was at home, Saul ordered his soldiers to seize David in the morning and kill him. David heeded his wife Michal's plea for him to save his life and to follow her escape plan for him. She let him down an outside wall through a window and then put an image in his bed as a ruse (v. 12).

How humiliating this stealthy getaway must have been for David. As a faithful shepherd, he had slain both lion and bear to protect his sheep. As a victorious warrior, he had withstood legions of Philistines and boldly charged and defeated a giant. However, none of his previous adversaries had been circumcised (i.e., under a covenant with Jehovah), nor were they the Lord's anointed. Consequently, facing Saul in combat was not an option, but neither did David want to perish under the king's evil agenda. Seeing no other recourse, he yielded to his wife's counsel, which caused him to break out of his own home and escape under the cover of darkness.

After David departed, Michal placed an image in David's bed and covered it with clothes and even used goats' hair to replicate David's head (v. 13). The image that Michal revered was a *teraphim*, which, though inferior to a pagan idol, was a demi-god of sorts in the household where it resided. Michal did not worship it, but rather ascribed a certain level of importance to it in household affairs (something like the regard some would give to a religious statue of a saint, or like the idea that good luck is obtained by the possession of a four-leaf clover or a rabbit's foot). Her esteem for this image revealed what was in her heart, suggests Peter J. Pell:

> Michal loves David and saves his life, but she does not follow him in the path of rejection. She fails to say to him what Ruth said to Naomi – "Where you go I will go." When David is away, she brings upon the

scene what never should have been harbored in the house – an image. First she treasured it secretly, then, she brought it out openly. She meant to shield David by her deception, but she ensnares herself, and to turn away her father's wrath she sullies David's character.[69]

For those who truly love the Lord Jesus, it is a great privilege to follow Him in His rejection no matter what the personal cost of doing so. God forbid that we claim to love the Lord, but dwell where He cannot to avoid suffering reproach with Him. To become satisfied with a mere form of Christianity, and not to cherish communion with the living, eternal One who sacrificed Himself for us, is a disposition to be most abhorred. As we have already seen, David was a believer who valued the Lord above all else, but Michal was a secret idolater and therefore lacked the motive and the ability for holy consecration and self-sacrifice.

When Saul's men came to arrest David, Michal said that he was sick, implying that he could not be disturbed in his bed (v. 14). The king, however, anxious to end David's life, ordered that David be brought to him in his sickbed (v. 15). After returning to David's house to seize him, the men discovered the subterfuge (v. 16). Saul angrily interrogated his daughter Michal to determine why she had deceived her father and let David, his enemy, escape (v. 17). Previously, Michal had lied to permit David's flight; now she lied to preserve her own life, saying that David had commanded her, *"Let me go! Why should I kill you?"* Lying to and deceiving others is an affront to the truth, and thus to the God of truth (Ps. 31:5).

Solomon reminds his son that there are seven things God hates: a proud look, a lying tongue, murder, devising wicked schemes, a swift inclination to do mischief, a false witness, and those who sow discord among God's people (Prov. 6:16-19). Lying is never permissible for the child of God (Eph. 4:25). Rather, believers are to speak the truth in love, or be silent and entrust the consequences of either of these honorable responses to the Lord (Eph. 4:15). When things go wrong, we should not go wrong with them! The belt of truth is spiritual armor that should be worn by believers at all times (Eph. 6:14).

Michal justified her sin for a perceived higher motive – protecting the lives of herself and her husband. However, the Lord was quite able to protect His anointed king from Saul's murderous attempts without Michal's finagling. Sadly, she valued David's life more than his integrity and what she thought was justifiable behavior only tarnished David's public testimony. What kind of man threatens his wife with death and prompts disloyalty to the king in order save his own life? Though a lover of David, Michal is the daughter of a man living after the flesh and she likewise acts in the flesh to achieve what the flesh wants – its preservation. She behaved quite differently than Jonathan, who defended the behavior and character of the one he dearly loved (at great risk) without compromising the truth.

David then fled to Ramah to find the one man in Israel who could guide, strengthen and encourage him, the prophet Samuel. Because he was a man also living in separation unto God, Samuel received God's anointed without hesitation and without fear of one whom God had rejected – Saul. David told the elderly prophet all that Saul had done against him (v. 18). Knowing that Saul would be searching for David, the two men journeyed together to Naioth, a suburb of Ramah. There may have been a school of the prophets located there (as in Bethel and in Jericho later; 2 Kgs. 2:3-5).

Pursuing and Prophecy (vv. 19-24)

It did not take long before Saul discovered that David was with Samuel at Naioth (v. 19). Saul sent men to Naioth to seize David, but Samuel was waiting for Saul's envoy with a group of fellow prophets. As Saul's soldiers approached the group, *"the Spirit of God came upon the messengers of Saul, and they also prophesied"* (v. 20). The Holy Spirit caused Saul's men to fall into a trance or some ecstatic state which was accompanied by utterances. This behavior, to the common observer, would have appeared similar to that of the prophets when speaking for the Lord. After hearing this news, Saul sent two more groups of men to arrest David, but each time the men were diverted from their evil objective by the Holy Spirit (v. 21). Frustrated by these reports, Saul decided to apprehend David himself.

The king traveled to Ramah and inquired, *"Where are Samuel and David?"* Samuel's crowning achievement was to anoint David, a man after God's own heart, as Israel's next king and as a type of Israel's coming Messiah. Samuel now receives the additional honor of being identified with David as a co-conspirator against the crown. Though David was despised and threatened by the God-forsaken king, the prophet rightly sided with God's anointed and was willing to protect him in a God-honoring way.

Saul journeyed to Naioth after learning that Samuel and David were there (v. 22). However, as Saul approached Naioth, the Spirit of God came upon him also. The king then stripped off his royal garments and prophesied all that day and night before Samuel. The sight of the king in his undergarments prophesying for such a long time caused some to ask, for a second time, *"Is Saul also among the prophets?"* (v. 23). T. Wilson observes that the visible effects of the Holy Spirit on Saul were more pronounced than those on the previous three companies of men that he had sent to arrest David:

> Whereas the Spirit of God came upon the first company and they prophesied as one man, the second company "prophesied likewise," and the third "prophesied also," of Saul we read: "the Spirit of God was upon him also ... he ... prophesied ... And he stripped off his clothes also, and prophesied before Samuel in like manner, and lay down naked all that day and all that night" (vv. 20-21, 23-24). The more determined the rebel, the more evident the power of God upon him. We also note the irony of the situation, as Saul, who came to arrest – perhaps even to execute – Samuel, is found prophesying before him. The moral authority of the prophet was greater than that of the man who now bore the scepter. We recall the Lord's words to Philadelphia: "I will make them of the synagogue of Satan ... to come and worship before thy feet, and to know that I have loved thee" (Rev. 3:9).[70]

When previously moved by evil, Saul had been a mouthpiece for the devil, but here God demonstrates His power to speak His Word through any mouth He chooses. The Lord has already demonstrated this ability through the false prophet Balaam and even his donkey, and would again at a later date through the high priest Caiaphas. But this outward exhibition of the Holy Spirit's power is not the same as His inward work in the heart which leads to repentance and spiritual regeneration. Saul was being controlled by the Holy Spirit, but he remained unconverted, just like Balaam.

God's power displayed in this chapter by protecting David and Samuel affirms Moses' previous words to be true: *"The beloved of the Lord shall dwell in safety by Him, who shelters him all the day long"* (Deut. 33:12). God honors and defends those who remain consecrated and faithful to Him, even when their deaths become necessary to advance God's purposes. As shown in the resurrection of the Lord Jesus Christ, God is able to overcome all evil powers and principalities to preserve and exalt those who are His (Eph. 1:19-21). Clearly, death is not a defeat, but a promotion into glory!

Samuel's honorable conduct of placing his trust in the Lord is in contrast to Michal's carnal attempt to save her husband's life. Samuel did not resort to the sword, to lying, or to deception, but rather permitted the Lord to intervene to thwart Saul's evil plans and to honor Himself by doing so. Regardless of our motives, God does not need our ungodly behavior to exalt His name, or to protect those who are His, or to fulfill His word!

According to the Hebrew superscript, Psalm 59 was penned shortly after the life-threatening scenarios of this chapter. David recounts his near escape from Saul's javelin and how he resorted to the throne of grace in breathless haste. David prayed to be delivered from blood-thirsty men, who did not deserve God's mercy, because he had done nothing to merit such ruthless hostility (Ps. 59:1-5). His would-be assassins were like snarling dogs prowling about at night; their words were perverse and as sharp as swords, yet in their arrogance they did not think God could even hear them (Ps. 59:6-7). God laughs at such ignorance and scoffs at such evildoers; therefore, David knew God would show mercy and preserve his life (Ps. 59:8-10). Hence, David was confident he would have further reason to sing praises to God, who was his strength, refuge, and defense. As witnessed in God's defense of David and Samuel at Naioth, God defends those who put their trust in Him!

Meditation

We rest on Thee, our Shield and our Defender!
We go not forth alone against the foe;
Strong in Thy strength, safe in Thy keeping tender,
We rest on Thee, and in Thy Name we go.

We go in faith, our own great weakness feeling,
And needing more each day Thy grace to know:
Yet from our hearts a song of triumph pealing,
"We rest on Thee, and in Thy Name we go."

— Edith G. Cherry

Loyalty to the True King
1 Samuel 20

While the unrobed king was prevented from doing evil by the Holy Spirit, David escaped Saul's clutches and traveled back to Gibeah to seek out Jonathan. David bemoaned to his friend, *"What have I done? What is my iniquity, and what is my sin before your father, that he seeks my life?"* (v. 1). David's queries of Jonathan remind us of the Lord's question put to an officer who had just struck him for answering Annas: *"If I have spoken evil, bear witness of the evil; but if well, why do you strike Me?"* (John 18:23). Like David (who wonderfully typifies the Lord in so many ways), we too can identify with Christ in a special way when falsely accused or suffering persecution though innocent of wrongdoing. God's people throughout the scriptural record can be likewise identified – all benefitting from the experience of suffering for the reproach of Christ (Phil. 3:10) or identifying with His people rather than seeking what the world had to offer them (Heb. 11:25).

Jonathan responded to David's questions by affirming that he would faithfully warn his friend if what he feared was true: *"By no means! You shall not die! Indeed, my father will do nothing either great or small without first telling me. And why should my father hide this thing from me? It is not so!"* (v. 2). Apparently, Jonathan was unaware of his father's recent attempts on David's life at Gibeah and at Ramah. David did not question Jonathan's devotion to him, but he was concerned about two matters (v. 3): First, that Saul, knowing of his son's loyalty to David, would likely conceal his evil intentions from Jonathan. Second, that Jonathan would put too much trust in his father to keep his oath of the last chapter.

To alleviate David's anxiety in this matter, Jonathan promised David, *"Whatever you yourself desire, I will do it for you"* (v. 4). David then informed Jonathan of his plan to assess the king's attitude towards him (vv. 5-7). The festival of the New Moon began the next day and David planned to be absent from the king's table and also the following day. If the king inquired about David, Jonathan was to say that David had asked to be excused to celebrate the feast with his family in Bethlehem. The king's response to this information would reveal his true disposition towards David. If the king acted favorably to David's absence, then all was well, but if he became enraged, then they would know that the king was determined to do evil against David. Jonathan was to notify David of the results of this test on the third day.

Because it was Jonathan who initiated the covenant between them, David gently reminded his friend that it was his moral responsibility to be true to him (v. 8). Nevertheless, Jonathan needed no such reminder. He loved David and affirmed that he would tell him the truth, no matter what the outcome was (v. 9). The two then made their way into a field where Jonathan vowed to relay accurate news to David of the king's intentions and that God should judge him if he failed to do so (vv. 10-13). Having stated his part of the covenant, Jonathan then rehearsed David's part:

And you shall not only show me the kindness of the Lord while I still live, that I may not die; but you shall not cut off your kindness from my house forever, no, not when the Lord has cut off every one of the enemies of David from the face of the earth." So Jonathan made a covenant with the house of David, saying, "Let the Lord require it at the hand of David's enemies" (vv. 14-16).

The souls of Jonathan and David were knit together in deep devotion and affection – either man would have gladly laid down his life for the other. Both men heartily affirmed the renewed covenant and then agreed as to how the information would be delivered covertly in three days. David would stay somewhere (presumably Bethlehem with his family) and then return on the third day to a hidden place near the stone Ezel (located on the south end of the field in which they were standing). Jonathan would also return with his bow and a lad to gather his arrows at the appointed time. If, after shooting three arrows, he said to the lad, *"Look, the arrows are beyond you,"* then David would know evil was determined against him by the king (vv. 18-23). In short, in three days – three arrows would tell all.

Jonathan returned to the king's table for the New Moon celebration, and, though the king noticed David's absence, he said nothing, thinking he was ceremonially unclean for some reason (vv. 24-26). The king's reasoning shows that Saul knew David to be a man of conscience and conviction – he would rather miss a religious feast than attend it in his uncleanness. However, on the second day, Saul inquired about David's empty chair and Jonathan informed the king that he had given David leave to attend the sacrifice and feast with his family in Bethlehem (vv. 27-29). The king, knowing his son's devotion to David, was infuriated by Jonathan's response:

> *You son of a perverse, rebellious woman! Do I not know that you have chosen the son of Jesse to your own shame and to the shame of your mother's nakedness? For as long as the son of Jesse lives on the earth, you shall not be established, nor your kingdom. Now therefore, send and bring him to me, for he shall surely die* (vv. 30-31).

Saul's slur was not intended to accuse his wife of any wrongdoing. Eastern families showed great respect and devotion to their mothers, so degrading one's mother was to add extra offense to the explicit insult. Though a carnal tirade, the king's words were more prophetic than he knew. Not only had God promised to remove the kingdom from Saul and his descendants, but a few centuries later the prophet Isaiah would confirm the title Saul gave David as one associated with the coming Jewish Messiah: *"There shall come forth a Rod from the stem of Jesse, and a Branch shall grow out of his roots"* (Isa. 11:1).

The house of David would be in spiritual decline, but suddenly, out of this decaying branch a fresh shoot of promise springs out. Hence, the Messiah, the *Rod* or *Branch* of David, will spring up from the *stem of Jesse*, but He will also be the *root cause* of this new life. David, as a son of Jesse, could rule over Israel with God's approval, but only the Son of God, who was also a descendant of Jesse, could bring life from what was dead.

As we have already seen, the prophet Samuel anointed David, a man after God's own heart, as the king of Israel; he was the eighth son of Jesse (17:12). In David's autumn years, the Lord promised him, through the prophet Nathan, that a new and everlasting dynasty would be established and one of David's descendants would sit on his throne forever:

When your days are fulfilled and you rest with your fathers, I will set up your seed after you, who will come from your body, and I will establish his kingdom. He shall build a house for My name, and I will establish the throne of his kingdom forever. I will be his Father, and he shall be My son. If he commits iniquity, I will chasten him with the rod of men and with the blows of the sons of men. But My mercy shall not depart from him, as I took it from Saul, whom I removed from before you. And your house and your kingdom shall be established forever before you. Your throne shall be established forever (2 Sam. 7:12-16).

Not only would David sit on the throne of Israel instead of Jonathan (as Saul surmised), but the royal line of kings through David would never end and would culminate with the coming of Israel's Messiah, the Lord Jesus Christ. There was much more at stake than just David sitting on the throne instead of Jonathan, and Saul, though he tried relentlessly, could not undermine the sovereign and providential purposes of God. David must be king and Jonathan knew it.

Jonathan tried to reason with his father, but his defense of David, his rival to the throne, only enraged the king, who threw a spear at him (vv. 32-33). Understanding that the king was determined to do evil against David, Jonathan arose from the table with fierce anger and grief over the king's unjust behavior toward his friend (v. 34). The next day, Jonathan and a lad returned to the field where David was waiting (v. 35). Jonathan shot the three arrows as previously planned and then delivered the coded message concerning the lad fetching the arrows; afterwards, Jonathan sent the boy and his bow back into town (vv. 36-40).

David then withdrew from his hiding place and fell on his face and bowed down three times before Jonathan. His loyal friend had kept his word and had come to warn him despite the cost to himself. The two men then warmly greeted each other with a kiss and wept together over the harrowing news (v. 41). Jonathan then said to David: *"Go in peace, since we have both sworn in the name of the Lord, saying, 'May the Lord be between you and me, and between your descendants and my descendants, forever'"* (v. 42). The gravity of the situation was sinking in and both men realized things would never be as they had been before. Yet, as Peter J. Pell notes, God was with them and that brought a sense of His peace into their turbulent trial:

But if the suffering was great for both, the consolation was mutual. Mingled with their bitter tears was the deep sense of the presence of God, and that brought peace. *"Go in peace,"* says Jonathan, *"and the Lord be between me and thee forever."* Thus they were not alone in their sorrow.[71]

True, their friendship in the future would be marked by separation rather than by joyful fellowship, but both men enjoyed communion with the One who ruled over all things and that was a solace to their souls.

Jonathan then returned to the city to remain under the authority of a God-forsaken king whose power was ever diminishing and would soon end. On the other hand, David, Israel's true king, would remain a fugitive until God ended Saul's reign. Likewise, the Lord Jesus Christ, David's royal son, will not return to the earth to receive His kingdom until God determines that the times of the Gentiles have ended. Then the majestic reign of the Jewish Messiah will be without end and He will receive the praise and honor He so richly deserves!

Meditation

Thou art the King of Israel,
Thou David's royal Son,
Who in the Lord's Name comes,
The King and blessed one:

All glory, laud, and honor
To Thee, Redeemer, King!
To Whom the lips of children
Made sweet Hosannas ring!

— Theodulph of Orleans

In God "Should" I Trust
1 Samuel 21

David Flees to Nob (vv. 1-9)

To escape Saul's jealous rage, David retreated south of Gibeah to the priestly city of Nob located in Benjamin's territory (v. 1; Neh. 11:32). Some think Nob was located on the ridge of the Mount of Olives just northeast of Jerusalem[72] and therefore was observable from Jerusalem (Neh. 11:32; Isa. 10:32). The high priest Ahimelech was afraid when he saw David, because he was alone (apparently the men with David were waiting nearby).

In recounting this story, Mark states that the Lord Jesus referred to the high priest as being Abiathar, not Ahimelech, his father (Mark 2:26). Some think that Mark may have simply recollected the names incorrectly, but the apparent contradiction is perhaps best clarified by either one of these explanations: First, the bread was given to David through Abiathar's intercession with the high priest (he was likely preeminent among the priests, as Darby suggests). Second, it may have been Abiathar's own portion that was given to David and he was then remembered in Scripture for his kindness. Abiathar, the only surviving priest of the Nob slaughter in the next chapter, will afterwards join David's renegade group in Keilah.

Fearing that he would not receive his help if Ahimelech knew he was a fugitive, David lied to the priest concerning his situation:

The king has ordered me on some business, and said to me, "Do not let anyone know anything about the business on which I send you, or what I have commanded you." And I have directed my young men to such and such a place. Now therefore, what have you on hand? Give me five loaves of bread in my hand, or whatever can be found (vv. 2-3).

David was a man with a tender conscience and he knew that the ninth of the Ten Commandments prohibited bearing false witness (Ex.

20:16), but it would seem that he did not regard lying as iniquity if one's life was at stake. Yet, the Lord does not approve of lying at any time (Eph. 4:25); His people are to properly represent Him by speaking the truth in love at all times (Eph. 4:15). God is quite capable of protecting what is His under any circumstance without His people's efforts to help Him out by spinning a yarn full of falsehoods. This chapter reminds us that prior to glorification, great men and women of faith still have feet of clay!

If we pause to evaluate David's story, we quickly spot a number of illogical statements. Why would the king send David on an important mission without supplies or weapons? Why did he have so few men with him? Why had David traveled only five miles in three days if he was on an urgent errand for the king? Why was David seeking weapons from priests who were not permitted to be soldiers? Ahimelech, however, had no reason to doubt the word of a nationally acclaimed warrior like David even though his story did not add up.

The priest told David that there was no common bread to give him. The only bread they possessed was the holy unleavened cakes just removed from the Table of Showbread (vv. 4, 6). The Law required these twelve cakes to be replaced every Sabbath and then the priests were to eat the holy bread in the courtyard of the tabernacle (Lev. 24:8-9). The fact that the twelve cakes had just been removed and had not been eaten meant that it was the Sabbath. The situation also indicated that the priests were likely short on food themselves and the unleavened cakes were a necessary portion of food for them.

David refers to this unleavened bread as *common*, not *holy*, and therefore lays claim to it. In reality, the bread had not been removed from before the Lord (which is what made it holy), because the Ark was still at Kirjath-jearim (7:1-2); it was not in the tabernacle at Nob. So the entire practice of replacing the unleavened bread weekly shows the religious confusion that was prevalent in Israel at this time. David understands that the bread is not really holy unto the Lord and requests five of the twelve cakes.

David's evaluation of the bread was a significant assertion and beyond the dictates of the Law. Yet, it was one that the Lord Jesus later approved of when the Pharisees accused the disciples of violating the Sabbath by picking and eating heads of grain on the Sabbath (Mark 2:23-28). Although the plucking of grain was permitted when walking through a neighbor's field (Deut. 23:25), such work was to be avoided on the Sabbath Day. The point of the Lord's rebuttal was this – He was man's Sabbath – true rest for the human soul could only be found in Him (Matt. 11:28-30). But He, like David, had been rejected by the same people who were given the legal system ordained by God which was to lead them into ultimate rest (i.e., point them to the Messiah).

The Sabbath and male circumcision were recurring signs of God's covenant to be observed by the Jews. Because the Jews disobeyed God's Law, Paul says they made mockery of circumcision, the sign of their covenant with God (Rom. 2:25-29). In the same way, the Jews mocked the Sabbath by rejecting the One the Sabbath spoke of. Consequently, Israel's weekly Sabbath (with all the particulars of the Old Covenant) was abolished because of the transgression of rejecting God's Son as their Sabbath – that is, their Savior and Messiah (Heb. 7:18, 8:13). This then permitted Christ to use the Sabbath as He saw fit to introduce the New Covenant which He would seal with His own blood to redeem repentant sinners (Heb. 8:8). David, also Israel's rejected king, likewise placed a different value on the showbread than the priests did under the Law by calling it "common" and, therefore, permissible for him and his men to eat.

Israel would have no rest until the rightful king, God's anointed, was seated on Israel's throne. David's rejection on the Sabbath occurred when Israel was in a state of religious confusion (e.g., the Ark of the Covenant was not with the tabernacle, and the high priestly line was through Ithamar, not Eleazer). This foretells Christ's own rejection as Israel's Sabbath while the Jewish nation was in religious confusion. There could be no rest for anyone until Christ accomplished the work of redemption at Calvary and its benefit is received by faith. Likewise, there will be no peace for Israel until the glorified Savior is seated on the throne of David.

David assured the high priest that he and his men had had no sexual contact with women in the previous three days and therefore were ceremonially *clean*. Under the Law, anyone touching the clothing and bedding associated with semen emissions was ceremonially unclean and had to wash and keep separated from others until evening (Lev. 15:16-18). This is why Moses mandated a three-day-abstinence condition on Israel before leading the nation before Mount Sinai to meet Jehovah (Ex. 19:15). Furthermore, David claimed that he and his men were holy because they had been *set apart* by the king for a special mission. Based on David's claim, Ahimelech gave him the showbread as requested (v. 5). Ahimelech had direct access to the Lord through the Urim and Thummin, but apparently chose not to use the sacred lots to verify David's story, much of which was not true.

Why did David ask for only five loaves of bread and not more? This is the second time David has specifically been identified with the number five, the first being the five smooth stones he took from the brook of Elah, one of which was used to strike Goliath in the head. Metaphorically speaking, the number five represents God's goodness and grace to meet human need or responsibility. For example, the Lord Jesus would confirm five ministries of grace to establish and edify the Church (Eph. 4:11). David was counting on God's grace to slay Goliath and again on God's grace to sustain him in his present crisis. About a millennium later, the greater David would take five loaves of bread (and two fishes) and satisfy the hungry bellies of approximately twenty thousand people (Matt. 14:16-21). The number five speaks of God's abundant grace in action!

Regrettably, one of Saul's herdsmen, Doeg, an Edomite, was also at the tabernacle and witnessed the conversation between Ahimelech and David (v. 7), which he later reported to Saul (22:9). Though David came for bread, seeing Doeg alerted David to his need of weaponry also. David asked the priest whether he had any swords and spears. He stated that they were unarmed because they were required to depart on the king's business in haste (v. 8). The priest said that the only weapon he had was the sword David had taken from Goliath in battle. It had been wrapped in a cloth and placed behind the ephod (i.e., where the high priest's shoulder-dress was hung when not in use; v. 9). Some think the sword was actually wrapped in a portion of Goliath's military cloak as part of a dedicated trophy.[73]

The fact that the sword was given such a place of honor in the tabernacle wonderfully illustrates a truth Jesus Christ would demonstrate later. Peter J. Pell writes:

> The witness of the greater victory of our Lord Jesus is seen in the sanctuary above. By death – the enemy's own weapon, wrested out of his hand – He slew death. "He death by dying slew." And now "His wounds in heaven declare" his triumph. The strength with which He slew death is available for us. One has well said, "Death is the best weapon in the arsenal of God, when wielded by the power of life."[74]

162

Goliath was the administrator of death, and his sword the instrument of death, but David conquered Goliath by slaying him with his own sword. Likewise, the cross was the instrument of death and the devil the administrator of death, but through His sacrificial crucifixion, Christ defeated Satan's death-hold on humanity. The writer of Hebrews put it this way:

> *Inasmuch then as the children have partaken of flesh and blood, He* [Christ] *Himself likewise shared in the same, that through death He might destroy him who had the power of death, that is, the devil, and release those who through fear of death were all their lifetime subject to bondage* (Heb. 2:14-15).

Given this symbolism of Goliath's sword, J. N. Darby explains how God is able to use death to give life:

> It was by the sword of Goliath, the power of death, that the Lord destroyed all his strength who had the power of death. Death is the best weapon in the arsenal of God, when it is wielded by the power of life.[75]

David was delighted to hear the news concerning Goliath's sword and said *"there is none like it"* (probably referring to its size and metallurgical tempering). Likewise, we too are weaponless against the enemy unless we have the one weapon which is like no other – the death and resurrection of Christ. And, as David shows us, such a unique weapon that confers life can only be found in God's sanctuary. Truly, *"there is none like it,"* and Satan can do nothing against the weapon which has already vanquished him and brought eternal life to the redeemed.

David requested and received Goliath's sword. However, as we will see shortly when David moves to Gath, the provision of God against the enemy will not help us if we are not being led by the Lord in its use. God's anointed has now been fed and armed from God's sanctuary. And God the Father continues to do so for all His people who exercise faith, for they have been blessed *"with all spiritual blessings in heavenly places in Christ"* (Eph. 1:3). All that is needed to live every day to the full for God's glory is found in the heavenly places in Christ. Through His death we possess all the wonders of His life.

David Flees to Gath (vv. 10-15)

After receiving bread and Goliath's sword, David then fled to the Philistine-controlled border town of Gath (v. 10). For David to seek asylum among his uncircumcised enemies indicates the severity of Saul's tyranny against him and how forlorn David must have felt. His family, Jonathan, and even Samuel could no longer assist him, so David fled with a handful of men into a hostile foreign land.

It does not seem likely that David entered Gath with their champion's sword dangling from his belt. About seven years had passed since Goliath's defeat, and David himself had matured from a teenager to a young man, so perhaps David thought that he might not be easily recognized. Nonetheless, David had gained much notoriety among his enemy as a warrior and his presence did not go unnoticed very long. He was seized and immediately taken to Achish, the king of Gath (v. 11). The text is unclear if David was actually arrested or was merely taken to the king as a person of interest. Given David and Achish's future association (28:1-2; 29:6), it seems likely that the king wanted to profit from an alliance with a skilled warrior, who, like them, was Saul's enemy too.

Being in Achish's clutches provoked stark fear in David's heart (v. 12). Fear, not faith, led David to Gath, so we should not be surprised that the predispositions of the flesh (e.g., fear, lying, deception, etc.) are ruling David's behavior. Without the Holy Spirit's convicting and controlling influence in our thinking, we all would be prone to such degenerate behavior.

David reasoned that the king would not make sport of a madman, so he acted like he was an insane fool. He even scrawled on the doors of the gate while permitting his saliva to run down his beard (v. 13). C. and A. De Rothschild surmise that David chose to trust in pagan superstition at this juncture: "To save himself, he pretended madness, well knowing that the insane were held inviolable, as smitten and protected by deity."[76] The man of God who in faith charged a giant in battle, the anointed king of Israel who wonderfully typifies the coming Messiah, now lowers himself to the unworthy strategy of faking insanity to preserve his life, but he does so at the cost of his integrity.

Achish was offended by the display or at least seemed to be. He may have known David was faking the whole thing, but did not want his servants to be aware of it lest they hurt David and forfeit any possible future alliance with him. The king therefore told his servants to remove the lunatic David from his home (vv. 14-15). David was promptly released from Philistine custody and immediately retreated to the cave of Adullam within Israel's borders (22:1).

By his behavior David had compromised the dignity which God had conferred upon him as His anointed. Like David, none of us are exempt from stumbling, but thankfully we can learn and profit from David's failure so as to avoid repeating his mistake ourselves. T. Wilson summarizes what we should glean from David's shameful experiences in this chapter:

> David had planned without God. He had met the Lord's priest but asked only sustenance and sword; he did not seek, or did not follow, the guidance of his God. His lies had done no more for him than exchange the fear of Saul for the fear of Achish, notes McShane, who tellingly remarks that "the man, who acted so wisely in the court of Saul, now acts the fool in the court of Achish." How easily a good man can change his behavior if out of touch with God! And how quickly even a good man can lose his listening ear! No longer attentive to his God, David was now straining to catch every whisper from Achish's court as he previously had been in Saul's.[77]

Obviously, if we keep near the Lord and count on Him for all the affairs of life, He will keep us from falling. The events of this chapter were deeply humiliating for David, but, as H. L. Rossier observes, it had a positive benefit for him also:

> David's heart was broken and his spirit overwhelmed because of this, but under this discipline he had learned to know himself and to know the Lord in a more intimate way, and what more could he desire? *"Jehovah is nigh to those that are of a broken heart, and saves them that are of a contrite spirit"* (v. 18).[78]

David wrote Psalms 34 and 56 to express what he had learned from his failure at Gath. According to the superscription, Psalm 34 was written shortly after David escaped from Abimelech (Achish by name) by feigning insanity. It is not his scheming that David boasts in, but rather how God answered his prayer and controlled the situation to preserve his life and secure his freedom (Ps. 34:2, 4). David hoped his passion to praise God *"at all times"* in this matter would prompt all the afflicted to seek the Lord's help, so that they might add their praises to his (Ps. 34:1, 3), might experience radiant joy, and not suffer shame (Ps. 34:5-6). All those who trust in the Lord for protection will be able to say with David, *"taste and see that the Lord is good"* (vv. 7-8).

In Psalm 56, David acknowledged that he was surrounded by his enemies and those loyal to him were just a few, but then he cried out to the Lord for mercy (Ps. 56:1-2). At first David acknowledges his fear, saying, *"Whenever I am afraid, I will trust in You"* (Ps. 56:3), but after a season of prayer he affirms: *"In God I have put my trust; I will not be afraid. What can man do to me?"* (Ps. 56:11). Notice how David flipped the order of his fear and his trust in these two verses to encourage his own heart. This illustrates the transforming effect prayer has on the believer's thinking, that is, when real faith in a sovereign God is exercised in ominous situations.

Meditation

Worry is a cycle of inefficient thoughts whirling around a center of fear.

— Corrie Ten Boom

It is good to remind ourselves that the will of God comes from the heart of God and that we need not be afraid.

— Warren Wiersbe

David on the Run
1 Samuel 22

Gath to Hereth Through Moab (vv. 1-5)

David departed Philistia altogether and took up residence in the cave of Adullam (v. 1). David likely sheltered in many caves during those years he was being hotly pursued by Saul. Samuel names two specific caves that David hid in: Adullam directly after escaping from the King of Gath (v.1; Ps. 56), and Engedi a few months later when David spared Saul's life (24:1-3). The cave of Adullam is located about twelve miles south-west of Bethlehem. David would visit this cave again years later, as it became the base of operation during a military campaign against the Philistines after he was recognized as Israel's king (2 Sam. 5:17-25, 23:13).

After hearing that David was in Adullam, his brethren left Bethlehem to be with David (most likely because they feared Saul's tyranny). They were not the only ones; many who were in debt and oppressed by Saul also flocked to David. The cave was a refuge from oppression, separated from wickedness; hence, anyone willing to identify with the rejected king was welcome. David's ranks quickly swelled and he became captain over four hundred men (v. 2). T. Wilson observes the similarity of these dissidents finding hope in David to that of repentant sinners finding full satisfaction and purpose in Christ:

> Generally speaking, men are not drawn to Christ until, like those that came to David, they see that elsewhere they cannot find the blessing they so much need. They too are then fashioned by their new Master to serve as good soldiers of Jesus Christ.[79]

Because David's parents were too old to suffer the daily hardship and danger that he was exposed to, David journeyed to Mizpah in Moab and asked the king of Moab to care for his parents. This separation was only until David knew *"what God will do for me"* (v.

167

3). Notice that David did not say "until I know what Saul will do to me." True faith reckons with God, not the adverse situation or the adversary threatening to rob us of our peace.

David's great-grandmother Ruth was a Moabite and that may explain why the king was sympathetic towards David and honored his request. However, based on Jewish tradition of the Midrash, the King of Moab eventually killed David's parents. Though David wanted what was best for his parents, he was wrong to put his confidence in the Lord's enemies instead of in the Lord to care for them.

The prophet Gad appeared to warn David to leave his stronghold for the land of Judah. David obeyed the word of the Lord and his band of dissidents departed to the forest of Hereth (v. 5). The only word that mattered in the king's camp was his own, but David was not self-willed and welcomed the one who bore the testimony of God's word.

Psalm 57 is similar in theme and construction to Psalm 56 discussed in the last chapter, but has a more celebratory tone. It was likely written not long after Psalm 56, as the Hebrew superscription notes David was hiding from Saul in a cave when it was penned. The tone and content of this psalm certainly fits the scenario occurring immediately after David's escape from Gath.

Despite his continuing crisis, David composes two stanzas to proclaim his trust in the Lord; each concludes with a refrain of aspiration for God to be exalted in the situation (Ps. 57:5, 11). Though hiding in an earthly cave, David knew the only safe refuge was under the shadow of God's wing – it is from this safe haven David would plead for mercy until all his calamities had passed (Ps. 57:1-3). David describes his surrounding enemies as prowling lions and ravenous beasts who sought to devour him through military conquest; however, God would exalt Himself through their defeat (Ps. 57:4-5). Because David had focused his heart on the Lord instead of fretting over his distresses, he was confident in the outcome and hence vows to sing a victory song to the Lord in the dawning day of liberation (Ps. 57:7-8). The poem concludes with the refrain: *"Be exalted, O God, above the heavens; let Your glory be above all the earth"* (v. 11). Whether in turmoil or in peace, whether impoverished or abounding, may this prayer be the aspiration of God's people.

Saul Slaughters the Priests at Nob (vv. 6-23)

After a paranoid Saul learned that David had returned to Judah, he berated those with him (especially Jonathan because of his covenant with David) for not disclosing David's whereabouts to him earlier (vv. 6-8). Saul shows us that the flesh is most evident in one's speech when it is obsessed with self, and is clouded with exaggerations to provoke an emotional response in others. He uses the first person singular seven times in verse 8, and employs several universal hyperboles: *"**All of you** have conspired against me, and **there is no one** who reveals to me ... **there is not one of you** who is sorry for me."* Poor, pitiful Saul gives the impression that everyone is out to get him by supporting the conspiracy of a young pretender who has no claim to his throne.

Once the king finished his tirade, Doeg, the Edomite, told Saul that he had seen David obtaining help from Ahimelech at Nob (v. 9): *"He [Ahimelech] inquired of the Lord for him [David], gave him provisions, and gave him the sword of Goliath the Philistine"* (v. 10). Saul summoned Ahimelech and the priests of Nob to interrogate them on the matter (vv. 11-13). After arriving, Ahimelech told the king the truth; they had innocently helped the king's son-in-law because he claimed to be on the king's business (vv. 14-15). He also reminded the king that this was not the first time that he had inquired of the Lord for David.

Saul began a new quest that day – to snuff out David's sympathizers in Israel; the royal tyrant decreed that all the priests of Nob should be executed (v. 16). The king then ordered his Jewish guards to carry out the verdict immediately, but they feared God more than they feared Saul and refused to strike down Jehovah's priests (v. 17). Saul then ordered Doeg to do it. Immediately he slew 85 righteous priests with his sword (v. 18) and then traveled to Nob and killed all their families, and even their livestock (v. 19). This graphically illustrates the end to which our self-willed nature will take us if not brought under the control of the Holy Spirit.

While in no way do we endorse David's deception which led to the slaughter of the priests, the entire situation is firmly in God's control. Doeg's murderous hand is actually bringing about the fulfillment of God's prophecy against Eli and his descendants (2:31-36, 3:11-14). God is able to accomplish His purposes by using either human carnality, or triumphs of faith.

One of the sons of Ahimelech named Abiathar was able to escape the slaughter and flee to David and informed him of all that had happened (vv. 20-21). David said to Abiathar, *"I knew that day, when Doeg the Edomite was there, that he would surely tell Saul. I have caused the death of all the persons of your father's house. Stay with me; do not fear. For he who seeks my life seeks your life, but with me you shall be safe"* (vv. 22-23). Abiathar then remained with David during all his fugitive years and later would oversee the tabernacle after David moved it and the Ark to Jerusalem. However, after David's death, he sided with Adonijah's pursuit of the throne (1 Kgs. 1), so after Solomon was anointed king, he removed him as high priest (1 Kgs. 2:26-27).

Abiathar also had the high priest's ephod with him, which permitted the use of the sacred lots to discern the mind of God (as seen in the next chapter). David's group of disgruntled and distressed followers was growing larger and now included several hundred soldiers, most of his family, a priest, and a prophet. William MacDonald further suggests that the scene portrays a charming picture of Christ patiently waiting for His vindication day:

> Prophet (Gad), priest (Abiathar), and king (David), all in exile together, picture Christ today as He waits until His enemies are made His footstool and His throne is set up on earth.[80]

Just as Saul was reigning in the place of David, Israel's rightful king centuries ago, the spirit of Antichrist pervades the world today and will continue to do so until Christ returns to reign over the earth (2 Thess. 2:7-8; 1 Jn. 4:2-3). As we see in this chapter, when the rule of God's people is controlled by that which opposes God, there is much human suffering. Clearly, the spirit of Antichrist is rampant today!

After hearing this news of Doeg's murderous doings, David wrote Psalm 52. In this poem, David contrasts his faith in the Lord (and God's resulting favor) with a sinful, treacherous man who receives God's displeasure. The Hebrew superscript identifies Doeg the Edomite as the man in question.

David was astonished that anyone who had so dishonored the Lord could ever boast of his own despicable deeds (Ps. 52:1). Doeg loved wickedness and used his deceitful tongue as a sharp sword to devour the innocent (Ps. 52:2-4). David reasoned Doeg would suffer a short life in divine retribution; this would strengthen the resolve of the righteous to trust in the Lord, rather than to pursue ill-gotten riches like Doeg had (Ps. 52:5-7). Knowing God would judge the wicked and that he himself had received God's favor for living righteously served to increase David's resolve to trust in the Lord's mercy forever (Ps. 52:8). Doing so meant he would always be able to praise the Lord with the upright (Ps. 52:9). David implores us to loathe treachery and its evil devices, and to put our confidence in the Lord's mercy and prevailing justice.

Meditation

Justice without force is powerless; force without justice is tyrannical.

— Blaise Pascal

If you take care of yourself and walk with integrity, you may be confident that God will deal with those who sin against you. Above all, don't give birth to sin yourself; rather, pray for those who persecute you. God will one day turn your persecution into praise.

— Warren Wiersbe

The Rescuer Is Rescued
1 Samuel 23

David Rescues Keilah (vv. 1-13)

We learn in this chapter that David was not idle during his wilderness years of evading Saul. Besides writing a number of lovely psalms, David also defended the oppressed and protected those near his hideouts. For example, after learning that the Philistines were robbing the threshing floors of Keilah, David was moved with compassion to do something, but wisely sought the Lord's counsel on the matter first. *"Shall I go and attack these Philistines?"* (v. 2). The Lord's answer was, *"Go and attack the Philistines, and save Keilah"* (v. 3).

It is unclear from the text how the Lord answered David's questions. He may have responded through the prophet Gad, as Abiathar did not arrive with the priest's ephod until after David had delivered Keilah. In any case, the man of faith wanted to discern the mind of the Lord before acting (v. 6). The Lord Jesus always behaved in this way. Accordingly David, the rejected king of Israel who acts in accordance with God's will to save His people, presents a wonderful picture of the future disposition and work of Israel's final King – Jesus Christ.

While speaking to the Lord, David humbly refers to himself three times as "Your servant." Before acting on the Lord's behalf, it is wise to seek His mind with a spirit of meekness and submission. We should want only what the Lord wants. Knowing his mind first will prevent us from opposing what He has determined to accomplish. For instance, we may respond in pity to the perceived need of another only to find out later that we enabled that person to continue in sin.

David's men, already on the run from Saul, were not as eager to confront an enemy that was not seeking them, especially a much larger one like the Philistines. David showed good leadership by not ignoring the reservations of his men. Rather, he sought the Lord's counsel a second time to be sure of His direction (v. 4). Again the Lord confirmed what David was to do, but gave the added promise that He would ensure a complete victory: *"Arise, go down to Keilah, for I will deliver the Philistines into your hand."*

Seeing that this was the Lord's battle, David obeyed and led his men against the Philistines, who were soundly defeated and despoiled of their livestock (v. 5). The fact that the Philistines had livestock with them meant that this was not just a raiding party, but a well-armed and well-supplied excursion into Israel with a long-lasting objective. David, with the Lord's help, saved Keilah and exemplifies true faith working for God's honor. Samuel Ridout suggests:

> As we look about us today, we see the vast ecclesiastical systems of the world, from Rome on, with high pretension, with wealth and all carnal machinery for the carrying on of a great work. The mistake is often made – alas, often by the children of God – of thinking that where there is such an enormous amount of machinery, there must be power. It is this that causes men of faith sometimes to shrink from the lonely and lowly path of separation, lest they be deprived of their activity in the service of the Lord, both in ministering to His people and in the gospel to the world. It is often objected that if one gives up association with some system, it will deprive him of his usefulness. Let David speak to us here. His equipment and opportunities were ample [though isolated and with few men]. But it was He who was largely doing the work for Israel.[81]

It did not take long for news of David's rescue of Keilah to reach the ears of Saul (v. 7). The deranged king actually believed that God, who had soundly rejected him, was showing kindness to him by entrapping God's "beloved" in a walled town so that he could be captured. It is the epitome of an evil spirit to think God is somehow for you when He is not with you at all. The king quickly assembled a sizeable complement of men to besiege Keilah and capture David and his men (v. 8).

Yet, David understood the evil heart of Saul and knew that the king would not rest until he was dead. Through Abiathar's use of the ephod, David inquires of the Lord:

> *O Lord God of Israel, Your servant has certainly heard that Saul seeks to come to Keilah to destroy the city for my sake. Will the men of Keilah deliver me into his hand? Will Saul come down, as Your*

servant has heard? O Lord God of Israel, I pray, tell Your servant (vv. 10-11).

Although he is the anointed king of Israel, David does not exalt himself in God's presence, but rather claims to be merely a lowly servant who desired to do God's bidding. Again David conveys a charming picture of the Lord Jesus Christ, who, knowing the Father's will, came to earth to accomplish it as a loyal Servant. Mark's gospel account is devoted to this humble presentation of Christ during His first advent. The Lord said, *"The Son of Man did not come to be served, but to serve, and to give His life a ransom for many"* (Matt. 20:28). Likewise, our sacrificial obedience and genuine humility thrill the heart of God, for it reminds Him of His own Son's devotion!

Jehovah's answer to David's inquiry was concise, *"He will come down."* David then asked the Lord if the men of Keilah would deliver him and his men into the king's hands. The Lord affirmed, *"They will deliver you"* (v. 12). Having discerned the mind of the Lord, David immediately left Keilah with his six hundred men and *"went wherever they could go"* (v. 13). Saul halted his advance on Keilah after learning that David had escaped into the wilderness.

David's response to his difficult circumstance was quite different than Saul's reaction to his challenging situation in chapter 13. With an enormous Philistine army gathered to confront Saul and his much smaller army which was dissipating through desertion, Saul decided to present burnt offerings himself, rather than wasting more time waiting for Samuel to arrive. Because of a stressful circumstance, Saul compromised the truth (i.e., he did what the Law prohibited). David, on the other hand, waits on the Lord to ensure he knows the truth before acting. David is victorious over the Philistines and rewarded for honoring the Lord. In contrast, Saul was told he would lose the kingdom for transgressing the priesthood.

This comparison reminds us that we should never compromise the truth to alleviate whatever circumstances are pressing down on us. The consequence of not having God with us in our trials will always be more costly than if we had continued in faith to do what He appreciates. As David shows us, it is best not to concede what we know is right but to let the Lord fight our battles for us! Matthew Henry commends David's willingness not to take matters into his own hands to end his long trial:

Commend his eminent virtues, his humility, modesty, fidelity to his
prince, and patient attendance on the providence of his God, that he
did not draw up his forces against Saul, fight him in the field, or
surprise him by some stratagem or other, and so avenge his own
quarrel and that of the Lord's priests upon him, and put an end to his
own troubles and the calamities of the country under Saul's tyrannical
government. No, he makes no such attempt; he keeps God's way,
waits God's time, and is content to secure himself in woods and
wildernesses, though with some it might seem a reproach to that
courage for which he had been famous.[82]

Indeed, David displays the prosperity of genuine faith, along with
the noble qualities befitting a king of Israel, that is, the moral
discernment and the intelligence of what truly pleased God. Despite
life's difficulties, living is so much more enjoyable when we walk with
the Lord.

The Lord Rescues David (vv. 14-29)

David hid in various mountain strongholds in the Wilderness of
Ziph and Saul unsuccessfully hunted for David every day (v. 14).
David was aware that Saul was seeking his life, but he was equally
aware that God was preserving him despite his aggressor's efforts (v.
15). Although Saul could not locate David, Jonathan had no difficulty
finding him in the forest of Ziph (v. 16). He says to David, *"Do not
fear, for the hand of Saul my father shall not find you. You shall be king
over Israel, and I shall be next to you. Even my father Saul knows that"*
(vv. 17-18).

Jonathan's visit is notable for at least two reasons. First, he shows
us that it is much easier to find common ground with those we love
than with those we do not – hence, the son of Saul had no difficulty
locating David. God's love is the binding agent that marks Christians as
a peculiar people in the world (John 13:35). Through the power of the
Holy Spirit, Christ's love draws those who previously had nothing in
common into intimate communion with each other. This is why Paul
exhorts believers to behave *"with all lowliness and gentleness, with
longsuffering, bearing with one another in love, endeavoring to keep
the unity of the Spirit in the bond of peace"* (Eph. 4:2-3).

Second, although love is a powerful agent to draw God's people
together, it cannot be divorced from the truth. While deeply devoted to

175

David, Jonathan permits his fancy to carry him beyond God's ordained will. Jonathan would choose not to remain with David, but rather to remain under his father's authority – a rulership empowered by the flesh and not the Spirit of God. Saul's kingdom was destined to die, for this is how God must deal with flesh. Hence, there was no possibility of Jonathan, whose allegiance was to the man of flesh, being at David's side when he gained the throne of Israel in God's timing. C. H. Mackintosh draws a clear application from the scene before us:

> We cannot walk with Saul and David at the same time. We cannot hold Christ and the world – we must take our choice. The Lord grant us grace to reject the evil and choose the good, remembering the solemn words of the apostle: *"This is a faithful saying; for if we be dead with Him, we shall also live with Him; if we suffer, we shall also reign with Him' if we deny Him; He also will deny us"* (2 Tim. 2:11-12). This is the time of suffering, the time for enduring afflictions and hardness; we must wait for the time of rest and glory.[83]

Regardless of the second point, Jonathan's visit was a great encouragement to David. It would be the last time that these two devoted friends would see each other. After they renewed their covenant, Jonathan returned home, but David remained in the woods. That is until the Ziphites came to Saul at Gibeah and revealed David's hiding place – the hill of Hachilah just south of Jeshimon. Many think David's stronghold may have been located two to three miles southeast of Hebron in a lone, conical-shaped, one hundred-foot high, flat-topped hill. These Ziph-betrayers even encouraged the king to move quickly to accost David before he had a chance to escape (vv. 19-20).

Knowing David's skill in eluding him and not wanting to go on another wild goose chase, Saul tasked the Ziphites with pinpointing David's exact location and then spying on his activities. Saul would continue his search for David throughout Judah, but would quickly move to apprehend David after they provided more precise information (vv. 21-23). The Ziphites left Saul to fulfill their secret mission, but as Saul suspected, they found that David and his men had already departed Hachilah.

David, apparently sensing the danger, moved his men about five or six miles further south of Jeshimon into the Wilderness of Maon (v. 24). Saul was subsequently informed that David was hiding in a rock stronghold near Maon (v. 25). Saul quickly took his troops to this location, but arrived on the side of the mountain opposite to what David was on (v. 26). While his prey was quickly circling away from him, Saul received an urgent message that the Philistines were invading the land, which prompted the king to abandon his quest for David (v. 27). Saul left to battle the Philistines, and David took the opportunity to relocate to the rugged, rocky region of En Gedi to the east (vv. 28-29). En Gedi was an oasis about ten miles south of Masada on the western shore of the Dead Sea, but it is evident in the next chapter that David did not camp anywhere near this haven of water and foliage.

God's providential care of David in this situation is somewhat ironic. The very people David just defeated at Keilah invaded Judah at just the right time to preserve him from Saul's hand. The wisdom and ways of God are never at a loss to care for His people and to accomplish His purposes in the process. In honor of God's protection, David afterwards referred to this locale as *the Rock of Escape*. God has already demonstrated in the life of David that He has many ways of delivering His own from trouble. Peter J. Pell writes:

> When Saul commanded all his servants to kill David, Jonathan's friendship preserved him (19:1-2). When the javelin was flung at him, a rapid movement on David's part saved him (19:10). From Saul's ambush he escapes with Michal's help through the window (19:12). Saul's messengers sent on three occasions are overpowered by the Spirit of God (19:20). Out of the hands of the men of Keilah he is delivered by the warning of word of God (22:5). At Ziph the messenger comes to Saul at the critical moment (23:27) and David sings, *"He hath delivered me out of all trouble"* (Ps. 54:7).[84]

No wonder David joyfully named the place "the rock of escape." David penned Psalm 54 shortly after the treachery of the Ziphites. In it, David urgently pleads with the Lord to deliver him from his vicious oppressors because they had no respect for God's name, which represents His person and character (Ps. 54:1-3). The latter portion of the psalm is an expression of David's trust in God, his Helper, to render justice and retribution on his enemies (Ps. 54:4-5). There was no doubt in David's mind that the Lord would grant his prayer. Thus, he promised to praise the Lord and to offer peace offerings to show his thankfulness (Ps. 54:6-7). Because God is good, His name is also good

– David knew that God would judge all those who dishonor His name by ill-treating those who treasure it.

May we too endeavor to honor the Lord's name in whatever we do (1 Cor. 10:31), and likewise to honor those that He honors for doing so. The psalms that David wrote during this season of his life show us that his heart was becoming more intimately bound to God's through each trial. For example, while avoiding Saul in the wilderness of Judah he expressed his deepening desire for God: *"My soul follows close behind You; Your right hand upholds me"* (Ps. 63:8). James teaches us that God uses progressive trials to add patience to our existing faith (Jas. 1:2-3), and David tells us that the wilderness experiences of life are worth having to obtain a higher experience with God.

Meditation

> Abide with me: fast falls the eventide;
> The darkness deepens; Lord, with me abide.
> When other helpers fail and comforts flee,
> Help of the helpless, O abide with me.
>
> I need your presence every passing hour.
> What but your grace can foil the tempter's power?
> Who like yourself my guide and strength can be?
> Through cloud and sunshine, O abide with me.
>
> Hold now your Word before my closing eyes.
> Shine through the gloom and point me to the skies.
> Heaven's morning breaks and earth's vain shadows flee;
> In life, in death, O Lord, abide with me.

— Henry Francis Lyte

David Spares Saul
1 Samuel 24

Shortly after Saul returned from battling the Philistines, he was informed that David had gone to the Wilderness of En Gedi (v. 1). The king chose three thousand of Israel's finest soldiers to pursue David and his men (v. 2). The area that David was thought to be hiding in was a labyrinth of rocky crags, ravines, and caves known as *"the Rocks of the Wild Goats."* Saul paused his search for David at En Gedi to enter one of its many caves to relieve himself; he was unware that David and his men were hiding in the recesses of the same cave (v. 3).

David's men believed that God had rewarded David's faithfulness by delivering his enemy into his hand (v. 4). However, that was not David's sense of the situation. Rather than smiting Saul, David quietly snuck up behind Saul and cut off part of his royal robe and then retreated from the king. The anointed king of Israel knew better than to strike down God's anointed; even cutting Saul's robe bothered David's conscience (v. 5). He obtained no personal satisfaction in ruining the king's attire, but needed irrefutable evidence that he meant Saul no harm.

Undoubtedly, David's comrades were hoping their long ordeal would soon be over with one thrust of David's sword, but it was not to be. David restrained his men and explained that God had the sovereign right to remove those He placed into authority in His timing, and that he had received no command from the Lord to strike Saul down (v. 6). Because Saul was God's anointed, David would not lift a finger against him; rather, he would wait for the Lord to resolve the situation. David encouraged himself in this cause: *"My soul, wait silently for God alone, for my expectation is from Him"* (Ps. 62:5). Only a man of principle who feared the Lord more than the wicked king who was trying to kill him would behave in such a way, and David was such a man. Our carnal nature seeks revenge at the slightest provocation, but true faith waits on God to resolve the matter.

After finishing his business, the king exited the cave and went his way (v. 7). Afterwards, David went to the mouth of the cave and called out to Saul, *"My lord the king!"* (v. 8). When Saul looked behind him, he saw David bowed with his face to the earth. David then challenged the king not to listen to those who said that David sought to harm him, for that very day he could have taken the king's life in the cave (vv. 9-10). The young fugitive then held up the piece of the king's robe that he had cut off to prove his claim (v. 11). The piece of cloth proved that he had no ill intentions towards Saul and was blameless in his conduct towards the king (v. 12).

Being innocent of wrongdoing, David was willing to let the Lord execute justice against Saul on his behalf (v. 13). From a practical standpoint, this meant that David was harmless and was not worth bothering with; should the king of Israel waste time searching for a dead dog or a flea in the wilderness? (v. 14). But even if Saul did continue to pursue righteous David, he was assured that the Lord would deliver him out of the king's hand (v. 15). Psalm 7 refers to David's righteous plea to Saul at En Gedi.

During his speech to Saul, David appeals twice to the Lord to act as Judge. How much less contention would there be in the Church today if believers permitted the all-knowing and all-powerful Lord to judge all the injustices, false gossip, and slander amongst us? In actuality, He will judge all such things completely and He will do a much better job than we ever could.

Not only did Saul recognize David's voice, but his words struck a deep blow in the king's heart, causing him to weep (v. 16). The scene shows us how powerful genuine grace and self-sacrifice are in softening the hardest of hearts to consider the truth. However, as T. Wilson notes, Saul's emotional exercise within his soul is not the same as his spirit acting on the truth unto genuine repentance:

> David with his harp *charmed* Saul but did not *change* him (16:23). Here David *challenged* Saul with his innocence but, again, did not *change* him. There were tears and protestations of repentance, but no change. The passage is one that should leave the reader with the realization that it is possible for an individual to be emotional without there having been any spiritual work in the soul. In dealing with souls, whether saved or unsaved, we need to recognize that mere emotion will accomplish nothing that will endure. The Spirit of God

also reveals that a man who does not have divine life could easily employ the language of spirituality.[85]

The emotionally distraught king then spoke to David:

You are more righteous than I; for you have rewarded me with good, whereas I have rewarded you with evil. And you have shown this day how you have dealt well with me; for when the Lord delivered me into your hand, you did not kill me. For if a man finds his enemy, will he let him get away safely? Therefore may the Lord reward you with good for what you have done to me this day. And now I know indeed that you shall surely be king, and that the kingdom of Israel shall be established in your hand. Therefore swear now to me by the Lord that you will not cut off my descendants after me, and that you will not destroy my name from my father's house (vv. 17-22).

By verbalizing what he knows will happen, Saul apparently comes to grips with God's will for the kingdom. He knows that David will one day reign over Israel, so the king asks David to vow that he would deal kindly with his family at that time. David does so, and the king returned home, but David and his men went up to the stronghold (v. 23).

Meditation

John Bunyan, who suffered years of imprisonment in England during the seventeenth century for preaching Christ, found that his joy in life rested in the sufficiency of Christ and through completely identifying with Him:

Therefore, I bind these lies and slanderous accusations to my person as an ornament; it belongs to my Christian profession to be vilified, slandered, reproached and reviled, and since all this is nothing but that, as God and my conscience testify, I rejoice in being reproached for Christ's sake.

Nabal and His Wife
1 Samuel 25

The Death of Samuel (v. 1)

Samuel, the last of the Israel's fifteen judges, died and was buried in his hometown of Ramah (v. 1). Josephus places the death of Samuel in 1012 B.C.[86] This date coordinates well with other historical events, which means he and Saul shared coregency over Israel for approximately eighteen years. Their coregency marked the end of the judges and the beginning of monarchial rule (Saul being the first king).

The lamenting of all Israel for Samuel indicates the deep respect the people had for the godly and selfless prophet. Regrettably, Samuel's absence meant that the Jewish nation, under Saul's leadership, would be out of touch with the mind of the Lord. Jews often mourned the deaths of notable leaders for thirty days (Num. 20:29; Deut. 34:8). It was during this period that David felt it was safe to leave En Gedi and journey to the Wilderness of Paran at the far south end of Judah's territory.

At this juncture, David had been on the run for about six years. Saul will die approximately two years after Samuel's death, which will bring David's fugitive years to an end. David's age is estimated to be twenty-eight years at the time of Samuel's death; he will begin reigning over Judah at the age of thirty.

David and Nabal's Wife (vv. 2-44)

We are next introduced to Nabal, a wealthy descendant of Caleb, living in Maon (a town about 25 miles southeast of Hebron; v. 1). Nabal also owned much land near the town of Carmel, which should not be confused with Mount Carmel far to the northeast (near the city of Haifa today). Although Nabal was a harsh and evil man, his wife Abigail (likely much younger than he) was a beautiful and wise woman (v. 3). Abigail's name means "the joy of her father," but we doubt that it was for joy that he gave his beautiful daughter to Nabal in marriage; more likely it was for the handsome dowry he received for her.

Nabal owned three thousand sheep and a thousand goats and was busy shearing his sheep as the story commences (v. 2). Because the wool trade was an important aspect of the Jewish economy, the time of sheep shearing was also a festive time of feasting (v. 4). Hearing that Nabal was shearing his sheep, David sent ten men to petition Nabal for food (vv. 5-9). David and his men had been living peaceably among Nabal's shepherds and had not taken anything from Nabal. Rather, they had protected his flocks and servants day and night from bandits and predators (v. 16). In this sense, David's men had acted like "Nabal's servants." The region was arid, making water and supplies scarce (v.11; Josh. 15:19), yet David did not steal from Nabal or presume an entitlement for services rendered; rather, he asked for provisions as a courtesy.

Nabal sheared his sheep, but David had been the good shepherd of those sheep. Nabal should have appreciated David's protection and willingly returned a portion of his abundance to David's men, but instead he spoke boorishly of David and denied his envoy's request:

Who is David, and who is the son of Jesse? There are many servants nowadays who break away each one from his master. Shall I then take my bread and my water and my meat that I have killed for my shearers, and give it to men when I do not know where they are from? (vv. 10-11).

Instead of rewarding David for his helpful generosity, Nabal upbraided the anointed king of Israel! He suggested that David was a rebel servant who had broken away from his master, like so many others were doing at that time. In saying this, Nabal was implying that this had not been a problem previously, but rather, David had set a bad example of rebellion that other servants were now following. In short, the wicked, wealthy man saw nothing lovely in the man that God had chosen, the one who was after His own heart. Nabal should have at least feared David's skilled militia just over the ridge, but, being a fool, he valued the worth of a few provisions more than his own life and the lives of those in his household.

The reason that Nabal was emotionally estranged from David was because *"he did not know him."* If Nabal had truly known the Lord's anointed, rather than listening to and agreeing with what others were saying about him, Nabal would have responded differently. This means that believers must have a clear vision of faith to be able to properly discern the true glory of Christ and cling to Him during His time of rejection. On this point C. H. Mackintosh writes:

> It is one thing to be a Christian, as people say, and another thing to confess Christ before men. Indeed, one can hardly find anything more selfish than the condition of heart which would lead us to take all the Lord Jesus has to give, and yield Him nothing in return. "Provided I am saved, all the rest is unessential." This is the secret thought of many a heart, and if thrown into a more honest form would be this, "If I am sure of salvation, it matters little about the glory of Christ." This was just Nabal's mode of acting; he reaped all the advantage he could from David, but the moment David put in his claim for sympathy and aid, his worldly spirit developed itself.[87]

After hearing of Nabal's churlish response, an enraged David assembled four hundred armed men to take vengeance on Nabal (vv. 12-13). Why did David embark on such a vicious quest after responding with much grace to Saul's ill will towards him? The answer to this question is one we know all too well; when a child of God is not in communion with the Lord, our flesh prompts us to resent every offense and to desire personal vindication. Close communion with the Lord ensures His mind will be our mind and His ways, our ways. Paul confirms that having the lowly mind of Christ eliminates nearly all of our problems (Phil. 2:1-5). But at this juncture, David's thoughts were not the Lord's thoughts and the enemy quickly took advantage of the situation. One who has received much divine blessing is in the position to act most carnally when prompted to unrighteous rage!

Considering his master too abrasive to approach on the matter, one of Nabal's shepherds informed Abigail about the situation, confirmed their positive experience with David and his men, and warned her of imminent peril (vv. 14-17). Indeed, Nabal had chosen to return evil for David's goodwill and David was determined to show no mercy in his retaliation (v. 21): *"May God do so, and more also, to the enemies of David, if I leave one male of all who belong to him by morning light"* (v. 22).

After hearing the servant's report, Abigail (without consulting her husband) worked quickly and diligently to prepare a large quantity of foodstuffs to take to David, which she hoped would avert his wrath (vv. 18-19). Some would fault Abigail for undermining her husband's authority, but Scripture contains no rebuke of her actions, but rather applauds her behavior. Subordinates are to respect the authority God places over them as unto Him, unless that authority opposes His expressed will. For instance, children are to honor their parents, but only as unto the Lord (Eph. 6:1) and citizens are not to resist God by disobeying their civil rulers unless they are clearly rejecting God's rule (Rom. 13:1-3; Acts 5:29).

Accordingly, wives are to respect their husbands' authority as unto the Lord, meaning that they are not obliged to follow their husband's leadership in matters of sin. Nabal was a wicked man who had rejected and insulted God's anointed king of Israel; Abigail acted quickly and prudently to try to right the wrong and hopefully save her husband's life. Abigail epitomizes the words of Solomon concerning a virtuous wife: *"A virtuous woman is a crown to her husband"* (Prov. 12:4; KJV) and *"She will do him good and not evil all the days of her life"* (Prov. 31:12; KJV).

Abigail had her servants load two hundred loaves of bread, two skins of wine, five sheep already dressed, five seahs of roasted grain, one hundred clusters of raisins, and two hundred cakes of figs onto donkeys and to go ahead of her. Apparently, she would not be able to travel as fast on a donkey herself and did not want to delay the arrival of her gift to David. Thankfully, she was able to meet David before David and his men arrived to take vengeance on Nabal (v. 20).

Abigail humbles herself before David and pleads for him to accept her peace offering to avoid bloodshed (vv. 23-31). Although she confesses to not having any part in the offense, she asks David to judge her for her foolish husband's behavior. Abigail's intercessory request to David is one of the longest discourses by a woman recorded in Scripture and indeed one of the most touching. Abigail pleaded with David not to *"regard this scoundrel Nabal. For as his name is, so is he: Nabal is his name, and folly is with him!"* (v. 25). In other words, she asked David to excuse her husband's actions because of his natural weakness of being foolish and because an utter fool could not pose any threat to David (v. 26).

Nabal's humble wife then complimented David's righteous character and affirmed that Jehovah would honor His promises to place him on the throne and protect both him and his long-lasting dynasty (vv. 28-30). Every point of her address touched David's heart. It was evil for him to avenge himself, especially on one so weak and foolish; rather, he should be fighting *"the battles of the Lord"* (v. 28). In short, Abigail delivered David from a great sin by causing him to look beyond the *present* petty offense to his *future* grandeur in Israel. Why should the heir of the kingdom lower himself to take vengeance on a foolish man insulting David over a few sheep? Much of what we do in the here and now would never occur if we too contemplated our glorious and blessed eternal future in Christ.

David was utterly astonished by Abigail's self-effacing discretion (v. 32). Clearly, God had used her to prevent him from slaughtering many innocent people because of their master's arrogant parsimony (vv. 33-34). Matthew Henry suggests that through Abigail's intercession David suddenly became aware of the great danger he was in of shedding innocent blood. This realization therefore magnified David's appreciation of God's mercy of deliverance through Abigail's wise words:

> David speaks of the sin as very great. He was coming to shed blood, a sin of which, when in his right mind, he had a great horror; witness his prayer, *"Deliver me from blood-guiltiness."* He was coming to avenge himself with his own hand, and that would be stepping into the throne of God, who has said, *"Vengeance is Mine; I will repay."* The more heinous any sin is, the greater mercy it is to be kept from it. He seems to aggravate the evil of his design with this, that it would have been an injury to so wise and good a woman as Abigail: *"God has kept me back from hurting thee"* (v. 34).[88]

As a result of Abigail's selfless and prudent intervention, David retreats to his stronghold with his men and sends her home in peace (v. 35).

Because Nabal had been feasting and was drunk with wine, Abigail did not inform him of what happened until the next day (v. 36). Her restraint in not censuring her husband in his drunken state shows the respect that Abigail had for her husband's position over her, though doubtless she did not esteem the man personally. Though she was well-cared for, her situation was one of bleak loneliness, for she was bound to an ungodly, egotistical fool. When she did inform him the next day of what happened, Nabal suffered instant paralysis likely caused by a heart attack or a stroke (v. 37). The Lord ended his miserable life ten days later (v. 38).

Interestingly, Nabal had never met David face to face, but the thought of David's avenging sword overwhelmed Nabal's soul with fear and in due course brought him down to Sheol. There is a day coming, when the Greater David will also strike fear into all the foolish Nabals on the earth. Then all those who do not know Him, and in fact have spoken ill of Him, will experience the second death, while all the Abigails of the world will be joined to the Son of David forever.

After hearing of Nabal's death, David recognized that Nabal's judgment and his own vindication had come directly from God (v. 39). Being impressed by Abigail, and realizing that God had also freed her from a horrible union, he sent messengers with a marriage proposal to Abigail (v. 40). The customary time of mourning for a deceased family member was seven days (31:13), so David probably waited until after this to propose marriage (e.g., 2 Sam. 11:26-27), an offer Abigail immediately accepted (v. 41).

For a second time we find Abigail riding a donkey in haste to David, but on this day it is in response to his love and generosity, not his wrath over an offense. It is noteworthy that David also would gain a wealthy estate through the marriage. While Saul was ever diminishing, David was constantly increasing in wealth, power, and fame. God was proving to the Jewish nation through His providential control that David had His endorsement to be Israel's next king.

Because of Abigail's humility and discretion, God delivered her from the miserable situation she was entrapped in and she became David's wife. The entire scene is a lovely picture of the refined remnant of Israel restored to their Beloved in the Millennial Kingdom after suffering terrible hardships for centuries under Satan's rule when they had no association with Christ. But, as J. N. Darby explains, once Christ comes into His inheritance and is again spiritually united with Israel (pictured in David's union with faithful Abigail), He will freely share all that He has with the Jewish nation:

> David's position changes when Abigail is brought in. Jonathan never separated from the system in which he stood, never united himself to

David, although loving him, and never shared his sufferings. But Abigail identifies herself with him; existing relationships do not prevent her acknowledging David, and she is united to him after her husband's death. Jonathan prefigures the remnant in the character of the remnant of Israel, who acknowledge the future king, and adhere to him, but go no farther. As regards old Israel, they come to nothing with it; they will be blessed as reigned over in the kingdom [i.e., in the era of Davidic kings], but not be associated with Christ on the throne. Jonathan does not suffer with David, and does not reign with him. He remains with Saul, and, as to that position, his career ends with Saul.

Abigail, and even the malcontents who joined David, shared his sufferings. Abigail separates herself completely from the spirit of her husband, and it is on account of her faith and wisdom that David spares Nabal's life. God judges the latter, and then Abigail becomes the wife of David. Historically David had nearly failed in his high standing. In fact it is on account of the faithful remnant, the Abigail of the foolish nation, that Israel itself has been spared, and the Lord's connection with the assembly is in the character of pure grace, not in that of the avenger (as hereafter with Israel). At this time it is that David, during his rejection, surrounds himself with those who will be the companions and the retinue of his glory in the kingdom. ... Abigail was forming for herself, without knowing it, the position of the assembly, in the future she was preparing for herself.[89]

The author closes the chapter by noting that David now had two wives who were with him, Abigail and Ahinoam of Jezreel, and that Saul had given his daughter Michal, David's first wife, to Palti of Gallim (vv. 42-44). This action publicly showed Saul's displeasure with David, and that he was disclaiming David as a son-in-law. But Saul had no right to undermine David's marriage covenant with Michal, which, as we will see later, will have severe judicial consequences.

Whether David married Abigail before Ahinoam cannot be determined from Scripture. Barnes notes that the listing of David's wives in 2 Samuel 3:2 and 1 Chronicals 3:1 place Ahinoam first, but this may have been because she bore David's firstborn son.[90]

The story of Nabal and Abigail reminds us that God deals with people according to the pride that is lurking in their hearts. The Lord Jesus said: *"For whoever exalts himself will be humbled, and he who humbles himself will be exalted"* (Luke 14:11). Both James and Peter put the matter this way, *"God resists the proud, but gives grace to the humble"* (Jas. 4:6; 1 Pet. 5:5). Nabal honored himself and perished under the hand of God, while Abigail humbled herself (even assuming the shame associated with her husband's wickedness) and God highly exalted her – indeed, she became the wife of Israel's king!

Meditation

A lowly spirit is demonstrated when one associates with the poor. It is this spirit alone which does not despise any who are created by God. God's presence and glory is manifested in the life of the spiritually humble. ... A lowly person is a teachable person, easily entreated and open to explanation. Many of our spirits are too arrogant: they can teach others but can never themselves be taught. Many possess a stubborn spirit: they stick to their opinions even if they realize they are wrong.

— Watchman Nee

David Spares Saul Again
1 Samuel 26

The Ziphites again betrayed David's whereabouts to Saul saying, *"Is David not hiding in the hill of Hachilah, opposite Jeshimon?"* (v. 1). This was either the same location or near to it where David camped in chapter 23. Saul immediately gathered 3,000 choice men of Israel to seek David in the Wilderness of Ziph (v. 2). As previously mentioned, the number *five* in Scripture is associated with God's grace meeting human need or responsibility. Interestingly, in both chapters 24 and 26, Saul brings 3,000 of his best soldiers to confront David and his 600 men, a fivefold difference. In each chapter, God intervenes with grace to not only foil Saul's attempt, but also to prompt the king to reconsider his actions. God's grace benefits everyone; it blesses the righteous and also causes the sinner to realize what they are missing.

David's spies confirmed that Saul had arrived and was encamped by a road at the hill of Hachilah (vv. 3-4). David is completely aware of Saul's approach; the text says that David "saw," "sent," and "understood." He is not ignorant of his enemy's devices, yet David is determined to trust in the Lord and to calmly wait for His salvation.

David then secretly journeyed to a place where he could overlook Saul's camp. Saul was sleeping in the midst of the encampment with his commander Abner and his soldiers positioned around him (v. 5). David wanted to venture down for a closer look and asked both Ahimelech the Hittite and Abishai, his nephew (Joab's son), *"Who will go down with me to Saul in the camp?"* (v. 6). Abishai agreed to go. At this juncture David could have easily positioned his men to ambush Saul and his men in their sleep, but that was not his intention. He certainly seeks safety for himself and those in his care, but he does not seek the ruin of Saul.

At nighttime, David and Abishai ventured into Saul's camp and found everyone sleeping, including the king who had his spear stuck in the ground by his head (v. 7). Abishai then said to David, *"God has*

190

delivered your enemy into your hand this day. Now therefore, please, let me strike him at once with the spear, right to the earth; and I will not have to strike him a second time!" (v. 8). But David barred Abishai from stretching out his hand against the Lord's anointed (v. 9). Then David affirmed that Saul would perish by the hand of the Lord and in His timing (v. 10). Before the two departed, David asked Abishai to rise up and take the spear and jug of water by Saul's head, which he did (v. 11).

It would normally not be possible for two adversaries to get so near the king without detection, for guards and watchmen would be posted throughout the night, but God caused everyone in Saul's camp, including the king, to enjoy a deep sleep that night (v. 12). After David scaled the hill opposite to the camp, he called out to Saul's general and chided Abner for doing such a poor job of protecting his king (vv. 13-15). David then displayed the king's spear and water jug to prove that his accusation was legitimate and that Abner deserved to die for his negligence (v. 16).

Saul immediately recognized David's voice and called out to him, *"Is that your voice, my son David?"* (v. 17). David answered the king and again asked why he pursued his servant who had done him no wrong (v. 18). David then reasoned that if the Lord had stirred up hatred in Saul's heart towards him, that he would present an offering to resolve the offense. However, if it were troublesome men who were arousing Saul's hostility toward him, then they should be cursed by God because they were preventing him from sharing their inheritance in the Lord (v. 19).

Not only had injustice driven David from his master, but it had also prevented David from coming to the central sanctuary to worship the Lord. Hence, those opposing David were, in effect, saying to him, *"Go, serve other gods."* This vexed David's soul, for he loved the Lord and longed to be before the Lord. David further argued that it was unreasonable for Saul to seek to kill him, for he had repeatedly shown that he meant the king no harm. So why would the king continue to seek out a harmless flea like David and relentlessly pursue him as if hunting a partridge in the wilderness (v. 20). Jamieson, Fausset, and Brown explain the ancient practice of hunting partridges in remote places:

The allusion is to the ancient method of taking these birds by throwing sticks. Wild animals of a large size were generally captured in nets and pitfalls. ... As to fowls, people in the East, in hunting the partridge and other game birds, pursue them until observing them becoming languid and fatigued; after they have been put up two or three times, they rush upon the birds stealthily, and knock them down with bludgeons. It was exactly in this manner that Saul was pursuing David: he drove him from time to time from his hiding place, hoping to render him weary of his life, or obtain an opportunity of accomplishing his destruction.[91]

Again David's sincere words and sound rationale penetrated Saul's hardened heart. The king said, *"I have sinned. Return, my son David. For I will harm you no more, because my life was precious in your eyes this day. Indeed I have played the fool and erred exceedingly"* (v. 21). The king admits that he has been foolish and had sinned against David. He also invited David back to his court in peace and promised not to pursue him anymore. David responded by suggesting that one of Saul's young men should come to retrieve his spear (v. 22) and then said:

May the Lord repay every man for his righteousness and his faithfulness; for the Lord delivered you into my hand today, but I would not stretch out my hand against the Lord's anointed. And indeed, as your life was valued much this day in my eyes, so let my life be valued much in the eyes of the Lord, and let Him deliver me out of all tribulation (vv. 23-24).

The king responded to David's second statement by commending his merciful conduct towards him and by predicting his advancement because God was with him: *"May you be blessed, my son David! You shall both do great things and also still prevail"* (v. 25). David then went his way and Saul returned to Gibeah.

Over the course of eight years, Saul made at least fourteen attempts on David's life, but the Lord delivered David out of every trap and hostile plot:

1. Javelin thrown at David (18:11)
2. Javelin thrown again at David (18:11)
3. Battling the Philistines to win Merab (18:17)
4. Battling the Philistines to win Michal (18:25-27)

5. Saul instructs servants and his sons to kill David (19:1)
6. Javelin thrown a third time at David (19:10)
7. Soldiers sent to David's house (19:11)
8. Soldiers sent to arrest David at Naioth (19:20)
9. Soldiers sent to arrest David at Naioth again (19:21)
10. Soldiers sent to arrest David at Naioth a third time (19:21)
11. Saul seeks David at Naioth (19:23)
12. Saul seeks David in the wilderness of Maon (23:25)
13. Saul seeks David in the wilderness of En Gedi (24:2)
14. Saul seeks David in the wilderness of Ziph (26:2)

After the events of this chapter, Saul will no longer seek David's life. The king finally accepts that he cannot out-maneuver the providential care and purposes of Almighty God. Saul's final days must have been most miserable, for he knew God was against him and that it was only a matter of time until David was seated on the throne of Israel, which meant his own death was imminent.

Meditation

The best way to deal with slander is to pray about it: God will either remove it, or remove the sting from it. Our own attempts at clearing ourselves are usually failures; we are like the boy who wished to remove the blot from his copy, and by his bungling made it ten times worse.

— Charles Spurgeon

Allied With the Philistines
1 Samuel 27

The brightness of David's noble release of Saul in the last chapter is eclipsed by his disgraceful dealings with Achish in this chapter. The most painful falls often occur directly after our great achievements. For whatever reason, David is not exercised to look upwards in faith, but rather at his circumstances, which permits doubt and discouragement to fill his heart. Regrettably, he plans the way of his escape without consulting the Lord. Peter J. Pell writes:

> David forgets momentarily the anointing by Samuel, the victory over Goliath, the escape from Saul's spear, the prophetic utterances of Jonathan and assurances of Abigail. Even the last words of Saul when he said, *"My son David, thou shalt both do great things and also thou shalt still prevail"* are forgotten.[92]

Despite the Lord's ongoing protection, David did not believe that Saul would end his hostility towards him. He thought his only escape from Saul was to dwell with the Philistines, for surely Saul would not hunt for him in Philistia. Plagued by doubt, David reasons: *"There is nothing better for me than that I should speedily escape to the land of the Philistines"* (v. 1). C. H. Mackintosh highlights the incongruity of David's confession:

> How completely must David have lost the sense of God's sufficiency when he could say, *"There is **nothing better** for me than that I should speedily escape into the land of the Philistines."* Nothing better for a man of faith than to go back to the world for refuge! Strange confession! It is the confession of one who had allowed circumstances to come between his soul and God. When we slip off the narrow path of faith, we are liable to run into the wildest extremes, and nothing can more forcibly exhibit the contrast between one looking at God and one looking at circumstance than David in the

Valley of Elah and David scrabbling to the doors of the Philistine king.[93]

Undeniably, David was dead wrong; his best recourse was to wait on the Lord and not leave the land of his inheritance and of his kingdom. How could he identify with Jehovah and claim to be an Israelite while living in Philistia? But this has always been the enemy's primary attack against God's people, that is, to muddle their identification and inheritance in Christ, and then associate them with worldly entrapments to provoke further complacency and compromise. The devil always provides a way of escape for the man or woman of faith in times of distress. Abraham took refuge in Egypt to avoid a drought; David headed to Gath to flee from Saul. But the devil's broad way leading to ruin is not the path of faith that ensures God's fellowship and blessing.

In actuality, David's resolution to flee to Philistia was flawed on several counts. First, the Lord had already proven repeatedly that He would not permit Saul to take David's life. Second, David had been chosen by God and anointed by Samuel as Israel's next king, but he had to reside in Israel to rule. Third, the prophet Gad had already instructed David to remain in Judah (22:5). Fourth, he had already asked God to curse those persuading Saul to hunt for him because they were, in effect, forcing him to flee into an idolatrous land and away from Jehovah's central sanctuary. Fifth, in Philistia, he was beyond the aid and counsel of those countrymen loyal to him.

As it would be unwise for about two thousand Jews with all their livestock just to stroll into the royal city of Gath on a whim, it seems likely that Achish had previously extended to David an open invitation to return. Dismayed, David took his two wives (Ahinoam and Abigail) and his six hundred men with their families to Gath (v. 2). Achish is a royal title, not a proper name, and the family distinction in verse 2 (i.e., the son of Maoch) suggests that this may not have been the same Achish of chapter 21. Regardless, the king of Gath warmly welcomed Saul's enemies to his city (v. 3). David's assessment of Saul's behavior was correct; after he heard that David was in Gath, *"he sought him no more"* (v. 4).

David did not want to be under the close scrutiny of Achish, so he asked the king for a place in the countryside, suggesting that it was not fitting for his lowly servant to reside with the king in his royal city (vv.

5-6). In time, David would learn the futility of seeking a place for himself in a land where the Ark of God years earlier found no place of rest.

Achish responded favorably to David and gave him the border town of Ziklag (v. 6). After the Canaan Conquest, Joshua had designated the border town of Ziklag as part of Simeon's territory, but the Jews did not secure it from the Philistines (Josh. 19:5). Simeon's borders were within Judah's tribal allotment, so in effect, through the enemy's generosity, David had finally obtained Ziklag as part of Judah's inheritance (Josh. 15:31).

David and his men lived among the Philistines for sixteen months (v. 7). Although the Lord would not forsake David during this time, J. N. Darby describes why it was a very disagreeable situation for David to be in.

> David, after all, is only a man, and immediately after this testimony that God was with him (a testimony that even Saul acknowledged; 26:25), his faith fails, and he passes over into the midst of the enemies of God's people. God, no doubt, makes use of this means to remove David from peril. But at the same time, he is tried and chastened, and is exposed to the dreadful necessity of appearing ready to fight against Israel. ... In the land of the Philistines he gains their king's favor, not by faith, but by prudence inconsistent with truth. It is an unhappy position; nevertheless, God does not forsake him. He chastises him, and in a painful manner, but He spares and preserves him.[94]

Indeed, this long excursion among uncircumcised pagans, Israel's enemies, was a spiritual low point in David's life. David's harp was silent in Gath, and Scripture contains no record of any psalms being composed by David during this miserable chapter of his life.

Rather than joyful accolades of praise, David led raiding parties against the Geshurites, the Girzites, and the Amalekites, even going as far south as the way of Shur leading to Egypt (v. 8). To ensure there would be no witnesses of his pillaging, David slaughtered every man, woman and child during his attacks and brought their livestock and apparel to Achish (vv. 9, 11). Whenever the king of Gath asked David about his plundering, he would say that he had raided the southern areas of Judah, of the Jerahmeelites, and of the Kenites (v. 10). David kept the truth of his plundering secret through a masterpiece of subterfuge while he lived in Ziklag (v. 11).

The Geshurites and Girzites were likely descendants of Amalek, who were a people God was determined to wipe out because they had attacked the weary Israelites journeying out of Egypt to Mount Sinai (Ex. 17). Because Saul had not obeyed the Lord concerning His ongoing conflict with the Amalekites, the kingdom was taken away from him and designated for David, a man after God's own heart (15:1-35). Although more brutal than necessary, David was willing to continue the age-old conflict between the Lord and the Amalekites because of Saul's unwillingness to engage them. In this sense, David was willing to fight the Lord's battles.

Regardless of how one views David's harsh military exploits while at Ziklag, there are at least three reasons for faulting David's conduct.

First, the Lord does not approve of deception and lying. David would later reflect on this and acknowledge the wrongness of such shameful behavior:

> *My soul melts from heaviness; strengthen me according to Your word.*
> *Remove from me the way of lying, and grant me Your law graciously.*
> *I have chosen the way of truth; Your judgments I have laid before me.*
> *I cling to Your testimonies; O Lord, do not put me to shame!* (Ps 119:28-31).

Lying was reprehensible for the king of Israel to engage in! The ruler of Israel was to reflect God's own character in all his actions and speech. The Jewish nation was to be a beacon of truth and holiness among the Gentile nations so that they could learn of Jehovah's greatness. Likewise, Christians are commanded to put away all lying and speak the truth in love (Eph. 4:15, 25). Such conduct permits Christ to be reflected to a sinful world that desperately needs to see the reality of His holy presence within His people (Eph. 4:25).

Second, the reason that David did not want Achish to know about his raiding practices was because he feared what would happen to him and his men if the Philistines found out the truth. If the Philistines knew that David was attacking their allies, they would be forced to move against him, to preclude retaliation for granting David safe haven among them. David must learn not to rely on carnal means and behaviors to resolve his problems; rather, he must fully trust in the Lord and commit his way to Him.

Third, though in faith David could engage the Lord's enemies, the Amalekites, David could no longer trust the Lord to preserve him from Saul's hand. The difference is that David was able to swing his sword in the former, but had to simply rest in God's providential care for the latter.

On the night of the Lord's arrest, Peter demonstrated his courage by facing down a band of soldiers coming to arrest the Savior by himself. The Lord Jesus told Peter to put his sword away, lest he perish by it, and then He repaired the damage that Peter's sword did to Malchus' ear (Matt. 26:52; John 18:10-11). A few hours later, Peter, challenged by a servant girl as to whether he was a disciple of Jesus, adamantly denied any association with Christ (Luke 22:56). Peter went to a solitary place and wept bitterly after this failure. He learned that day what all believers must realize – it is much easier to die once for the Lord than it is to die daily in order to live for Him. It is easier to swing a sword than to fully rest in the Lord.

Achish believed David's account of his raids and even gloated in the matter, *"He has made his people Israel utterly abhor him; therefore he will be my servant forever"* (v. 12). The king of Gath thought that David had outraged his countrymen and therefore had alienated himself from Israel for good. This meant that Achish could employ David in his own enterprises and profit from the association. However, as we will soon see, God will not permit His servant to side with the Philistines against His people. Jehovah would use the Philistines to end Saul's life, which will permit David to return to Israel and reign over the Jewish nation as promised.

Meditation

> God moves in a mysterious way
> His wonders to perform;
> He plants His footsteps in the sea
> And rides upon the storm.
>
> Deep in unfathomable mines
> Of never failing skill;

He treasures up His bright designs
And works His sovereign will.

Judge not the Lord by feeble sense,
But trust Him for His grace;
Behind a frowning providence
He hides a smiling face.

Blind unbelief is sure to err
And scan His work in vain;
God is His own interpreter,
And He will make it plain.

— William Cowper

Among God's Enemies
1 Samuel 28

The book of 1 Samuel follows the lives of three men: Samuel, Saul, and David. All three characters are mentioned in this dismal chapter: Samuel dies, Saul, being shunned by God, seeks the assistance of a medium, and David aligns with the Philistines to fight against Israel.

David Enlisted Against Israel (vv. 1-2)
We learn in verse 1 that the Philistines were gathering their armies together at Aphek (29:1) before advancing into Israel. Achish enlisted David and his men to be a part of his army. David responded to the king's request by identifying himself as an able servant for the king. Delighted by this commitment, Achish promoted David to be one of his *"chief guardians forever"* (v. 2). Only human failure can explain how the king of Israel, a Jehovah worshiper, could become the bodyguard of a pagan chieftain!

What a strange dichotomy of alliance this was for David: the next king of Israel is in league with Israel's chief enemy to slaughter the people he is destined to shepherd. His duplicity would have resulted in a great tragedy, but God will not permit it. In the next chapter, the Lord will intervene to deliver His servant and prevent him from doing what would greatly sadden His own heart.

Samuel Dies (v. 3)
God's faithful mouthpiece and the last judge of Israel dies and is buried in his hometown of Ramah (v. 3). The light of God's revelation within the Promised Land is all but snuffed out at this juncture. The fact that all Israel lamented for Samuel was a wonderful testimony to the selfless character of the faithful prophet. The people mourned his death because he had been a godly man who had done much good for the Jewish nation. There would be no such grief over Saul.

Saul Seeks a Medium (vv. 4-25)

Not only was Israel's next king in a bad way, Israel's present monarch was sinking deeper into despair and depravity. No doubt the death of Samuel, his friend and counselor, caused him to feel even more cut off from God. Additionally, Saul feared the sizable Philistine army now positioned against him at Shunem, so he inquired of the Lord for guidance (vv. 4-5). Shunem was a small village located within Issachar's borders near the Jezreel Valley and south of Mount Gilboa (Josh. 19:18). Because Saul had been rejected by the Lord, no answer came to the king through dreams, the Urim, or by the prophets (v. 6).

Ironically, the kingdom had been taken away from Saul earlier because he had not sought the Lord in his endeavors (13:13, 14:19, 15:11), but now that judgment was looming over his head, the king earnestly sought the Lord. The words of Isaiah ring true, *"Seek the Lord while He may be found, call upon Him while He is near"* (Isa. 55:6). The Lord was not near to Saul; therefore, it was too late for the king to call on Him expecting an answer. The Lord *"is longsuffering toward us, not willing that any should perish but that all should come to repentance"* (2 Pet. 3:9), but there are limitations to His offer of mercy!

The deafening silence from above caused Saul to seek guidance from below. He instructed his men to find a *"woman who is a medium, that I may go to her and inquire of her"* (v. 7). Rejected at the gate of heaven, the king now seeks comfort from the mouth of hell! Samuel's solemn words to Saul after he spared the spoil of Amalek and Agag ring true, *"Rebellion is as the sin of witchcraft"* (15:23). Though Saul's sinful actions were separated in time, the two sins cannot be detached from each other, for both come from the same fountainhead – Satan. Ongoing rebellion against God always leads to holding hands with the devil!

The king thought that finding a medium would be a difficult task because in his early years he *"had put the mediums and the spiritists out of the land"* (v. 3). Apparently, Saul had done so only to earn God's favor. That is, he acted merely as a legalist does – to earn God's favor, not to uphold God's honor. He was likely surprised then that his men were aware of such a woman, a medium at En Dor.

The Law of Moses demanded that witches be put to death – there were no second chances for those rebelling against God's sovereignty by consorting with fallen angels under Satan's authority. Mediums supposedly consulted the dead for counsel, but were actually conferring with familiar spirits who imitate the deceased. During life these demonic foes gather information by observation and then later pose as the souls of departed loved ones. Today, séances, channeling, and tools such as ouija boards are used in the practice of necromancy. Edward Dennett further explains this evil occupation:

> The essential idea of a witch was commerce with spirits, which finds its counterpart in the spiritualism of the present day. Hence in Leviticus she is described as *"a woman that hath a familiar spirit."* (Lev. 20:27). The witch of En Dor is the exemplification of her kind, for we read that Saul went to her and said, *"I pray thee, divine unto me by the familiar spirit, and bring him up whom I shall name unto thee"* (1 Sam. 28:8). This is the very thing that spiritualists profess to do — to bring the inquirer into communion with departed spirits. Like Saul, unable to obtain communications from God, they seek information concerning things unknown and unseen through the agency of spirits. It is, in fact, a turning from God to Satan. The whole system, whether in Israel or our own day, is Satanic. A witch, therefore, was to be destroyed.[95]

Because Saul wanted to secretly consult with Samuel through a medium, he disguised himself and journeyed to En Dor under the cover of night with only two men (v. 8). The masquerading king asked the witch to conduct a séance to bring up from Sheol an individual he wanted to speak with. The woman was suspicious of a trap, for King Saul had previously commanded that mediums and spiritists be killed or driven out of Israel (v. 9). However, Saul swore in the Lord's name that no harm would come to her for conducting the occult ritual (v. 10). William MacDonald comments on the ludicrousness of this scene: "How Saul could promise protection in the name of the Lord, who had decreed the death of such persons, or how the medium could be assured of safety by an oath sworn to that God, is an enigma."[96]

The king's oath in Jehovah's name to endorse the very thing Jehovah hated illustrates to what depths Saul's depraved mind had plumbed. In a lapse of faith, David had temporarily sided with the Philistines against God's people, but Saul had sold himself out to the devil because God had rejected him. The woman asked Saul, *"Whom shall I bring up for you?"* and the king immediately responded,

"Samuel" (v. 11). The witch then began to use her occult arts as requested. The profound silence of Scripture as to what her charms or enchantments were confirms that believers are not to know about or to covet forbidden things associated with *"the depths of Satan"* (Rev. 2:24). Samuel Ridout explains how Satan uses familiar spirits through the black art of necromancy to lure undiscerning souls into his grasp:

> All the so-called revelations from departed spirits which are being made nowadays are, when not impostures, as many of them are, lying messages from an evil spirit with whom the medium is communicating. God does not use unholy channels for the communication of truth, and while it is quite possible for the demon to tell of various events which have taken place in one's past life, or the lives of his acquaintances, and to give "revelations" which are in accord with the habit of mind of the person who has departed, they never emanate from the departed. This explains why such reassuring messages are returned, professedly from the spirit world, to those who are living in sin. They are assured that the departed are perfectly happy, and enjoying every pleasure, and that God is too loving to punish any, and that they can go on in their course without fear. All of this is so evidently satanic, that it shows how the world instinctively turns to Satan for reassurance.[97]

As previously mentioned, familiar spirits observe the living and then are able to accurately imitate them after death to deceive loved ones of the deceased. Satan cannot call up anyone out of Hades. The Lord Jesus made it clear in Luke 16 that there was no escape from their imprisonment until resurrected to stand before the Lord Jesus Christ at the Great White Throne judgment (Rev. 20:11-15)!

The notoriety of the witch's profession indicates that she had regularly summoned familiar spirits, but what happened next profoundly startled her. She screamed out and then confronted her visitor: *"Why have you deceived me? For you are Saul!"* (v. 12). The king no longer tried to conceal his identity, but rather attempted to calm the woman, so that she would continue, *"Do not be afraid. What did you see?"* (v. 13). The witch replied that she saw a spirit ascending out of the earth. Saul inquired about the form of the spirit and the woman responded, *"An old man is coming up, and he is covered with a mantle"* (v. 14). Perceiving that this description represented Samuel, Saul stooped down and bowed his face towards the ground.

We pause momentarily to consider what we have just read. Notice that whatever the witch considered to be the normal outcome of the séance did not occur. Perhaps a familiar spirit which she was accustomed to communicating with alerted her to Saul's presence, as that realization seems to occur prior to Samuel's arrival. Or it may have been that her first sight of Samuel coming up was not the normal illusory form that she was accustomed to. In either case, this explains her sudden fright – she recognized the presence of a power far superior to her enchantments, and that her life was in jeopardy.

Following her frightened gasp, the Lord permitted the soul of Samuel to rise up from Sheol, while at the same time opposing any demonic interference with the prophet's message to the king (e.g. Dan. 10:10-21). The text specifically states that it was Samuel and not a familiar spirit speaking to Saul. Furthermore, Samuel delivered a prophetic word to Saul concerning the events of the following day, which all came to pass, proving that it indeed was the Lord speaking through Samuel.

Samuel reproved the king, *"Why have you disturbed me by bringing me up?"* (v. 15). Saul then explained why he had sought the prophet's help (though through a medium). He was greatly distressed because the Philistines were amassing against him and God would not speak to him. Samuel then told Saul exactly what was about to happen and why:

> *So why do you ask me, seeing the Lord has departed from you and has become your enemy? And the Lord has done for Himself as He spoke by me. For the Lord has torn the kingdom out of your hand and given it to your neighbor, David. Because you did not obey the voice of the Lord nor execute His fierce wrath upon Amalek, therefore the Lord has done this thing to you this day. Moreover the Lord will also deliver Israel with you into the hand of the Philistines. And tomorrow you and your sons will be with me. The Lord will also deliver the army of Israel into the hand of the Philistines* (vv. 16-19).

Samuel first rebukes Saul for seeking counsel from him, since he, being a prophet of God, could only speak for God, and God was not speaking to the king. Then, for the third time, Samuel tells Saul that God was ripping the kingdom from him and giving it to David (v. 17, 13:14, 15:28). Saul already knew that the Lord had rejected him, would not communicate with him, and that David would be the next king of

Israel. However, the king was overcome with fear after Samuel told him that God considered him His enemy and that he and his three sons would die the next day by the hand of the Philistines.

The king lost all his strength and fell limply to the ground (v. 20). H. L. Rossier observes: "It is only when man finds himself before his inevitable fate that he really appreciates all its bearing. Until then there is always room for some illusion which hides the horror of our future from us."[98] But alas, Saul can no longer hide behind self-concocted illusions – the end has come and being estranged from the Lord, there is no comfort for his soul. What a miserable plight it must be for someone to stand on the threshold of death and to peer into the unfamiliar corridors of eternity and see no light, no love, no hope, and no God.

What did Samuel mean when he said to Saul, *"tomorrow you and your sons will be with me"*? Jamieson, Fausset, and Brown explain that the prophet simply meant that they would be in the state of the dead: "The expression 'with me' does not imply that the condition of Saul and his sons would be the same as that of Samuel, but that they would be, like the prophet, in the receptacle of departed spirits, though each would have his own place."[99] Jews in the Old Testament understood that death was unavoidable, and that beyond the grave their souls would be sequestered in a spiritual abode called Sheol.

The Hebrew word translated "Sheol," but sometimes rendered "grave" in the Old Testament, is the equivalent of the Greek *Hades*, used in the New Testament. The Lord Jesus taught that this spiritual domain houses disembodied spirits in one of two compartments (Luke 16:19-31). Abraham's Bosom is where faithful souls consciously await resurrection unto life through Christ, and the second is a place of torment where the wicked reside until their resurrection unto final judgment in the Lake of Fire. It is the author's opinion that the realm of Abraham's bosom was emptied after Christ's resurrection (Matt. 27:52; 2 Cor. 5:8).

The Lord Jesus said that you will know a tree (a true believer) by whether he or she bears good fruit or not (Matt. 7:17-18). If we apply the Lord's statement: *"Therefore by their fruits you will know them"* (Matt. 7:20) to Saul and Jonathan, it would seem that Jonathan was a man of faith and integrity, while his father was an egotistical, self-serving man who did not regard the Lord or His word. If this assessment is correct, then Jonathan would have joined Samuel in

Abraham's Bosom, but Saul would have been deposited in Hades to suffer affliction with the souls of all the wicked up to that time. Saul probably thought things could not get worse for him, but he would learn the following day that eternity apart from God is much worse than anything man might suffer among the living.

Besides the emotional trauma resulting from Samuel's judicial decree, the king was weak physically because he had not eaten that day. Seeing his desperate condition, the witch petitioned the king to eat something, but he refused (vv. 21-22). But, after his two men and the woman all insisted that he eat something, Saul heeded their voice (v. 23). The woman had a fatted calf in the house with her, which she killed and prepared for Saul with some freshly baked unleavened bread (v. 24).

Saul and his servants ate what the woman prepared and then they departed into the darkness of the night (v. 25). Saul had eaten his last meal – in a few hours he would be dead. The same prophet who had announced Saul's kingship forty years earlier had also foretold its end.

Meditation

Take care of your life and the Lord will take care of your death.

— George Whitefield

You have been used to take notice of the sayings of dying men. This is mine: that a life spent in the service of God, and communion with Him, is the most comfortable and pleasant life that anyone can live in this world.

— Matthew Henry

Separation and Restoration
1 Samuel 29

The day finally came in which David's identification with the Philistines posed an inescapable predicament for him. He was with the Philistines and they were preparing to war with Israel. How could David draw back from the confrontation after deceiving his supposed master about his enterprises and his sympathies? Furthermore, how could he fight against Saul, whose life he had spared twice because he was God's anointed? How could he lift up a sword against his beloved Jonathan?

David was learning that it was easier to set off down the wrong pathway than to forsake it later and suffer the consequences of one's folly. Clearly, David was in a bad way, but thankfully the Lord had not abandoned him. God was going to intervene to ensure that David would not fight against His covenant people but also to chasten David in such a way that his faith and his way would be restored.

Chronologically speaking, this chapter and the next occur before Saul's journey to see the medium, which occurred just a few hours before his death (28:3-25). In this chapter, the Philistine armies are still gathering their forces at Aphek, a city about ten miles east-northeast of Joppa. In chapter 28, the Philistines had already moved their combined forces about forty miles northeast to Shunem, a village located in the Jezreel Valley (Josh. 19:18). (This large valley forms the Plain of Esdraelon and is also known as the Valley of Armageddon.) At the same time, Saul and his troops were encamped by the fountain at Jezreel (v. 1). Keil and Delitzsch describe this location:

This fountain is the present Ain Jalûd, a very large fountain, which issues from a cleft in the rock at the foot of the mountain on the northeastern border of Gilboa, forming a beautifully limpid pool of about forty or fifty feet in diameter, and then flowing in a brook through the valley.[100]

Saul's camp then would be east of the town of Jezreel, and therefore located between Shunem to the north and the summit of Gilboa to the south.[101]

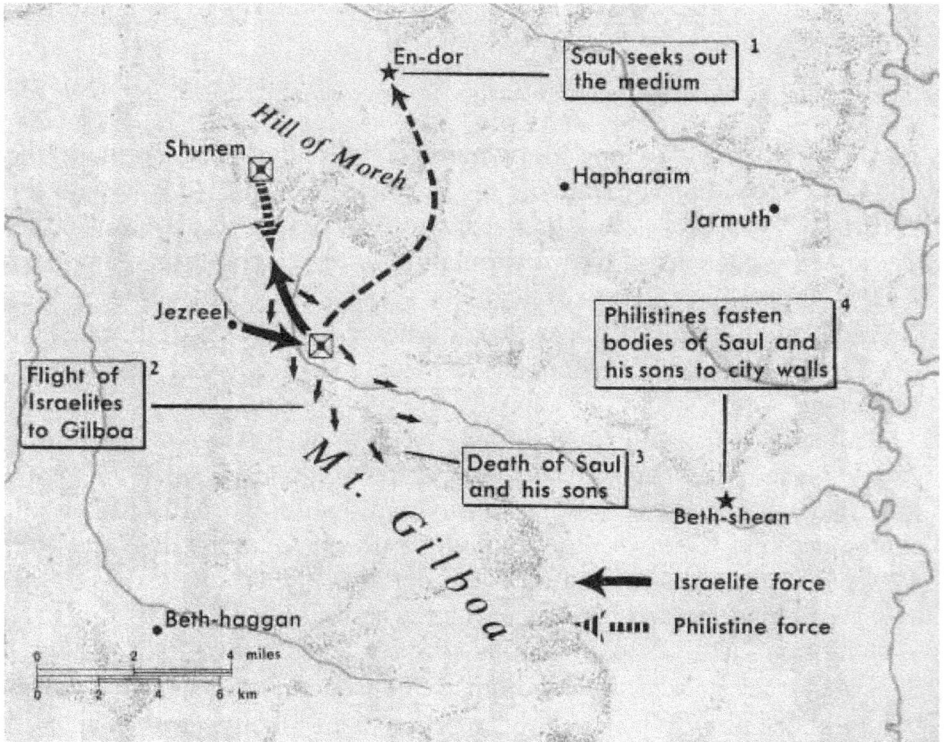

During the days of the judges, Barak (with Deborah's encouragement) defeated a much larger and better equipped Canaanite army here, and then Gideon with 300 men wiped out a large host of Midianites at this location. Those great victories proved that no army could oppose Israel when God fought for His people. However, the Lord will not be fighting alongside Saul on this occasion. Rather, He will be using the Philistines to end the king's life and to remove all possible successors to Israel's throne.

At Aphek the ranks of the Philistine soldiers were reviewed by their princes (v. 2). It was soon discovered that Achish had a band of renegade Hebrews as his rear guard and the Philistine commanders resented their presence: *"What are these Hebrews doing here?"* (v. 3).

H. L. Rossier suggests that this illustrates what happens when a believer places himself in a false position by seeking the world's protection:

> David cannot gain the world's confidence unless perhaps the world is depending upon him like Achish because he has made God's people abhor him and has given himself into bondage in this way. Moreover, Achish, we must observe, has still other motives for confidence, and we cannot help but see in him a certain natural nobility, won over by the *apparent* uprightness of David's character (Alas! it is not even apparently so in God's sight.) Hence, Achish defends David before the princes.[102]

A child of the devil may put their confidence in a child of God, when they have been observed to consistently strive against the Lord and His people. However, this is a flawed confidence, for God will not permit His children to continue in evil without chastening them (Heb. 12:6). As we are about to observe, a child of God can find no lasting help from those who oppose God, nor can the child of the devil obtain lasting security from a wayward child of God. The Philistine lords had rightly realized the inconsistency of the Hebrews being among them. They knew that their very identity prohibited any true union with them. Achish had been duped into a false fellowship with David, but the lords were not fooled; they rightly said, "What are these Hebrews doing here?" Today, worldlings might well recognize the same contradiction of union by asking, "What are these Christians doing here?"

The other Philistine lords (presumably four, Achish being the fifth) did not want to go into battle having Hebrew soldiers both in front of them and behind them. Achish protested by defending David: *"Is this not David, the servant of Saul king of Israel, who has been with me these days, or these years? And to this day I have found no fault in him since he defected to me"* (v. 3).

Nevertheless, Achish's endorsement of David did not satisfy their concern and they demanded that he and his men be removed from their ranks before engaging Israel in battle (v. 4). The other lords feared that during battle, David might have second thoughts of fighting his old master and turn on them. Then they reminded Achish that this was the same David the Hebrew women danced before while singing: *"Saul has slain his thousands, and David his ten thousands"* (v. 5).

Achish informed David that though he had not observed any offense in him, the Philistine princes did not favor his presence with them and therefore he must withdraw in peace and return to Ziklag (vv. 6-7). Of course, Achish did not know that David had been secretly raiding their Philistine allies, or he would not have been so willing to defend him.

Clearly, the Lord had intervened to deliver David out of his terrible predicament; yet, David chose to dispute the decision barring him from the Philistine army: *"But what have I done? And to this day what have you found in your servant as long as I have been with you, that I may not go and fight against the enemies of my lord the king?"* (v. 8). David's protest may have been deceptive to maintain the appearance of loyalty to Achish, his master. Regardless, Achish consoles David by affirming his esteem for him, but the decision of the lords was final (implying that he had been out-voted 4 to 1). The king requested that David return to Ziklag at first light the following morning (vv. 9-10). The next day David and his men began their fifty-mile journey south to Ziklag while the Philistine army headed northeast to Shunem in the Jezreel Valley (v. 11).

Thankfully, the Lord had used the disdain of the Philistine lords to redirect His servant's steps. Later, David would realize that God's providential care spared him the humiliation and shame which would have been attached to his name if he had gone into battle with the Philistines. He would write: *"The steps of a good man are ordered by the Lord and He delights in his way. Though he fall, he shall not be utterly cast down; for the Lord upholds him with His hand"* (Ps. 37:23-24). But at this juncture, David is self-willed; he is not delighting in the path that God has chosen for him. He must learn that deliverance from trouble is not the same as restoration to God; he must, therefore, come under God's chastening rod for disobedience.

The writer of Hebrews reminds us that such correction is proof of God's love for His children and that He loves us too much to leave us the way we are:

"My son, do not despise the chastening of the Lord, nor be discouraged when you are rebuked by Him; for whom the Lord loves He chastens, and scourges every son whom He receives." If you endure chastening, God deals with you as with sons; for what son is there whom a father does not chasten? But if you are without

chastening, of which all have become partakers, then you are illegitimate and not sons (Heb. 12:5-8).

The Lord's chastening will not be of David's choosing, nor will he be consulted about it beforehand. None of us, naturally speaking, would desire to select a punishment that would best expedite our brokenness. Thankfully, God knows how to accomplish that goal best. Dear believer, be thankful that God's rod of affliction is always tempered with mercy! He desires to accomplish the greatest result within us without unnecessarily marring our souls by extreme harshness.

Samuel Ridout reminds us that, like David, God's sheep still wander from His fold today and must be firmly attended to by the Shepherd's crook:

> We have probably all seen some cases of recovery. One has wandered from God and apparently been left for a time to his own devices. He may have been successful in worldly affairs, and all seems to have gone well, even though he has manifestly compromised his pilgrim character and his integrity as a man of faith. God has kept silence. Then perhaps when the shame of such a course is most glaring, the stroke has fallen. Property has been swept away, dear ones perhaps have been taken, and the afflicted man is left somewhat as Job. And now, instead of the pride and self-sufficiency and the hypocrisy which had previously marked him in his course, we find a humbled and a chastened spirit. God is turned to, and the proud soul has found in its affliction the only meeting point between a wandering saint and a holy God. Such can say with David, *"It is good for me that I have been afflicted"*; *"before I was afflicted I went astray; but now have I kept Thy word."*[103]

God will now cause David to come face to face with his sin. His servant will learn again the joy of pursuing the heart of God. This is why the writer of Hebrews exhorts us to *not despise the chastening of the Lord*! We will be the happiest when we yearn for what God wants, and detest what He hates. His rod of correction is His blessed incentive to get us to do just that! Praise the Lord for His loving care of all His people, especially the wayward.

Meditation

I was a wandering sheep,
I did not love the fold;
I did not love my Shepherd's voice,
I would not be controlled.
I was a wayward child,
I did not love my home;
I did not love my Father's voice,
I loved afar to roam.

The Shepherd sought His sheep,
The Father sought His child;
They followed me over vale and hill,
Over deserts waste and wild:
They found me nigh to death,
Famished and faint and lone;
They bound me with the bands of love,
They saved the wandering one.

I was a wandering sheep,
I would not be controlled;
But now I love my Shepherd's voice,
I love, I love the fold.
I was a wayward child,
I once preferred to roam;
But now I love my Father's voice,
I love, I love His home.

— Horatius Bonar

David Despoils the Amalekites
1 Samuel 30

Evidently, the news that the Philistines had gathered their armies to attack Israel in the north made its way to the Amalekites in the far south. They raided southern Philistia while it was unguarded. It took David and his men three days to travel the fifty miles from Aphek to Ziklag. When they arrived, they found that Ziklag had been burned and all the people (including the children and infants) had been taken away (v. 1). David experienced the very horror that he had inflicted on the same people group previously (27:8). The fact that the burned-out town was not littered with bodies meant that their wives and children had been enslaved and not slain (vv. 2-3). That offered a glimmer of hope to the weary husbands and fathers in David's company.

David's men, already exhausted from their journey, wept over the loss of their loved ones until they had no more strength to do so (v. 4). David too was distressed by the capture of both of his wives, Ahinoam and Abigail, but the situation worsened when some of David's men blamed him for this tragic state of affairs and spoke of stoning him (v. 5).

Moses had promised that when the men of Israel appeared before the Lord three times a year at the appointed feasts, they could leave their homes defenseless in perfect confidence that He would protect what was theirs (Ex. 34:24). However, Moses gave no such promise for those choosing a path of disobedience. David was not before the Lord, but had left Israel altogether and associated himself with the enemies of God. He could not, therefore, expect the Lord to watch over his interests while he neglected the Lord's interests. On the contrary, God touched what was most precious to David to awaken him to his need of repentance and restoration. David acutely felt the welts of God's rod.

No doubt the sixteen months of living among the uncircumcised and away from the Lord's presence had taken an emotional toll on David's men. But they were correct; David was responsible. Their

213

leader should have expected the Amalekites to avenge themselves and therefore should have left some men behind to protect their families. Yet that was merely a matter of bad judgment; the deeper issues which spawned the disaster were David's disobedience in not remaining in Judah, and in identifying himself with and then aiding Israel's enemy.

David knew his God, and realized that the entire situation was too well crafted to have happened by chance. Having recognized the hand of God, a contrite David *"strengthened himself in the Lord his God"* (v. 6). The fact that the Amalekites had struck shortly after David had impudently gone to fight with the Philistines, but not a single person belonging to David was killed, demonstrated God's control of the entire situation. David had slaughtered every man, woman, and child of the Amalekites during his raids and that should have been their retribution towards David, but it was not.

God was judging His servant, but He was doing so in measure to bring about David's restoration, not his crushing, and David realized it. Jehovah would not permit the Amalekites to harm what was His servant's, nor would he allow David and his men to resolve the situation on their terms or with their resources. The Lord had wrung out of them every ounce of human energy and determination so that they would have no alternative but to turn to Him and then advance with Him against their enemy.

Although everyone and everything seemed to be against David at this moment, he knew to whom to turn for comfort and help in his dire crisis. So while David's men further disheartened each other, David chose to permit God's grace to work in his own heart; he thus remained calm and optimistic. God's grace is magnified in man's failures, and the more keenly our ruin is felt, the more we appreciate God's grace. The fact that David never retaliated against those who publicly challenged him verifies the depths of serenity that grace achieved in his soul. J. N. Darby summarizes what God accomplished for David through the Amalekite raid:

> The Amalekites strip him of everything and burn Ziklag, and his followers are ready to stone him. All this is grievous, but the grace of God raises him up again, and the effect of this chastisement is to bring him back to God, for he was ever true to Him in heart. David encouraged himself in Jehovah his God, and inquires of Him what he

shall do. What patience, what kindness in God! What care He takes of His people, even while they are turning away from Him![104]

Even though the right course of action was apparent to everyone and every moment that passed only increased the distance between the men and their families, David paused to seek God's direction in the matter. He says to Abiathar the priest, *"Please bring the ephod here to me"* (v. 7). The priesthood was God's link between Him and His people and David's request for the ephod brought him back in touch with God. Abiathar immediately did so and then David asked the Lord, *"Shall I pursue this troop? Shall I overtake them?"* The Lord promptly answered David *"Pursue, for you shall surely overtake them and without fail recover all"* (v. 8). Because the Lord's answer was not merely a "yes" but conveyed a promise, it does not appear that the Urim and the Thummim in the high priest's breastplate were used, but rather God gave a prophetic word to David through Abiathar.

This scene likely confirms that Abiathar and the priest's ephod were with David and his company while accompanying Achish, otherwise the Amalekites would have confiscated both at Ziklag. If this assumption is correct, we must wonder why David did not consult the Lord about marching into battle with the Philistines. It suggests that David knew what he was doing was wrong, but out of pride, or perhaps fear, he did it anyway.

This is the first time we have read that David sought the Lord's mind since arriving in Philistia sixteen months earlier. He realizes that his past folly has created his present distress and he is determined to look beyond the smoldering ruins and faithless friends to obtain the blessing of His changeless God. Matthew Henry suggests that David's renewed resolve to commit all things to the Lord is what all His people should do:

> David had no room to doubt but that his war against these Amalekites was just, and he had an inclination strong enough to set upon them when it was for the recovery of that which was dearest to him in this world, and yet he would not go about it without asking counsel of God, thereby owning his dependence upon God and submission to him. If we thus, in all our ways, acknowledge God, we may expect that he will direct our steps, as he did David's here, answering him above what he asked, with an assurance that he should recover all.[105]

David demonstrates his utter loyalty to Jehovah by seeking and waiting for God's counsel even on a matter in which the answer was blatantly obvious. Because he did, the Lord promised a happy ending to his crisis – all that was lost would be recovered! A life pleasing to God does not merely seek to do what He approves, or permits, but rather pursues Him to achieve what will best honor His name (Phil. 1:20-21).

The young commander and his six hundred weary and emotionally distraught men then pursued hard after the Amalekites (v. 9). However, by the time David and his men reached the Brook Besor (about fifteen miles southwest of Ziklag), two hundred of his men could go no further. (This brook is thought to be Wady Ghazza, which runs from Beersheba to the southwest and then the northwest until it enters the Mediterranean Sea southwest of Gaza.) These men did not have the strength to ford the brook, so they stayed behind with whatever supplies and baggage the other four hundred determined they could do without to move faster (vv. 10, 24). This situation again tested David's faith, but despite one-third of his men failing him, he chose to move forward in the confidence that God would keep His word.

God is honored when His people trust His character and promises even when they do not understand what He is doing. If we fully understood the mind of God, we would naturally revere Him less! It is right for us, then, during the storms of life, to acknowledge that God is God, and to count on Him to accomplish what is beyond reason and is outside our control. This is why Paul did not boast in his sufferings while serving the Lord, but rather in the manifestation of God's grace in his difficulties. This focus caused him to highly extol the Lord, instead of complain: *"Oh, the depth of the riches both of the wisdom and knowledge of God! How unsearchable are His judgments and His ways past finding out!"* (Rom. 11:33).

David and his remaining men continued to pursue the Amalekites. They discovered an ill Egyptian lying in a field and learned from him that he was an Amalekite slave that had been abandoned to die (vv. 11, 13-14). The man was weak, for he had not eaten or drunk water in three days. This information meant that the attack on Ziklag had occurred while they had been in Aphek, and that the Amalekites had at least a four-day head start on them.

The Egyptian was given bread and two clusters of raisins to eat and water to drink (v. 12). After the man regained his strength, he informed David that the Amalekites had *"invaded the southern area of the*

216

Cherethites, in the territory which belongs to Judah, and of the southern area of Caleb; and we burned Ziklag with fire" (v. 14). David asked the Egyptian if he would lead them to the encampment of the Amalekites (v. 14). The man agreed to do so if David would swear to God that he would neither kill him, nor return him to his master (v. 15). David assured the man of his life and freedom. Peter J. Pell observes that David did for this poor Egyptian slave what Christ has done for believers:

> Abandoned by our master in the field (the world) and left to perish, Christ ministers to our fainting soul the consolation of His own grace and mercy. Abundant provision is ours: life, strength, health, and joy. Although found and fetched and fed, the young man could not be happy until fully assured of complete and final deliverance from his former bondage. This David gives him. We also receive from Christ not only the forgiveness of all our sins, but full justification and acceptance. We are placed beyond the reach of all our foes in Christ the Risen One. We who were once the slaves of Satan now make inroads on his territory; deliverance has placed us in the service of our Deliverer.[106]

And to this wonderful life and liberation in Christ we say, "Praise the Lord."

There is an obscure detail in the text that we should not pass over, as it explains the meaning of an often used Jewish idiom. Notice that the sick Egyptian had not eaten bread or drunk water *"for three days and nights,"* but in the next verse he tells David that he was left three days earlier, not four (vv. 11-12). This shows that the term "one day and one night" was a Jewish idiom for indicating a day, even when only a part of a day was indicated.

Matthew 27:63 shows that the Pharisees understood the Lord's vernacular concerning His resurrection. He said, *"After three days I will rise again,"* but then they asked Pilate for a guard to the secure the tomb *until* the third day. If the term "after three days" were not interchangeable with "the third day," the Pharisees would have asked for a tomb to be guarded for four days, but they did not do so. In summary, the idiom "three days and nights" and the expression "three days" were commonly used interchangeably. It would be no different than a woman expressing that she was in her ninth month of pregnancy, which could describe one day after eight months of being pregnant or up until her due date.

Returning to the narrative, the Egyptian man did guide David to the Amalekites encampment (v. 16). The Hebrews found their enemy in a sprawling celebration because of the great spoil they had taken from the Philistines and from Judah (v. 16). Clearly, they were not anticipating a counterstrike from anyone, and why should they? David and his men and the Philistine armies were over a hundred miles northeast of their position.

David and his men rested briefly and then attacked the Amalekites from dusk until the following evening the next day; they slaughtered the drunken Amalekites, except four hundred young men who escaped on camels (v. 17). Just as the Lord had said, David recovered all that the Amalekites had taken, including his two wives; nothing was lacking (vv. 18-19). David, as the commander, claimed the captured sheep and cattle as his spoil, which he will later distribute as gifts in Israel (v. 20). All the other plunder within the camp (including arms, ornaments, jewels, money, clothing, camels, and donkeys) was divided among David's men.

When the group rejoined the two hundred men left behind at the Brook Besor, there were some wicked men with David who did not want to share the spoil with the two hundred men because they had not engaged in the battle (v. 21). They suggested that these men should only be rejoined with their families (v. 22). But David warmly greeted the two hundred waiting men and then reproved the selfish soldiers who wanted to deny them a share of the spoil:

My brethren, you shall not do so with what the Lord has given us, who has preserved us and delivered into our hand the troop that came against us. For who will heed you in this matter? But as his part is who goes down to the battle, so shall his part be who stays by the supplies; they shall share alike (vv. 23-24).

The two hundred men had stayed at the brook and guarded their baggage and therefore had contributed to the victory. Though they had lacked strength, they were still useful to David and, therefore, their brethren should not despise them! Likewise, all believers share their identity in Christ, all will share in His riches (Rom. 8:17; Eph. 1:3) and therefore none should be despised. It is understood that some brethren are weaker than others in recognizing sin and resisting its destructive power (1 Cor. 8:9-13). For this reason Paul says, *"comfort the fainthearted, uphold the weak, be patient with all"* (1 Thess. 5:14); this is the type of grace David shows his weaker brethren. He knew that the blessings of the Lord should not be hoarded by the strong, but rather shared among His people to ensure that no one suffered lack. His decree became a statute in Israel from that day forward (v. 25).

We find that the early Christians held a similar view of sharing their possessions and, as a result, enjoyed wonderful unity and fellowship together: *"Now the multitude of those who believed were of one heart and one soul; neither did anyone say that any of the things he possessed was his own, but they had all things in common"* (Acts 4:32). Paul taught that there should be equality among the brethren:

For I do not mean that others should be eased and you burdened; but by an equality, that now at this time your abundance may supply their lack, that their abundance also may supply your lack -- that there may be equality (2 Cor. 8:13-14).

If a brother is in need and another brother is able to meet that need, he should readily do so. Equality is not communism. Holding all things in equality is not the same as everyone having equal portions. When God's people value God, the things of God, and His people, there is unity, but if their focus is on temporal things, envy, dissatisfaction, and coveting occur. David took steps to ensure that greed would not cause division in his ranks.

After returning to Ziklag, he demonstrated his commitment to his own edict by sending portions of the spoil to friends and to the elders of various settlements throughout or near to Judah (vv. 26-30). He was rewarding those who had been loyal to him and had permitted him and his men to abide with them during his years of fleeing Saul (v. 31). Notice that the betraying Ziphites received no part of David's generosity. Likewise, there is a day coming when in grace the Lord Jesus will divide His spoil and amply reward every kindness done to Him or to another in His name, but woe to those who sided against Him (Matt. 25:31-46)!

At Ziklag, David learned a valuable lesson – a child of faith must trust in the Lord's character and promises even if all appears to be bleak and threatening. With David's experience in mind, we close this chapter with a challenge to our own hearts from C. H. Mackintosh:

> Are we able to lean on the Lord amid the ruin around us? Is He beyond everyone and everything to our souls? Can we encourage ourselves in Him when all without and within seems directly against us? Is His name dear to us in this day of faithlessness and cold formality? Are we prepared to pursue the rest of our course through the desert in solitariness and desertion, if such should be needful? It may be, we have learnt to cease looking, in any way, to the children of this world, but are we prepared to lose the approval and confidence of our brethren? David's companions spoke of stoning him, but the Lord was more to him than all; the Lord was *"his refuge."* Do we know the power and comfort of this?[107]

Meditation

Marvelous grace of our loving Lord,
Grace that exceeds our sin and our guilt,
Yonder on Calvary's mount out-poured,
There where the blood of the Lamb was spilt.

Marvelous, infinite, matchless grace,
Freely bestowed on all who believe;
You that are longing to see his face,
Will you this moment His grace receive?

— Julia H. Johnston

Saul's End
1 Samuel 31

We have in this chapter the continuation of the account which began in chapter 29. The Philistines did not engage Saul in the central highlands, which would have been to his advantage, but rather moved quickly from Aphek to the central part of the Jezreel Valley. Their intention was probably to move all the way to the Jordan River and completely cut off Saul from the northern tribes and seize control of Galilee. This tactic forced Saul to move down from the hill country and to engage the Philistines in the southern Plain of Esdraelon, which was to their advantage.

Saul had already been told by Samuel that he would die in this battle; David also foretold that this would be the way Saul would perish (26:10). The day of God's retribution had arrived and Saul will now answer for sparing the Amalekites, for intruding on the priesthood, for spilling the blood of the innocent priests and their families at Nob, and for relentlessly hunting David like a dog for eight years.

The Philistine army moved south from Shunem to engage Saul and his troops coming north into the Jezreel Valley from the fountain at Jezreel. Israel's army quickly fell into disarray and was repelled and driven back. The Jews did not widely employ the use of the bow as the Philistines did, and it seems that when the ranks of Israel's army drew near for hand-to-hand conflict, they were battered by volleys of arrows from Philistine archers as they came into range. As a result, Israel's army was in chaos before the clang of clashing swords could ever be heard. This is why David, while later lamenting the death of Jonathan, commanded that the children of Judah should be taught the skill of archery (2 Sam. 1:18).

Many soldiers perished as Israel's army retreated up the southern slopes of Gilboa (v. 1). The Philistines followed hard after Saul and his sons (v. 2). Apparently, Jonathan, Abinadab, and Malchishua were quickly slain by archers and the king *"was severely wounded by the archers"* (v. 3). The language suggests that Saul was struck by more than one arrow. The only son of Saul to survive this battle was Ishbosheth, whose name means "the man of shame." But as expected, his very survival would later perpetuate the awful dishonor that fell upon the house of Saul.

Preferring not to die at the hands of his enemy, Saul commanded his armorbearer: *"Draw your sword, and thrust me through with it, lest these uncircumcised men come and thrust me through and abuse me"* (v. 4). Even at the threshold of death, the self-righteousness of Saul's uncircumcised heart despised the uncircumcised Philistines, but his spiritual vitality was no better than theirs.

Apparently, the armorbearer drew his sword, but was afraid to strike down his king, for he was answerable for the king's life. Saul then took the drawn sword, positioned in such a way that he could fall on it and then ended his own life. Seeing that the king was dead, his armorbearer then took back his sword from Saul's body and also fell on it and killed himself (v. 5). He was a loyal bodyguard who, though declining to kill his king, did not refuse to die with him. The king, his three sons, and his armorbearer all perished in the same day (v. 6). Adam Clarke offers further insight into the scene we have just witnessed:

> Saul and his armorbearer died by the same sword. ... "Draw *thy* sword," he says to him, and thrust me through; which, when he refused, Saul, the text says, "took *the* sword," the very sword, "and fell upon it." What sword? Not his own, for then the text would have said so; but, in the plain natural grammatical construction, the sword before mentioned must be the sword now referred to, that is his armorbearer's sword (1 Chron. 10:4-5). It is established Jewish tradition that this armorbearer was Doeg, and I see no reason why it should be discredited, and if so, then Saul and his executioner both fell by that weapon with which they had before massacred the priests of God.[108]

Seeing that Saul and his sons had perished, and Israel's army was soundly defeated, the Jews in the region of the Jezreel Valley fled for their lives, and the Philistines dwelt in their cities (v. 7). The next day, while the Philistines were stripping the slain Israelites of valuables, they discovered the bodies of Saul and his three sons on Mount Gilboa (v. 8). They cut off Saul's head and stripped off his armor and sent both to pagan temples throughout Philistia as trophies of victory (v. 9). Though the text does not specifically state this, the Philistines probably cut off and paraded the heads of Saul's sons also. Saul's armor was placed in the temple of Ashtaroth (Astarte), but his body and the bodies of his sons were fastened to the wall of Beth Shan as a public spectacle (v. 10). This also indicates that the Philistines had captured and occupied Beth Shan and likely other Jewish cities extending eastward to the Jordan.

News came to the men of Jabesh Gilead of the dishonorable way the Philistines had treated Saul's body. The thought of their king who had previously saved them from the Ammonites (chp. 11), having no proper burial and the birds of prey feasting on their rotting corpses was more than they could bear. The valiant men of Jabesh then traveled to Beth Shan after dark, took all four bodies down from the wall, and then carried the bodies back to Jabesh and burned them (v. 12). Cremation was not a normal practice in the Jewish culture, but was used here because the bodies were badly mutilated.

These brave men accomplished quite a feat. They crossed the Jordan River and journeyed through a narrow, upland passage some twelve miles to retrieve the four headless bodies, which were probably guarded, and then they carried the bodies back the same route all in one night. After the bodies were burned, they collected the bones, buried them under a tamarisk tree at Jabesh and then fasted for seven days (v. 13). It was customary in the Ancient Near East to mourn the dead for seven days and nights.

We are saddened to see Jonathan, the one who deeply loved David, come to such a terrible end, but his allegiance to his father (a man of the flesh) ensured that he would never have a place in David's kingdom. What a sorrowful ending for Saul also. Everything is lost: the battle, his sons, and his kingdom, and his only perceived escape – suicide. But Saul would soon find out that his illusion of relief through death was only another manifestation of his selfish heart.

H. L. Rossier suggests that the book of 1 Samuel concludes with the ending of everything, so that the kingdom of God's beloved, David, can commence without opposition:

> Here we see the end of the priesthood, of the judges, of kingship according to man. Everything crumbles; God allows it, for this is exactly what is necessary. Everything must fall before David. Let *him*

abide: that is enough. This defeat, this judgment, this ruin of man are, for God, the dawn of the reign of the beloved![109]

Meditation

O King of Glory! David's Son!
Our sovereign and our friend!
In Heav'n forever stands Thy throne,
Thy kingdom hath no end.

Oh now to all men, far and near,
Lord, make it known, we pray,
That as in Heav'n all creatures here
May know Thee and obey.

— Martin Behm

2 Samuel

Devotions in 2 Samuel

David Learns of Saul's Demise
2 Samuel 1

Introduction

As previously mentioned, 1 and 2 Samuel were originally one book, and remain so in the Hebrew text. The book was first divided in Alexandria in the third century B.C. to maintain conventional scroll size for such manuscripts. This means that 2 Samuel is not a new book, but rather the continuation of the narrative from 1 Samuel.

First Samuel began with the ruin of the Levitical priesthood, which had failed to keep Israel in a proper relationship with God. He withdrew from them and permitted them to suffer under Saul's carnality. Although God was judging the corrupt priesthood, was punishing his people through devastating Philistine victories, and the Ark was estranged from the tabernacle, God mercifully raised up a godly prophet, Samuel, to communicate with His wayward people. He introduced a new type of relationship that God would have with Israel through His chosen king, before whom a faithful priest should always minister. Second Samuel picks up on this latter prophecy. We will see that God's anointed, who has a heart for God, but who still suffered in the midst of his brethren, will gloriously reign over Israel. This man is God's beloved and his name is David.

David's suffering ends when he, by God's direction and power, attacks and vanquishes the Amalekites (1 Sam. 30). Amalek is a picture of the flesh under Satan's control, and David accomplishes what Saul was commanded to do, but could not because he was a man of the flesh. Before Saul's rejection, God enabled him to overcome the Philistines, but afterwards, God used the Philistines to remove Saul from office. That is where 1 Samuel ends, the death of Saul. Second

227

Samuel begins with the dawning of a wonderful era in which God's man, David, will reign over Israel for forty years.

The man who defeated the Amalekites will rule over Judah for seven years before being recognized by all Israel as their king. David was thirty years of age when he began to rule in Judah. The theme of 2 Samuel is the establishment of David's power as a king of grace. Of course, all of this is a lovely portrayal of the Lord Jesus, who also suffered in Israel to vanquish the enemy that had ensnared humanity by death. As a result, Christ can extend grace to the condemned, so that they may join Him in His glorious, eternal kingdom.

The Report of Saul's Death (vv. 1-16)

Three days after David returned to Ziklag (after slaughtering the Amalekites), a man from Saul's camp with his clothes torn and dust on his head entered the city and prostrated himself on the ground before David (vv. 1-2). Evidently, it was widely known that David resided in Ziklag at that time. The timing of both David's and then the Amalekite's arrival at Ziklag suggests that while the Lord was restoring to David what the Amalekites had taken, He was at the same time stripping everything from Saul. The visitor's appearance in rent garments, with earth upon his head, and in great haste all suggested that he had survived a terrible calamity, but, as we shall soon see, the man was an imposter.

After learning that the man had fled from Israel's encampment against the Philistines, David inquired how the battle had gone (v. 3). The man answered, *"The people have fled from the battle, many of the people are fallen and dead, and Saul and Jonathan his son are dead also"* (v. 4). Although this report would have grieved David, especially for Jonathan's sake, the news would not have been surprising, as he had already foretold how Saul would die. David continued his interrogation of the man by asking how he knew Saul and Jonathan were dead (v. 5). The young survivor then gave the following account:

> *As I happened by chance to be on Mount Gilboa, there was Saul, leaning on his spear; and indeed the chariots and horsemen followed hard after him. Now when he looked behind him, he saw me and called to me. And I answered, "Here I am." And he said to me, "Who are you?" So I answered him, "I am an Amalekite." He said to me*

228

again, "Please stand over me and kill me, for anguish has come upon me, but my life still remains in me." So I stood over him and killed him, because I was sure that he could not live after he had fallen. And I took the crown that was on his head and the bracelet that was on his arm, and have brought them here to my lord (vv. 6-10).

Solomon tells us that *"In the multitude of words sin is not lacking, but he who restrains his lips is wise"* (Prov. 10:19). The Amalekite would have probably fared better if he had not spun such a lengthy yarn. As H. L. Rossier explains, David's third question unmasked his lies:

David, a spiritual man, already suspects the unlikelihood of this story: "I happened *by chance* to be upon mount Gilboa." What? By chance – in the thick of battle? "Behold, Saul leaned on his spear; and, behold, *the chariots and horsemen* followed hard after him." Here the Word itself convicts this man of lying. It was not the horsemen but the *archers* who had threatened him (1 Sam. 31:3-4). The remainder of his account is a bare-faced lie. Saul could not have asked the Amalekite to end his life, for the king's armorbearer did not kill himself until he *"had seen that Saul was dead"* (1 Sam. 31:5).[110]

While much of the man's story appears to be fabricated, he did hold Saul's crown and bracelet in his hands, which testified of the king's demise. At this, David tore his clothes in mourning and so did his men. David and his comrades wept, grieved and fasted until evening for their fallen countrymen (vv. 11-12). One wonders how they would have been able to genuinely grieve over Saul's death, had the Lord permitted them to fight with the Philistines against Israel.

That evening David asked the young man two more questions. The first question was, *"Where are you from?"* and as the man had already let slip his origins earlier, he could not contradict himself now. He answered, *"I am the son of an alien, an Amalekite"* (v. 13). The only reason that an Amalekite would be on the battlefield of Gilboa would be to rob the dead of their valuables. Because of the danger, these scavengers would not immediately rush onto an active battlefront (1 Sam. 31:8). This meant that several hours would have passed after Saul had fallen on his sword, ensuring that he would have bled to death from multiple mortal wounds before the Amalekite arrived. Accordingly, Saul could not have been hobbling along on his spear as the Amalekite claimed. After finding Saul's body, the Amalekite saw an opportunity for advancement in David's kingdom, or at least the possibility of financial reward. So he brought the royal crown and bracelet to David. (The bracelet was worn above the elbow and was a sign of royalty in the Ancient East.)

Those who are the Lord's should follow David's example of scrutinizing those we do not know by first examining their origin – with whom do they identify? The pivotal question is, *"What think you of Christ?"* (Matt. 22:42). A true child of God will acknowledge that Christ is the Son of God, who came down from heaven and was born of a virgin to be God's sacrificial Lamb for human sin (John 1:29; 1 Jn. 4:2-3). Those who deny this truth (i.e., that Jesus Christ is the Son of God who came from heaven) cannot be saved (John 8:24; 1 Jn. 4:15). Satan, though appearing as *"an angel of light,"* cannot permit his followers to identify with Christ, for *"no one can say that Jesus is Lord except by the Holy Spirit"* (1 Cor. 12:3; 2 Cor. 11:14). The Amalekite was a child of the devil and therefore could not have allegiance to Israel, and in fact, Israel had been commanded to exterminate the Amalekites, for they were God's enemies. The matter of origins settled the issue with David; an Amalekite could not be trusted, nor could he join his ranks.

David's final question to the Amalekite was framed as a rhetorical indictment: *"How was it you were not afraid to put forth your hand to destroy the Lord's anointed?"* (v. 14). David then instructed one of his young men to execute the Amalekite, which he did (v. 15). David then pronounced sentencing over the dying Amalekite: *"Your blood is on your own head, for your own mouth has testified against you, saying, 'I have killed the Lord's anointed'"* (v. 16). By his own mouth he had given evidence of his crime.

David had the man executed for several reasons. First, he was an Amalekite under God's judgment. Second, he claimed to have killed God's anointed, but yet was not a soldier of either army – Saul was to die at the hands of his enemies. Third, the man came to David with Saul's crown hoping to profit somehow from telling David the tragic news of Saul's death, but he misjudged David's reaction to the matter.

How are we to understand the Amalekite's testimony of Saul's death since it disagrees with the account in the final chapter of 1 Samuel? There we learned that Saul, being mortally wounded, fell on a sword and killed himself, and then his armorbearer, seeing that his master *was dead,* likewise fell on his sword and also ended his life.

Since the Amalekite had Saul's crown and bracelet, he must have come across Saul's dead body a few hours after the battle concluded and he took the articles. His story of finding Saul hobbling along with spear in hand could not possibly be true, as Saul had already been immobilized by mortal wounds from arrows and then had fallen on a sword to end his own life. The most likely explanation of the contrasting reports is that the Amalekite, a symbol of the flesh, fabricated the story to honor himself in David's eyes and to hopefully reap some reward for bringing David Saul's crown. However, the flesh should never be permitted to glory in the providential workings of God; rather, the flesh (i.e., the Amalekite) was rightly put to death.

Ironically, Saul lost the kingdom for not exterminating the Amalekites, as commanded by the Lord (1 Sam. 15), and yet it is an Amalekite who removed his crown from his head and took credit for his death. If Saul had obeyed the Lord, then there would have been no Amalekites available to glory in his demise. The Lord often uses what we value more than obedience to Him as an instrument of our own chastening.

The Song of the Bow (vv. 17- 27)

While David was grieving over Saul and over Jonathan, *"the beauty of Israel,"* he wrote the *Song of the Bow* which was to be taught to the children of Judah (v. 17). It was also recorded in the Book of Jasher, meaning the "Book of the Upright." This may have been a poetic record of Israel's leaders and their endeavors. This book has since been lost (i.e., the Holy Spirit did not preserve the book to become a part of the canon of Scripture).

The Philistine archers had inflicted heavy losses on Israel's army, and David's song instructs future Jewish soldiers to learn the skill of archery, like brave Jonathan had (v. 22). Evidently, Saul did not have many archers with him, but we learn from 1 Chronicles 12:1-7 that a band of archers from the family of Kish in Benjamin had joined David at Ziklag. Even in Philistia, the Lord provided David what he needed, while Saul had to do without the Lord's help.

Every portion of David's lament is a lovely expression by a man of God full of the grace of God, of the benefit of being refined and restored through chastening. Even after eight frightening years of fleeing Saul's sword, there is not one note of resentment, fault-finding, or even a complaint in David's song. He first confirms Israel's heavy losses on the heights of Gilboa while engaging the Philistines, but then adds *"tell it not in Gath"* (vv. 19-20). Israel's new king did not want the Philistines to hear the news and rejoice in Saul's death and Israel's terrible defeat.

Although Saul and Jonathan fought as bravely as lions and were swifter than eagles, they both perished in battle. This meant that Saul's shield would no longer be oiled for future battles (vv. 22-23). Because the battlefield of Gilboa was stained with the blood of many of his countrymen, David requested that it receive no rain or dew (v. 21). In effect, David was poetically asking God to memorialize the battlefield by perpetual barrenness.

David further requested that the daughters of Israel weep over Saul for the prosperity that his forty years of leadership brought to Israel (v. 24). The song then offers a tribute to beloved Jonathan. Jonathan was a friend most pleasant to David. Their bond of brotherly devotion surpassed even the natural love that a husband has for his wife (vv. 25-26). The refrain which began the poem, is then repeated for a third time to conclude the lament, *"How the mighty have fallen, and the weapons of war perished!"* (v. 27).

Meditation

Think about how much falsehood and deceit there is in the world! How much exaggeration! How many untruths are added to a simple story! How many things are left out, if it does not serve the speaker's interest to tell them! How few there are around us of whom we can say that we trust their word without question!

— J. C. Ryle

Civil War Over Two Kings
2 Samuel 2

David Anointed King of Judah (vv. 1-7)

With Saul removed from office, David inquired of the Lord if he should dwell in a city in Judah. This communication was probably accomplished by Abiathar's use of the sacred lots in the high priest's shoulder dress. Having been chastened and restored to the Lord, David shows us where his real strength resided – not in his sword, but in his dependence on the Lord. Like David, we too, through correction, must learn dependence to properly pursue God's will in all things – following our will leads to independence from God and trouble!

The Lord's answer to David's question was "Go up." David then inquired to which city he should go and the Lord directed him to Hebron (v. 1). Hebron was about eighteen miles northeast of Ziklag, and there would be many loyal to David residing in the vicinity. The young king then took his two wives, Ahinoam and Abigail, to Hebron and his men brought their families there also.

The elders of Judah then anointed David as their king (v. 4). They also informed David that it was the men of Jabesh Gilead who had recovered the mangled bodies of Saul and his sons and had given them a proper burial. David appreciated this deed and sent messengers to Jabesh Gilead to commend their valor and kindness:

> *You are blessed of the Lord, for you have shown this kindness to your lord, to Saul, and have buried him. And now may the Lord show kindness and truth to you. I also will repay you this kindness, because you have done this thing. Now therefore, let your hands be strengthened, and be valiant; for your master Saul is dead, and also the house of Judah has anointed me king over them (vv. 5-7).*

Although a laudatory message, David also promised to defend them if there was any reprisal for their kind deed done for Saul's house.

Furthermore, David indirectly invited the valiant men of Jabesh Gilead to recognize him as their king, as Judah had already done.

Ishbosheth Recognized as Israel's King (vv. 8-11)

Apparently, it took Saul's general, Abner, about five years to remove the Philistines from northern Israel and to secure the region so that Saul's only remaining son, Ishbosheth, could reign as king. Abner took Ishbosheth to Mahanaim (located in the Transjordan) and made him king over Gilead and the northern tribes of Israel (vv. 8-9). Abner also had family ties with Ishbosheth; he was Saul's cousin (i.e., Abner was the son of Ner, Saul's uncle; 1 Sam. 14:50).

Ishbosheth, whose name means "the man of shame," was forty years old when he began to reign over Israel. He ruled for two years before being murdered by his servants (v. 10). His older brother Jonathan would have been in his early forties when he was smitten by the Philistines five years earlier. Saul was a man of the flesh, meaning that Ishbosheth was an extension of the same system which opposed the mind of God and His anointed – David.

Although the writer will describe the ensuing civil war in a moment, he paused to summarize David's reign in Hebron. David was king over Judah seven years and six months before being recognized as Israel's king (5:1-5). Although he was God's anointed king of Israel, David did not force the matter. He did not send messengers throughout Israel demanding that the people swear their allegiance to him or else! Rather, David was content to wait on the Lord's timing to resolve the matter of Israel's loyalty. Apparently, for the first five years in Judah, David was able to avoid conflict with a rival leader altogether. Nonetheless, that was all about to change.

Civil War (vv. 12-32)

Abner and the servants of Ishbosheth departed from Mahanaim to the pool of Gibeon where they met Joab and some of David's servants (vv. 12-13). Abner would have been at least thirty years older than Joab and consequently was the more battle-hardened of the two leaders. Abner had led Saul's army for over thirty years and had actually survived the massacre in the Jezreel Valley which ended Saul's life.

Abner must have been the one who chose Gibeon (his hometown; 1 Chron. 8:29-30) as the site for this parley with Joab. He would have been intimately familiar with the region; plus it was in Benjamin's territory, and near to Saul's hometown. This meant there would be a good number of Ishbosheth sympathizers nearby. The two factions set opposite each other on either side of the pool of Gibeon; apparently, neither side wanted to instigate a war with their brethren.

The silence was broken when Abner suggested that the best young men from both sides should compete against each other to prove whether Israel or Judah possessed the better warriors (v. 14). Joab agreed to this contest and twelve Benjamites (followers of Ishbosheth) engaged twelve of David's servants (v. 15). This entire event was of the flesh, conceived in the flesh and engaged in the flesh – both the Lord and David are completely absent from the scene. What is of the flesh ends in destruction, so it is of little wonder that what began as a sporting event quickly turned into a bloody fiasco.

Each participant attempted to grab his opponent's beard while at the same time thrusting his sword into his victim's body (v. 16). The conflict ended in a draw with all the men dying of their wounds, hence the place was named "the Field of Sharp Swords." Because the matter was of the flesh, the cause of David is not advanced by this struggle, but rather twenty-four fellow brethren lay dead! There was nothing of God or for God accomplished at Gibeon.

May we learn the lesson illustrated for us here: the cause of Christ cannot be advanced in our own strength and wisdom, but rather only by resting in Him in heavenly places (Eph. 2:6). David, God's anointed in Hebron, was absent from this struggle and would have never endorsed it; thus, the conflict lacked God's blessing and ended in sorrow. If Christ is not in our labors, all that we do is in vain, and often results in shame being attached to His name.

With no clear victor, the championship did not terminate the rivalry, but rather the shedding of blood served to inflame vicious passions on both sides which escalated the fight. An all-out confrontation ensued, which soon turned Abner's men on their heels as they fled from David's servants (v. 17). David's three nephews, Joab, Abishai, and Asahel, were all in the fray. These were the sons of David's sister Zeruiah (2 Sam. 2:13; 1 Chron. 2:16). The youngest of the three, Asahel, was exceptionally fast on his feet; he was likened to a wild gazelle (v. 18).

Because of family ties, the sons of Zeruiah attempted to claim rank in David's kingdom according to the flesh, but in actuality they had no claim at all. When David's mighty men are later listed in chapter 23, we find that Abishai did not attain to the "first three," and that Asahel was listed among "the thirty," although he died at a young age. Though brave and clever, and the leader of David's army, the third brother, Joab, is not named among David's mighty men. No doubt his self-willed, often cruel ambitions and his deceitful ways negated such an honor. Joab served David as it best served himself.

Returning to the narrative, Asahel pursued Abner relentlessly (v. 19). After Abner verified that it was Asahel chasing him, he told the young Asahel to turn aside and be satisfied with capturing one of his younger soldiers (v. 20). However, Asahel continued after Israel's general, who pleaded a second time with Asahel to *"lay hold on one of the young men and take his armor for yourself."* In other words, he should take a lower ranking soldier as a prisoner. Abner told Asahel that he did not want to kill him, for that would only further antagonize Joab against him (v. 22). Abner's superior strength and battle experience would be no match for the young warrior, despite all Asahel's zeal and speed. But Asahel remained undeterred from his glory-seeking quest, so Abner impaled him through the stomach with the blunt end of his spear. Asahel died almost immediately. Some of David's men who had been chasing the Benjamites were utterly stunned by the gory sight. Instead of continuing the chase, they just stood over Asahel and gaped at his corpse (v. 23).

Asahel's two brothers, Joab and Abishai, who did not know what had happened to their brother, did not pause from pursuing Abner as he fled eastward from Gibeon. As the sun was going down they had traveled all the way to the hill of Ammah, which was about half the distance between Gibeon and Jericho (i.e., about 8 miles east of Gibeon; v. 24).

The Benjamites following Abner regrouped on the hill of Ammah and Abner reformed their lines (v. 25). This was a strong defensive position, so Abner called out to Joab, *"Shall the sword devour forever? Do you not know that it will be bitter in the latter end? How long will it be then until you tell the people to return from pursuing their brethren?"* (v. 26). In other words, "enough is enough; you are the victor this day; let the conflict end without invoking bitterness, for we are all brethren." He was the one who had foolishly instigated the jest of combat which led to the deaths of twenty-four young men. But he now seems shocked by the outcome of that original sporting event, especially since he was on the losing side and his life was being threatened. Matthew Henry comments on Abner's abrupt change of heart in the conflict:

> How easy it is for men to use reason when it assists them who would not use it if was against them. If Abner had been the conqueror, he would not have been complaining of the voraciousness of the sword and the miseries of a civil war, nor pleading that both sides were brethren. But, finding himself beaten, all these reasonings are mustered up and improved for the securing of his retreat and the saving of his scattered troops from being cut off. How the issue of things alters men's minds. The same thing which looked pleasant in the morning at night looked dismal.[111]

Abner's foolish suggestion had backfired on him, proving the wisdom of the proverb: *"Go not forth hastily to strive, lest thou know not what to do in the end thereof, when thy neighbor hath put thee to shame"* (Prov. 25:8). Given David's aversion to shedding the blood of his countrymen, Joab had likely been ordered to take a defensive posture in his interaction with Abner. But since Joab had been provoked into the fight by Abner (v. 14), he was ready to pursue Abner and his men all night if necessary. But knowing the king's mind on the matter, he wisely heeded Abner's plea, no doubt partly because of his higher-ground position (v. 27). Joab blew his trumpet to signal his men to withdraw from the chase and regroup (v. 28). T. Wilson observes:

> Three times we read of Joab blowing the trumpet to avoid unnecessary slaughter, and each of them in connection with an opponent of David. The opponents were: Abner (2:28), Absalom (18:16) and Sheba (20:22). This time it allowed Abner, by forced march overnight, to reach Mahanaim before the news of Asahel's death reached Joab's ears.[112]

Though exhausted, Abner did not take any chances; he knew that Joab would probably seek revenge and renew his attack after learning that he had killed his younger brother. Abner and his men therefore journeyed northeastward all night. They crossed the Jordan River and traveled all the way to Mahanaim, Ishbosheth's capital city (v. 29). The location of Mahanaim is believed to be about ten miles east of the Jordan River and near the Jabbok River. If this placement is correct,

Abner and his men in one day journeyed over 45 miles total to escape
David's troops under Joab's leadership.

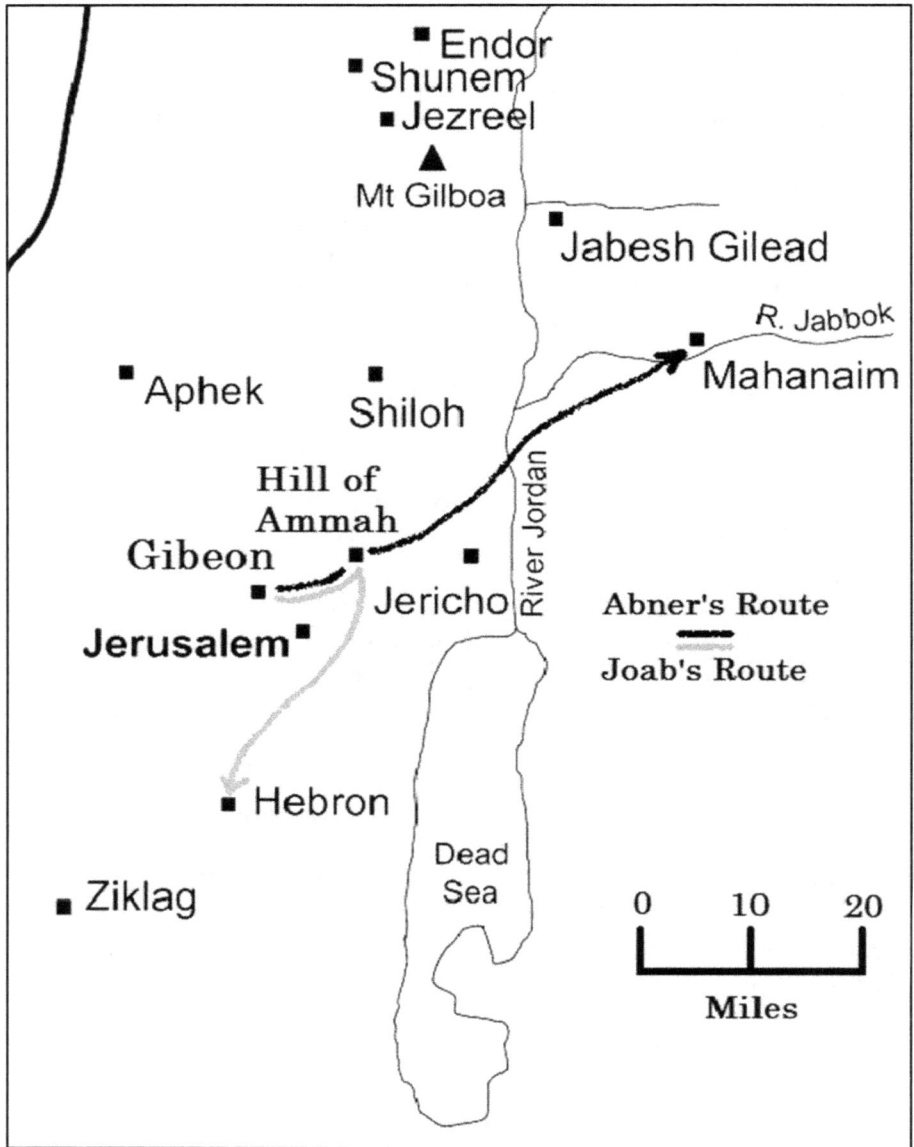

Joab numbered his men after they were reassembled; including
Asahel, a total of twenty men had perished in the confrontation (v. 30).

Abner and his Benjamites sustained a much higher number of casualties; 360 men were lost (v. 31). Not wanting to remain in hostile territory, Joab and his men traveled through the night back to Hebron, arriving there at daybreak. Their total trek from Gibeon to the Hill of Ammah, and then through the rugged terrain to Hebron was approximately 33 miles. Astoundingly, by the next morning after the altercation, the two factions were sixty miles apart.

Asahel was buried in his father's tomb, which was at Bethlehem (v. 32). It is unknown how his body was moved from Gibeon to Bethlehem. Regrettably much death and mourning will mark Israel's violent struggle over the next two years before everyone would honor God's anointed as king. The Lord's beloved David must be seated on the throne in Jerusalem for Israel to enjoy God's peace. Likewise, the earth will continue to suffer the ill-effects of sin, such as sorrow, pestilence, injustice, poverty, and death until the Greater David, God's beloved Son, sits on the throne of Israel in Jerusalem. When the Lord Jesus Christ has His rightful place in Israel, then the Jewish nation will finally be at peace and the entire planet will benefit from His glorious kingdom.

Meditation

When the King of kings triumphantly returns from heaven above,
He will reign on earth supreme wielding power framed in love,
Sickness, sadness, wars, and famines will forever cease,
And Israel, with all the nations, will enjoy everlasting peace.

— W.A.H.

David Increases as Saul Diminishes
2 Samuel 3

David's Power and Family Expand (vv. 1-5)

During the next two years there was persistent warring between the house of Saul and the house of David, *"but David grew stronger and stronger, and the house of Saul grew weaker and weaker"* (v. 1). This is a reminder that God's means of recompensing evil and establishing His Word are not always prompt, but are sure nonetheless.

As a young man, David had endured Saul's reckless evil spirit in Gibeah for about seven years. Then, for the next eight years David was a fugitive, followed by the rejection and rebellion of the northern tribes for another seven years. Through these years of harsh trials, David had learned what James later wrote to be true: *"Knowing that the testing of your faith produces patience. But let patience have its perfect work, that you may be perfect and complete, lacking nothing"* (Jas. 1:2-4). David lived to be seventy years old, meaning that he spent about one third of his life enduring hardships resulting from the envy, injustice and treachery of others. Consequently, David could genuinely encourage others to *"wait on the Lord; be of good courage, and He shall strengthen your heart; wait, I say, on the Lord!"* (Ps. 27:14).

After arriving at Hebron, David took four more wives (for a total of six) and his family quickly expanded. Although there may have been daughters born to him, six sons are mentioned. The firstborn was Amnon by Ahinoam; the second, Chileab by Abigail; the third, Absalom by Maacah; the fourth, Adonijah by Haggith; the fifth, Shephatiah by Abital; and the sixth, Ithream, by Eglah (vv. 2-5).

Perhaps the writer included the birth of David's six sons to highlight that his strength was on the rise, whereas, Saul had lost three of his four sons, and his house was diminishing. With that said, David is acting independent from God and following his own will in his family life. God's will and God's word are the same; Moses had warned future kings not to multiply wives to themselves (Deut. 17:17).

As discussed in 1 Samuel 1, polygamy was a departure from God's original design for marriage of one man and one woman for life. David sets a bad example to his successors in two ways: polygamy and marrying a foreigner.

David's marriage to Maacah, the daughter of Talmai, the king of Geshur (a state in the Aramean kingdom), was likely to strength his interests. But Jewish men were not permitted to marry foreign women, lest Jewish families suffer spiritual corruption (Deut. 7:13; Ezra 9:1-11; Neh. 10:31). Though it seems unlikely, it is possible that Maacah had been captured in a raid and David chose to take her as a wife per the allowance of Deuteronomy 10:10-13, but she would have been a pagan nonetheless. David's error in marrying a foreigner become obvious later as the union produced Absalom, who brought shame to David's house. Absalom raped his half-sister Tamar and later nearly succeeded in stealing the kingdom from David.

David also took several concubines who bore him many children (1 Chron. 3:9). Though Scripture does not advocate the wife of second degree (i.e., a concubine), such unions were common in the Ancient East. Unfortunately, both of David's mistakes (marrying foreigners and polygamy) were repeated by the next king of Israel, Solomon. Tragically, his many foreign wives prompted him to worship their false gods and anger the Lord.

As David had learned and would learn again, independence from God always leads His people into trouble. Likewise, Christians would do well to heed Paul's instructions to marry only in the Lord (1 Cor. 7:39) so that husbands and wives will not be spiritually unequally yoked together (2 Cor. 6:14). A child of the devil and a child of God have nothing in common, which means their relationship can result only in trouble.

Abner Defects to David (vv. 6-39)

During the civil war, Abner's fame and position in the house of Saul became strong, meaning that Ishbosheth was basically a puppet-king (v. 6). Ishbosheth apparently resented the arrangement because he publicly challenged Abner for having sexual relations with Rizpah, one of Saul's concubines. In his mind, the act disrespected his father's memory. Whether the offense was true or not, the narrative does not say. If the accusation was true, Saul's son may have believed that

Abner was trying to take control of the kingdom by the indiscretion (v. 7). In either case, Ishbosheth's lack of prudence insulted Abner.

Given all that Abner had done to establish Ishbosheth in Israel and to protect him from David, making a public spectacle of Abner over a woman was indeed foolish (v. 8). Abner never denied the charge (which probably meant that he was guilty), but rather addresses the matter of his loyalty. Abner asks Ishbosheth, *"Am I a dog's head that belongs to Judah?"* This statement implied that he was not a worthless traitor; in fact, he had never shown loyalty to Judah in the past. Abner then pledged to Ishbosheth that he would tirelessly labor to ensure that what God had sworn to David would be realized – the transfer of the kingdom from the house of Saul to David (vv. 9-10). Ishbosheth was stunned by Abner's vow and could not answer him because he feared his formidable general (v. 11).

Abner then sent messengers to David confirming that he should be king over all of Israel and also Abner's desire to enter into a peace covenant with David (v. 12). David agreed on the condition that Saul's daughter, Michal, David's rightful wife, be returned to him (v. 13). After David became a fugitive, Saul gave Michal to Paltiel in marriage, which was against the Law and constituted adultery. The matter may have been brought to Ishbosheth's attention already, but he had not responded to David's request. About fifteen years had passed since David knew Michal as his wife.

David reminded Abner that he had paid a high price for her – the lives of a hundred Philistines (v. 14). The purpose of David's request appears to be more about testing Abner's commitment than getting Michal for himself, as their interaction afterwards was frosty, to say the least. Through Abner's influence, Ishbosheth ordered that Michal should be taken from Paltiel (who resided at Gallim) and be returned to David at Hebron (v. 15). This also furnished Abner a legitimate and timely opportunity to journey to Hebron to speak with David about a peace treaty. A weeping Paltiel followed Michal for about three miles (Bahurim was about three miles northeast of Jerusalem) before Abner commanded him to return home, which he did (v. 16).

Abner then used his influence to rally the northern tribes to David by reminding them that David had been their choice for king previously (v. 17). He also affirmed that David was also God's choice for Israel: *"By the hand of My servant David, I will save My people Israel from the hand of the Philistines and the hand of all their enemies"* (vv. 17-

18). Abner, with twenty of his men, then appeared before David in Hebron to confirm that all Israel was ready to acknowledge his rule (v. 19). David made a feast to welcome Abner and his men (v. 20). After the feast Abner proclaimed, *"I will arise and go, and gather all Israel to my lord the king, that they may make a covenant with you, and that you may reign over all that your heart desires"* (v. 21). This plan pleased David who sent Abner away with his blessing and in peace.

Joab Murders Abner (vv. 22-30)

Shortly after Abner had peacefully departed Hebron, Joab and his men returned from a profitable raid (v. 22). After learning of the new covenant between David and Abner, Joab complained to David that he had been deceived by Abner, who only came to Hebron to spy out David's defenses (vv. 23-25). The king did not change his mind. However, Joab sent messengers after Abner requesting, in David's name, that he return to Hebron (v. 26). David was completely unaware of Joab's scheme to avenge his younger brother Asahel's death.

The messengers found Abner and his men at the well of Sirah (about a mile northwest of Hebron) and after delivering the message, Abner and his men returned to Hebron as requested. Joab greeted Abner at the city gate and took him aside privately where he stabbed Abner in the stomach and he died. Joab had avenged Asahel's death (v. 27). However, the author reminds us that Joab had no right to revenge because Asahel had died in battle; Abner had not murdered him (v. 30).

Ironically, Hebron was a City of Refuge (Num. 35:22-25) which made Joab's crime doubly wrong – Abner was entitled to a fair trial to decide the matter, but was not granted one. Furthermore, Joab openly and without shame settled his revenge at the gate of the city, the place where justice was to be ministered. He deceitfully murdered a man while under a covenant of peace, against his king's wishes, in a City of Refuge and at the seat of civil justice. What mockery of God's authority and righteousness! It is therefore no surprise that David, after learning of Joab's crime, publicly pronounced a severe curse on Joab:

My kingdom and I are guiltless before the Lord forever of the blood of Abner the son of Ner. Let it rest on the head of Joab and on all his father's house; and let there never fail to be in the house of Joab one who has a discharge or is a leper, who leans on a staff or falls by the sword, or who lacks bread (vv. 28-30).

David condemnation requested that Joab's descendants would consistently suffer: illness, leprosy, lameness, death by slaughter or in battle, and abject poverty for generations to come. Besides the sorrow and pain of death, disease, and starvation, to have an ongoing discharge meant that a Jew was ceremonially unclean and could not appear before the Lord (Lev. 15).

Joab was an ambitious man seeking to advance himself in David's kingdom. As shown in the narrative, he will support a righteous cause or oppose an unrighteous cause to the degree that it agrees with his own interests. Joab was a stranger to the life of faith that his king enjoyed; therefore, his leadership of David's army could only run counter to David's rule. David should have executed Joab, but did not. That mistake would cost the king much later, as it was Joab who brought back David's rebellious son Absalom to Jerusalem. H. L. Rossier characterizes the type of man Joab was:

> Nothing stops him; he has no scruples in satisfying his ambition. Someone has said of him: "We find Joab wherever there is evil to do or much to gain." Joab is a figure of political flesh. It is to his advantage to support David's cause. If we compare Abner with Joab, Abner is the better man. Nevertheless, Joab comes on the scene as a *champion of the testimony*. [But as we know] the moment the flesh takes over the testimony, see the result: ruin, nothing but ruin. One man is fighting for David and the other for one whom God no longer recognizes. Is one better than the other? When the flesh is supporting David – or Christ – the results are no better than when the flesh is supporting the Antichrist.[113]

Both Joab and Abner were carnal men; the former is on the right side concerning the kingdom, while the latter holds more integrity, but still acts against his conscience to oppose God's man. Can there be any doubt as to why this narrative is besmirched by acts of pride, envy, deceit, and murder – these are deeds of the flesh (Gal. 5:19-21) and both men are of the flesh.

David's Mourns for Abner (vv. 31-39)

Not wanting to see a civil war continue, David commanded Joab and his men to tear their clothes, to gird themselves with sackcloth, and to mourn Abner's death (v. 31). David even followed the coffin in the funeral procession. Abner was buried with honor in Hebron and all the people, including the king, wept at Abner's grave (v. 32). David then sang a lament over Abner: *"Should Abner die as a fool dies? Your hands were not bound nor your feet put into fetters; as a man falls before wicked men, so you fell"* (vv. 33-34).What does David mean when he said Abner died "as a fool?" The Hebrew word translated "fool" is *nabal*, also used to identify Abigail's first husband whom the Lord struck down because of his malicious foolishness. The same word is translated "the vile person" twice in Isaiah (Isa. 32:5-6). As T. Wilson explains, this is the idea conveyed by David's usage of *nabal* in his song:

> This word [*nabal*] does not concern weakness of the mind, nor is it related to inappropriate behavior. It is a word related to that used for one who "brought folly in Israel" (Gen. 34:7). "Folly in Israel was the most reprehensible kind of folly, because it was the desecration of an ideal," comments Strahan. It describes someone with no conscience, whose "sin is dark in proportion to the glory of the religion which it violates ... The shameless person who committed folly in Israel was a profligate who defiled what was sacred to the Lord." ... Abner died as an outcast or criminal in chains might have died. The best translation of the noun is probably "profane" or "ungodly."[114]

David lamented both Abner's death and the manner of it; he died as an ungodly person should and he did not deserve that. By his statement, David confirmed the unjust nature of Abner's death – he was a victim of wicked deceitfulness.

To show his brokenness over Abner's death, David refused to eat. He even uttered an oath that he would not eat until after the sun set (v. 35). All Israel took note of and approved of David's behavior and were satisfied that the king had nothing to do with Abner's murder (vv. 36-37). The chapter closes with the king praising Abner as a great man and rebuking the harsh sons of Zeruiah for their treachery and foretelling that the Lord would repay them for their wickedness (vv. 38-39). And He would!

Whether David's grief over Abner's death was legitimate or not, we do not know. However, the way in which the king humbled himself to honor Israel's fallen general stayed further hostilities and secured the kingdom for David. This chapter illustrates the many instabilities and ills caused by the flesh when those who identify with God do not rest in Him and His will.

Meditation

God may allow His servant to succeed when He has disciplined him to a point where he does not need to succeed to be happy. The man who is elated by success and is cast down by failure is still a carnal man. At best his fruit will have a worm in it.

— A. W. Tozer

Carnal Christians tend to show off their differences and superiorities in clothing, speech or deeds. They desire to shock people into recognizing all their undertakings. ... Carnal believers are moved easily. On one occasion they may be extremely excited and happy; on another occasion, very despondent and sad. In the happy moment they judge the world too small to contain them, and so they soar on wings to the heavens; but in the moment of sadness they conclude that the world has had enough of them and will be glad to be rid of them... their lives are susceptible to constant changes, for they are governed by their emotions.

— Watchman Nee

Ishbosheth Is Murdered
2 Samuel 4

Saul's son Ishbosheth was distressed with all Israel after hearing of Abner's death at Hebron (v. 1). The historian pauses to introduce us to Jonathan's son Mephibosheth, who was five years old when his father died (about seven years earlier). After hearing of the tragedy at Jezreel and fearing that the Philistines would slaughter all the civilians, Mephibosheth's nurse had picked him up in haste, but the lad fell and became lame in both his feet (v. 4).

The introduction of Jonathan's lame son in a section of narrative detailing Ishbosheth's murder seems out of place. With the last of Saul's sons soon to be dead, the writer may have mentioned young and crippled Mephibosheth (the only remaining male heir of Saul) to show that restoring a descendant to Saul's throne was a hopeless cause. David would be Israel's new king and would have a lasting dynasty as promised.

We are also introduced to two captains in Israel's army, Baanah and Rechab, who were sons of Rimmon the Beerothite (vv. 2-3). Beeroth was previously a Gibeonite city in Benjamin's territory (Josh. 9:17). Why Rimmon fled with his family from Gath and came to Beeroth is unknown. During one hot afternoon, these two came into the king's house pretending to get a supply of wheat, and stabbed the king to death while he was resting on his bed (vv. 5-6). Barnes supposes that the Beerothites were originally Canaanites living in the region, meaning that Baanah and Rechab might have killed Ishbosheth to avenge Saul's massacre of the Gibeonites, their countrymen, whom they dwelt with (21:1-2).[115]

The two brothers then cut off Ishbosheth's head, escaped, and traveled throughout the night to bring their bloody token of triumph to the king of Judah at Hebron (v. 7). They boasted of their accomplishment to David and declared that the Lord had avenged him of Saul and his descendants (v. 8).

After listening to the two pompous murderers, David addressed Rechab and Baanah, but not in the way they were expecting:

As the Lord lives, who has redeemed my life from all adversity, when someone told me, saying, "Look, Saul is dead," thinking to have brought good news, I arrested him and had him executed in Ziklag – the one who thought I would give him a reward for his news. How much more, when wicked men have killed a righteous person in his own house on his bed? Therefore, shall I not now require his blood at your hand and remove you from the earth? (vv. 9-11).

Rechab and Baanah would receive no reward for murdering an innocent man in his own house (his sanctuary per se) and while completely defenseless – asleep on his bed. Rather, they would reap David's righteous indignation. The king commanded his young men to execute the two brothers, then to cut off their hands and feet and hang them by the pool in Hebron (v. 12).

The display of their mutilated bodies would publicly declare David's disclaim for their crime in murdering Israel's king and his complete innocence in the matter. All Israel would know that David was completely opposed to the annihilation of the house of Saul. Rechab and Baanah certainly deserved death, but we wonder why Joab did not receive the same decisive judgment for an equally appalling crime (i.e., murdering an innocent man). Ishbosheth's head was buried in Abner's tomb at Hebron.

Meditation

Justice without force is powerless; force without justice is tyrannical.

— Blaise Pascal

David King Over Israel
2 Samuel 5

David Reigns Over All Israel (vv. 1-5)

After David had reigned for seven and a half years over Judah, all the tribes of Israel gathered at Hebron to recognize him as king over the entire Jewish nation. The northern tribes proclaimed to David:

> *Indeed we are your bone and your flesh. Also, in time past, when Saul was king over us, you were the one who led Israel out and brought them in; and the Lord said to you, "You shall shepherd My people Israel, and be ruler over Israel" (v. 2).*

The elders of Israel made a covenant with David at Hebron and anointed him king over Israel (v. 3). David was thirty years old when he began to reign over Judah in Hebron; he would now reign over the entire nation in Jerusalem for the next thirty-three years (vv. 4-5). David would be 37 or 38 years old when this event occurred.

Recognizing God's Shepherds

This portion of Scripture provides a lovely three-step process for recognizing those God has called to oversee his people as shepherds. Teaching gift and leadership ability are qualities easily recognized because of their obvious blessing to the local assembly; however, identifying those men with shepherd hearts requires more discernment. The fact is that many male teachers, exhorters, counselors, and administrators are not called to be shepherds, or to the more specific office of eldership. Just because a brother can wonderfully expound God's Word does not mean that he is an elder. Likewise, a successful businessman may have no shepherding aptitude whatsoever. If skill and success are not criteria, how can a local assembly be sure to appoint a man that God has called to be an elder?

The Bible records many spectacular and specific calls of God's people into various ministries, some by the Lord Himself. Should believers expect a voice from heaven, a vision, or a prophetic utterance to confirm God's calling for their lives? During the early days of the Church Age, prophets were given to the Church as a check against false teachers – they confirmed the oral transmission of the Word of God by the apostles before it was written down. Since believers have a divine anointing to understand truth (1 Jn. 2:20, 27) and the Word of God is now complete (Jude 3; 1 Cor. 13:9-10), modern Christians should not expect prophetic confirmations of ministry, at least in the normative sense. God may reveal Himself directly, but He should not be expected to do so.

Furthermore, the book of Acts, through its record of early Church history, reveals a clear transition from "apostles" to "apostles and elders" to just "elders" (speaking of local church leaders). All of this is to say that today we should not expect a specific revelation to confirm God's calling for us in ministry. Practically speaking, how would you know a supernatural sign or a prophetic utterance was from God, anyway? It might be from the devil to lead you astray. Moreover, we tend to read into situations that which we want to be true.

Rather than waiting for some supernatural sign to divinely confirm church elders, it seems wise to be guided by the scriptural pattern that God uses to recognize leadership. In the life of David, for example, three distinct stages of affirmation of his call as the leader of Israel are recorded in verses 1-3.

The southern kingdom (Judah) had recognized David as their king seven years earlier; thus David had been reigning over them in Hebron. Now the northern kingdom of Israel had decided to anoint David as their king also. What led them to this decision? First, they recognized that David had a divine calling; he had been personally selected by God for the purpose of ruling over them. Second, they recognized that it was David who had led them in the practical affairs of the nation even when Saul was king. Understanding this, they prudently recognized David as their king. David had a divine call, an internal call (i.e. he had an internal compulsion to do the work of leading), and then he was recognized by all.

When God places a divine call on a person, with time and with proper spiritual maturity this calling becomes actively lived out in his or her life and others take notice. A believer often gains a sense of where he or she is going in ministry long before it happens – in some respects this can be a bit unsettling and may result in anxiety. In time, others will recognize what God is doing and will verify the believer's call to service.

This three-stage process of calling is the same for church elders: the Holy Spirit calls (appoints) them (Acts 20:28), the internal call is shown by active, selfless service (1 Tim. 3:1), and eventually the serving shepherd will be morally and spiritual scrutinized according to the requirements of Titus 1 and 1 Timothy 3 and then be publicly recognized as an elder. If a brother with a blameless testimony just cannot keep from doing shepherding work in the assembly, and is marked by faithfulness despite the personal cost to himself, he is likely God's man. The man who cries "Pick me" is most assuredly not God's choice. Rather, God's man respects the office and is often leery of the responsibility because he can already identify with the work and the cost of doing it.

Those who are elders and those who may be recognized as elders are not perfect men, but they should be blameless brothers of high moral standards and character. A prospective elder who is drawn to shepherding work and exhibits the qualities of 1 Timothy 3:1-7 is most likely the man that God has raised up *from among His sheep* (Acts 20:28) to be *shepherds among His sheep* (1 Pet. 5:1). Recognizing in haste a man whom God has not called will be one of the most painful mistakes an assembly can make. However, engaging in prayer and careful observation, while waiting on the Lord to make it obvious to everyone will be the safe approach in recognizing those He has called to shepherd. Likewise, David was called by God to shepherd, was shepherding God's people, and then was recognized by everyone as God's shepherd for Israel.

The Conquest of Jerusalem (vv. 6-16)

Now that the tribes of Israel were united under one king, David recognized that the seat of government must be further north than Hebron, but not too far from Judah. With this in mind, David set his sights on capturing the stronghold at Zion (Jerusalem) in Benjamin's territory, which the Jebusites had occupied for centuries. Of the five high places in which the future city of Jerusalem would be built (Zion, Akra, Bezetha, Moriah, and Ophel), only Zion to the south was

251

inhabited at this time. The Jebusites' fortification there was so impregnable that they taunted David by saying they could put blind and lame on the wall battlements to keep him out (v. 6).

Although the Jebusites did not believe that David could overcome them, he conquered their fortification and renamed it "the City of David" (v. 7). The writer even chronicles how David accomplished this. The king discerned that the underground shaft supplying water to the city was vulnerable to attack, so he put out a challenge to his men: *"Whoever climbs up by way of the water shaft and defeats the Jebusites (the lame and the blind, who are hated by David's soul), he shall be chief and captain"* (v. 8).

Apparently, a small group of David's men (led by Joab; 1 Chron. 11:6) were able to navigate the water shaft, enter the city undetected, and open the gates to allow David's main force to access the city. Unfortunately, this accomplishment earned carnal Joab the privilege of leading David's army. Interestingly, the Jebusites' sarcasm about their "blind and lame" defeating David became a proverb of David's when speaking of his overconfident enemies.

After the victory, David moved from Hebron to the City of David. He began fortifying his new stronghold by leveling and filling in areas between the hills (Zion and Ophel) and then erecting retaining walls and embankments to protect the city, especially from the Jebusites in the north (v. 9). Jamieson, Fausset, and Brown describe David's construction efforts:

> David built round about from [the] Millo and inward – probably a row of stone bastions placed on the northern side of Mount Zion, and built by David to secure himself on that side from the Jebusites, who still lived in the lower part of the city. The house of Millo was, perhaps, the principal corner-tower of that fortified wall. Such was the small beginning of Jerusalem.[116]

David had accomplished what no Jew had been able to do since Israel entered Canaan under Joshua's leadership – remove the Jebusites from Zion (Josh. 15:63). The feat gained him much renown throughout Israel – everyone knew that *"the Lord God of hosts was with him"* (v. 10).

Besides Jerusalem being the central location for Israel's throne, Zion and the surrounding area has special significance to the Lord throughout Scripture. The Lord told Abraham to go to a specific mountain in the land of Moriah (Jerusalem) and to offer his only son Isaac whom he loved as a burnt sacrifice (Gen. 22). A millennium later, David would offer a burnt sacrifice to God on Mount Moriah to halt a judgment of pestilence against Israel (2 Sam. 24; 1 Chron. 21). A generation afterwards, his son Solomon would build a spectacular temple at that same location where the Lord had appeared to David when he offered the sacrifice to avert the plague (2 Chron. 3:1). Another millennium later, the Lord Jesus Christ would be tried and crucified on or near Mount Moriah. In a future millennium, the Lord Jesus will reign from this location in a new temple, which will then be honored as the religious capital of the world (Zech. 14:16-17).

Seeing all that God would accomplish at Jerusalem, it is no surprise then that His heart is attached to that place:

For the Lord has chosen Zion; He has desired it for His dwelling place: "This is My resting place forever; here I will dwell, for I have desired it (Ps. 132:13-14).

His foundation is in the holy mountains. The Lord loves the gates of Zion more than all the dwellings of Jacob. Glorious things are spoken of you, O city of God! (Ps. 87:1-2).

Jerusalem is where God's throne of grace will be established on earth. There His Son's name will be vindicated and He will reign supreme over all the nations!

Seeing David's military aptitude, Hiram, the king of Tyre wanted to secure peace with David. His good intentions were demonstrated by supplying cedar trees, carpenters, and masons for the construction of David's new city (v. 11). The long years of Philistine oppression had left Israel with a short supply of craftsmen and masons, so Hiram's assistance was greatly appreciated. God was supplying everything that David needed to establish his kingdom and David was excited to see the Lord honor His promise to him. The new king realized that his position was not for his own honor, but rather he had been divinely appointed to be king for the good of Israel (v. 12).

Unfortunately, David took more concubines and wives after moving from Hebron to Jerusalem. More wives also meant more sons and daughters, so the writer paused to list the names of some of the males born to David in Jerusalem: Shammua, Shobab, Nathan, Solomon, Ibhar, Elishua, Nepheg, Japhia, Elishama, Eliada, and Eliphelet (vv. 13-16). This listing is understood to be a historical summary, as Solomon, for example, would not be born for several years (12:24).

Given the amount of Bible prophecy that centers in the city of Jerusalem, we may wonder why the tribe of Judah chose to dwell peaceably with the Jebusites for five centuries, rather than driving them out of that city as demanded by the Lord in the days of Joshua (Josh. 15:63; Judg. 1:21). That question is answered in this chapter. David, who pictures the coming Messiah in so many ways, was the only one who could capture the city. The former Jebusite stronghold was renamed to the City of David and became the capital of Israel. In time, Jerusalem would expand north and west from the original City of David, and God's temple would be constructed just north of the Hill of Ophel on Mount Moriah (Neh. 3:26).

Isaiah and Zechariah inform us that when Messiah returns to the earth to establish His kingdom, He will rule from Jerusalem (Isa. 66:10-21; Zech. 14:8-21). In a coming day, a descendant of David, the Lord Jesus Christ, will return to Jerusalem, and when He does, He will rule all men forevermore (7:16-17; Ps. 89:34-36).

The Philistines Defeated (vv. 17-25)

During the years of Israel's civil war, the Philistines were content to let the Jews kill each other, rather than giving them a reason to unify by attacking the Jewish state. However, after David became king over all the tribes, the Philistines moved quickly to attack before David could get his government and army fully established. So the Philistines began searching to find David's location (v. 17). After hearing this news, David retreated to his stronghold at the cave of Adullam (1 Chron. 11:15) and inquired of the Lord if he should engage the Philistines who had gathered against him in the Valley of Rephaim, west of Jerusalem (v. 18).

This is when three of David's mighty men broke through the enemy's lines to fetch David a drink of water from the well of Bethlehem after discerning what would delight their king (1 Chron. 11:16-19). Because they jeopardized their lives to bring him the water, David could not drink it, but poured it out on the ground to the Lord.

The Lord answered David's request and instructed him to fight the Philistines, for He would ensure his victory (v. 19).

After learning that the Lord would be fighting his enemy for him, David engaged the Philistines at Baal Perazim and was triumphant (v. 20). David was quick to give the Lord the credit for the achievement: *"The Lord has broken through my enemies before me, like a breakthrough of water"* (v. 20). The suddenness of Israel's attack caught the Philistines off guard, which meant that they had no time to collect their images. Adam Clarke writes: "It was the custom of most nations to carry their gods with them to battle. In imitation of this custom the Israelites once took the ark and lost it in the field (1 Sam. 4)."[117] David's men collected the abandoned images and destroyed them by fire (v. 21; Deut. 7:5, 25; 1 Chron. 14:12). The victory then was not just over the Philistines, but also over their gods. For that reason, David named the place "Baal Perazim" meaning Baal is broken.

After their first defeat, the Philistines deployed a second time in the Valley of Rephaim (v. 22). Again, David inquired of the Lord as to what he should do. The Lord answered David:

You shall not go up; circle around behind them, and come upon them in front of the mulberry trees. And it shall be, when you hear the sound of marching in the tops of the mulberry trees, then you shall advance quickly. For then the Lord will go out before you to strike the camp of the Philistines (vv. 23-24).

The mulberry trees may have actually been aspen, poplar, or balsam trees, which rustle with the slightest movement and are found in many of the ravines of southern Palestine. The idea seems to be that the Philistines expected David's attack to be a frontal assault from the south, but God directed him to place his troops on the northern side of the valley. As the Philistines marched by the edge of the tree groves, God would cause a sound to be heard that they would believe to be an army marching against them from the south. For the Philistines it was an army they could not see, but for David, it was God on the march and his signal to begin attacking his enemy's flank and rear guard.

The sound of marching ahead and David's sudden assault from behind panicked the enemy's ranks and David routed the Philistines. Because David did exactly what the Lord commanded him to do, the Philistines from Geba (Gibeon) were driven back to Gezer (v. 25). The

Philistines were now completely removed from the Judean highlands. When the Lord fights for His people, no power on earth or in high places can oppose them!

Meditation

Jerusalem, lift up thy voice!
Daughter of Zion, now rejoice!
Thy King is come, whose mighty hand
Henceforth shall reign over every land.

He comes to every tribe and race,
A Messenger of truth and grace:
With peace He comes from heaven above
On earth to found His realm of love.

Let all the world with one accord
Now hail the coming of the Lord:
Praise to the Prince of heavenly birth
Who bringeth peace to all the earth.

— Johan O. Wallin

The Ark Comes to Jerusalem
2 Samuel 6

The Right Thing the Wrong Way (vv. 1-11)

Other than a passing reference in 1 Samuel 14, we have not heard anything about the Ark of the Lord since it was brought to Abinadab's home about seventy years earlier (see 1 Sam. 7 discussion of timing). David selected thirty thousand choice men to accompany him to "Baale Judah" to bring the Ark of *"the Lord of Hosts, who dwells between the cherubim"* back to the City of David (vv. 1-2). Baale Judah was situated on a hill about ten miles west of the City of David. The city is also known as Kirjath-Baal (Josh. 15:60) and Kirjath-Jearim (1 Sam. 6:21).

The Ark was carried out of Abinadab's home and put on a new cart (v. 3). Despite the emotional hype of this occasion, this is our first indication that trouble was ahead. David should have known God's thoughts concerning the transport of His Ark and have acted on them. But instead, he permits those serving God to adopt the ways of the world in the matter (i.e., to repeat the method the Philistines used to return the Ark to Israel years earlier). The Philistines were not judged for their actions, because they were not Jehovah's covenant people and did not know better – but Israel had no excuse. Whenever God's people tread the religious paths blazed by worldlings, they will always do damage to their own souls.

Two sons of Abinadab, Uzzah and Ahio, guided the cart; Uzzah was on the cart and Ahio was leading the oxen (v. 4). Barnes observes that Abinadab could not possibly be alive and that Uzzah and Ahio were likely his grandsons:

> It does not at all follow that Abinadab was still alive, nor can we conclude from Uzzah and Ahio being called sons of Abinadab, that they were literally his children. They may well have been sons of Eleazar and grandsons of Abinadab, or yet more remote descendants,

since there is no distinct evidence that Abinadab was alive even when the ark was brought to Kirjath-jearim. The house may have retained the name of "the house of Abinadab" long after his death.[118]

A joyous musical procession accompanied David as the people played various stringed instruments and percussion pieces (v. 5). Wilson notes that the cornet "consisted of rings hanging loosely on iron rods and was played by shaking it."[119] When the cart came to Nachon's threshing floor (meaning it was at a high place), the oxen stumbled, and Uzzah put out his hand to hold the Ark steady (v. 6). Recall that the Ark had been carried from Mount Sinai to Canaan, an arduous thirty-nine-year journey, on the shoulders of the Levites and not once does Scripture record that they stumbled. Though we may not understand why God commands what He does, and there may seem to be a better way to accomplish what He commands, it will always be best to obey Him and to rest in His grace. The Lord will enable us to do what He wants us to do and will impede everything else.

Uzzah apparently felt the Ark needed to be safeguarded, as if God were not sufficient to protect what is His. But his casual act of touching what was most holy to God only underscored the fact that Israel was dishonoring the Lord by what they were doing. Jehovah had previously commanded that the Ark be moved by staves carried by the Kohathites:

And when Aaron and his sons have finished covering the sanctuary and all the furnishings of the sanctuary, when the camp is set to go, then the sons of Kohath shall come to carry them; but they shall not touch any holy thing, lest they die. These are the things in the tabernacle of meeting which the sons of Kohath are to carry (Num. 4:15).

Uzzah's act aroused the Lord's anger and he was immediately struck dead. Had Uzzah acted with sincere intentions? We are not told; perhaps the Lord saw something in his heart that was offensive and judged it accordingly. For instance, Uzzah may have been showing off his daring familiarity with the Ark to impress the crowd. Regardless of what prompted God's instant wrath against Uzzah, the matter greatly displeased David who had genuinely desired to revere God by bringing His Ark to Jerusalem (v. 8). The king's error was not his zeal, however, but his lack of reverence for God's sacred things for which He is jealous.

David then called the place of judgment *Perez Uzzah*, meaning "outburst against Uzzah." The king said, *"How can the ark of the Lord come to me?"* (v. 9). David was full of joy and excitement about reestablishing proper worship of Jehovah at a central sanctuary in Israel. He did not understand why God had acted against him and feared moving the Ark any further lest more people die. Sadly, David was doing what the Lord wanted, but the wrong way; then, he ceased to do what he was supposed to do because God objected to the way it was being done.

There is valuable lesson for us in this; the believer should discern both the *what* and the *how* in serving the Lord. What is done must be in obedience to Him, and how it is done must reflect His character. The Corinthians learned this painful lesson in observing the Lord's Supper. The local church was obeying the Lord's command to break bread in remembrance of Him, but then changed the meeting into something it was not – a drunken and gluttonous love feast (1 Cor. 11:20-34). H. L. Rossier notes that the Corinthian believers were judged accordingly:

> What happened to David here also happened to the Corinthians who had introduced a carnal element at the Lord's table. God could not tolerate such a thing. "On this account many among you are weak and infirm, and a good many are fallen asleep" (1 Cor. 11:30). God was a consuming fire for them, as well as for Uzzah, and we must remember this. David was forced to understand this. The Lord had made a breach *before him against the Philistines* at Baal-perazim; now God's judgment makes a breach *against him.* "He called that place Perez-uzzah [breach of Uzzah]" (v. 8).[120]

Believers should never adopt a the-end-justifies-the-means mentality in the work or worship of the Lord. It is God who sanctifies the means, or the end means nothing. Just as the Levites were to labor to bear up the Ark, Christians are to labor to bear up the name of Christ. There is no easy secular way of accomplishing this. Rather, God's way leads believers into suffering (2 Tim. 3:12) and then into glory (Rom. 8:18).

David later realized his mistake in how the Ark should be moved (1 Chron. 15:13). His error reminds us that true worshipers of God must labor in His Word to understand what God has revealed about Himself and how He wants to be revered. The value of our worship relates directly to how we commune with God in spirit and in truth (John 4:23-24). Only as the Holy Spirit leads believers in worship that is founded in truth can we offer anything to God that He will appreciate. C. H. Mackintosh offers this helpful insight:

> There can be no real power where truth is sacrificed. There may be the appearance of it, the assumption of it, but no reality. How can there be? God is the source of power, but He cannot associate Himself with what is at variance with His truth. Hence, although *"David and all Israel played before God with all their might,"* there was no divine power. God's order was shut out by the human arrangement, and all ended in confusion and sorrow.[121]

Expressions of adoration towards God have value only if they affirm what has God's approval. Pious acts with good intentions may look good to others, but if what we do affronts God's character or word, we invite His chastening hand, not His pleasure. This would be the lesson David would glean from this sorrowful experience – he would wait on the Lord and then only do what had His approval.

The festive procession dispersed and instead of bringing the Ark to the City of David, it was taken into the house of Obed-Edom the Gittite (v. 10). It is not likely that the Ark had traveled too far from Abinadab's home. The writer tells us that his house was on a hill, meaning that a steep slope may have contributed to the oxen stumbling. Obed-Edom was a Levite of the family of Merari (1 Chron. 15:18-24, 16:38). The ark of the Lord remained at his house for three months and the Lord blessed him and his household during that time (v. 11).

David Brings the Ark to Jerusalem (vv. 12-23)

The king was informed that the Lord had blessed Obed-Edom because the Ark resided in his home (v. 12). This showed David that the Lord appreciated Obed-Edom's care of the Ark and that God did not oppose the relocation of the Ark. The king was reminded that standing aloof from the Ark (which represents God's presence among His people) caused the loss of His blessing, but approaching God in reverential respect and holiness prompted God's goodness. Believers today must understand the same concept: to stand apart from God is death (spiritual separation) and to come into His presence wrongly causes the same. It is only by being sanctified in Christ, with sins cleansed by His blood, that we can enter God's presence with joy and have confidence of His acceptance.

David again led the nation to fetch the Ark, but this time the Ark was appropriately carried by the Levites. The location of Obed-Edom's home is not stated, but the journey from Kirjath-Jearim to the City of David would be less than ten miles. The priests were presenting burnt offerings of oxen and fattened sheep about every six paces along the route the Ark traveled (v. 13). Exactly what distance this represents is unknown. It is ironic that on their first attempt, they had a new cart (picturing their disobedience), but no sacrifices (they did not worship), but on their second attempt, they had no cart, but offered their complete obedience and many sacrifices to the Lord. As we will see, the people's genuine adoration for God forged in obedience was the difference between failure and success – the same is true today!

Psalm 68 likely celebrates David's conquest over the Jebusites in Zion, his bringing the Ark to Jerusalem, and its placement in a tabernacle that he had pitched there (v. 17). We learn from 1 Chronicles 16:37-40 that the previous tabernacle (with the holy articles, but not the Ark) somehow found its way to a high place in Gibeon. The prayer in Psalm 132 also recounts how the Ark of the Covenant was joyfully found in Ephrathah, after being returned by the Philistines and how David conveyed it to Jerusalem (Ps. 132:6-8). As observed in the previous chapter, the City of David (Jerusalem) was now the capital of Israel and the only proper place to worship Jehovah.

Not only did the priests present many burnt offerings on makeshift altars as the Ark journeyed along, but also the king leading the procession was busy honoring the Lord as well: *"David danced before the Lord with all his might; and David was wearing a linen ephod"* (v. 14). The people were ecstatic over the sight; all Israel shouted and the trumpets blasted their exuberant approval (v. 15). The psalmist tells us that it is most appropriate for God's people to be cheerful in spirit and joyful in praise before Him:

> *Let Israel rejoice in their Maker; let the children of Zion be joyful in their King. Let them praise His name with the dance; let them sing praises to Him with the timbrel and harp. For the Lord takes pleasure*

in His people; He will beautify the humble with salvation (Ps. 149:2-4).

But not everyone was happy in the Lord. Michal had not joined the festive entourage and when she saw David leaping and whirling before the Ark as it entered the City of David, she despised him (v. 16).

The Ark was placed in the tabernacle that David had erected and when all the burnt and peace offerings were concluded, David blessed the people and sent them home (vv. 17-18). But he did not send them away empty-handed. Each person received a loaf of bread, a piece of meat and a cake of raisins (v. 19). David then returned to bless his own household.

Michal's Rebuke and Judgment (vv. 21-23)

Michal was waiting for him with a sarcastic taunt: *"How glorious was the king of Israel today, uncovering himself today in the eyes of the maids of his servants, as one of the base fellows shamelessly uncovers himself!"* (v. 21). Interestingly, Michal is never referred to as "David's wife" in this passage, but rather "Saul's daughter." Their sharp interaction is on this basis – the daughter of the man of the flesh, Saul, could not understand why the king would so openly humble himself before the Lord.

But David's retort to Michal affirmed that the king of Israel should be lowly before the Lord, which is why the kingdom was taken from her father – he was a proud, self-focused man:

> *It was before the Lord, who chose me instead of your father and all his house, to appoint me ruler over the people of the Lord, over Israel. Therefore I will play music before the Lord. And I will be even more undignified than this, and will be humble in my own sight. But as for the maidservants of whom you have spoken, by them I will be held in honor* (vv. 21-22).

David considered himself nothing; he was vile in God's sight and would gladly debase himself further to ensure he remained self-effacing before the Lord. Therefore, the king had gladly put off his royal apparel (outer garments) to dance before the ark as it was being carried into Jerusalem. David's behavior was appropriate, for *"no flesh should glory in His presence"* (1 Cor. 1:29-30) and *"the Lord lifts up the humble; He casts the wicked down to the ground"* (Ps. 147:6). The king understood that he must remain low before the Lord to rule over His people with His approval and blessing.

Concerning the charge of indecency, the nation saw David without his kingly attire and wearing a linen ephod. This was an unusual sight, but David had laid aside only his royal glory, not his moral integrity. But his uninhibited, humble behavior brought a charge from his estranged wife, Michal, that he had shamefully uncovered himself in front of Israel's maidens.

The king told Michal that his behavior was prompted by joy in the Lord – there was nothing perverse about his actions. He then reproves her by pointing out that her father's pride did not enhance his leadership, but rather caused him to be rejected by God, and cost him the kingdom. Accordingly, David did not think anything which contributed to the glory of God was too much for him to do. So, even though Saul's daughter did not approve of his actions, David was content to be honored by the maidservants of Israel.

The king had demeaned himself before the Jewish nation to show his esteem for Jehovah, but he did it in such a way that still honored Moses' law prohibiting public indecency (Ex. 20:26, 28:42). For her insolence, Michal would remain barren the remainder of her life (v. 23). Whether this was a curse of sorts or if David was simply stating that he was withdrawing marital rights from her is unknown. Regardless, she would never know the satisfaction of conceiving, bearing, and nurturing children of her own. Like David, only those who love and obey the Lord experience the joy of His presence.

Meditation

Joyful, joyful, we adore You,
God of glory, Lord of love;
Hearts unfold like flowers before You,
Opening to the sun above.

Melt the clouds of sin and sadness;
Drive the dark of doubt away;
Giver of immortal gladness,
Fill us with the light of day!

— Henry van Dyke

Your Kingdom Come
2 Samuel 7

God's Covenant With David (vv. 1-17)

This chapter picks up a few years after David brought the Ark to Jerusalem and put it in a tabernacle that he had fabricated and erected for it. By God's hand, David enjoyed rest from all his enemies and was living in a fine house he had constructed in the City of David. David, who had been forced to endure a nomadic life for eight years while fleeing Saul's wrath, was enjoying his new residence. However, as he contemplated the matter, he did not feel it was appropriate that he should have such a fine home, while the Ark was residing in a mere tent.

The king notified the prophet Nathan of his intentions to build God a permanent house among His people, saying, *"See now, I dwell in a house of cedar, but the ark of God dwells inside tent curtains"* (vv. 1-2). David wanted the Lord to have a permanent structure, not just a cloth tent to reside in. This sounded good to the prophet Nathan, who replied, *"Go, do all that is in your heart, for the Lord is with you."*

As a prophet, Nathan was close to the Lord's thoughts, but as Matthew Henry suggests, he was not perfect in discerning God's mind concerning the temple. Therefore, God gave a word to Nathan that very night to correct his statement to David:

> The same night, that Nathan might not continue long in an error nor David have his head any further filled with thoughts of that which he must never bring to pass. God might have said this to David himself immediately, but he chose to send it by Nathan, to support the honor of his prophets, and to preserve in David a regard to them. Though he be the head, they must be the eyes by which he must see the visions of the Almighty, and the tongue by which he must hear the word of God. He that delivered this long message to Nathan assisted his memory to retain it, that he might deliver it fully (he being resolved to deliver it faithfully) as he received it of the Lord.[122]

Godly believers will not always perfectly discern the mind of the Lord, but the Lord does grant correction, reproof, and further instruction for those humbly walking with Him. Such was the case with Nathan; he originally spoke out of his knowing God, but God intervened with a direct message, so that he might know His specific thinking on the matter. This message, received through a vision, was then immediately delivered to David (v. 17):

Go and tell My servant David, "Thus says the Lord: 'Would you build a house for Me to dwell in? For I have not dwelt in a house since the time that I brought the children of Israel up from Egypt, even to this day, but have moved about in a tent and in a tabernacle. Wherever I have moved about with all the children of Israel, have I ever spoken a word to anyone from the tribes of Israel, whom I commanded to shepherd My people Israel, saying, "Why have you not built Me a house of cedar?"'" Now therefore, thus shall you say to My servant David, "Thus says the Lord of hosts: 'I took you from the sheepfold, from following the sheep, to be ruler over My people, over Israel. And I have been with you wherever you have gone, and have cut off all your enemies from before you, and have made you a great name, like the name of the great men who are on the earth. Moreover I will appoint a place for My people Israel, and will plant them, that they may dwell in a place of their own and move no more; nor shall the sons of wickedness oppress them anymore, as previously, since the time that I commanded judges to be over My people Israel, and have caused you to rest from all your enemies. Also the Lord tells you that He will make you a house.

When your days are fulfilled and you rest with your fathers, I will set up your seed after you, who will come from your body, and I will establish his kingdom. He shall build a house for My name, and I will establish the throne of his kingdom forever. I will be his Father, and he shall be My son. If he commits iniquity, I will chasten him with the rod of men and with the blows of the sons of men. But My mercy shall not depart from him, as I took it from Saul, whom I removed from before you. And your house and your kingdom shall be established forever before you. Your throne shall be established forever'" (vv. 3-16).

First, the Lord reminded David that He had dwelt in a tabernacle among His people since the time of the Egyptian Exodus. It is a lovely reflection of God's grace that He Himself came down from heaven to "walk" alongside His people as they journeyed through the wilderness to Canaan. During those years, it was necessary that God's holy things be in a portable tent, but now that the Jews were settled in the land, the time had come for a permanent temple for Him to be constructed (vv. 6-11).

Second, God promised that David would have a son (Solomon) who would build His temple – David would not be permitted to because he had shed too much blood (vv. 12-15). If this son sinned, God promised to chasten him, but with tempered mercy so that David's dynasty would continue. David's life work had been characterized by fighting, not building. Yet, until King Saul, the man of the flesh, was removed and Israel's surrounding enemies had been subdued, no temple foundation could have been laid. David's life ministry was a preparatory work to clear the way for the temple's construction, which would be completed by his son Solomon. In grace, the Lord had taken David out of the obscurity of a sheepfold and raised him up to rule over His people, thus paving the way for his son to build a lasting testimony of Jehovah's presence in Israel, that all nations would note.

Third, God promised David that a new and everlasting dynasty would be established and that one of his descendants (the Messiah) would sit on his throne forever (vv. 16-17). As Psalm 89 confirms, God's covenant with David created a special father/son-like relationship between them, with God vowing to bless and protect David and to make him victorious before his enemies. Although at times God would chasten His covenant people for their rebellion, He would not forget His promise to David of an everlasting dynasty!

The Coming Kingdom

The book of Ecclesiastes shows us how far short Solomon came from fulfilling the promises of God to David in this chapter. His failure would cause Israel, and us too, to look for one *"greater than Solomon,"* through whom God would honor His covenant with David. Matthew 12:42 tells us that the Lord Jesus Christ will be that Person and Israel's final king. Christ is a descendant of King David (Matt. 1:1) and the rightful heir to his throne, which God has promised to establish forever (vv. 13-16). Though the Lord has already been highly exalted in heaven, He presently sits upon His Father's throne and is waiting to return to establish His earthly kingdom (Rev. 3:21, 11:2-3). However, Paul, pondering the wonderful grace extended to him, the chief of sinners, declares the Lord Jesus Christ now: *"the King eternal, immortal, invisible, to God who alone is wise, be honor and glory forever and ever"* (1 Tim. 1:17). Amen.

While the Lord Jesus does hold the title-deed to His kingdom, He has not exercised His kingship authority as King of kings and Lord of lords. At present, He sits on His Father's throne in Heaven awaiting the day when He will triumphantly return to earth (Rev. 3:21). After the Church Age is complete and at the conclusion of the Tribulation Period, Christ will return to the earth to destroy the Antichrist and his armies at the battle of Armageddon. Then He will establish His throne in Jerusalem (Isa. 66:11-14; Zech. 14; Rev. 19:11-21). At that time a remnant of the refined Jewish nation will be restored to Him (Zech. 8:6-12).

As the nations are not presently seeking the Lord (Zech. 8:22) or esteeming the Jewish people (Zech. 8:23), we can safely declare that the events Zechariah is foretelling have not occurred yet. To this date, the Jews have not received all the land promised to Abraham (Gen. 15:18-21), the throne of David has not been established forever (2 Sam. 7:14-17), the Gentiles have not been subdued (Jer. 30:8; Zech. 14:16-17), and they certainly are not the esteemed people of the Earth (Zech. 8:23; Isa. 66:10-18). God is a covenant-keeping God and He will honor all that He says He will do!

God is not finished with the Jewish nation. Israel will be nationally established in prosperity, Jerusalem will be the religious center of the world, Jehovah will be worshiped by the nations, and the Gentiles will greatly esteem the Jewish people. At present, the Jewish nation is locked in spiritual blindness while Christ is building His Church. When the "fullness of the Gentiles" is complete, that is, when the last Gentile soul has been added to the Church and it has been removed from the earth, God will awaken His covenant people of old during the Tribulation Period (Rom. 11:25). This seven-year period is the final week in Daniel's prophecy (Dan. 9:27).

Christ's literal kingdom on earth is promised and is coming, but today it is on the earth in spiritual form only. Those who respond to the gospel message will be citizens of Christ's kingdom to come. During the Kingdom Age, glorified saints and spiritually revitalized Israel will live on the earth with faithful Tribulation survivors in a wonderful utopia in which the prophecies of this chapter will be fulfilled. Until that time, may our hands be strong as we labor for what we know is coming – the kingdom of the Lord Jesus Christ!

David's Praise to God (vv. 18-29)

God had revealed to David, not only His great plans for David and Israel, but also how He would honor and exalt Christ. After hearing the marvelous extent of God's covenant with him, David was beside himself. He went to the tabernacle and in utter amazement and self-effacement sat before the Lord. In the stillness of the quiet and solitary place, David, overwhelmed by God's goodness, was prompted to praise and worship Him:

> *Who am I, O Lord God? And what is my house, that You have brought me this far? And yet this was a small thing in Your sight, O Lord God; and You have also spoken of Your servant's house for a great while to come. Is this the manner of man, O Lord God? Now what more can David say to You? For You, Lord God, know Your servant. For Your word's sake, and according to Your own heart, You have done all these great things, to make Your servant know them* (vv. 18-21).

This is a wonderful picture of unhindered communion with God – David sharing his deepest thoughts of appreciation and admiration while sitting before the Lord in complete freedom and confidence. David is contrite before God; he has no thoughts of himself, but rather rejoices in what God is determined to accomplish for him and for Israel. C. H. Mackintosh reminds us that when we lose sight of ourselves before the Lord, our souls are liberated to pour out holy adoration for God and appreciation for His ways:

This is true worship, and is the very reverse of human religiousness. The former is the acknowledgement of God by the energy of faith; the latter is the setting up of man in the spirit of legalism. No doubt, David would have appeared, to many, a more devoted man when seeking to build a house for the Lord than when sitting in His presence. In the one case, he was trying to do something; in the other, he was apparently doing nothing. It is like the two sisters at Bethany, of whom one would seem, in the judgment of nature, to have been doing all the work, and the other to have been sitting idle. How different are God's thoughts! David sitting before the Lord was in a right position, rather than seeking to build.[123]

David pondered why God had selected him for such honor, a mere shepherd boy, the youngest of his brethren, and from an unknown family in a remote town in Israel. The king also pondered God's many mercies that took him from obscurity to the throne; David had survived numerous battles with multiple enemies and diverse hostilities from within Israel to be God's chosen victor.

Overwhelmed by his contemplations, the king affirmed why he was still alive and had been so richly blessed: *"Therefore You are great, O Lord God. For there is none like You, nor is there any God besides You, according to all that we have heard with our ears"* (v. 22). All that had happened to David was under his great God's control, to bring Himself glory and to honor His covenant with Abraham – to cling to and bless a nation of his lineage (vv. 23-24). God had redeemed a people out of Egypt that would forever be His!

In verse 25, we come to David's prayer which concludes the chapter. H. L. Rossier writes:

> Here we find the character of *a true prayer of communion*: Do as Thou hast desired to do and as Thou hast said. *"Let the house of Thy servant David be established before Thee. For Thou...hast revealed to Thy servant, saying, I will build thee an house...Let it please Thee to bless the house of Thy servant...for Thou, Lord Jehovah, hast spoken it"* (vv. 26-29). Let us take this attitude as a model for ourselves. Having received divine communications in our hearts, let us sincerely request of God the things that He Himself has promised us. He loves to give us the things we ask of Him, to grant them according to our thoughts and our desires, for since these are the fruit of communion with Him they are His own thoughts and desires.[124]

David expresses his full agreement with God's plan to build up his house and then asks the Lord to fulfill His word so that His name will be magnified forever: *"The Lord of hosts is the God over Israel"* (vv. 25-29). In the Church Age, believers also have the opportunity to enjoy unhindered communion with God and to humbly request, in the name of the Lord Jesus Christ, that God will honor Himself by answering our prayers (John 15:16, 16:23-24). May we, like David, rejoice in the amazing providential goodness of God, who has determined to enrich His people for the honor and glory of His name!

Meditation

The Lord unto His Christ has said,
"Sit Thou at My right hand,
Until I make Thine enemies
Submit to Thy command.
A scepter prospered by the Lord
Thy mighty hand shall wield;
From Zion Thou shalt rule the world,
And all Thy foes shall yield.

"Thou shalt subdue the kings of earth
With God at Thy right hand;
The nations Thou shalt rule in might
And judge in every land."
The Christ, refreshed by living streams,
Shall neither faint nor fall,
And He shall be the glorious Head,
Exalted over all.

— Henry S. Cutler

Conquest and Order
2 Samuel 8

David's Kingdom Expands (vv. 1-14)

The writer details David's further conquests to solidify his kingdom and the various individuals he appointed to give order to it. David left the holy repose of the Lord's presence to fight His battles with heightened zeal. He now understood that he was to clear the way so that another after him could lay the foundation of the Lord's house. Chapters 8-10 record David's preparations to this end. The man of war was to clear the land of enemies so that his son, enjoying the peace his father had secured, could erect a testimony to Jehovah among the nations. The judicial shedding of blood during David's reign secured the blessing which would be wonderfully evident in Solomon's majestic rule. This is the apex of Israel's glory to date, but Israel's returning Messiah will achieve much more!

In God's providential purposes, He called David to be a fighter and Solomon to be a builder – both are essential in the triumphal work of God and represent both advents of Christ. C. H. Mackintosh affirms this typological understanding and reminds us that the Church's hope of glory is in Christ alone:

> At the cross we behold the stroke of justice falling upon the spotless Victim, and then the Holy Ghost came down to gather men around the person of Him who was raised from the dead. Just as David began to gather the hewed stones, and the materials for the joinings of the house, the moment the place of the foundation was settled. The Church is the temple of the living God, of which Christ is the chief corner stone. The materials for this building were all provided, and the place of its foundation purchased, in the season of Christ's trouble, for David represents Christ in His sufferings, as Solomon represents Him in His glory. David was the man of war; Solomon represents Him in His glory. David was the man of war; Solomon, the man of rest. David had to grapple with enemies; Solomon was able to

say, *"There is neither adversary nor evil occurrence"* (1 Kgs. 5:4). Thus do these two kings shadow forth Him who, by His cross and passion, made ample provision for the building of the temple which shall be manifested in divine order and perfectness in the day of His coming glory.[125]

Having secured the loyalty of his countrymen throughout Israel, David begins purging the pagan inhabitants remaining in Israel and reclaiming lost territory. He begins by conquering the Philistines (v. 1). Notice that David took control of the Philistine city Metheg Ammah (i.e., Gath; 1 Chron. 18:1). The city in which, as a younger man, he became fearful and played the madman to preserve his life was now his! Metheg Ammah means the "bridle of the capital" – David now held the key of power.

The Philistines dwelt directly west of the Judean foothills in Philistia and had been Israel's enemies since Joshua led the Israelites into Canaan (Judg. 3:1-4). During the era of the Judges, the Philistines had repeatedly attempted to expand their dominion by invading Jewish territory. The conflict raged back and forth for hundreds of years until David finally subdued Philistia, a necessity before the temple could be constructed.

Next, David defeated the Moabites, the people of his great-grandmother Ruth. The king commanded that two out of every three prisoners captured be put to death; surviving Moabites then became David's servants and paid him tribute (v. 2).

The king's uncharacteristic brutality towards the Moabite is generally explained in two ways. First, Barnes suggests that Psalm 60 indicates "that David had met with some temporary reverse in his Syrian wars, and that the Moabites and Edomites had treacherously taken advantage of it, and perhaps tried to cut off his retreat."[126] Second, Jewish tradition suggests that David's severity against the Moabites was because they had killed his parents whom he had put into their care during his fugitive years (2 Sam. 22:3-4). It is possible that both explanations are true. Regardless, David exacted severe retribution for Moab's treachery.

David then set his sights on the loosely joined Syrian (Aramean) city-states to the north. Israel first attacked Zobah, north of Damascus, because their king Hadadezer and much of his army were engaged in a campaign to recover territory near the River Euphrates (v. 3). David took one thousand chariots, seven hundred horsemen, and twenty thousand foot soldiers from Hadadezer, and hamstrung all but one hundred chariot horses (v. 4). In song, David alludes to why he did not preserve the bulk of the warhorses: *"Some trust in chariots, and some in horses; but we will remember the name of the Lord our God"* (Ps. 20:7). While Gentile armies prized their war-chariots and cavalry in battle, David, by hamstringing the captured horses, demonstrated that his strength for conquering was solely in the Lord.

The Syrians from Damascus moved to cut off David and his men before they could return to Jerusalem with their spoils of war. This proved to be a huge tactical mistake, for 22,000 Syrians were slain by Israel's army (v. 5). This gave David control of two chief cities in the north, Zobah and Damascus. He placed a Jewish garrison in Damascus (likely in Zobah as well) and these vassal city-states served David and paid him tribute (v. 6).

Why was David so successful in opposing larger and better armed forces? The reason was that *"the Lord preserved David wherever he went."* David confiscated Hadadezer's shields of gold and much bronze and brought these metals to Jerusalem – the king was stockpiling construction materials for the temple (vv. 7-8).

After Toi, the king of Hamath, heard that David had defeated Hadadezer (his enemy also), he sent his son Joram to congratulate David and to provide him with articles of gold, silver, and bronze (vv. 9-10). All that David received or confiscated from Moab, Ammon, Philistia, Syrian cities, and the Amalekites was dedicated to the Lord (vv. 11-12). David's fame became even more notable after slaughtering 18,000 Syrians in the Valley of Salt (south of the Dead Sea); this victory occurred under Abishai and Joab's leadership (v. 13; 1 Chron. 18:12; Ps. 60).

Eugene H. Merrill explains that there is a textual quandary as to whether those defeated were actually the Syrians or the Edomites:

Though "Aram" (i.e., "Arameans") is in most Hebrew manuscripts, the Septuagint and some other versions have "Edom," a reading that is also supported by a few Hebrew manuscripts and by 1 Chronicles 18:12. The difference in the original language is in only one letter: *d* (as in Edom) and *r* (as in Aram), easily confused in Hebrew. If "Aramean," it may be that the Edomites had solicited Aramean help against Israel. In any event, David again prevailed and brought Edom also under his hegemony.[127]

Whether the Syrians assisted the Edomites or not, Edom's rebellion was subdued and David placed garrisons throughout their land (v. 14). The writer again notes, *"The Lord preserved David wherever he went."* David had a heart for God, knew what God wanted him to accomplish, and God enabled him to do it – thus, he was unstoppable. H. L. Rossier reminds us that when we commune with God and think as He does, we also triumph in ways that only He can bring about.

> The victories of this chapter grow out of David's communion with his God just as the victories of 2 Samuel 5 were the fruit of his dependence and obedience. When we are in communion with Him, God has no need to discipline us as He did with Uzzah. Communion lets us advance, sure of being in God's pathway without needing special instruction to show this pathway to us. "I will instruct thee and teach thee the way in which thou shalt go; I will counsel thee *with Mine eye upon thee*" (Ps. 32:8) will become reality to us. Our path becomes God's path because our thoughts do not differ from His. Thus it is said twice in this chapter: *"The Lord preserved David wherever he went"* (vv. 6, 14).[128]

David wrote Psalm 60 to inform others of the powerful benefits of communion with God and trusting His promises. The poem is based on David's military experiences confronting the Syrians in the north and the invading Edomites in the south (vv. 8-13; 1 Kgs. 11:15-16). At this point in the Syrian war, the main Hebrew army was in the north, which meant David's troops were spread thin in the south where the Edomites launched a surprise invasion. This resulted initially in terrible Jewish losses; the Jews had been forced to unfurl a banner of retreat (Ps. 60:1-4).

The king surmised the defeat was from the Lord, because He was angry with Israel. Victory is at the hand of God, so David petitioned the Lord on behalf of those He loved, to turn their divinely-orchestrated calamity into a God-directed triumph (Ps. 60:5). Joab was sent south to fend off the Edomites and God did grant a tremendous victory to his forces. Reviewing the entire situation, David reminds his countrymen of God's previous promise: since all Jewish territories were His, He would ensure Israel's inevitable victory over their enemies (Ps. 60:6-8).

David's Administration (vv. 15-18)

Israel's king desired that his kingdom be governed with justice and equality (v. 15). The writer then lists the chief officers in David's cabinet: Joab commanded Israel's army, Jehoshaphat was David's recorder, Zodok and Abiathar (i.e., Ahimelech's son; see 1 Sam. 22:20 discussion) were priests, Seraiah was the secretary, Benaiah was in charge of the king's security, and some of David's sons were chief ministers (vv. 16-18).

At this juncture, David maintains Abiathar (a descendant of Aaron's son Ithamar through Eli and Phinehas II) as Israel's high priest, likely because of his long association with David during his fugitive years. Later, Solomon will remove Abiathar from this position and Zadok alone served as high priest. Zadok was a descendant of Aaron through Eleazar and Phinehas I, and of the rightful pedigree to be high priest (see discussion in 1 Sam. 2). Solomon's action fulfilled God's judgment against the house of Eli.

Conquest and order marked the expansion of David's kingdom. This would permit glory and blessing to be the main characteristics of his son Solomon's reign. Only through Christ's well-ordered victory at Calvary can we reap the vast goodness of an eternal God, who will exalt His Son over all that He has created. How unimaginable Christ's coming kingdom will be – what will it be like to bask in the splendor and love of God without any distractions, no carnality, no limitations, and no sorrow?

Meditation

> If you can really make a man believe you love him, you have won him, and if I could only make people really believe that God loves them, what a rush we would see for the Kingdom of God!
>
> — Dwight L. Moody

Mephibosheth Invited to the King's Table
2 Samuel 9

With his kingdom advancing, David paused to consider his promise to his dear deceased friend Jonathan. The king inquired of his servants: *"Is there still anyone who is left of the house of Saul, that I may show him kindness for Jonathan's sake?"* (v. 1). Recall that David had promised Jonathan to show kindness to his *"house forever"* (1 Sam. 20:15).

An inquiry was made, and a servant of the house of Saul, Ziba, was brought before David (v. 2). After verifying Ziba's identity, David repeated his earlier question, but added that he wanted to *"show the kindness of God"* to the house of Saul (v. 3). Given all the years Saul had oppressed David, there is only one explanation for David's gesture – God's grace was at work in David's heart.

Ziba answered the king, *"There is still a son of Jonathan who is lame in his feet"* (v. 3). David then inquired of his location and Ziba informed the king that he was in the house of Machir in Lo Debar (v. 4). Lo Debar was located just east of the Jordan and about ten miles south of the Sea of Galilee. David sent men to bring Mephibosheth, the son of Jonathan, before him (v. 5). Observing the vast power of David's kingdom and being a surviving grandson of the previous king, Mephibosheth likely thought his days were numbered. He fell on his face before the king and answered the king's inquiry as to his identity with a humble reply, *"Here is your servant"* (v. 6).

David then said to Mephibosheth what the Lord Jesus often did to gain the trust of a fearful soul, "Fear not." The king did not want the son of his dear friend to be dreading what was not on his mind – wrath – but rather to be overwhelmed by what was – grace! This reflects God's own character: He is slow to anger (without being negligent to act) and quick to forgive (Prov. 14:17, 16:32). God demonstrates that anger is to be a secondary, not a primary, emotion. This is why Scripture does not represent Jehovah as an angry vindictive God yearning to vanquish the wicked, but rather as a God of love who desires to extend grace and mercy to those needing His help (1 Jn. 4:8, 16).

Hence, David, reflecting the heart of God, says, *"Do not fear, for I will surely show you kindness for Jonathan your father's sake, and will restore to you all the land of Saul your grandfather; and you shall eat bread at my table continually"* (v. 7). This is one of those moments in Scripture that defies human capacity and reason – God's grace is exemplified in such an impressive way that it stuns the hearer and prompts wonder and admiration. David had not confiscated Saul's property, which was typically done by the rising monarch of a new dynasty. Rather, David ensured that Mephibosheth would receive all that belonged to his grandfather. Mephibosheth again bowed before the king and exclaimed, *"What is your servant, that you should look upon such a dead dog as I?"* (v. 8).

The king informed Ziba that he had restored to Mephibosheth what belong to Saul, and that he (Ziba), his sons, and servants would manage Mephibosheth's assets so that he would always be provided for (at that time Ziba had fifteen sons and twenty servants; vv. 9-10). Additionally, David informed Ziba that Mephibosheth, his master, would always have a seat at the king's table. Ziba agreed to do all that David had commanded, for David's decree had presented him with a lucrative opportunity also (v. 11).

David then publicly announced his ruling, *"As for Mephibosheth, he shall eat at my table like one of the king's sons."* This distinct privilege of eating at the king's table is recorded four times in the narrative. The writer then notes that Mephibosheth, probably around thirty years old, had a young son whose name was Micha (v. 12). T. Wilson notes that the meaning of Micha's name is in keeping with Mephibosheth's humble and thankful disposition towards the Lord:

> Interestingly, Micha's name means "Who is like unto the Lord (or Jah)?" We, who have tasted grace richer than Mephibosheth did, can understand that sentiment. However, Mephibosheth had named that child Micha before David fetched him from Lo-debar, and after he had been handicapped by a cruel accident (4:4), and dispossessed of the family estate. Clearly, humility was not the only grace to be seen in Mephibosheth; genuine gratitude to his God was another.[129]

Indeed, broken down, death-bound men who have tasted the goodness of the Lord should be thankful! The chapter concludes by noting that Mephibosheth then lived in Jerusalem and regularly sat at the king's table (v. 13).

The story of King David's kindness to Mephibosheth, the crippled son of Jonathan, is a fitting allegory of the Lord's Table. Normally, a new king would exterminate all remaining heirs of the previous dynasty in order to prevent a potential takeover. However, King David, because of his love for Jonathan and the covenant he had made with him (1 Sam. 18:3), set a place at his table for Mephibosheth for the remainder of his life. Mephibosheth was treated like the king's son.

Mephibosheth never had to worry about where his next meal would come from, and he could enjoy daily fellowship with the king. Similarly, though once the enemies of God, believers in Christ now have the opportunity to enjoy fellowship with Him and with other believers at His table and to receive daily wherewithal to serve Him. Those in Christ are treated as God's honored children.

Often the biblical term "the Lord's Table" (which speaks of a spiritual table where believers receive blessings and enjoy fellowship in Christ – see 1 Corinthians 10) is confused with the biblical term "the Lord's Supper" (which refers to the remembrance meeting of the local church – see 1 Corinthians 11). Consequently, most of Christendom refers to the Lord's Supper with the non-scriptural term "the communion service." There is *communion with Christ* at the Lord's Table, but more specifically, there is a *remembrance of Christ* at every Lord's Supper – the value of His death is proclaimed afresh. The Lord's Table is spiritual and is set by Him, whereas the table at the Lord's Supper is physical and is set by us; at the former we receive provisions from the Lord, but at the latter we worship and remember Him.

To summarize, the Lord's Table speaks of the sum total of the spiritual blessings we have in Christ, while the Lord's Supper refers to the remembrance meeting of the Church. In the sense that the souls of believers are refreshed through Spirit-led worship, the Lord's Table probably includes the Lord's Supper, but the distinct terminology and significance of each should not be lost. It is a great privilege to remember and refresh the Savior during the Lord's Supper, and it is a blessing to the heart of every believer to commune with and receive from the Savior at His Table.

Note that the glorious relationship David established with Mephibosheth did not change his physical condition. The final statement of the text says, *"he was lame in both his feet."* No doubt outsiders feasting with David had disparaging thoughts towards one so pitiful that he had to be carried to the king's table. But to David, Mephibosheth was a son who occupied the highest position he could bestow on him.

Likewise, pathetic sinners saved by the King of Grace are co-seated with Him at His table in heavenly places (Eph. 2:6-7). Being seated at David's table did not change Mephibosheth's *condition* (he was still lame), but it did change his *position* in the eyes of the king. Believers, like everyone else living in the world today, still have sin-crippled bodies. The difference, however, is that those justified in Christ have a righteous position before God and enjoy a loving relationship with Him as His children. While fellowship can be broken because of personal sin, the reality of this great privilege can never be lost (John 5:24).

Paul understood that there was nothing in him that was lovely and pleasing to God; it was only what he was in Christ that mattered to God. It is only Christ, through the power of the Holy Spirit, who sanctifies us to be pleasing to God and also enables us to please God:

For I know that in me (that is, in my flesh) nothing good dwells (Rom. 7:18) – Paul's condition.

So then, those who are in the flesh cannot please God [i.e., the practice of sin displeases God]. *But you are not in the flesh but in the Spirit, if indeed the Spirit of God dwells in you* [i.e., positionally in Christ, God no longer sees us in the flesh; not dead in sin, but alive in Christ] (Rom. 8:8-9).

This is why believers are to have no confidence in the flesh, otherwise they will displease God. Rather, believers are to remain seated at the Lord's Table, and live as His Spirit-filled children. Paul therefore exhorts the believers at Corinth not to remove themselves from the Lord's Table to partake of the world's resources; to do so is to fellowship with demons:

I do not want you to have fellowship with demons. You cannot drink the cup of the Lord and the cup of demons; you cannot partake of the

Lord's table and of the table of demons. Or do we provoke the Lord to jealousy? Are we stronger than He? (1 Cor. 10:20-22).

May each believer realize the importance of eating at the Lord's Table and, accordingly, choose to abide with Him there. Failure to do so will provoke the Lord's jealousy and His chastening hand. Why would a believer ever want to sever his or her communion with the Lord? It is a great privilege and honor to sup at His Table!

Meditation

Lord, at Thy Table we behold the wonders of Thy grace;
But, most of all, admire that we should find a welcome place.
What strange, surprising grace is this, that we, so lost, have room!
Jesus our weary souls invites, and freely bids us come!

— Thomas Gibbons

The Ammonites and Syrians Defeated
2 Samuel 10

Nahash, the king of Ammon, died, and David desired to show kindness to his son Hanun because of his father's previous unspecified generosity to David (vv. 1-2). Until this time, Ammon had remained loyal and had not resisted David's efforts to secure the region.

David sent comforters to the land of Ammon to console the new king. As some fifty years had passed since Saul's confrontation with Nahash, the deceased may have been the son of the former Nahash. Regardless, David's gesture represents a lovely picture of the Lord Jesus Christ who extends an offer of lavish grace to "whomsoever will" (not just to His covenant people, but to the Gentiles also). However, as we will soon see in the story of Hanun, God's goodness can still be refused.

Certain advisors told Hanun that David's ambassadors were not what they claimed to be, but were rather spies gathering information for an inevitable invasion (v. 3). The young Ammonite king heeded their counsel. Before dismissing David's servants, Hanun's men shaved half their beards and cut their garments off to an indecent length (v. 4). Barnes summarizes the magnitude of the offense: "Cutting off a person's beard is regarded by the Arabs as an indignity equal to flogging and branding among ourselves. The loss of their long garments, so essential to Oriental dignity, was no less insulting than that of their beards."[130] In the Ancient East, a man's beard was held in such high respect that men often swore by their own beards in matters of great importance.

Because the Law prohibited trimming their beards in accordance with pagan practices (Lev. 19:27), Jewish men permitted their beards to grow naturally. This meant that the Ammonites' insult was doubly disconcerting, because the Jews would have to shave the other half of their beards to ensure, that their facial hair grew back evenly.

After hearing about their shameful treatment, David told his emissaries to remain in Jericho until their beards had sufficiently grown back (v. 5). Interestingly, Isaiah will later prophesy Moab's final ignominy and doom, but employing a colorful reminder of their shameful deed in this chapter, *"Moab will wail ... on all their heads will be baldness, and every beard cut off"* (Isa. 15:2).

Instead of regretting their mistake of humiliating David's envoy (a declaration of war, so to speak), the Ammonites began soliciting allies to bolster their ranks against David's imminent retaliation. The Ammonites hired 20,000 Syrian foot soldiers from Beth Rehob and Zoba, 1,000 men from Maacah, and 12,000 from Ish-Tob (v. 6). Maacah was in Transjordan just to the north of Manasseh's territory but south of Mount Hebron. Tob was south of Maacah, situated about forty miles east of the Jordan River and ten miles south of the Sea of Galilee.

After learning of Syria's rebellion (for David had already subdued them; chp. 8) and that Ammon had secured an alliance with Syria, David sent Joab and all Israel's mighty men to confront the Syrians and Ammonites (v. 7). The Ammonites put themselves in array to protect the gate of Rabbah (Rabbath), their capital city, while the mercenary forces skirted Israel's army in an outflanking maneuver (v. 8).

When Joab saw that the battle lines were on either side of him, he chose some of Israel's best soldiers and arrayed them against the Syrians, the better warriors (v. 9). The remainder of Israel's army would be commanded by Abishai, Joab's brother, and would engage the Ammonites (v. 10). Joab instructed Abishai:

> *If the Syrians are too strong for me, then you shall help me; but if the people of Ammon are too strong for you, then I will come and help you. Be of good courage, and let us be strong for our people and for the cities of our God. And may the Lord do what is good in His sight* (vv. 11-12).

Basically, Joab told his men to be strong and fight for Israel's honor and for the sake of her cities and that the Lord would do what seemed good to Him. The idea was, "Maybe God will help, maybe He will not; if He does, we will not refuse His help." Joab is a carnal man and his implied message to his men is the extent of his piety: "Heaven will help those who help themselves."

During the battle, Joab repelled the Syrians and they fled before Israel's mighty men (v. 13). That sight demoralized the Ammonite soldiers who then retreated from Abishai into their walled city (v. 14). Although Joab was victorious that day, it was a meaningless achievement – the Ammonites were secure in their fortification and the Syrians merely withdrew to regroup later. No one was conquered, just temporarily beaten back.

Joab returned to Jerusalem to inform David of Israel's hollow victory. In type, flesh can never achieve a lasting victory over flesh. Aspirations of change and techniques for reformation work only for the weekend; enduring victory over carnal impulses must be gained through the power of the Holy Spirit (Rom. 8:13). David, the one called by God to subdue Israel's enemies and empowered by the Holy Spirit, needed to be leading Israel's army to victory under the Lord's direction, not carnal Joab. David learned that he could not delegate his responsibility to a fleshly man and expect anything but a carnal outcome. The Lord was with David, so he must lead the next assault for there to be a spectacular victory.

The Syrians regrouped and fortified themselves at Helam. Hadadezer even brought Syrian soldiers from beyond the Euphrates River to bolster their position at Helam (v. 16). The commander of Hadadezer's army was Shobach. David gathered Israel's full army and led them into battle against the Syrians first; he would not repeat Joab's mistake of getting trapped between two battlefronts (v. 17).

The Syrians fled before Israel, who killed seven hundred charioteers, forty thousand horsemen, and Shobach (v. 18). After witnessing the appalling slaughter of the Syrians, the kings who had aligned with Hadadezer pursued peace with David and thereby became his servants (v. 19). The Syrians concluded that it would be foolish to assist the Ammonites against Israel again. The following map illustrates the various battles David fought as described in this chapter and in chapter 12.[131]

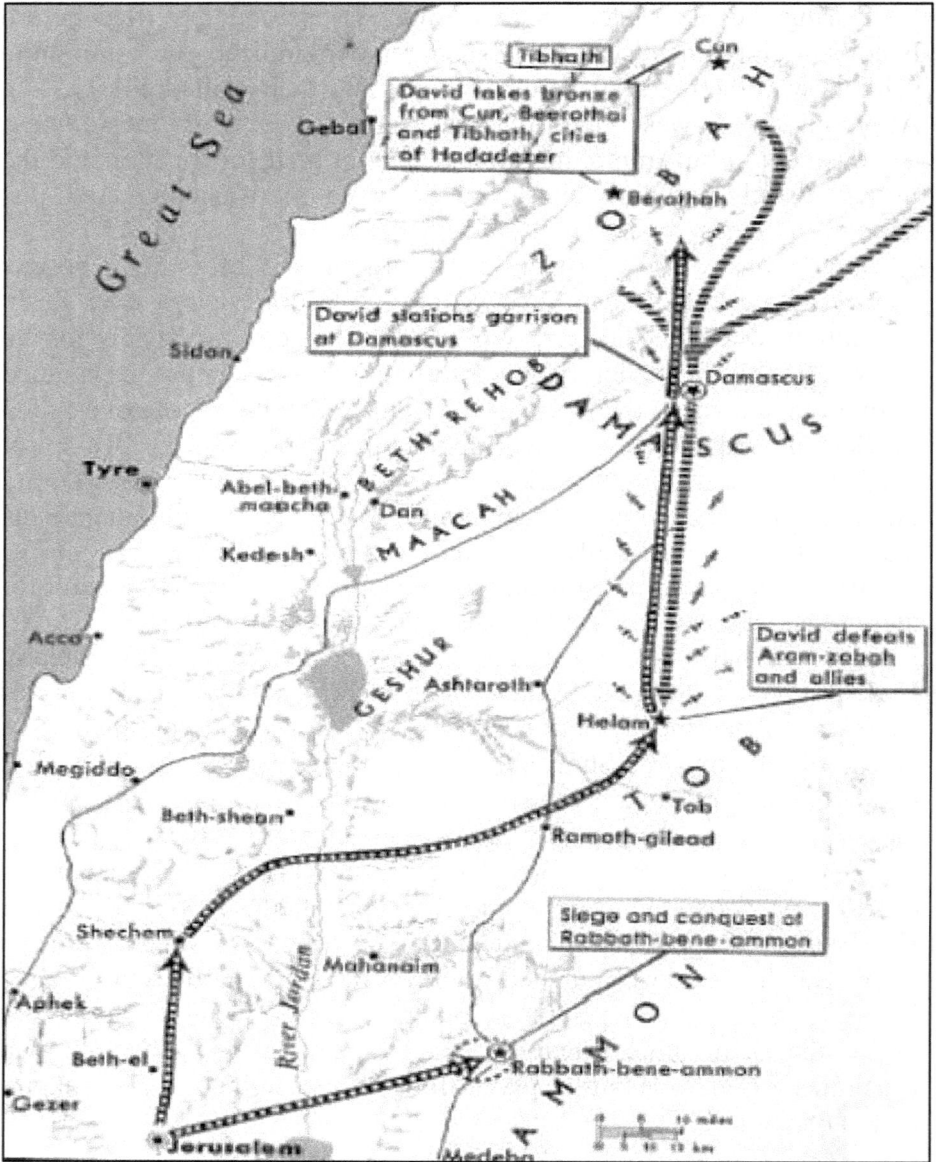

David's escapades of conquering and despoiling those opposing Israel and showing grace to the destitute and brokenhearted (chapters 8-10) wonderfully typify the coming advent of Christ, suggests J. N. Darby:

David exercises his power in bringing his enemies into subjection. The Philistines, who dwelt within the land of Israel, are subjugated. ... Moab is subdued and made tributary. At length the outward enemies, the Syrians, also, are either conquered or submit themselves. The Edomites become David's servants, and Jehovah preserves David wherever he goes. In all this we have again the man of faith and the type of the Lord Jesus, King in Zion, who is victorious over the enemies of Israel, and puts Israel in possession of the Promised Land (Gen. 15:18) as far as the Euphrates. He dedicates the spoil to Jehovah. He reigns over all Israel, and executes judgment and justice unto all his people. The companions of his pilgrimage participate in the glory of His kingdom – a type, in all this, of the kingdom of Christ.[132]

David penned Psalm 21 as an expression of thanksgiving by the congregation for answering their prayers to preserve their king in battle. The historical setting of this psalm seems to have been David's victory over the Ammonites and Syrians in this chapter. The returning king praises the Lord for displaying His majestic power in battle and for granting him the desire of his heart – the preservation of his life and a complete triumph (Ps. 21:1-6). David affirms that his prayer was granted because he fully trusted in the unfailing love of the Most High (Ps. 21:7). The king is then addressed by the congregation, who state they knew he would be completely victorious over his enemies because he trusted in the Lord (Ps. 21:8-10). They realize God would grant him future victories for the same reason, despite the ongoing efforts of David's enemies to overcome him. The congregation declares they will sing praise to God alone for flexing His might and power on behalf of their king (Ps. 21:11-12).

When God is on your side, every temptation and every conflict can be overcome, that is, if we side with Him! God is with David and David's heart is with the Lord and as a result Israel is unstoppable! Sadly, the next chapter records how David's heart became entangled in a web of sin, which resulted in serious consequences to himself, to his family, and to the entire nation. Consequently, there is an interruption of the narrative concerning the battle for Rabbah beginning in the next chapter through 12:25.

Meditation

Since the days of Pentecost, has the whole church ever put aside
every other work and waited upon Him for ten days, that the Spirit's
power might be manifested? We give too much attention to method
and machinery and resources, and too little to the source of power.

— Hudson Taylor

David's Great Sin

2 Samuel 11

David, superbly enabled by the Lord, has faithfully set out to establish his kingdom, which will then permit his son to build Jehovah's temple undistracted by war or lack of resources. Unfortunately, the king's terrible sin recorded in this chapter halts the expansion of his kingdom, and results in discipline and consequences that will plague his family for years to come. From a typological standpoint, David, in previous chapters, represented the Lord Jesus' first advent, which was marked by suffering, obedience, and victory. After chapter 10, embroiled in sin and deception, David no longer typifies the victorious Jewish Messiah doing God's will during His first advent.

The victories described in the previous chapter were largely against the Syrians, meaning the Ammonites, who were secure in their capital city of Rabbah, had yet to be punished for insulting David's ambassadors. With the winter months over, it was time to recommence military operations against the Ammonites by putting Rabbah in siege (v. 1). A siege of a large walled city was a time-consuming venture, so the king tasked Joab with the effort. David chose to remain in Jerusalem instead of going to war.

The Sin (vv. 2-5)

It is difficult to precisely place David's age at this time. Given the biblical chronology of events, he must be between 39 and 49 years of age. (The latter age seems more likely, as Solomon was thought to be about 19 years old when he became king and David later died at the age of 70). David suffers a mid-life crisis, so to speak. The consequences of his unchecked lusting will have severe and lingering ramifications for his entire family and the Jewish nation.

The king spent a leisurely afternoon in his bed. It was not uncommon for those in the Ancient East to rise with the sun, to take a

287

short nap during the heat of the day, and then to enjoy the cooler air on one's rooftop in the evening. David arose from his siesta sometime after three o'clock and then strolled out on the flat roof of his house to view the city (v. 2). The king saw a beautiful woman bathing and inquired about her.

It would have been inappropriate for a woman of the Ancient East to bathe in an open court so that anyone could see her from a rooftop. Because of her lack of feminine modesty, someone did see her – the king. Proverbs 7 teaches us that the sexual sin of the woman is *to lure* and of the man is *to follow*. Some commentators suggest Bathsheba was intentionally flaunting herself and hoping the king would notice her, but there is nothing in the text to suggest this assumption is accurate.

Actually, the entire chapter keeps to a factual account of the events without expressing what motivated wrong behavior. The text, therefore, reveals Bathsheba as a beautiful woman, not an alluring one, though certainly her lack of discretion was what stirred David's passions. Regardless, the lion's share of guilt falls squarely on the one God put into authority and who was to represent God's character in executing his royal office, David.

If David had been at Rabbah fighting the Lord's battle with his army, then his eye would have never rested on the object which the devil hoped would arouse the king's corrupt nature within (which all of us inherited from Adam). For this reason, C. H. Mackintosh exhorts us to be vigilant in what we should be doing, so that we do not do what we ought not to be doing:

> It is well to be ever on the watch, for we have a watchful enemy. *"Be sober, be vigilant,"* says the apostle, *"because your adversary, the devil, as a roaring lion, walks about, seeking whom he may devour."* Satan watches his opportunity, and when he finds a soul unoccupied with his proper service, he will surely seek to involve him in evil. It is, therefore, safe and healthful to be diligently engaged in service – service flowing out of communion with God, for we are thus in an attitude of positive hostility to the enemy, but if we are not acting in hostility, he will use us as instruments for his own ends. When David failed in energy as the captain of the hosts of Israel, he became the slave of lust. Sad picture! Solemn, most solemn warning for our souls![133]

If our hearts are filled with Christ, there will be no room for what does not have His approval. It is only when Satan prompts us to desire something apart from Christ that he can succeed in drawing us after his things. It is only when we know "the Lord is my portion" that we will be safe from the seductive attempts of the enemy. Satisfaction in Christ is the best defense against sin. At this particular juncture, it was not so for the king of Israel; he was coveting what the Lord disapproved of.

The king was informed that the name of the woman he saw bathing was Bathsheba, the wife of Uriah the Hittite, one of his soldiers (v. 3). David was probably thinking that, if the young woman was unmarried, he would take her as his wife, but that was not the case; she was married. An unspecified amount of time from his initial lustful impulse (perhaps a few days) had transpired, but the king chose not to extinguish his cravings which he knew were against God's will.

The king sent messengers to bring Bathsheba to him. Regrettably, David had sexual relations with Uriah's wife. Afterwards Bathsheba purified herself (bathed, per Lev. 15:18) and returned home in the evening (v. 4). Amazingly, she ignored God's command against adultery and so was punishable by death (for she did not cry out for help), but yet observed the ceremonial aspects of the Law because she desired to be clean before the Lord! But in God's sight, neither of them was *clean*. They were defiled by gross sin for which there was no Levitical sin or trespass offering by which one could be reconciled to God. A few weeks later Bathsheba informed David that she was pregnant with his child (v. 5).

Bathsheba may have been bathing initially because of some ceremonial pollution per the Law (v. 2). For example, a menstruating Jewish woman was unclean for seven days (regardless of how long her period actually lasted) and then was to bathe after this time to become ceremonially clean again (Lev. 15:19-24). If this was the case, Bathsheba would have been ovulating just a few days after such a ceremonial washing and this would explain why her encounter with David resulted in conception.

Being the granddaughter of David's counselor Ahithophel (23:34) and being childless (i.e., she likely had not been married long) meant that Bathsheba was likely some thirty years younger than the king. Her younger age, and the king's status as a great man, may explain why she consented to the adulterous rendezvous (as there is no evidence that she was forced). Although married and apparently a chaste woman, perhaps she thought that yielding to such a renowned king would not be a sin. David's conduct proves the old adage: "Absolute power corrupts absolutely." But God would hold David accountable for abusing the authority He had bestowed on David.

David's folly and sin abound in this chapter. First, he neglected the business of suppressing the Lord's enemies as he had been personally tasked to do (5:2). Second, the king did not consult the Lord as to who should lead the troops against Ammon. Third, he became slothful – something we have not previously witnessed in David. Fourth, he is guilty of a wandering eye and lusting for what displeases God. Fifth, he used his power to lead a subordinate into sin. Sixth, he committed adultery. Seventh, instead of admitting his sin, he tried to cover it up. Eighth, he had Bathsheba's husband, one of his valiant servants, murdered. Ninth, the king made Joab an accomplice to the murder of Uriah. Tenth, other faithful soldiers died with Uriah in David's cover-up scheme. Eleventh, David used his position to steal what was not his; David took what belong to Uriah, Bathsheba (Matt. 1:6). Twelfth, David carried on as if God had not noticed what he had done or would not act against him!

Regrettably, it was not long after slothful David neglected the things of God that he then rejected the word of God. Likewise, we never read of Noah having a drinking problem before the flood, because he was engrossed in the work of building God's ark. *"Because of laziness the building decays, and through idleness of hands the house leaks"* (Eccl. 10:18). Many of God's people have fallen into sin because their hands were idle. David proved the old axiom: "Idle hands are the devil's workshop." He had acquired enormous prosperity and had nearly vanquished all his enemies. It was springtime, the appropriate time to capture the last Ammonite stronghold of Rabbah and have total control of the kingdom. But, instead of engaging God's enemy in battle, David tarried in Jerusalem and took up a position against God.

David's idleness made him restless and afforded him too much time to think about what he should not have been musing on, and consequently he fell into sin. If David had been attending to the Lord's business, he would have been tired and enjoyed a good night's rest and Bathsheba would have been nowhere in the vicinity to notice. His temptation resulted from idleness. The prophet Ezekiel informs us that the perverse city of Sodom had an *"abundance of idleness"* (Ezek.

16:49). Solomon eloquently warns the Lord's people of this evil, *"Whatever your hand finds to do, do it with your might; for there is no work or device or knowledge or wisdom in the grave where you are going"* (Eccl. 9:10). Many of the devil's temptations will be avoided if we stay busy in the Lord's work.

We know that David had a routine of praying three times each day (especially during his trouble-filled early years; Ps. 55:17). Apparently, David was not before the Lord on this day, which meant he was more vulnerable to temptation. Matthew Henry wisely remarks, "Idleness gives great advantage to the tempter. Standing waters gather filth. The bed of sloth often proves the bed of lust."[134] Straying from the Lord's will, His work, and His presence will always lead us into trouble! Dear believer, by staying near to God and keeping busy in His work we afford the devil fewer opportunities to recruit us into his business.

The king gave in to his lust! In Joshua 7, Achan admitted to taking from Jericho a beautiful Babylonian garment, two hundred shekels of silver, and a wedge of gold weighing fifty shekels (Josh. 7:20-21). The narrative shows the progress of his sin to its full development: Achan "saw," he "coveted," and he "took." These were the same three steps leading to death that Eve made when she ate the forbidden fruit in Eden (Gen. 3:6), and the same David followed when he stole Bathsheba, Uriah's wife. Achan, Eve, and David sinned for the same reason you and I do today; we first think about, then lust after, and then do what is outside of God's will.

David lusted for what God said he could not have, and then entered into sin. James puts the matter this way: *"But each one is tempted when he is drawn away by his own desires and enticed. Then, when desire has conceived, it gives birth to sin; and sin, when it is full-grown, brings forth death"* (Jas. 1:14-15). Our bodies are equipped with mechanisms to keep us healthy and to procreate, but when we lust for what is beyond God's design for our behavior, we enter into sin and suffer broken fellowship with the Lord. This is what David did and we learn in the next chapter that he remained in this miserable spiritual condition for about a year!

The Cover-Up Effort (vv. 6-13)

Pregnancy is a difficult condition to hide for very long, so David had little time to plan a cover-up scheme to prevent their sin from becoming public. Adultery was punishable by death, so the offense also put Bathsheba's life in jeopardy (Lev. 20:10).The most logical choice was to withdraw Uriah from the battlefront so that he could spend some time with his wife. Then everyone would think that Bathsheba was pregnant with her husband's child.

David sent word to Joab to send him Uriah (v. 6). After his arrival in Jerusalem, the king quizzed Uriah about the details of the siege effort and troop morale to make it appear that his recall was legitimate (v. 7). Then David sent Uriah home to his wife, even providing a gift of food. However, loyal Uriah did not go home, but rather he slept at the door of the king's house (vv. 8-9). Some commentators believe that Uriah had heard that his wife had been in the king's court and therefore was suspicious about her. He was therefore determined not to come near her. While this is possible, it seems that Uriah would have opened David's later dispatch to Joab, if he actually believed that the king was conspiring against him.

After learning from his servants that Uriah did not go home, the king asked Bathsheba's husband why he did not go home to be with his wife after being away for so long (v. 10). Uriah's reply to the king's question affirmed that he was an upstanding man:

> *The ark and Israel and Judah are dwelling in tents, and my lord Joab and the servants of my lord are encamped in the open fields. Shall I then go to my house to eat and drink, and to lie with my wife? As you live, and as your soul lives, I will not do this thing* (v. 11).

We learn from this verse that Uriah was not just an ethical man, but a spiritual one also. His first concern was that the Ark should have a permanent dwelling place, not just a tent. This meant that Israel must overcome Ammon; the campaign that he was now engaged in must succeed. Furthermore, Uriah did not feel it was appropriate for him to enjoy marital intimacy with his wife while his comrades were away from their homes battling the Ammonites. Uriah's response of devotion for God and his countrymen must have had a convicting effect on the king's guilty conscience. While his loyal servant was concerned about God's honor and the wellbeing of others, the king was attempting to hide how he had taken advantage of Uriah in such a deplorable way.

Not giving up on his plan, David instructed Uriah to remain one more night in Jerusalem and that he would return him to Joab the following day (v. 12). That night David called Uriah to a feast and the host ensured that his guest got quite drunk, again hoping that high-minded Uriah would go home to his wife in a drunken stupor (v. 13). But it was not to be; Uriah slept among David's servants that night and did not go home.

The Murder (vv. 14-25)

The next morning David returned Uriah to Joab, with sealed orders (v. 14). David instructed Joab to put Uriah in the forefront of the hottest battle and then to withdraw from him so that he would be struck down by the enemy (v. 15). Faithful and innocent Uriah delivered his own death sentence to Joab, who carried out David's command. The valiant warrior, willing to die for the king's honor, will instead die for the king's sin. Uriah was positioned by Joab where he knew that there were valiant enemy soldiers (v. 16).

After Israel began engaging the Ammonites, the evil plot was sprung. Uriah and those with him were apparently pressing forward in the center when both flanks were summoned to withdraw from them, leaving them exposed to archers on the wall (v. 17). Not only did Uriah die in David's cover-up, but many other men devoted to David did too.

Joab sent a courier to David with a report on the siege effort against Rabbah (v. 18). The messenger was told to first relay the sorrowful news of how some of the king's men were slain. Then, after David became angry and began to criticize Joab for getting too close to the wall, the courier was to inform the king that Uriah had also perished in the battle (vv. 19-21). This scheme permitted Joab to take advantage of Uriah's murder to smooth over with the king some of his own errors in military tactics. In the future, Joab would have more freedom to do as he pleased because he could hold this deceitful matter over David's head to gain his own way (i.e., blackmail David).

The messenger did as Joab ordered and brought the king news from the battlefront (v. 22). He told the king that the Ammonites had come out of Rabbah to confront Israel, and at first were prevailing, but then were driven back into the city, but that archers positioned on the wall killed several soldiers, including Uriah (vv. 22-24). After hearing the report, David gave the courier a message to encourage Joab, *"Do not let this thing displease you, for the sword devours one as well as another. Strengthen your attack against the city, and overthrow it"* (v.

293

25). Calloused David had no remorse over his evil deed and even justified Uriah's death as a normal cost of war.

David Takes Uriah's Wife (vv. 26-27)

Bathsheba mourned the death of her husband (v. 26). After the normal period of mourning was over (usually seven days), David hastily sent for her. Bathsheba became David's eighth wife, and she bore him a son (v. 27).

David planned out everything necessary for him to enjoy his forbidden fruit (Bathsheba) and without the consequences of doing so. But there was one thing that David forgot to consider – what the Lord thought about his horrendous behavior. The writer does not forget this detail: *"But **all** that David had done in this matter greatly displeased the Lord!"* (v. 27). Nothing that David had done had escaped God's awareness. A holy God must judge sin, especially in His beloved children, and particularly those in authority.

Meditation

> Man-like it is to fall into sin,
> Fiend-like it is to dwell therein;
> Christ-like it is for sin to grieve,
> God-like it is all sin to leave.

> — Friedrich Von Logau

David Repents
2 Samuel 12

Nathan Reproves David (vv. 1-15)

God sent the prophet Nathan to confront David over his adultery with Bathsheba and the murder of her husband to conceal it (v. 1). It is not likely that Nathan had spoken to David since his wrongdoing in the previous chapter, or that David had solicited Nathan's counsel. David, like our first parents after they ate the forbidden fruit, tried to hide from God. This meant that Nathan's sudden arrival at the palace was unsolicited, unannounced, and probably unwelcomed.

Might there be more Nathan-like believers in the Church today who will not ignore those believers spiritually suffocating in sin. It takes real courage to lovingly rebuke those we love despite their social or religious rank. Let us remember that David was the king of Israel and could have effortlessly ordered Nathan's execution. May we all be encouraged to stand in the light of God's truth and *"have no fellowship with the unfruitful works of darkness, but rather expose them"* (Eph. 5:11). Nathan practiced what Paul exhorted the Christians in Thessalonica to do:

> *But as for you, brethren, do not grow weary in doing good. And if anyone does not obey our word in this epistle, note that person and do not keep company with him, that he may be ashamed. Yet do not count him as an enemy, but admonish him as a brother* (2 Thess. 3:13-15).

Nathan loved David and in obedience to God's command sought to restore David by confronting him over his sin. The prophet spoke in a parable, and spiritually despondent David had no clue that he was the actual perpetrator in the story. Nathan told the king about a wealthy man who seized a poor man's only ewe lamb, which he greatly treasured, in order to serve a meal to an unexpected visitor (vv. 2-4).

David was enraged over the tale: *"So David's anger was greatly aroused against the man, and he said to Nathan, 'As the Lord lives, the man who has done this shall surely die!'"* (v. 5). Even though the king was himself under the heavy yoke of sin himself, David quickly and severely judged the lesser offense of another.

The prophet used this story to express God's anger over David's sin. David had abused the power of the throne which God had given him; thus, stern judgment would be forthcoming. David's anger aroused by Nathan's story was just, but hypocritical (v. 6). David upheld the Law's fourfold restitution for stealing, but also demanded the death of the guilty party; yet, under the Law, the consequences for David's more grievous sin was the death penalty. David was enraged at the injustice done to the poor man, yet he had committed a much worse offense and had remained unrepentant for about a year. It demonstrates how easy it is for anger to cloud rational thinking and logical conclusions. When we are not in communion with God, our anger has the greatest opportunity to be provoked and to result in ungodly behavior.

Unknowingly, David had pronounced his own sentence – he deserved death! It is at this moment that we, in our mind's eye, see the brave prophet raising his shaking finger and pointing it at David to voice God's indictment:

You are the man! Thus says the Lord God of Israel: "I anointed you king over Israel, and I delivered you from the hand of Saul. I gave you your master's house and your master's wives into your keeping, and gave you the house of Israel and Judah. And if that had been too little, I also would have given you much more! Why have you despised the commandment of the Lord, to do evil in His sight? You have killed Uriah the Hittite with the sword; you have taken his wife to be your wife, and have killed him with the sword of the people of Ammon. Now therefore, the sword shall never depart from your house, because you have despised Me, and have taken the wife of Uriah the Hittite to be your wife." Thus says the Lord: "Behold, I will raise up adversity against you from your own house; and I will take your wives before your eyes and give them to your neighbor, and he shall lie with your wives in the sight of this sun. For you did it secretly, but I will do this thing before all Israel, before the sun" (vv. 7-12).

The prophet's rebuke is carefully crafted. He first acknowledges the goodness of God to David before identifying David's crimes against God: *"I anointed you ... I delivered you ... I gave you ... and gave you ... I also would have given you much more!"* (vv. 8-9). The indictment contrasts God's manifold blessings with the unreasonableness of David's wicked behavior: *"Why have you despised the commandment of the Lord, to do evil in His sight?"* (v. 9). The prophet then reveals the sordid details of David's covert and abhorrent crimes – nothing had escaped the attention of David's omniscient God. Notice that the secret murder of Uriah and the stealing/marrying of his wife are mentioned twice.

In David's wretched spiritual state he was numb to his accountability for his own sin, even after Nathan aroused his sense of justice with the parable of the stolen ewe lamb. However, when Nathan indicted David, *"You are the man"* the hidden sin was traced to its source and David instantly became a conscience-smitten, broken-hearted sinner in the presence of a holy God. All was revealed, there could be no more hiding and David readily confessed his sin against the Lord.

Nathan's rebuke of David should remind us that, though others may not know our secret sins, God knows and we know all about them. *"Be sure your sin will find you out"* (Num. 32:23). Nathan also told David the cost of his sin, *"the sword shall never depart from your house"* ... *"I have raised up adversity against you"* ... *"I will take your wives"* from you and another will publicly defile them. We wonder what went through David's mind after hearing that his children would be a grief to him, his enemies would oppress him, and that another man would sexually assault his wives to shame him? He must have realized that a few moments of wanton pleasure was not worth the grave and enduring consequences to himself and his household. No doubt he wondered why he had preferred his sin over joyful fellowship with God and for such a long time. Sin always has a hidden price tag; it costs far more than we expect and has consequences that last a lot longer than we ever anticipated.

As David affirmed to Nathan, the Law demanded that four lambs be given in restitution for a stolen lamb that had been killed (Ex. 22:1-2). The Law's retribution for theft was particularly steep and would be a deterrent against stealing another's possessions. Centuries later, a repentant Zacchaeus referred to this provision of the Law when he told the Lord Jesus, *"If I have taken anything from anyone by false accusation, I restore fourfold"* (Luke 19:8). David had stolen what was not his and had then killed Uriah, and God would exact from him the life of four of his own sons for that crime: his newborn son conceived in adultery with Bathsheba, Amnon (who raped his own half-sister), Absalom (who led a national rebellion against his father), and Adonijah (who unsuccessfully conspired to be king).

David felt God's rebuke keenly and confessed his sin to Nathan, *"I have sinned against the Lord"* (v. 13). When a child of God humbly and honestly confesses his or her sin, God is then able to put it away for good (1 Jn. 1:9). Indeed, Nathan avowed that the Lord had chosen to pass over David's sin, in that he would not die for his offenses. But then the prophet adds a painful "however." Because David's transgression had caused God's enemies to blaspheme Jehovah's name, Bathsheba's newborn son would die (v. 14). Matthew Henry explains how David gave an occasion for Jehovah's enemies to blaspheme the Lord and exhorts us not to do the same:

> The wicked people of that generation, the infidels, idolaters, and profane, would triumph in David's fall, and speak ill of God and of his law, when they saw one guilty of such foul enormities that professed such an honor both for him and it. "These are your professors! This is he that prays and sings psalms, and is so very devout! What good can there be in such exercises, if they will not restrain men from adultery and murder?" They would say, "Was not Saul rejected for a lesser matter? Why then must David live and reign still?" not considering that God sees not as man sees, but searches the heart. … There is this great evil in the scandalous sins of those that profess religion and relation to God, that they furnish the enemies of God with opportunity to reproach and to blaspheme (Rom. 2:24).[135]

After delivering God's message, the faithful prophet left the palace (v. 15). We wonder why the Lord permitted David to remain in his sin for approximately an entire year before sending Nathan to censure him. The answer is partly revealed in Psalm 32, for David informs us that he was miserable during this time:

Have mercy on me, O Lord, for I am in trouble; my eye wastes away with grief, yes, my soul and my body! For my life is spent with grief, and my years with sighing; my strength fails because of my iniquity, and my bones waste away (Ps. 31:9-10).

Clearly, the Lord had been using David's wounded conscience and the lack of communion with Himself to break His servant. Our private sins are no secret to us or to the Lord and will be a burden to our souls until rightly dealt with. Thankfully, as foretold by Nathan, David did receive unmerited forgiveness and was restored to God. He pens Psalms 32 and 51 to acknowledge all that God had accomplished through mercifully chastening him.

In Psalm 31, although David did not know how God could forgive him, David knew by faith that his transgressions were forgiven (Ps. 32:1-2). David recalls the time he was silent in his sin and under God's heavy hand: he groaned deep in his bones day and night; he grew old and his vitality dried up as crops in a long summer's drought (Ps. 32:3-4). The way out of this pitiful spiritual condition was to confess his sin and ask for forgiveness (Ps. 32:5). Given the outcome of his experience, he counsels others not to linger in denying their sin, but to get right with the Lord while He may be found, rather than being overwhelmed by the mighty waters (i.e., correction by calamity; Ps. 32:6). Having confessed his sin, David had grown to appreciate the Lord as his Hiding Place – God is a Refuge to those who trust in Him (Ps. 32:7).

Although under the Law the punishment of adultery and murder demanded David's death, God's righteousness would be upheld in executing judgment – David would lose four sons! Because of His covenant with David, God spared his life, but God's justice cost David dearly and his household never knew peace afterwards. No doubt as David looked back over his life, he greatly regretted his unchecked lust and carnal conniving. The message of the Law is that *"the wages of sin is death"* (Rom. 6:23) and that God will judge all that offends His holy character. Yet, David also experienced God's mercy in a way that he did not know was possible. Such an expression of divine grace does not undermine God's governmental authority, but rather complements it! H. A. Ironside comments on this important distinction:

All believers today are under the government of God the Father who, without respect of persons, judges according to every man's works (1 Pet. 1:17). It is true today, as in past ages, that whatsoever a man sows, that shall he also reap (Gal. 6:7). This is true of all men whether saints or sinners. There are temporal consequences that follow sin, which may go on all through life, even though God has forgiven the sin itself as in David's case. Nathan said by divine authority, *"The Lord also hath put away thy sin."* But he added, *"The sword shall never depart from thy house"* (2 Sam. 12:7-15). ... Both these have to do with the divine government in this world and not with the question of how a guilty sinner may be cleansed from his sin and saved for eternity.[136]

The matter of salvation is settled through the cross of the Lord Jesus Christ and cannot positionally be lost by the personal sins of the saint, though every sin has some consequence to the believer from a practical standpoint. David was forgiven, but the repercussions of his sin, as we will see in the next few chapters, will plague him for the remainder of his life.

As just described, Psalm 32 expresses David's joy of being forgiven and restored to God after His discipline had ceased. Although the Hebrew superscript of that poem does not give the particulars, it seems likely that it follows on the heels of Psalm 51, which does pertain to his adultery with Bathsheba and the murder of her husband Uriah. David shows us in Psalm 51 that true repentance assumes personal responsibility for one's own actions:

Have mercy upon me, O God, according to Your lovingkindness; according to the multitude of Your tender mercies, blot out **my transgressions***. Wash me thoroughly from* **my iniquity***, and cleanse me from* **my sin***. For I acknowledge* **my transgressions***, and* **my sin** *is always before me. Against You, You only, have* **I sinned***, and done this evil in Your sight* (Ps. 51:1-4).

Although deserving death for his offenses, David could sing this ecstatic penitential song acknowledging God's forgiveness. Nathan had told David that he would not die for his crimes. David also knew Jehovah to be a covenant-keeping God and that He had made unconditional promises to him. So even though David did not know how God could righteously forgive his sin, he believed by faith that he had a means of doing so beyond what the Law revealed.

The writer of Hebrews later reveals that this means the blood of Christ, which sealed a New Covenant between Jehovah and the Jewish nation (Heb. 8:8). The original covenant, the Law, could not save, as no one could keep it; its purpose was to show sin and point sinners to the Savior, Christ (Rom. 3:20; Gal. 3:24). David's rule among Jewish kings is rare. David began well and finished well, after experiencing moral failure in the midst of his tenure. David cherished God's unwarranted forgiveness for the remainder of his life and that kept him on course as God's humble servant. Likewise, the same realization keeps believers close to the Lord today as they journey on the narrow and high road of holy living.

David's Son Dies (vv. 16-23)

As part of the discipline pronounced on David, his newborn son by Bathsheba was struck with illness (v. 15). The child was probably less than three months old, as Joab is again in active warfare, meaning that winter had passed. If this is correct, Nathan visited David about a year after his adulterous affair with Bathsheba. It also meant that the child had been in the home long enough for all to rejoice over him and to bond with him; this made God's judgment all the more sorrowful.

The king humbly prostrated himself before the Lord to fast and to pray for the child (vv. 16-17). On the seventh day the child died. David's servants were afraid to tell him the news because of his despair; they feared that David might harm himself (v. 18). However, David heard his servants whispering, and, perceiving that the child had died, asked his servants if that was the case (v. 19).

After learning of his son's death, *"David arose from the ground, washed and anointed himself, and changed his clothes; and he went into the house of the Lord and worshiped"* (v. 20). Afterwards he returned to his home and requested that food be set before him. His servants were perplexed because David had fasted and wept for the child while he was alive, but then wanted to eat after learning that the child had died (v. 21). David answered them:

> *While the child was alive, I fasted and wept; for I said, "Who can tell whether the Lord will be gracious to me, that the child may live?" But now he is dead; why should I fast? Can I bring him back again? I shall go to him, but he shall not return to me* (vv. 22-23).

David's response reveals his complete confidence in the Lord to do what was right, even in matters of his chastening. MacDonald writes,

"Before the blow fell he prayed, knowing that Jehovah was a *God of mercy*. After the blow fell he worshiped, knowing that Jehovah was a *God of righteousness*."[137] True repentance agrees with God about the matter of sin, rests in His mercy, and willingly accepts His justice – this is what David did.

Speaking of the deceased baby, the king told his servants, *"I shall go to him, but he shall not return to me"* (v. 23). Whether he was merely referring to the grave, or more specifically to Sheol, the realm of disembodied souls in the Old Testament, is unclear. Regardless, David anticipated seeing his deceased infant son again after death (i.e., a conscious reunion of departed souls).

There are only a few passages of Scripture which address this matter. The Lord Jesus informs us that a rich man suffering in Hades (the place of temporary torment for the unjustified dead) knew who Abraham and Lazarus were and also who his brothers (still living) were. Those who had been martyred during the Tribulation Period and had gone to heaven were fully cognizant of what had happened to them and requested that God take vengeance on their oppressors (Rev. 6:9-11). The disciples, though a bit confused at first, recognized the Lord Jesus after His resurrection (Luke 24:31; John 20:20).

Apparently, death does not prohibit us from recognizing loved ones, even if they have not yet experienced resurrection – we intuitively know their spiritual essence. There must, then, be the ability of individuals to distinguish other souls even when there is not a body; thus, it would stand to reason that individuals after experiencing resurrection would still be discernable (i.e., the resurrected body would contain the same soul that was recognized before). Paul tells us that the resurrected body of the believer draws characteristics from its mortal body (1 Cor. 15:37-39). This allows it to be similar in appearance to its previous earthly form. The resurrected body will represent God's best design for each individual; perhaps this is the reason that when angels appear in human form, they never appear as children or as elderly.

David believed that he would someday see his deceased newborn son in heaven. Though born condemned in Adam (John 3:18; Rom. 5:12), such souls, never having the opportunity to choose life in Christ, are *apparently* made trophies of God's grace through Christ. There is one thing that we can be sure of in this matter: *"Shall not the Judge of all the earth do right?"* (Gen. 18:25). Yes, God will do what is right! And like David, we should simply rest in the flawless character of God.

Solomon Is Born (vv. 24-25)

David, now having grace flowing out of him again, is able to comfort Bathsheba after losing their firstborn son. The Lord blessed Bathsheba, for she quickly conceived again and bore another son. H. L. Rossier observes that this was a declaration of God's grace towards Bathsheba:

> Grace brings Bathsheba, whom defilement would prevent from having a portion in God's blessings, into the Messiah's line of descent (Matt. 1:6). She becomes the mother of the king of peace and glory. Grace delights to work on behalf of fallen creatures whom it associates with Christ in order to show its "exceeding riches" in the ages to come.[138]

Bathsheba's second son was named Solomon (v. 24). As the verb form of Solomon's name means "to amend" or "to restore," we gain a sense that Solomon was God's replacement son for David and Bathsheba, after striking down their first child in judgment. Solomon was God's symbol of *peace* (the meaning of his name) to his parents. Nathan called the newborn, Jedidiah, which means "beloved of Jehovah" (v. 25). Jehovah loved Solomon! We later learn that Solomon had been chosen by God to carry on David's dynasty and to build His temple, which would fulfill God's promise to David in chapter 7.

Rabbah Falls (vv. 26-31)

Because of David's slothfulness and sin, chapters 11 and 12 interrupted the narrative concerning the conquest of Rabbah, the capital of Ammon (v. 26). Joab had continued his siege efforts that had begun the previous year and was able to capture the city's water supply, which meant it would fall soon (v. 27). Joab sent word for David to gather Israel's full army and come to Rabbah, so that he would not be the one accredited with the victory (v. 28). This was a noble and loyal gesture by Joab, who often employed carnal methods to accomplish personal agendas.

David journeyed to Rabbah and Israel conquered the city (v. 29). The king's crown, weighing a talent of gold with many precious stones, was removed from the king of Ammon's head and placed on David's (v. 30). The people of Rabbah and other Ammonite survivors became David's servants (to make bricks, to hew wood, and perhaps to mine) and Israel's army returned to Jerusalem (v. 31).

Meditation

Measure your growth in grace by your sensitiveness to sin.

— Oswald Chambers

Sin is the dare of God's justice, the rape of His mercy, the jeer of His patience, the slight of His power, and the contempt of His love.

— John Bunyan

Trouble at Home
2 Samuel 13

Amnon Rapes Tamar (vv. 1-22)

It did not take long before David began to reap the painful consequences of his sins committed in chapter 11. Paul reminds us that *"God is not mocked; for whatever a man sows, that he will also reap. For he who sows to his flesh will of the flesh reap corruption"* (Gal 6:7-8). Grace does not set aside the consequences of the believer's sin; corrupt seed must eventually bear its carnal fruit. The forgiven sinner may experience restoring grace and enjoy sweet and deep communion with God again, while at the same time being under the rod of God's discipline for past offenses against Him. This was the painful reality that David experienced for much of the remainder of his life.

Nathan had told David that *"the sword shall never depart from your house,"* meaning that David's children would cause him much anguish and sorrow. Because Amnon was the oldest son of David, he may have thought that he would be the next king of Israel and could therefore take certain liberties, without fear of retribution.

He particularly was fond of Tamar, David's daughter by Maachah (3:3) and Absalom's sister (v. 1). Tamar was a virgin and as the king's daughter every precaution was in place to maintain her purity. Because of her protective seclusion and guardianship, lusting Amnon became quite distraught over not being able to have sexual relations with his half-sister, so much so that it affected his health (v. 2). His cousin and friend Jonadab noticed his declining health and inquired about it; Amnon told him of his tormenting predicament (vv. 3-4).

Crafty Jonadab suggested that Amnon pretend to be bedridden with sickness and to ask the king to send Tamar to his home to make some cakes for him, that he might eat from her hand (vv. 5-6). Since David did not appoint any of his brothers to notable positions within his government, the son of David's brother Shammah (1 Sam. 16:9) may have been acting in spite against his uncle. Regardless, his scheming made him an accomplice to Amnon's crime.

David consented to Amnon's request, and directed his daughter to visit Amnon at his house and to do as he had requested (vv. 7-8). Tamar did as asked; she prepared and cooked the cakes and brought them to Amnon in a pan, but he refused to eat (v. 9). Instead, he commanded everyone to leave the premises and for Tamar to bring the cakes into his bedroom, so that he could eat them there from her hand (v. 10). Tamar obliged her brother, but then when she was alone with Amnon, he grabbed her and said, *"Come, lie with me, my sister"* (v. 11).

By asking Tamar, a modest and virtuous young woman, to consent to such a lewd act reveals just how malignant with sin Amnon's mind had become. In his lustful state, he actually thought she might approve of the idea. Tamar, however, was repulsed by Amnon's demand and quickly blurted back her objection:

> *No, my brother, do not force me, for no such thing should be done in Israel. Do not do this disgraceful thing! And I, where could I take my shame? And as for you, you would be like one of the fools in Israel. Now therefore, please speak to the king; for he will not withhold me from you* (vv. 12-13).

As a last resort to preclude her rape, she encouraged Amnon to ask their father for her hand in marriage. She told Amnon that surely he would approve. It seems doubtful that Tamar was actually giving her consent to marry Amnon, as such unions were unlawful (Lev. 18:9-11). Rather, her suggestion was an attempt to check Amnon's passions through reason without rejecting him outright. But her wise attempt went unheeded, and Amnon, being stronger than her, raped his sister (v. 14). As David did not marry Maacah, Tamar and Absalom's mother, until after he was king in Hebron (3:3), we can place Absalom's age at this time (as based on details in the next chapter) at 27 to 29 years, meaning that Amnon was approaching thirty. Tamar was likely in her late teens or early twenties and clearly no match for Amnon.

Paradoxically, after Amnon's animalist appetite was gratified, he then despised his sister intensely and demanded that she leave, but she would not (v. 15). Apparently, feelings of guilt and regret overwhelmed his conscience, and perhaps the realization of punishment gripped his mind. His actions show us that lust is not love and that carnal impulses are very much linked together – hate, envy, murder, and lust are akin to each other. Sin is not reasonable, and unchecked lust will lead us into insane behavior, as David has already learned.

Amnon's command was deeply insulting to Tamar, for not only had she been violated against her will, but now she was being rejected also. Under the Law, a man was to marry a virgin that he had defiled (Deut. 22: 28-29), but clearly Amnon had been driven by lust, without any genuine concern for his sister. Amnon would not listen to Tamar's tearful appeal, but instead commanded his servant to put her out of his house and bolt the door after her (v. 17).

Tamar wore attire fitting for one of the king's virgin daughters, "a robe of many colors" (in actuality, this was probably a tunic with long sleeves; v. 18). But after she was cast out, she tore her special robe, put ashes on her head, and went home weeping bitterly with her hand on her head (v. 19). After her brother Absalom learned that Amnon had raped Tamar, he consoled his sister and told her to hold her peace about the matter (v. 20). Absalom was not making light of the offense, but was resolved to handle it in his own way, rather than relying on the king to properly punish Amnon. Being unwanted by Amnon, Tamar was forced, by no fault of her own, to bear her shame alone; she lived with Absalom and remained unwed.

David was angry when he heard what had happened, but he did not punish Amnon for his crime. According to the Law, incest was punishable by death (Lev. 20:17). How could David publicly rebuke his son, when he too had been carried away by lust to take a woman unlawfully (v. 21)? Absalom had rightly discerned that the king would not properly judge Amnon for his crime. Although he hated Amnon for what he had done to his sister, Absalom guarded his speech, so that no one would know that he planned to avenge Tamar (v. 22).

Absalom Murders Amnon (vv. 23-33)

Two full years passed before Absalom moved to retaliate for Tamar's rape (v. 23). Sheep-shearing was always a festive occasion in the Ancient East, so Absalom invited David, with all his brethren, to feast with him at Baal Hazor (about eight miles northeast of Jerusalem and near Ephraim; v. 24). Because the king did not want to burden Absalom with such an expense, he decline to attend (v. 25). Absalom then requested that his brethren, including Amnon, be permitted to attend (v. 26). The king initially rejected the idea, but then consented after Absalom pressed him on the matter (v. 27).

Apparently all, or nearly all, of David's adult sons, including Amnon, attended the celebration. Absalom commanded his servants to slay Amnon on his signal, for he intended to wait until Amnon had been drinking for a while before executing his plan (this would minimize Amnon's ability to defend himself; v. 28). The time came when Absalom gave the signal and his servants killed Amnon. Seeing their brother murdered while sitting at the banqueting table caused David's other sons to panic and flee to Jerusalem on their mules (v. 29).

The initial report of the incident to the king was that Absalom had killed all his sons (v. 30). After hearing this appalling news, David arose, tore his garments and fell to the ground; his servants likewise tore their garments (vv. 30-31). But, Jonadab, the son of David's brother Shimeah (the one who had originally counseled Amnon on how to rape Tamar), told the king not to fret, for all his sons were not dead; Absalom had killed only Amnon because he raped his sister Tamar (vv. 32-33).

Absalom Flees to Geshur (vv. 34-39)

The Law provided no wiggle room for premeditated murder – it was a capital offense (Num. 35:21). Having achieved his long-awaited objective, Absalom fled across the Jordan northward to Geshur; there he would live with his maternal grandfather Talmai, who was the king of Geshur (vv. 34, 38).

Being the oldest son of David, Amnon was the one most likely to succeed David to the throne. There was only one other son of David older than Absalom, Chileab, but because he is not mentioned in adulthood, it is presumed that he died as a child. If this is correct, two of David's first three sons were dead and the third, deserving death for his crime, was living in exile.

Meanwhile in Jerusalem, Jonadab called the king's attention to his sons returning home by the road on the hillside (v. 35). David and his servants were overcome with relief and wept liberally because of the safe return of all David's sons, except for Amnon (v. 36). David was comforted over Amnon's death, but longed for and mourned Absalom's absence for the next three years (vv. 37, 39). For a second time, the king's affection for his son distorted proper justice for a crime he had committed. If David had appropriately punished Amnon, he would have gained Absalom's esteem, but because he did not, he lost two sons. True, Absalom was alive, but the king did not have his heart – as we will soon see, he was lost to the king all the same.

In future years, the king would be reminded many times of just how devastating the consequences of his uncontrolled lust were to his family. No doubt Nathan's decree *"the sword shall never depart from your house"* was a burden that David bore his entire life. Thankfully, Scripture presents a solution to sin and death: *"For the wages of sin is death, but the gift of God is eternal life in Christ Jesus our Lord"* (Rom. 6:23). We choose our sin, but it is God who chooses the consequences of our sin and offers consoling grace for those who regret and repent of their sin. God's infinite grace and forgiving heart ensure that failures are never final unless we choose to wallow in self-pity rather than find refuge in His grace. David chose the latter, Absalom the former – their ends tell the story of which choice is better!

Meditation

When the root is bitterness, imagine what the fruit might be.

— Woodrow Kroll

If you're a follower of Jesus but you feel distant from Him during this era of your life, if you're having difficulty resting easy in His forgiveness, could it be because you're blatantly refusing to let go of your animosity toward another person?

— Lee Strobel

Absalom Returns
2 Samuel 14

Three years have passed since the events of the preceding chapter. Joab perceived that David yearned for his son, so he solicited a wise woman from Tekoa to pretend to be a distressed and mourning mother who urgently needed the king's assistance (vv. 1-2). Joab told her what to say if she was granted an audience with the king (v. 3). The woman was brought before the king and after she requested the king's assistance, David inquired as to what her trouble was (vv. 4-5).

The supposed mother then spun her yarn before the king:

> *Indeed I am a widow, my husband is dead. Now your maidservant had two sons; and the two fought with each other in the field, and there was no one to part them, but the one struck the other and killed him. And now the whole family has risen up against your maidservant, and they said, "Deliver him who struck his brother, that we may execute him for the life of his brother whom he killed; and we will destroy the heir also." So they would extinguish my ember that is left, and leave to my husband neither name nor remnant on the earth* (vv. 6-7).

David was moved with compassion over the widow's plight, but it was an awkward situation because the Law required that her guilty son be executed for his crime. Not wanting to issue a rash decree that would exonerate a murder, David told her that he would look into the matter and make a ruling (v. 8). However, this did not satisfy the fictitious widow, who then offered to assume the guilt associated with a favorable decision that would preserve the life of her only living son (v. 9). David again tried to defer a ruling in the case by promising to protect her family until he did (v. 10). However, she was not content with this answer either and again pressured David to promise to protect her son from the avenger of blood and David vowed to do so (v. 11).

The trap was set and David had sprung it on himself by agreeing to protect her guilty son. Being pleased with the king's ruling, the woman then petitioned the king to listen to an additional request, which he agreed to do (v. 12). She asked the king why, if he would grant her guilty son a pardon, he was not moved to restore his own banished son, Absalom (v. 13)? She suggested, like spilled water on the ground, what Absalom did to Amnon was in the past and could not be undone. Furthermore, God has his ways of judging such sinners, which are not always immediate, and He is also able to forgive and restore the same to himself (as David well knew; v. 14). If God acts in this manner, should not the king also grant forgiveness to his son? T. Wilson summarizes the three elements of her case before David:

> In beguiling simplicity, she highlights the three principal parties in the case Joab was forcing the king to consider: First, *Amnon* is dead, and no act of justice can bring him back, though some think this sentence is pointing out to David that Absalom might die in exile. Second, God will eventually deal impartially with *Absalom*, if he is guilty; the RV and JND render the second statement as, "neither does God take away life." The sense would then be that God has not taken away Absalom's life, but is intent on his return. The woman is attempting to show that mercy can triumph over justice. Third, *David* should do what God has done and find means to bring back Absalom.[139]

However, Joab's reasoning through the woman had a vital flaw – God does not forgive those who do not desire to be forgiven by acknowledging the wrongness of their sin. Absalom had not humbled himself and repented of his sin, whereas a contrite and broken David had acknowledged his offenses against God, was therefore forgiven, and restored to God. The Lord Jesus told His audience that, *"unless you repent you will all likewise perish"* (Luke 13:3). He also instructed when to declare forgiveness to another individual: *"If your brother sins against you, rebuke him; **and if** he repents, forgive him"* (Luke 17:3-4). Believers are to mentally release the offenses of others to the Lord immediately to deal with (Eph. 4:32), and only then declare forgiveness to a repentant offender. It is unbiblical to grant forgiveness to those still in sin, for such an act endorses the continuance of sin.

The woman, pleading on behalf of Absalom, then told the king that it was appropriate that he, who had granted her fictitious son compassionate clemency, should do the same for his banished son (vv. 15-16). After making her appeal, she adds some flattery into the mix (perhaps to soothe the king's anger), comparing David's powers of discernment to that of an angel of God (v. 17).

Sensing that he had been set up by Joab, David asks her if Joab had put her up to this clever subterfuge; she told David the truth; Joab had put his words into her mouth (vv. 18-20). The king then addressed Joab, *"All right, I have granted this thing. Go therefore, bring back the young man Absalom"* (v. 21). Joab sensed the king's displeasure and fell to the ground before David and thanked him for showing favor to him by granting his request through the woman from Tekoa (v. 22).

Joab then departed for Geshur and brought Absalom to Jerusalem (v. 23). However, the king made the stipulation that Absalom could reside in his own home, but he was not to see David's face (v. 24). Joab may have been looking out for himself in this episode, for David was aging and Absalom, as David's oldest living son, was the prime candidate to succeed his father to the throne. Thus, by bringing Absalom back to Jerusalem, Absalom would be indebted to Joab. Nonetheless, as we will soon see, Joab's conniving backfired. It was dangerous for David to permit a rebellious and estranged son to have access to the people he governed. The entire situation had not been handled righteously and therefore nothing good could come from it.

Absalom was a handsome young man without any blemishes (v. 25). His good looks were further embellished by his long, thick hair, which he cut once a year because it became too heavy to manage (v. 26). The historian notes that Absalom had three sons and one daughter whom he named after his sister Tamar (v. 27). Because the names of the sons are not mentioned, it is generally thought that they perished in their infancy.

Tamar is said to have been *"a woman of beautiful appearance."* This statement gives us a clue to Absalom's age at this juncture; he must be at least in his early thirties to have a daughter referred to as a woman. Absalom was not born until David was king in Hebron (the king was thirty at that time) and David died at seventy years of age. This would indicate that David was probably in his mid-sixties during the events of this chapter. Later, Absalom's granddaughter Maachah was Rehoboam's favorite wife (2 Chron. 11:21). Rehoboam was David's grandson, through Solomon, who reigned as Israel's king after his father's death.

Two full years passed without Absalom being granted a meeting with his father (v. 28). He had twice requested a meeting with Joab to discuss the matter, but was ignored (v. 29). To gain Joab's attention, Absalom ordered his servants to set fire to one of Joab's barley fields that was near one of Absalom's fields (v. 30). That prompted Joab to immediately come to Absalom's house to protest, *"Why have your servants set my field on fire?"* (v. 31). Absalom said that it was to gain an audience with him, so he could deliver his petition to the king: *" 'Why have I come from Geshur? It would be better for me to be there still.' Now therefore, let me see the king's face; but if there is iniquity in me, let him execute me"* (v. 32). Absalom was right, either he was guilty and deserved to be punished or he should be granted full amnesty by the king and have a normal father-son relationship.

Joab relayed Absalom's message, and the king summoned Absalom. David had not seen his rebel son in five years, so we can only imagine his emotions when Absalom appeared and bowed his face to the ground. Sadly, David kissed the murderer Absalom, a token of his forgiveness which made mockery of God's Law which demanded Absalom's death (v. 33). There had been no confession of sin, no judgment of sin, and no atonement of the sin, which meant there would be more trouble ahead for David's house.

We must wonder if Solomon was thinking of his own family's situation when he later wrote: *"He who justifies the wicked, and he who condemns the just, both of them alike are an abomination to the Lord"* (Prov. 17:15). David's judicial mistake would result in a great upheaval in Israel, culminating in a civil war and a great loss of life. It is a reminder that whenever we rationalize disobeying God's Word, things can only get worse!

Meditation

When we walk with the Lord in the light of His Word,
What a glory He sheds on our way!
While we do His good will, He abides with us still,
And with all who will trust and obey.
Trust and obey, for there's no other way
To be happy in Jesus, but to trust and obey.

— John Sammis

Absalom's Treason
2 Samuel 15

Absalom's Treason (vv. 1-12)

Although David had spared Absalom's life, the rebellious schemer began immediately to plot his father's death in much the same way that he had Amnon's demise. He often traveled with an entourage of supporters (v. 1). He frequently inserted himself into legal matters being heard at the city's gate, posing as one who would be a true advocate for the people and a champion of justice (vv. 2-3). By his comments he was suggesting that his father had been negligent and partial in legal matters, and if he were given the opportunity to judge Israel, he would ensure everyone would benefit from equitable justice (v. 4).

So Absalom courted the favor of the people in this manner; he also warmly greeted those who came to the king for judgment, but in a way that promoted himself to the detriment of his father (v. 5). Absalom's politicking tactics were successful. Over time, he *"stole the hearts of the men of Israel"* (v. 6).

After "forty years" Absalom petitioned the king for permission to journey to Hebron to fulfill a vow he made in connection with the Lord returning him to Jerusalem from Geshur (vv. 7-8). The number "forty" is obviously a scribal error; it is generally thought that the correct number is "four" (as Josephus, the Syriac and Arabic texts all affirmed). But what period of time is actually being marked is unknown. It seems reasonable to assume that four years had passed since Absalom had returned to Jerusalem. Regardless of when Absalom's conspiracy was initiated, David granted his request and gave him leave (v. 9).

After leaving Jerusalem, Absalom sent secret messengers throughout all the tribes of Israel, saying, *"As soon as you hear the sound of the trumpet, then you shall say, 'Absalom reigns in Hebron!'"* (v. 10). Hebron would be the location for all those loyal to Absalom to assemble and then they would return to Jerusalem in force to overthrow David. Using a religious disguise, Absalom invited 200 influential men to accompany him to Hebron; these men knew nothing of the unfolding plot, but would be nonetheless caught up in it (v. 11). Because these men were well-respected and had gone with Absalom, many would think they were in favor of his insurrection – though in actuality most, if not all, were quite loyal to David. Absalom may have also included in this group some fickle soldiers who he thought might desert David if given the opportunity. Hebron, being eighteen miles south of Jerusalem, was a day's journey. This meant that the 200 men with Absalom would not be able to affirm their loyalty to David nor be able to support him, and thus they became a propaganda tool to bolster Absalom's cause.

The rebel son also sent for David's counselor Ahithophel living in Giloh to attend his sacrifice and feast in Hebron (v. 12). Ahithophel was a logical choice, not only because of his wisdom and knowledge of tactics, but, being the grandfather of Bathsheba (whom David publicly shamed), he would have just cause to hold a grudge against the king. Absalom's thorough planning caused the conspiracy against David to quickly expand – the number gathering to him was steadily increasing. H. L. Rossier suggests that Absalom's character is clearly that of a reprobate child of the devil, who, as the Lord Jesus said, was *"a murderer from the beginning"*:

All the evil instincts of Absalom's nature are unleashed to attain their object. He uses flattery and puts on an appearance of righteousness, disinterestedness (vv. 3-4), and love (v. 5) in order to steal the hearts of the men of Israel (v. 6). He deceives the simple (v. 11) and makes a pretense of worshiping and serving the Lord (vv. 7-8) in order to seize the kingdom and to take the place of the Lord's anointed, yes, of his own father, on the throne – for he hates his father; he hates everyone but himself.[140]

Saul had been a self-focused carnal man, but he was nothing like Absalom, who typifies the satanic methods and wicked character of the Antichrist. Humanity will largely follow him against God's anointed during the Tribulation Period, in much the same way Israel was now rallying around Absalom.

It is hard to imagine what would cause such a massive defection from a righteous king who had delivered Israel from all their enemies to a devious, self-focused man like Absalom. Yet, David was now old; he probably had been negligent in attending to judicial matters, just as Absalom suggested. Furthermore, his kingdom had diminished because of his sin with Bathsheba; his good reputation had been tarnished, and God had permitted Israel's enemies to rise up again to confront David. The apex of David's glory had long passed, and there seems to have been a general dissatisfaction in Israel as to the ways things were. The people were looking for a rising star to provide for and to protect them, as David once had done.

David Flees Jerusalem (vv. 13-37)

A loyal informant made David aware of Absalom's insurrection: *"The hearts of the men of Israel are with Absalom"* (v. 13). Rather than remaining boxed in at Jerusalem and causing a civil war that would decimate the city and result in many casualties, David decided to retreat into the wilderness (v. 14). This would permit David time to assess the strength of the opposition, and to choose a more conducive location for the inevitable confrontation. Time would also permit reason to set in once the emotional hype of recognizing a new king dissipated.

Those loyal to David quickly packed up what they could and hurried to join their escaping king; David left ten concubines to keep his house in Jerusalem in his absence (vv. 15-16). The king probably thought that, being women, Absalom would not murder them, and because of their age and association to him, they would not be raped, but God's prophetic word against David still had to be fulfilled (12:11).

The king paused on the outskirts of town to take note of those who had chosen to come with him (v. 17). All David's servants passed before him, as did all the Cherethites and the Pelethites under the command of Benaiah, as did the 600 Gittites under Ittai's leadership (v. 18). The latter band, David's bodyguard, were Philistines who had become loyal to David while he was at Gath and Ziklag and then returned with him to Israel after Saul's death and converted to the Jewish faith to remain with Israel's new king. David addressed Ittai the Gittite:

Why are you also going with us? Return and remain with the king. For you are a foreigner and also an exile from your own place. In fact, you came only yesterday. Should I make you wander up and down with us today, since I go I know not where? Return, and take your brethren back. Mercy and truth be with you (vv. 19-20).

But Ittai responded by declaring his loyalty to the king with a vow that wherever *"the king shall be, whether in death or life, even there also your servant will be"* (v. 21). Though an alien and not long in Israel, Ittai had high thoughts of his king and hence would not abandon the one he loved. David could not refuse such profound allegiance, hence Ittai and his men were granted the privilege of passing over the Kidron and suffering reproach alongside their rejected king (v. 22).

This is a wonderful picture of Gentile believers in the Church Age. Though Christ came to Israel first, they rejected Him, allowing the Gentiles to have an opportunity to receive the rejected King and enjoy the vast blessings promised to Israel (Eph. 3:1-12). All those devoted to God's chosen king, Jew and Gentile alike, were ready to journey into the wilderness with the one who had been betrayed and rejected (v. 23).

The priests Zadok and Abiathar brought the Ark of God (as carried by a group of Levites) to David (v. 24). Apparently, Absalom's charm had little effect on those closest to the Lord – the priests and Levites were loyal to God's anointed. David referred to Zadok as a prophet whose rightful place was in Jerusalem. It is possible that, like Jeremiah, he was a prophet and a priest, but it may be that David was merely referring to his possession of the Urim and Thummim to discern the mind of the Lord. In the days of apostasy ahead, David was concerned that the Word of God still be faithfully declared to God's people.

Accordingly, the king commanded the priests to carry the Ark back to Jerusalem, so that worship of Jehovah and the declaration of His word to the Jewish nation would continue (v. 25). David expressed his hope to be able to return and worship the Lord again in His tabernacle. With this said, David does not presuppose God's will in the matter, but rather he is resolved to rest in God's providential care and permit Him to end the insurrection as He deemed best (v. 26).

There was another reason that David wanted the priests and their sons to return to the city. David would wait in the wilderness to hear their assessment of the situation before deciding to flee Israel altogether or to make a stand if there were still many in Israel loyal to him (vv. 27-28). The priests obeyed David's instructions and returned with the Ark to Jerusalem (v. 29).

Having crossed the Kidron, David ascended the western slope of the Mount Olives with his head covered and barefoot to declare his deep grief over the events of the day (v. 30). Adam Clarke observes that David's humble and subdued departure illustrates his faith in the Lord to honor Himself in the trial:

> There does not appear any reason why such a person, in such circumstances, should not act on the defensive; at least until he should be fully satisfied of the real complexion of affairs. But David appears to take all as coming from the hand of God; therefore he humbles himself, weeps, goes barefoot, and covers his head! He does not even hasten his departure, for the habit of mourners is not the habit of those who are flying before the face of their enemies. He sees the storm, and he yields to what he conceives to be the tempest of the Almighty.[141]

While ascending the mount, David learned that Ahithophel was among the conspirators (v. 31). David asked the Lord to *"turn the counsel of Ahithophel into foolishness!"* David later wrote Psalm 40 to express how shocked and disturbed he was to learn that his trusted counselor had defected. David wrote of being betrayed by a false friend (likely Ahithophel) in Psalm 55: *"You, a man my equal, my companion and my acquaintance. We took sweet counsel together, and walked to the house of God in the throng"* (Ps. 55:13-14). Psalm 40:9 presents Ahithophel as a prophetic type of Judas Iscariot, one of the twelve closest disciples to the Lord Jesus, who betrayed Him into the hands of Jewish leaders for thirty pieces of silver. And like Ahithophel, Judas will also hang himself shortly after betraying the true king of Israel.

After arriving at the summit, David paused a second time to look out over Jerusalem. Though brokenhearted and tearful, the king was not hindered from praising the Lord (v. 32). David's thoughts at this juncture are recorded in Psalm 3 for us to appreciate. The deposed king was determined not to be bitter about his forced exile, but rather to meekly submit to whatever the Lord would allow. This is a deeply touching scene. Throughout his departure from Jerusalem we witness the grace of God shining out of David perhaps more than at any other time. He is settled, submitted, lowly (even barefoot) and does not strike back at those who denounce him, nor does he deprive the rebels in Jerusalem of the Ark of God.

Biblical and Church history has shown that God often uses an individual for great feats only after He has wounded him or her deeply. Accordingly, much of the praise recorded in Scripture comes from those crushed by oppression, betrayed by companions, or exposed to various hardships, yet all rejoice in their God! This is why Paul exhorts believers to *"Rejoice always, pray without ceasing, in everything give thanks; for this is the will of God in Christ Jesus for you"* (1 Thess. 5:16-18). True prayers of faith are marked by rejoicing and thanksgiving, even when all the evidence suggests that there is no reason to do so.

We get the sense that, though time was critical, David stops at the Kidron and on the Mount of Olives. The fact that he is walking barefoot gives a better semblance of a royal procession leaving Jerusalem rather than a hasty retreat. Hushai the Archite caught up with David while he lingered on the summit; his robe was torn and he had dust on his head (v. 32). Hushai seems to be God's immediate answer to David's prayer about thwarting the counsel of Ahithophel.

It is generally believed that Hushai was an old man and would have been a burden to David if he had come with him. Accordingly, David told Hushai that he could better serve his king as a spy in Jerusalem (v. 33). The ruse would require him to pledge his loyalty to Absalom. Because Hushai was one of David's high-ranking servants, Absalom would think that he could benefit from Hushai's counsel (v. 34). If Absalom did welcome Hushai as an advisor, David was hopeful that Hushai's words might undermine Ahithophel's advice, which David much dreaded (v. 35). We will learn in the next chapter that this is exactly what happened.

David also informed Hushai that he would be able to secretly convey information to him through the priests Zadok and Abiathar, who then could have their sons, Ahimaaz and Jonathan respectively, deliver his message to him (v. 36). Although the plan had considerable risk to Hushai, for Absalom might execute him on the spot, he, being David's trusted friend, did all that the king requested (v. 37). Hushai arrived back at Jerusalem just minutes before Absalom and his anti-David forces entered the city.

Meditation

Our Lord is now rejected, and by the world disowned,
By the many still neglected, and by the few enthroned;
But soon He'll come in glory! The hour is drawing nigh,
For the crowning day is coming by-and-by.

The heavens shall glow with splendor, but brighter far than they,
The saints shall shine in glory, as Christ shall them array.
The beauty of the Savior shall dazzle every eye,
In the crowning day that's coming by-and-by.

— El Nathan

David Flees Into the Wilderness
2 Samuel 16

Mephibosheth's Servant (vv. 1-4)

Ziba, the servant of Mephibosheth, met David as he descended the backside of the Mount of Olives. He brought David two donkeys laden with two hundred loaves of bread, one hundred clusters of raisins, one hundred summer fruits, and a skin of wine (v. 1). In response to the king's inquiry, Ziba confirmed that the donkeys were for the king's household to ride on, and the provisions were to sustain them in the wilderness (v. 2).

Then David asked Ziba about his master Mephibosheth. Ziba told David that he had remained in Jerusalem, saying, *"Today the house of Israel will restore the kingdom of my father to me"* (v. 3). In response to this information, David gave Ziba all that belonged to Mephibosheth and Ziba graciously acknowledged the king's generosity to him (v. 4).

Was Ziba telling the truth? Not likely. Rather, he saw an opportunity to improve his situation by taking advantage of his crippled master who could not come to David without help. The two saddled and laden donkeys may have actually been a gift from Mephibosheth to David that Ziba took credit for. Given his covenant with Jonathan, and that the Law required two witnesses to collaborate a valid testimony, David was wrong to convict Mephibosheth of treason and strip him of his property. At a minimum, the king should have waited to hear both sides of the story.

Later, the son of Jonathan will have an opportunity to tell David what happened to him and how he was prevented from coming to David at this juncture (19:24-30). Given the wonderful privileges and fellowship that David had extended to Mephibosheth and that Scripture never presents him as an ambitious, glory-seeking man, we conclude that Ziba lied to David. If David did write Psalm 116, and if the poem pertains to his deliverance from Absalom, then the reference by the psalmist to believing a lie and making a hasty decision probably pertains to this situation (Ps. 116:10-11).

Shimei Curses David (vv. 5-14)

When King David came to Bahurim, he was met by antagonistic Shimei from the house of Saul (v. 6). Bahurim was about three miles northeast of Jerusalem, and was where Abner forced a weeping Paltiel to return home from following Michal as she was being returned to David in Jerusalem (3:16). Shimei positioned himself above David on the hillside and cursed him and threw stones at the royal column as it journeyed down the road (vv. 7, 13). Shimei maliciously called David a bloodthirsty scoundrel who was now receiving just punishment from God for his evil doings; consequently, his son Absalom would rule the kingdom in his place (vv. 8-9).

David's nephew Abishai wanted to lop off Shimei's head for insulting the king. However, David rejected Abishai's noble attempt that would divert him from the path of humble submission to God's discipline and said, *"Let him curse, because the Lord has said to him, 'Curse David.' Who then shall say, 'Why have you done so?'"* (v. 10). The king then acknowledged to everyone that being from the house of Saul, Shimei had a more legitimate reason for disdaining him than his own son Absalom had. So David was content not to interfere with his slander (v. 11).

The king even thought that by permitting Shimei to add to his sorrow and affliction now, the Lord might be moved more quickly to show David favor later (v. 12). Knowing that his distress was for a greater good, David was patient and submissive to the anguish God had permitted him to suffer. Because the people were weary, the group rested briefly at Bahurim to refresh themselves before journeying further northeast into the wilderness.

Ahithophel's Counsel (vv. 15-23)

Having arrived in Jerusalem, Absalom gathered his followers and Ahithophel was with him (v. 15). Hushai (David's friend) also came to Absalom and proclaimed, *"Long live the king! Long live the king!"* (v. 16). In response to Absalom's inquiry as to why he did not depart Jerusalem with his friend the king, the older Hushai said, *"No, but whom the Lord and this people and all the men of Israel choose, his I will be, and with him I will remain"* (vv. 17-18). Hushai then pledged to serve the king's son as he had served the king (v. 19). Hushai, though clearly deceptive, crafts his words wisely to affirm his allegiance not merely to the people's choice, but to whom God anointed as Israel's king. That was clearly David, not Absalom. Duped by his own pride, Absalom accepted Hushai into his court.

Absalom then asked Ahithophel for counsel as to what should be the next step to secure the kingdom (v. 20). Ahithophel told Absalom that he should have sexual relations with his father's ten concubines who were left behind. In the Ancient Near East, the wives of the conquered king became the property of the conqueror; possessing them was evidence of who actually held the kingdom. Such a lewd act by Absalom would show everyone that he now possessed the kingdom and would also cause David to detest his son (v. 21). By this depraved act, Ahithopel was ensuring that father and son could never be reconciled.

Note that Hushai did not oppose Ahithophel's plan concerning David's concubines, a decision which seemingly affirmed his loyalty to Absalom. He does not appear to be a part of Absalom's inner circle of advisors (17:5-6), so he may not have even been present when the matter was decided. If later he had tried to defend the honor of these women after all the elders had already agreed with Ahithophel, Absalom would undoubtedly not have sought his counsel in the next chapter, which Absalom did heed. So because Hushai picked the best conflict to engage in, he was able to save David and those with him. Indeed, ten women were sadly shamed, but there was nothing Hushai could do about it. However, waiting for the best opportunity to assist David, he might save thousands of lives.

There is much to be gleaned from this wise example in Christian ministry today. All too often believers get sidetracked into permissible or even good things, but suffer loss because they neglected the best that God had for them. Before engaging in any new ministry, believers need to seek the Lord for guidance while assessing their biblical priorities (e.g., one's children and spouse should not be neglected), their spirit giftedness, and their calling within the Body of Christ. Sometimes, believers waste time entertaining goats instead of caring for God's sheep. Doing good things but neglecting the best things is still an error which results in diminished blessing.

Ahithophel's abhorrent proposal was agreed to. A tent was pitched on top of the royal house and Absalom publicly defiled David's ten concubines (v. 22). Albert Barnes adds the following insight concerning this hideous act:

> Taking possession of the harem was the most decided act of sovereignty (e.g., 1 Kgs. 2:22). It was also the greatest offense and insult that could be offered. Such an act on Absalom's part made reconciliation impossible. A further motive has been found in this advice, namely, the desire on the part of Ahithophel to make David taste the bitterness of that cup which he had caused others (Uriah and all Bathsheba's family) to drink, and receive the measure which he had meted withal.[142]

Ironically, the place where Absalom sexually assaulted David's wives was likely the same location that David's wandering eye first caught sight of a naked Bathsheba (11:2). Clearly, God's justice against David was being carried out as previously decreed by the prophet Nathan (12:11).

The historian then notes that the aged Ahithophel was well-known as being an extremely wise and highly valued counselor (v. 23). The people believed that he spoke as if he had inquired from God. But however wise Ahithophel may have been, the Lord would never have directed Absalom to commit adultery with David's concubines; such a hideous act was a capital offense under the Law (Lev. 20:11). Regardless of his ethics, both David and Absalom profited from Ahithophel's counsel.

In Psalm 41, David recounts a previous prayer (possibly from Ps. 39) for divine retribution against those who had deceitfully spoken against him. Psalm 41:9 likely refers to the betrayal of David's trusted counselor Ahithophel. On the eve of His crucifixion, the Lord referred to this verse, which states, *"Even my own familiar friend in whom I trusted, who ate my bread, has lifted up his heel against me,"* which foretells the betrayal of Judas, one of His disciples (see Mark 14:18-21). However, we note that although Christ addressed Judas as a friend, He never trusted him. While David likely had his trusted friend, Ahithophel, in mind when he penned those words, the statement had a greater fulfillment in the life of Christ.

Since the Lord Jesus knew from the beginning that Judas would betray Him (John 6:70-71), He only referenced the portion of the verse which was messianic in nature. This ensured the betrayer would be properly identified when the Lord Jesus, the host of the Passover feast, passed Judas the sop in fulfillment of this prophecy (John 13:18-19). Although David had prayed for God to judge his treacherous foes, the Lord repeatedly showed kindness to Judas, even calling him "friend" in the Garden of Gethsemane just before His own arrest (v. 10; Matt. 26:50). Thankfully, at His First Advent the Lord came to seek and to save the lost, not to condemn sinners.

Meditation

Hail, thou once despised Jesus! Hail, Thou Galilean king!
Thou didst suffer to release us; Thou didst free salvation bring.
Hail, Thou universal Savior, bearer of our sin and shame!
By Thy merit we find favor; life is given through Thy name.

Paschal Lamb, by God appointed, all our sins on Thee were laid;
By almighty Love anointed, Thou hast full atonement made:
All Thy people are forgiven through the virtue of Thy blood;
Opened is the gate of heaven; peace is made between man and God.

— John Bakewell

Hushai Protects David
2 Samuel 17

Hushai's Counsel (vv. 1-23)

After Absalom had intercourse with David's ten concubines, Ahithophel counseled Absalom to quickly gather 12,000 choice soldiers and to pursue David that very night (v. 1). His idea was to confront the king while those fleeing with him were weary and unorganized and that perhaps only the king would be slain and the remainder of the people preserved (v. 2). This plan was appealing because it minimized the shedding of blood and ensured that David could not retake the throne (v. 3). Ahithophel's counsel initially pleased Absalom and Israel's elders, for no one wanted to enter into a bloody civil war (v. 4).

Before executing this plan, Absalom summoned Hushai to hear his thoughts on Ahithophel's counsel (vv. 5-6). The elderly Hushai told Absalom: *"The advice that Ahithophel has given is not good at this time,"* citing David and his mighty men's vast experience in guerilla tactics of desert warfare (vv. 7-8). Hushai's counsel to Absalom was framed in poetic imagery and figurative language and was designed to appeal to both Absalom's emotions and his pride. In short, Absalom should not gamble on a quick scheme that, if unsuccessful could turn public opinion against him (for everyone knew that David was a valiant warrior; vv. 9-10). Rather than staying in the palace, Absalom should lead Israel's full army against David; this would force him into a walled city which would then be thrown into the river through overwhelming force (vv. 11-13). This meant that David would be so hopelessly outnumbered that his sudden defeat would be assured and Absalom would be recognized by everyone as the victor.

Absalom and all the men of Israel agreed that Hushai's counsel was better than Ahithophel's advice (v. 14). This did not happen on account of Hushai's colorful and persuasive words, but rather because the Lord was working *"to defeat the good advice of Ahithophel, to the intent that the Lord might bring disaster on Absalom."* In actuality, Ahithophel's plan was Absalom's best chance of overcoming David, but the Lord ensured that Hushai's counsel was followed to provide David more time to escape and to organize himself for battle.

Hushai informed the priests Zadok and Abiathar of all that had transpired and that they should tell David not to tarry in the wilderness overnight, but to quickly cross over the Jordan into safety (vv. 15-16). Although the elders had agreed to his proposal, Absalom could suddenly reverse that decision and pursue David. The priest's sons, Jonathan and Ahimaaz remained at En Rogel (a spring on the southeast outskirts of Jerusalem) rather than risking being seen coming and going into the city (v. 17). The priests gave the information to a female servant who then carried it to Jonathan and Ahimaaz, but a lad saw the exchange and took his news back to Absalom (v. 18).

Jonathan and Ahimaaz departed quickly from the fountain and headed to a man's house in Bahurim. The two men hid in a well in the courtyard (the well was likely dry at this time). A woman then put a cover over the well and spread ground grain over it (v. 19). When Absalom's servants arrived, they did not find the two men and being told by the woman that they had fled over the brook, went after them (v. 20). Later, Absalom's men returned to Jerusalem without their prey, and the two men climbed out of the well and warned David that he needed to cross the Jordan River swiftly because Ahithophel had counseled Absalom to immediately pursue David (v. 21). David heeded their warning and by dawn the next morning all in David's company were in the Transjordan (v. 22).

Ahithophel was humiliated that his counsel was ignored and saw no good outcome of future events for himself. If David regained his throne, he would certainly be put to death as a conspirator and if Absalom defeated David, Hushai would be the esteemed counselor of his court. So Ahithophel saddled his donkey, went home, put his house in order, and hung himself (v. 23). He was buried in his father's tomb.

David Helped at Mahanaim (vv. 24-29)

David went to Mahanaim, which ironically was Ishbosheth's capital when he ruled the northern tribes against David (v. 24). Meanwhile, Absalom crossed the Jordan with Israel's full army and encamped in the land of Gilead (v. 26). Absalom made Amasa captain of the army. He was the son of Abigail (David's sister and Joab's aunt) and was conceived apparently out of wedlock to an Ishmaelite named Jithra, an Israelite proselyte (v. 25; 1 Chron. 2:17). This meant that the generals of both armies, Amasa and Joab, were actually cousins and both were David's nephews. (The Nahash here likely refers to Jesse, David's father.)

The chapter closes by identifying three men in the Transjordan who greatly assisted David with much needed provisions and encouragement: Shobi, an Ammonite of nobility, Machir who once sheltered lame Mephibosheth, and the elderly Barzillai, a Gileadite. The recent wars with Ammon and past conflicts with the house of Saul would naturally dictate that these men should oppose, or at least be leery of, David. For example, Shobi, possibly the son of the deceased Ammonite king Nahash and hence the brother of Hanun, whom David defeated (10:1-2), would have every reason to despise David. But since David had shown him kindness when Rabbah was taken, he behaved favorably towards David now. Clearly, God had worked in the hearts of these men to assist His anointed. These three men provided bedding, cooking vessels, and food to David and those with him.

Clearly, the time of David's sorrow had exposed what men truly thought about their king. Those most unlikely to assist the betrayed king during his rejection, Shobi, Machir, and Barzillai, gladly stepped forward to do so. Shimei railed against David; Zeba sought to profit from the situation, and most of the Jewish nation rejected their king. David learned through this heartbreaking experience who really loved him and who merely tolerated him.

No doubt, when David returned to the throne, he had a deeper appreciation of and confidence in those whose genuine affection had been proven. Likewise, those willing to identify with the Lord Jesus Christ in His sorrow and rejection prove the validity of their faith and love for their Savior. He too appreciates those who cling to Him, even when the masses blaspheme His name, try to profit from His teachings, and reject His claims.

The internal evidence suggests that Psalm 61 was written by David while fleeing from Absalom through the rocky and desolate wilderness east of Jerusalem. He lodged temporarily in this wilderness until Hushai, David's spy, sent word for them to hurry across the Jordan to escape their pursuers. As we have just read, the situation was bleak; they were greatly outnumbered and the people were hungry, weary, and thirsty (v. 29).

There are several Hebrew words in the Psalms rendered "cry," but *rinnah* in Psalm 61:1 denotes a shrill sound; the tone of David's prayer was then one of desperation. Perhaps David was inspecting the defenses of their temporary encampment when the Lord drew his sight upward from the surrounding rock formations to his heavenly Rock of defense (Ps. 61:2-3). David knew there was no safer abiding place than God's presence and he expresses his resolve to remain there forever (Ps. 61:4). God had promised David a royal dynasty, so, on that basis, David prays for God's abiding protection, a lasting heritage of souls loyal to Jehovah, and a prolonged life to serve the Lord (Ps. 61:5-7). David's prayer demonstrates an unwavering faith in a tremendous God, the One who completely controlled his situation and would ensure the manifestation of His glory in it.

Meditation

Rejoicing in the Lord when distressed moves the hand of God. Praising God nourishes a hungry soul, and giving Him thanks rejuvenates a parched spirit. Rejoicing is a choice, and one that secures the believer's mind in hope and prompts God to do the impossible (Phil. 1:18)!

— W.A.H.

The Insurrection Dies with Absalom
2 Samuel 18

War in Ephraim's Forest (vv. 1-18)

David numbered his men, organizing them into divisions of thousands and hundreds, and appointing captains over each (v. 1). He placed a third of his troops under Joab's command, another third under his brother Abishai, and the remaining third was led by his new friend Ittai the Gittite (v. 2). David demonstrates a good principle for us to follow in the Lord's work – organize whatever you have to accomplish as much as you can. With the Lord's blessing, good order and discipline usually compensate for what we lack. The king was greatly outnumbered, so he organized his troops in an efficient command structure.

The king, now in his late sixties, planned to go out to war also, but everyone insisted that he was too valuable and should remain safe in the confines of the city (v. 3). Their objection demonstrates their faith in the Lord and their love for their king; they were engaged in a righteous cause, hence, David's presence or absence on the battlefield made no difference to them.

The king yielded to their objection and stood by the city gate as his troops departed for battle (v. 4). In the hearing of the people, the king addressed Joab, Abishai, and Ittai, *"Deal gently for my sake with the young man Absalom"* (v. 5). Although David's love for his wayward son is touching, his command to his troops to be merciful with the traitor who was trying to kill them and their king was disconcerting. As we will see in a moment, Joab chose to ignore the king's emotional command and misplaced affection.

The confrontation occurred in the thick woods of Ephraim to the east of the Jordan River (perhaps just north of the Jabbok River). Although the battle took place in Gad's territory, the forest was identified with Ephraim probably because of their memorable victory there during the days of the judges. David's servants slaughtered

20,000 of Absalom's soldiers (vv. 6-7). The battle ranged throughout the countryside and many men died from various injuries sustained while fighting in the dense forest (v. 8). These probably occurred from pits, bogs, thickets, and possibly wild beasts.

In order to be credited with the forthcoming victory, proud Absalom was with his troops as advised by Hushai. He was riding on a mule and became separated from his troops (or those with him were slaughtered). After meeting some of David's men, Absalom tried to escape by fleeing under a great terebinth tree. However, his head got caught in one of the low hanging boughs and his mule rode off leaving him hanging by his head (either his neck was caught in a fork or his long hair was tangled in the twisted branches; v. 9). Matthew Henry comments: "He hung 'between heaven and earth,' as unworthy of either, as abandoned of both; earth would not keep him, heaven would not take him, hell therefore opens her mouth to receive him."[143]

One of David's men reported the sight to Joab (v. 10). The commander rebuked the man for not killing Absalom, saying he would have given him ten shekels of silver and a belt (v. 11). However, the soldier said that he had heard the king tell his commanders to be favorable to his son, implying that he should be captured alive if possible (v. 12). Consequently, he would not kill the king's son even if offered a thousand shekels of silver, for such a deed would constitute insubordination, demanding severe punishment (v. 13).

Knowing that the death of Absalom would end the war and that every minute that passed would result in more of his countrymen dying, Joab grabbed the first thing he saw, which was three darts (small spears) and quickly departed to find Absalom. Joab found Absalom alive and still hanging in the tree by his head as reported. Without hesitation he thrust all three darts into Absalom's chest, his heart being the target (v. 14). However, seeing that Absalom was still alive, Joab's ten young armorbearers surrounded him and repeatedly struck him until he perished (v.15). Joab blew the trumpet to recall his troops – the battle was over (v. 16). Absalom's body was then cast into a deep pit within the forest and covered by a large heap of stones (v. 17). Absalom's men dispersed and everyone went home.

The historian then reveals an unrelated detail: since Absalom had no living sons to carry on his name (14:27), he had set up a pillar in the King's Valley to be remembered by (v. 18). The King's Valley, according to Josephus, was located about one quarter mile east of

Jerusalem in the Kidron Valley.[144] Yet, such a monument to one's life has no value if that person did not live for the Lord and Absalom did not. Rather, he opposed God's anointed, his king and father. His cunning deception and overt betrayal cost him his own life and the unnecessary deaths of thousands of his countrymen!

Men waste time and resources erecting monuments in an attempt to compel others to remember them, instead of living in such a way that others are benefitted long after they are laid to rest. Absalom would not be remembered well in Israel, but his loving father would grieve for him nonetheless.

News of Death and Victory (vv. 19-32)

Ahimaaz, the son of Zadok, asked Job if he could run to David to inform him that the Lord had avenged him of his enemies (v. 20). But Joab declined Ahimaaz's request because of the sensitive nature of the report and not knowing how the king might respond to the one bearing news of his son's death (v. 21). Instead of Ahimaaz, he chose a Cushite (probably his servant) to run to the king and inform him of what he had witnessed. But Ahimaaz, being caught up in the euphoria of the moment, still wanted to run to the king with the tidings of victory (v. 22). Joab pointed out that there was no reason for him to run to the king, as he had nothing to report that would not be first delivered by the Cushite (v. 23). However, Ahimaaz was insistent, so Joab consented for him to run also (v. 23). Ahimaaz was fast on his feet and took a slightly longer, but less difficult route through the plain, so that he actually arrived at the city before the Cushite traversing the hills did.

Back at Mahanaim, David was sitting between the two gates waiting for news when a watchman noticed a lone runner approaching the city (v. 24). The king realized that this was a carrier with a dispatch from the battlefront for him (v. 25). (If his forces had been defeated, there would have been many soldiers fleeing back to the city.) Then the watchman informed the king that he observed a second man running after the first and David discerned that the man also was bringing him news (v. 26). The watchman then identified the first runner as Ahimaaz, which delighted the king, who thought that since he was a good man, he must have good news (v. 27).

Ahimaaz arrived slightly before the Cushite and reported that all was well and that the Lord had delivered David from those who had opposed him (v. 28). However, Ahimaaz did not want to be the one who informed the king of Absalom's death, so he deflected the king's question about his son by claiming ignorance (v. 29). Shortly afterwards, the Cushite arrived and repeated Ahimaaz's news of victory, but he did not hesitate to inform the king of Absalom's death when the king inquired about his son (vv. 30-31).

The news of Absalom's death deeply impacted David, who went up to a private chamber over the gate to weep. His remorse was so profound that he wished that he had died in his son's place (v. 32). David's emotional response was inappropriate – weeping for his insolent son who was responsible for a civil war that had resulted in tens of thousands of Jewish casualties? The king was wrong to ignore the incredible deliverance that God had granted him and he also neglected to thank all those who had risked their own lives to save his. In the next chapter, Joab will rightly reprove David, who, seeing his mistake, then wholeheartedly honors those who honored him.

David had earlier written: *"The sacrifices of God are a broken spirit, a broken and a contrite heart – these, O God, You will not despise"* (Ps. 51:17). But a true sacrifice must be self-abasing. David's brokenness is self-focused; his weeping does not honor God's righteous judgment in the matter. For example, Aaron was not permitted to weep over the deaths of his two sons after they were judged for bringing strange fire before the Lord. We learn from this that a broken spirit is a good thing only when it is completely void of self-focus.

Meditation

Search me, O God, and know my heart today;
Try me, O Savior, know my thoughts, I pray.
See if there be some wicked way in me;
Cleanse me from every sin and set me free.

Lord, take my life, and make it wholly thine;
Fill my poor heart with thy great love divine.
Take all my will, my passion, self, and pride;
I now surrender, Lord – in me abide.

— J. Edwin Orr

333

David Returns to Jerusalem
2 Samuel 19

Joab Rebukes Mourning David (vv. 1-8)

The sword of sovereign retribution that had been promised to never depart from David's house had struck another blow. David's intense grief over Absalom's death caused his loyal servants to feel ashamed and guilty (vv. 1-2). Because David had covered his head in mourning, those returning victorious from battle were not greeted at the city's gate with celebratory fanfare or the king's praise, but rather with a somber silence befitting a terrible defeat (vv. 3-4).

After realizing what was happening, Joab sternly rebuked the king. He challenged David with showing more concern for the rebels that had tried to kill him than for those who had risked their own lives to protect him and his family (vv. 5-6). Joab then told David that, if he did not appear in public to honor those loyal to him, they would all forsake him by nightfall. David then uncovered his head and sat in the gate of the city to show his devoted servants his appreciation (vv. 7-8). Those on the losing side returned to their tents in Israel.

David heeded Joab's request, not out of respect for Joab, but rather because he knew God to be just in all His actions towards him. Absalom, the rebel and murderer, deserved to die and David knew that he must accept God's judgment of his son, even if by the hand of Joab. While it was true that Joab had ended the civil war by killing Absalom, David would not forget his cruel disobedience or his murderous ways. Before his death, David will instruct Solomon to judge Joab for the murders of Abner and Amasa during a time of peace (1 Kgs. 2:5).

David Returns to Jerusalem (vv. 9-18)

David demonstrated wise patience in not hastening back as a conqueror to retake his throne. The people needed to reaffirm him as their leader rather than him ruling them by force. Absalom's death caused the northern tribes to reconsider David's return to Jerusalem;

after all, he had delivered them from their enemies, including the Philistines (v. 9). Although some questioned David's fitness to lead, it did seem prudent for them to recognize a proven warrior as their king, especially since their self-appointed ruler had died in battle (v. 10). The debate about David shows the inconsistent nature of the nation: while tens of thousands of Jewish families were mourning their dead (as a result of following Absalom instead of David), they were also considering David's return to the throne. After learning that the northern tribes were discussing the matter, the king sent the priests Zadok and Abiathar to inquire of Judah's elders:

> *Why are you the last to bring the king back to his house, since the words of all Israel have come to the king, to his very house? You are my brethren, you are my bone and my flesh. Why then are you the last to bring back the king?* (vv. 11-12).

Since David was from the tribe of Judah, it seemed only appropriate that his own kin should be the first to want his return. However, since Judah had largely supported Absalom, many were fearful that David would retaliate against them if he was permitted to return to Jerusalem.

The priests also had a message for Absalom's general, Amasa, *"Are you not my bone and my flesh? God do so to me, and more also, if you are not commander of the army before me continually in place of Joab"* (v. 13). In an effort to sway the hearts of the people, David pledged to make his nephew Amasa the general of his army instead of Joab, whose overbearing ways he could no longer tolerate. By now, David had probably learned that it had been Joab who had killed Absalom. By pardoning and promoting the leader of Absalom's army, David accomplished three things. First, he was preventing any attempt by Amasa to reunite Israel against him. Second, he minimized the threat of retaliation in the minds of those who had followed Absalom. Third, his removal of Joab indicated the king's disapproval of his actions and ensured that those involved with the dissension would not be punished by a murderous general acting on his own authority. The king's amiable actions and questions moved the elders of Judah to request his return, *"Return, you and all your servants!"* (v. 14).

David then journeyed west to the Jordan River, while all Judah came to Gilgal to greet their returning king (v. 15). The railing Shimei, with a thousand men of Benjamin, and Ziba with his fifteen sons and twenty of his servants were among the procession also (v. 16). These crossed over the Jordan in order to properly escort the king and his family back into Israel; a ferryboat was used to transport the royal family over the river (vv. 17-18).

Shimei Receives Mercy (vv. 19-23)

After the king crossed the river, Shimei fell down before David and begged for mercy:

> *Do not let my lord impute iniquity to me, or remember what wrong your servant did on the day that my lord the king left Jerusalem, that the king should take it to heart. For I, your servant, know that I have sinned. Therefore here I am, the first to come today of all the house of Joseph to go down to meet my lord the king* (vv. 19-20).

But Abishai, whom David previously had prevented from killing Shimei for his railing (16:9), again insisted that he be put to death for cursing the Lord's anointed (v. 21). Though the sons of Zeruiah, David's sister, were mighty warriors, they were a constant thorn in David's side because of their hot-headed zeal and personal agendas. Although Shimei did deserve death for his insolence, David refused Abishai's request because he wanted the day of his return to be a joyous occasion unmarred by executions (v. 22).

Shimei's apology was likely not genuine. It is probable that he humbled himself to preclude certain death. Regardless, David accepted Shimei's acknowledgment of sin and granted his request for mercy by promising that he would not be executed for his offense (v. 23). Yet, we later learn that David did not forget Shimei's disrespect, for he ordered Solomon to deal mercilessly with the foulmouthed Benjamite, and Solomon did so later when justice demanded it (1 Kgs. 2:8-9).

David and Mephibosheth (vv. 24-30)

Crippled Mephibosheth also came to meet the king. The fact that he had not cared for his feet, washed his clothes, nor trimmed his mustache since David had departed Jerusalem indicated that he had been mourning David's absence, not rejoicing in it as Ziba had suggested (v. 25). The Hebrews cut off the hair on the upper lip (e.g., Lev. 13:45) and cheeks, but in times of mourning let it grow carelessly, as on the chin.[145] Mephibosheth's behavior during David's absence proved that he had no ambition of being crowned king in Israel.

In a harsh tone, David inquired of Mephibosheth as to why he had not come with him when he left Jerusalem (v. 26). Mephibosheth then refuted Ziba's earlier tale to the king. Mephibosheth asserted that he had wanted to go with David, but being crippled was unable to do so because he had been abandoned by Ziba, who then brought donkeys and food to the king and slandered him to achieve personal gain.

Mephibosheth praised David's character and ability to wisely judge such matters and therefore was pleased to rest in his judgment on the matter (v. 27). Mephibosheth does affirm that he had nothing to gain by being disloyal to David, who had seated him at his own table and treated him kindly even though he was from the house of Saul (v. 28).

Certainly, there would have been many witnesses to testify to Mephibosheth's loyalty during David's estrangement from Israel, but rather than investigating the matter further and rendering a just verdict in the matter, David chooses a swift resolution for the sake of peace. That is, he merely revised his early ruling in favor of Ziba, to indicate that Saul's property should be divided between Mephibosheth and Ziba, his servant (v. 29). David probably meant that his first decree concerning the land was still valid – that Mephibosheth owned the property, but Ziba had possession of it and should pay his master rent (9:10). However, this was an inappropriate decision, for David had now legally bound Mephibosheth to his crooked servant who had slandered him and then been rewarded for doing so by the king. David had chosen to ignore the Law's demand that a verified false witness be punished (Deut. 19:15-20).

Mephibosheth's response to this pitiable ruling is honorable: *"Rather, let him take it all, inasmuch as my lord the king has come back in peace to his own house"* (v. 30). Crippled Mephibosheth's disheveled appearance, his appreciation of David's abounding grace, and his meek response all indicate that he was innocent in the matter and that Ziba had tried to profit from the situation. The one who had enjoyed fellowship with the king at his table was overjoyed that the king was in his rightful place again; hence, the property in question was immaterial in comparison to David's return. Ziba sought an inheritance, but Mephibosheth wanted only to be near the king!

Mephibosheth longed for the king's return – not material wealth! Oh that the Church might be motivated by this same desire, *"If anyone does not love the Lord Jesus Christ, let him be accursed. O Lord, come!"* (1 Cor. 16:22). The Church does not need more cold formalism to regulate her complacency, rather more fervent affection for the Person of Christ and longing for His imminent return. Have not we, like Mephibosheth, feasted at the Lord's Table and experienced the kindness of God – should we not also then eagerly be looking for His appearing? All who yearn to see His face will be prompted to live purely (1 Jn. 3:2-3) and will be rewarded for doing so (2 Tim. 4:8).

David's Kindness to Barzillai (vv. 31-39)

Barzillai, the wealthy eighty-year-old Gileadite who had lavished David with kindness at Mahanaim, also came down from Rogelim to escort the king across the Jordan River (vv. 31-32). David invited Barzillai to accompany him to Jerusalem and to benefit from his hospitality, but the aged man declined, saying that he did not want to be a burden to the king (v. 33). He realized that his faculties had waned to such an extent that he would not be able to enjoy any celebrations; additionally, he knew that his time on the earth was short, and he wanted to die in his own land and be buried with his deceased kin (vv. 34-35). Rather than joining the king, Barzillai said he would go a short distance into Israel with David and then would turn back, but that his son Chimham would take his place and the king could show him any kindness he desired (vv. 36-37).

This was agreeable to David, who said he would honor Chimham in Barzilliai's place, in whatever way the esteemed father thought would be best (v. 38). After this discussion, the king and all the people crossed the Jordan. Then the king kissed Barzillai and blessed him and he returned to his home (v. 39). Before his death, David would charge Solomon to care for and protect all of Barzillai's sons (1 Kgs. 2:7). Apparently, Chimham was inducted into David's court (perhaps at Barzillai's request) and was then treated well by Solomon, as shown by Jeremiah's mention of his estate over four centuries later (Jer. 41:17).

Quarreling Over the King (vv. 40-43)

The king then went on to Gilgal, with his honored guest Chimham. All the people of Judah and about half of the people of Israel escorted the king in his journey (v. 40). Apparently, David decided to return to Jerusalem after Amasa arrived with the escort from Judah and not to wait for all the northern tribes to be present.

Just when all seemed to be going well, some men from Israel arrived and confronted the king, *"Why have our brethren, the men of Judah, stolen you away and brought the king, his household, and all David's men with him across the Jordan?"* (v. 41). David's preferential treatment of Judah resulted in bitter jealousy among some in the northern tribes, especially since they had been the ones to originally suggest that David be brought home.

The men of Judah answered this challenge, *"Because the king is a close relative of ours. Why then are you angry over this matter? Have we ever eaten at the king's expense? Or has he given us any gift?"* (v. 42). The implied answer was "no." This meant that David's kin were not expecting any tangible gain by escorting their king to Jerusalem; rather, they simply desired that David be restored to Israel's throne.

However, this answer did not satisfy the offended Israelites. They then suggested that, because David was the king of all Israel, the ten northern tribes had more right to him than the two tribes of Judah and Benjamin did (v. 43). As the next chapter shows, there was no winner in this shouting match. The historian does note that Judah's retorts were fiercer than Israel's ranting. But as we all know too well, when emotional rhetoric replaces prudent reasoning, only harm can result.

Quarreling rarely ends well; pride and favoritism led Israel into another costly civil war. Regardless of all the squabbling, David was God's anointed and the rightful heir to Israel's throne. Hence he would return to Jerusalem victorious over all opposition. T. Wilson notes the propensity of some in the Church today to permit division on the merits of family association, rather than the pursuit of truth:

Even in our day, there is a danger of divisions occurring that may not be caused by doctrinal issues. Family feuds can disrupt the unity of the saints, as they did in David's kingdom. Where elders are strong and have a single eye for Christ's glory, the danger should be less; where leadership is weak and carnal, the ground is prepared to receive seeds of dissension.[146]

Meditation

Opposition is not only evidence that God is blessing, but it is also an opportunity for us to grow.

— Warren Wiersbe

339

Sheba's Revolt
2 Samuel 20

Sheba's Brief Rebellion (vv. 1-22)

Sheba, a rebel from the tribe of Benjamin, blew a trumpet to summon the northern tribes to follow him (v. 1). The rallying cry was that Judah had laid claim to David and that, even though Israel had more tribes and were more numerous, they had no inheritance in the son of Jesse (v. 2). Notice how quickly emotional reasoning causes vacillation between extremes: Israel went from having ten parts in David to having no part in him in only one breath. Beware of people employing words such as "never" and "always" to try to substantiate their position. God always does what is right and never does what is wrong, but we all find ourselves somewhere in between those perfect extremes.

So Sheba, who had probably been part of Absalom's revolt, provokes the men of the northern tribes to desert David again. Those in Judah remained loyal to their king and escorted him to Jerusalem. David could have probably prevented this with words of appreciation or a brief commendation of their zeal, but his silence only convinced the northern tribes of his tribal partiality.

Solomon wrote: *"A soft answer turns away wrath, but a harsh word stirs up anger"* (Prov. 15:1). The men of Israel (as led by Sheba) and the men of Judah both stirred up angry feelings through harsh speech. David chose not to speak soft words which could have defused the situation. Dear believer, regardless of the world's injustices and our sufferings, what we do when we feel angry is our choice. We are completely responsible to God for the way we respond when angry and to others who are angry. Neither past hurts, nor enduring wrongs, nor physical adversity is holy ground for inflicting others with unrighteous behavior. Despite the circumstances, a Christian should seek to secure a right response to the wrong behavior of others. The goal is to serve others by provoking them to proper behavior (love and good works), not to incite them to greater sin through self-focused behavior. Harry A. Ironside explains that the wise person is one who possesses restraint when his or her feelings are moving otherwise:

> It takes far more true character to meet an angry man in quietness of spirit, and to return cool, calm words for heated, hasty ones. The man who controls his tongue shows that he has his personal feelings in subjection. The man who returns malice for malice reveals that he does not yet know how to rule his spirit. Grievous words only add fuel to the flame; a gracious demeanor will go far towards cooling the angry passions of another.[147]

After arriving at his house in Jerusalem, David took his ten concubines that had been shamefully defiled by Absalom and put them in a separate and private house (v. 3). They would be protected and cared for, but would live in widowhood for the remainder of their lives (David would not have marital relations with them).

David ordered his new commander, Amasa, to organize his troops and to set out after Sheba within three days to capture him (v. 4). However, Amasa delayed longer than the time allotted, so David tasked Abishai with defeating Sheba before he could get his resistance movement established or take refuge in a fortified city (vv. 5-6). Abishai's demoted brother Joab and his men, with the Cherethites, the Pelethites, and all the mighty men headed out of Jerusalem to find and defeat Sheba (v. 7).

Amasa caught up with Abishai's men at the stone marker at Gibeon (v. 8). Joab was wearing battle armor and purposely caused his sword to come out of its sheath and fall on the ground as he was approaching to greet Amasa. Joab casually picked up the sword with his left hand and warmly greeted unsuspecting Amasa, *"Are you in health, my brother?"* (v. 9). When Joab took Amasa's beard with his right hand to kiss him, Joab slashed Amasa in the stomach with the sword in his other hand such that Amasa's entrails poured out on the ground (v. 10). In God's timing, Joab will be rightly judged for his brutal and treacherous behavior.

Instead of finishing off Amasa, Joab left him in the middle of the highway to wallow in his blood and dying a slow, agonizing death. Meanwhile, he and Abishai headed northward to pursue Sheba. One of Joab's men yelled, *"Whoever favors Joab and whoever is for David –*

follow Joab!" (v. 11). But the call fell on deaf ears because the people were mesmerized by the gory sight of Amasa's shuddering body. The man then dragged Amasa into a field and covered him with a garment; then the soldiers resumed their quest for Sheba (vv. 12-13).

Their search for the Benjamite led them to the city of Abel of Beth Maachah on the far northern edge of Israel's territory (about a hundred miles north of Jerusalem; v. 14). Joab and his men besieged the city, built up a siege mound against the city's wall, and began striking the wall with a battering ram (v. 15). A wise woman in the city cried out to Joab and asked him to listen to her petition, which he agreed to do (vv. 16-17). She asked Joab why he wanted to destroy a mother in Israel, that is, a city in Israel widely known for imparting beneficial wisdom to others (vv. 18-19).

Joab explained that he had no interest in destroying the inheritance of the Lord, but rather was after a rebel named Sheba, the son of Bichri, who had rebelled against the king and was hiding in her city (v. 20). Joab promised that if the citizens of Beth Maachah delivered Sheba to him, then he and his men would depart in peace. The woman then promised that Sheba's head would be thrown over the city's wall shortly, and it was (v. 21). Joab then blew the trumpet, and David's forces withdrew. Each man returned to his tent, but Joab returned to Jerusalem (v. 22).

Although Sheba had a glorious moment at Gilgal, his insurgence was not strong, nor was it well-organized. The entire rebellion, including the initial delay in Jerusalem, time searching for Sheba, traveling to northern Israel, and then building a siege ramp probably did not last more than two to three weeks. *"The great God who formed everything gives the fool his hire and the transgressor his wages"* (Prov. 26:10). The wages of sin is death and Sheba died a fool's death because he chose to die for what God could not permit.

David's Officials (vv. 23-26)

The historian pauses to again list key officials in David's government. This list largely agrees with that of 8:15-18 (when Joab was still over all the army of Israel). Benaiah the son of Jehoiada was over the Cherethites and the Pelethites (v. 23). Adoram was in charge of revenue; Jehoshaphat the son of Ahilud was David's recorder (v. 24). Sheva was scribe; Zadok and Abiathar (the son of Ahimelech) were the leading priests (v. 25). Ira the Jairite was David's chief personal minister (v. 26).

Meditation

There are two kinds of people: those who say to God, "Thy will be done," and those to whom God says, "All right, then, have it your way."

— C. S. Lewis

Now we may infer from any defeat of ours that it is due either to lack of faith or failure to obey. No other reason can suffice.

— Watchman Nee

Gibeonites Avenged and Giants Fall

2 Samuel 21

The remainder of 2 Samuel reads like an appendix and represents additional key events in David's life, most of which happened in the early years of his kingdom. Consequently, most of the narrative in this section does not fall chronologically after the previous chapter.

David Avenges the Gibeonites (vv. 1-14)

David inquired of the Lord why Israel had suffered three years of famine. (This famine occurred many years prior to Absalom's and Sheba's revolts detailed in the previous chapters.) The Lord answered David, *"It is because of Saul and his bloodthirsty house, because he killed the Gibeonites"* (v. 1). To rectify the situation the king summoned the Gibeonites so that he could speak with them. Although David had not been responsible for this particular sin, as the king of Israel he was obliged to appease God's anger over the wrong done to the Gibeonites.

The writer pauses to explain the historical aspects of the injustice committed:

> *The Gibeonites were not of the children of Israel, but of the remnant of the Amorites; the children of Israel had sworn protection to them, but Saul had sought to kill them in his zeal for the children of Israel and Judah* (v. 2).

Just before his death, Moses commanded the Jews to wipe out the inhabitants of Canaan to ensure that they would not later ensnare them into idolatry (Deut. 12:28-30). However, a short time after Joshua led the Israelites into Canaan, they were deceived into making a peace treaty with the Gibeonites, who had posed as foreigners, but were actually a people residing in Canaan (Josh. 9). Because Israel's leaders had not sought counsel from the Lord and had issued this covenant in

His name, He would not permit the slaughter of the Gibeonites (who were Hivites). Instead, they were to be Israel's servants in the land (Josh. 9:19-20). The writer associates them with their near clan, the Amorites, who were one of the seven nations present in Canaan when Israel invaded the land.

Joshua and the elders chose not to correct one wrong with another, but to submit themselves to Jehovah and suffer the consequences for one rash mistake, rather than two. Israel honored this covenant for centuries until the time when King Saul attempted to eliminate the Gibeonites from Israel by slaughtering them (v. 5). For this reason, the entire nation was suffering God's chastening by a long famine.

David asked the Gibeonites what could be done to make atonement for Saul's evil and then vowed to do whatever they asked (vv. 3-4). The Gibeonites' grievance was with the house of Saul, not with the Jewish nation as a whole. They did not want silver or gold from Saul's estate, nor did they want David to perform any executions on their behalf. However, they did request that seven men, descendants of King Saul, be delivered to them. These men would be hung in Gibeah (Saul's hometown) showing that their deaths were to recompense for Saul's evil against them (v. 6).

Without consulting the Lord, David agreed to the Gibeonites' terms. Although not faulting David's desire to render justice, J. N. Darby faults David for not seeking the Lord's counsel on the matter:

> However, in yielding to the Gibeonites, David did not consult Jehovah as to what he should do. We see the government of God as to Saul's house and Saul's act towards those he had wronged, but though in its general character righteous and upright, had he consulted Jehovah, some happier way of being righteous might have been found.[148]

David gave the Gibeonites the two sons of Saul's concubine Rizpah (Armoni and Mephibosheth) and the five sons of Michal, Saul's daughter who, after marrying David, was given to another man while David was a fugitive (vv. 7-8). David spared Jonathan's son Mephibosheth because of his oath to Jonathan. (After this chapter he is likely the lone male survivor of Saul's house.)

Three clarifications are offered on these verses. First, the Mephibosheth to be hung is Saul's son, not Jonathan's. Second, Michal was barren and not the wife of Adriel, which suggests a scribal error in verse 8 (i.e., Merab was meant instead of Michal, per 1 Sam. 18:19). The Hebrew word *yalad* rendered "brought up" means "to give birth" to children, not to rear them up. Apparently, rather than admit a textual error, the translators chose to imply an unusual meaning of *yalad*. While it is possible that Merab died and Michal did raise up her sons as her own, the Hebrew text does not support that assumption. Third, Adriel was not the son of the Barzillai who later helped David during Absalom's revolt.

Hence, not only was God avenging the Gibeonites for Saul's evil against them, but He was also executing justice against Saul for breaking his vow to David concerning Merab, his oldest daughter. Saul had promised to give Merab to David as a wife (his reward for slaying Goliath), but then he gave her to Adriel (1 Sam. 18:19). Not only were these men hung, but their bodies were secured in the place of execution until the judgment for shedding innocent blood in the land was lifted by God (i.e. the famine).

This sentence seems to undermine Moses' command that *"fathers shall not be put to death for their children, nor shall children be put to death for their fathers; a person shall be put to death for his own sin"* (Deut. 24:16). However, we have limited information on the matter and Saul's extended family may have been implicated in Saul's attack on the Gibeonites or they may have sanctioned it. This understanding is shown in the Lord's indictment in verse 1; His wrath is not just against Saul, but also *"his bloodthirsty house."* Additionally, the house of Saul was implicated in various offenses committed against David, as described above. While time tends to dull our memories, God does not suffer from that affliction. He remembered every detail of Joshua's covenant with the Gibeonites, which was uttered in His name four centuries earlier, and He was going to judge those who had violated it.

Saul's concubine Rizpah took sackcloth and spread it for herself over a rock as a makeshift tent. From the time her sons were hung at the beginning of barley harvest (i.e., normally in mid-April) until the late rains came, she protected her sons' bodies day and night from predatory birds and beasts (v. 10). The late rains may refer to the rainy season in the fall (normally in October), or more likely that the bodies were publicly displayed until God ended the drought – meaning that His judgment was complete in the matter.

David was informed of Rizpah's tireless vigil and was moved with compassion (v. 11). He commanded that the bones of Saul and Jonathan that had been buried by the men of Jabesh Gilead (after their headless bodies were taken down from the wall of Beth Shan) be exhumed (v. 12). Their bones and the remains of Rizpah's two sons were to be brought to the tomb of Kish, Saul's father, and all were to be properly buried (vv. 13-14).

Once God's anger for Saul's offense was appeased, the public display of Rizpah's sons' rotting bodies was no longer needed to represent the shame of the crime. Because Saul's offenses had been properly judged, God heeded the prayers of the people to restore the land to fruitfulness.

Philistine Giants Fall (vv. 15-22)

The book of Chronicles places the following Philistine battles immediately after the fall of Rabbah and the defeat of the Ammonites (1 Chron. 20:4-8). This would place them a few years after David's sin with Bathsheba. If this assumption is correct, David would have been in his early fifties.

The king led his men into battle again against the Philistines (v. 15). David fought against a giant named Ishbi-Benob, who had a bronze spear weighing three hundred shekels and a new sword, who desired to kill David (v. 16). Seeing that David had become weary and was in trouble, Abishai rescued the king and killed the giant. Although at times Abishai was presumptuous, he did not exhibit the tendency to depravity of his brother Joab. Abishai's courage and loyalty to his king here are admirable, and confirms why his name is listed among David's mighty men.

Age had affected David more than he realized. His men were determined not to permit their king to return to the battlefield in the future, *"lest you quench the lamp of Israel"* (v. 17). They knew that David was God's anointed and represented His favor on the nation; if David died in battle, the nation would lose hope of God's blessings. Based on Romans 8:37 and James 4:6-8, Matthew Henry suggests a practical application for us to consider from David's example:

> David fainted, but he did not flee; though his strength failed him, he bravely kept his ground, and then God sent him help in the time of need, which, though brought him by his junior and inferior, he

thankfully accepted, and, with a little recruiting, gained his point, and came off a conqueror. Christ, in his agonies, was strengthened by an angel. In spiritual conflicts, even strong saints sometimes wax faint; then Satan attacks them furiously, but those that stand their ground and resist him shall be relieved, and made more than conquerors.[149]

Though David was old, he did not desire to live out his final days in ease. Rather, he desired to do what he could to preserve and enhance the kingdom. God blessed him for his faithful diligence; consequently, despite some setbacks, David never lost a battle against his enemies (though that cannot be said for conflicts in his home). As he already had plenty of glory at his age, David's actions in this chapter were not for personal gain, but for the good of Israel. David had learned firsthand the repercussions of idleness and leisure when God still had a work for him to do (i.e., he sinned with Bathsheba because he did not go out to war). The king is determined not to repeat that mistake, and we likewise should learn from his example, lest we too suffer from the consequences of idleness.

During another battle at Gob, Sibbechai the Hushathite killed Saph, also one of the sons of the Philistine giant from Gath (v. 18; 1 Chron. 11:29). During a subsequent altercation at the same location, the Bethlehemite Elhanan (23:24) killed another giant, a brother of Goliath, whose spear-shaft was like a weaver's beam (v. 19). A fourth giant from the same family had six fingers and six toes and was killed at Gath by David's nephew Jonathan, the son of Shimea (vv. 20-21).

It is possible that Goliath had four brothers who were the sons of one giant residing at Gath and that all were then slain by David or by his near-relatives (v. 22). As the Hebrew word *Rapha* is used to represent the father of these five giants, it may be that all five were merely descendants of the Rephaite family at Gath and may not be direct siblings. Regardless, they were all remnants of the aboriginal Canaanite giants discovered by Joshua previously and driven out of Hebron by Caleb (Josh. 11:22, 15:14). Their demise fulfilled the prophetic analogy of David taking five stones from the brook on the day he slew Goliath over thirty years earlier (1 Sam. 17:40). Truly, God enables those who will stand as His pilgrims on the victorious ground of Calvary to be triumphant in the land of giants!

Meditation

He who would valiant be against all disaster,
Let him in constancy follow the Master.
There's no discouragement shall make him once relent,
His first avowed intent to be a pilgrim.

Who so beset him round with dismal stories
Do but themselves confound – his strength the more is.
No foes shall stay his might; though he with giants fight,
He will make good his right to be a pilgrim.

Since, Lord, Thou dost defend us with Thy Spirit,
We know we, at the end, shall life inherit.
Then fancies flee away! I'll fear not what men say,
I'll labor night and day to be a pilgrim.

— John Bunyan (from
Pilgrim's Progress)

Praise to God
2 Samuel 22

David's song of thanksgiving for God's deliverance recorded here follows closely to Psalm 18, with a few variations. The timing of the poem is not stated, but H. L. Rossier concludes that it "historically belongs at the beginning of 2 Samuel 7 but is placed here because the last enemy of David and of his people has just been defeated (21:21)."[150]

Portions of this text are quoted in the New Testament and applied to Christ (e.g., Rom. 15:9; Heb. 2:13). God chose to use this inspired poem about David's God-enabled triumphs over death and the grave to wonderfully foreshadow Christ's future victory over the same, but after death. Paul describes the great spiritual battle that occurred at Christ's resurrection:

> *What is the exceeding greatness of His power toward us who believe, according to the working of His mighty power which He worked in Christ when He raised Him from the dead and seated Him at His right hand in the heavenly places, far above all principality and power and might and dominion, and every name that is named, not only in this age but also in that which is to come. And He put all things under His feet, and gave Him to be head over all things to the church, which is His body, the fullness of Him who fills all in all (Eph. 1:19-23).*

This poem is meant to draw our attention beyond David's victories over his enemies to the time when the most terrible conflict raged about the tomb of Christ. All the powers of hell were against the resurrection of Christ, but God overcame all opposition to raise His Son from the dead and to highly exalt Him on His throne. C. H. Mackintosh comments on this prophetic imagery within David's exaltation:

What language is here! Where shall we find anything to equal it? The wrath of the Omnipotent, the thunder of His power, the convulsion of creation's entire framework, the artillery of Heaven – all these ideas, so glowingly set forward here, outstrip all human imagination. The grave of Christ was the center round which the battle raged in all its fierceness, for there lay the Prince of life. Satan did his utmost; he brought all the power of hell to bear, all "the power of darkness," but he could not hold his captive, because all the claims of justice had been met. The Lord Jesus triumphed over Satan, death, and hell, in strict conformity with the claims of righteousness. This is the sinner's joy, the sinner's peace. It would avail nothing to be told that God over all, blessed forever, had vanquished Satan, a creature of His own creation. But to be told that He, as man's representative, as the sinner's substitute, as the Church's surety, gained the victory, this, when believed, gives the soul ineffable peace, and this is just what the gospel tells us![151]

David begins by expressing his love for the Lord and declaring what the Lord is to him: his Rock, Fortress, Refuge, Shield, Stronghold, and Horn of Salvation (vv. 1-3). David exclaims with joyful praise to the Lord, *"My Savior, You save me from violence."* All the king's experiences had taught him that there was only one thing to do in desperate circumstances – *"call upon the Lord, who is worthy to be praised"* (v. 4). Only the Lord could completely deliver David from his enemies.

In verses 5-20, David poetically describes how he was in the clutches of death many times, but the Lord had intervened and delivered him from his enemies. He lyrically describes his anguish as one surrounded by canopies of darkness and in the sorrows of Sheol, the snare of death (v. 6).

As previously mentioned, the Hebrew word *sheol* is rendered "pit," "grave," or "hell" throughout the Old Testament. It is the equivalent of the Greek word *hades*, used in the New Testament. In Luke 16, we learn that this spiritual domain secures disembodied spirits in one of two compartments: Abraham's Bosom where faithful souls await Christ's resurrection unto life, and a place of torment where the wicked continue to wait for their resurrection to stand before the Lord at the Great White Throne. Their eternal punishment in the Lake of Fire will follow.

Not having divine revelation on the topic of heaven, Old Testament saints, like David, hoped to enjoy God's presence on the earth after escaping the cold confines of Sheol through resurrection (e.g., Job 19:26; Dan. 12:2). Old Testament saints understood that death was unavoidable and that beyond the grave their souls would be sequestered in a spiritual abode called Sheol. The Lord spoke of this place during His earthly sojourn: redeemed souls were consciously residing in Abraham's bosom, while the wicked were suffering in Hades (Luke 16:19-31). The realm of Abraham's bosom was emptied after Christ's resurrection (Matt. 27:52; 2 Cor. 5:8).

Though not afraid of death itself, David was not too enthusiastic about the finality of death or his future stay in Sheol: *"The sorrows of Sheol surrounded me; the snares of death confronted me"* (v. 6; Ps. 18:5). Yet, he rejoiced and hoped in his future resurrection from Sheol in a new body:

Therefore my heart is glad, and my glory rejoices; my flesh also will rest in hope. For You will not leave my soul in Sheol, nor will You allow Your Holy One to see corruption (Ps. 16:9-10; also Ps. 86:13).

David is still waiting for his new resurrected body. His earlier body did see corruption in the grave, but the body of Jesus Christ, of whom David spoke prophetically, did not; He was raised from the grave after three days. This event not only fulfilled David's words, but also indicates his hope for a future resurrection. This is why Old Testament saints do not speak about dying and going to heaven – that is a mystery not revealed until the New Testament, as a result of Christ's finished work at Calvary (2 Cor. 5:8; Phil. 1:23). There is a day coming when the redeemed dead shall receive glorified bodies and shall stand with the restored nation of Israel to sing songs of praise to their Redeemer – the Lord Jesus Christ. May God guard our hearts and minds with His perfect peace until we are with Him forever.

Having said this, the gravity of what Sheol meant to the Jew graphically illustrates how keenly David felt the sorrow and torment of being constantly threatened by his foes. However, the Lord chose to rescue David from his adversaries and David suggests the reason in verse 21: *"The Lord rewarded me according to my righteousness; according to the cleanness of my hands He has recompensed me."* David firmly believed that God honors those who humbly walk in His ways and refrain from the filth of the world, and that He also opposes the arrogant and perverse (vv. 21-28). David felt he had received the Lord's help because he had walked in righteousness and maintained his integrity; he had clean hands before the Lord.

The panoramic view of all God's goodness prompted David to praise God for His faithfulness and to thank Him for all His splendid benefits (vv. 29-51). Because David knew God was his Lamp, Strength, Rock, Shield, and Tower of Salvation, he was able to overcome his enemies and trample them under his feet. With a thankful heart the king exclaims, *"The Lord lives! Blessed be my Rock! Let God be exalted, the Rock of my salvation!"* (v. 47).

David's song began with allusion to the horrific warfare associated with Calvary and Christ's tomb, but concludes with suggestions of Christ's coming kingdom. The king writes, *"the foreigners submit to me"* (v. 45), *"I will give thanks to You, O Lord, among the Gentiles"* (v. 50), and God *"shows mercy to His anointed, to David and his descendants forevermore"* (v. 51). This prophetic song begins at the foot of Christ's cross and concludes with His blessed kingdom. Christ's own example is a pattern that those who are His must follow – suffering precedes glory! Paul understood this truth and marveled at its outcome: *"I consider that the sufferings of this present time are not worthy to be compared with the glory which shall be revealed in us"* (Rom. 8:18). Christ was victorious over death, hell, and the devil himself, in order that those who choose Him as Lord and Savior might be with Him in glory forever!

During a turbulent time in David's life, he once wrote: *"I would hasten my escape from the windy storm and tempest"* (Ps. 55:8). It is not natural for us to crave threatening circumstances or to desire ongoing pain; David wanted to flee from the storm that was pursuing him. However, at the end of his life, David could write, *"God is my strength and power, and He makes my way perfect"* (v. 33). God could make David's way perfect because God's way is perfect (v. 31). Despite the many hardships he had endured, David had learned that God's way and God's word are perfect! May we also rest in that same eternal reality and long for Christ's coming glory.

Meditation

Off the west coast of Scotland lies a small group of islands called the Hebrides. Between 1949 and 1952 a great revival swept through these islands in answer to the prayers of God's people. Instrumental in this revival was the evangelist Duncan Campbell. He came to the Isle of Lewis to conduct a two-week evangelistic campaign, but stayed two years because of the ongoing revival. The following is one of many accounts of the power of intercessory prayer during this mighty movement of God which swept thousands of souls into His kingdom.

In a small cottage by the roadside in the village of Barvas lived two elderly women, Peggy and Christine Smith. They were eighty-four and eighty-two years old. Peggy was blind and her sister was almost bent double with arthritis. Unable to attend public worship, their humble cottage became a sanctuary where they met with God to pray for revival. They also excited various elders and deacons to commit extended times in prayer to usher in the forthcoming revival. One night several men that were praying in a barn experienced a foretaste of coming blessing. A young deacon rose and read part of the twenty-fourth Psalm: *"Who shall ascend into the hill of the Lord? Or who shall stand in His holy place? He that hath clean hands and a pure heart; who hath not lifted up his soul unto vanity, nor sworn deceitfully. He shall receive the blessing from the Lord."* Turning to the others he said: "Brethren, it seems to me just so much humbug to be waiting and praying as we are, if we ourselves are not rightly related to God." Then lifting his hands toward heaven he cried: "Oh God, are my hands clean? Is my heart pure?" He got no further, but fell prostrate to the floor. An awareness of God filled the barn and a stream of supernatural power was let loose in their lives. They had moved into a new sphere of God-realization, believing implicitly in the promise of revival.[152]

May we all ponder David's testimony of the divine power available when God's people lift clean, open hands heavenward and expect the Lord to come down in power to revive what is near death and to deliver those ensnared by spiritual darkness. *"Sow for yourselves righteousness; reap in mercy; break up your fallow ground, for it is time to seek the Lord, till He comes and rains righteousness on you"* (Hos. 10:12).

Last Words and Mighty Men
2 Samuel 23

The Mighty Messiah (vv. 1-7)

David, *the anointed of the God of Jacob*, wrote at least 73 of the 150 songs in Psalms. The first seven verses in this chapter contain the final inspired poem of *"the sweet psalmist of Israel."* The NIV renders this portion of text as *"the man anointed by the God of Jacob, Israel's singer of songs"* (v. 1). In other words, David was the lovely one whom God enabled to sing Israel's songs of praise to Him. We know from the first two chapters of 1 Kings that David lived a short time after penning these "last words" in order to seat Solomon on Israel's throne. Hence, we understand the phrase in verse 1 to refer to David's last *official* words.

The Holy Spirit inspired David to write his songs, but verse 3 seems to indicate that the Rock of Israel spoke directly to David concerning the future of his family. The Lord told David that the ideal king for His people would be perfectly just and would rule in utter awe and reverence for the Lord (v. 3). When such a ruler reigned in Israel, it would be like a morning without clouds, such that the sun would reflect its radiance in every direction off the shimmering dew-soaked grass (v. 4).

When the "Light of the World" does return to the earth, all will see the radiance of His divine beauty, His moral excellence, and His immense goodness. Christ's glory will shine out everywhere and will especially be reflected in His saints. Isaiah informs us that during the Kingdom Age a faithful remnant of the Jewish nation will be restored to Jehovah, and His light will reflect through Israel as a beacon to draw the nations to Jerusalem to worship:

> *Arise, shine; for your light has come! And the glory of the Lord is risen upon you. For behold, the darkness shall cover the earth, and deep darkness the people; but the Lord will arise over you, and His glory will be seen upon you. The Gentiles shall come to your light, and kings to the brightness of your rising* (Isa. 60:1-3).

David realized that he was not the king God was speaking about, but rejoiced in God's eternal covenant that ensured that One of his descendants would be. He would properly order all things to make His people secure and to bless them with much increase (v. 5). The coming Messiah would judge the sons of rebellion and would eliminate all unrighteousness from His glorious kingdom (vv. 6-7).

The king's "last words" give us a delightful pattern to follow: David does not hide his shortcomings, error, and failures, or the painful consequences of such, but his heart is overcome with joyful thoughts of the coming kingdom. None of us is perfect in deed or thought, but the more our hearts are filled with the glory of Christ, the more our consciences will be unhindered to serve Him!

David's Mighty Men (vv. 8-39)

At the end of his reign, David lists the men who had contributed most to his kingdom; there is a parallel (almost identical) account in 1 Chronicles 11:10-47. Missing from the list is David's nephew Joab who was over the king's army for much of his forty-year reign and was indeed a valiant warrior. Notwithstanding, his name is obviously missing because he killed Absalom and murdered Abner and Amasa. Although David did not punish Joab during his lifetime, Solomon will heed his father's instructions and put Joab to death after he becomes Israel's next king (1 Kgs. 2:5-6, 28-34).

In listing the names of his faithful warriors, David divided them into three classes. The three mightiest are listed first (Josheb-Basshebeth, Eleazar, and Shammah), then the second class (Abishai and Benaiah) and then the third class, "the thirty," over whom Asahel was chief.

The first three of David's mighty men are listed in verses 8-12 and are given special recognition above the others: The Eznite, Josheb-Basshebeth (also called Adino), who slew eight hundred (this number may be three hundred, per 1 Chron. 11:11) men at one time with a spear. Eleazar, the Ahohite, continued slaying the Philistines after his fellow soldiers retreated. When his comrades later returned to strip the slain of valuables, they found Eleazar still gripping his sword; apparently because of weariness his cramped muscles could not let it loose. Shammah, the Hararite, stood alone in a field of lentils and fought the Philistines with a great slaughter.

David then tells a story of three of his mighty men who came to him while he was encamped in the cave of Adullam fighting the Philistines located in the Valley of Rephaim (vv. 13-17). Although David resided in many caves during his fugitive and military years, the book of Samuel records only two specific caves: Adullam directly after escaping from the King of Gath (1 Sam. 22:1; Ps. 56), and at Engedi a few months later when David spared Saul's life (1 Sam. 24:1-3). David took refuge again in the cave at Adullam years later during the military campaign that is discussed in 1 Samuel 5 and 1 Chronicles 11.

The Philistines either had control of David's hometown of Bethlehem or were well-positioned between David and Bethlehem. The king casually expressed his longing for a drink of water from the well in Bethlehem (i.e., he did not intend for anyone to take his request seriously). Three men did hear David and desired to please their king. Without conferring with their commander, and at great risk to themselves, they broke through enemy lines, drew water from the well in Bethlehem and brought it to David.

The king was so overcome by this immense gesture of loyalty that he poured the water out on the ground as a sacrifice to the Lord – it cost too much to drink and thus was deemed a worthy offering. Perhaps David also felt foolish for uttering vain words of an indulgent nature that risked the lives of his highly esteemed men. In either case, David would not gratify his palate knowing the peril that his soldiers had placed themselves in to retrieve the fresh water. Commenting on this story Blaikie Williams writes:

> Those who live close to the Lord Jesus hear the longings of His heart for draughts of love from Africa and India and China; and, like these three mighty men, they turn their backs on home and wealth, and risk or lay down their lives to win for Christ the affection and service of nations held as hopelessly in the power of Satan as the well of Bethlehem was in the hands of the Philistines.[153]

David then names two more illustrious warriors in verses 18-23. Abishai, Joab's brother, was apparently the commander of the three men just mentioned. On one occasion, he lifted up his spear and slew three hundred opponents. Abishai was the one who, in holy zeal, wanted to slay both David's nemeses, Saul and Shimei, but was prevented from doing so by David. Benaiah, the son of Jehoiada, killed two lion-like warriors from Moab, slew a lion in a pit on a snowy day, and killed an Egyptian with his own spear (he having only a staff). David appointed Benaiah over his guard. These two men were more honorable than those listed next, but yet did not attain to the outstanding status of the first three mentioned in verses 8-12.

The remaining "thirty" (or thirty-seven) mighty men are then listed in verses 24-39. William MacDonald explains the numbering nuances in this section:

> Some numbers in this chapter need to be explained, such as the thirty chiefs (vv. 13, 24), the thirty-seven (v. 39), etc. The thirty may have been an elite military group, but counting all those who had served in it at one time or another, the total was thirty-seven. There were three in the first group: Josheb-Basshebeth (or Adino), Eleazar, and Shammah (vv. 8-12). Two were in the second group: Abishai and Benaiah (vv. 18-23). In the third group (vv. 24-39), the number "thirty" may have been a technical term, like "the twelve" for the apostles, even if one or more were not always there. It could also be quite literal, but the extra men beyond thirty may have been replacements for those who died in battle, such as Uriah the Hittite, the last valiant man in the list and Bathsheba's husband.[154]

David rejoiced to honor the names of those men who had hazarded their lives to bravely serve him: Asahel, Elhanan, Shammah, Elika, Helez, Ira, Abiezer, Mebunnai, Zalmon, Maharai, Heleb, Ittai, Benaiah, Hiddai, Abi-Albon, Azmaveth, Eliahba, Jonathan, Shammah, Ahiam, Eliphelet, Eliam, Hezrai, Paarai, Igal, Bani, Zelek, Naharai, Ira, Gareb, and Uriah.

At the judgment seat of Christ, the Lord Jesus will likewise honor all who have honored Him with their lives (Rom. 14:10-12; 1 Cor. 3:11-15; 2 Cor. 5:10). Our wonderful Savior does not forget any act done in His name that is accomplished in His power! Matthew Henry reminds us that faithfulness to Christ will be rewarded more than any honor that David could bestow on his devoted mighty men:

Christ, the Son of David, has his worthies too, who like David's, are influenced by His example, fight His battles against the spiritual enemies of His kingdom, and in His strength are more than conquerors. Christ's apostles were His immediate attendants, did and suffered great things for Him, and at length came to reign with Him. They are mentioned with honor in the New Testament, as these in the Old (as especially seen in Rev. 21:14). Nay, all the good soldiers of Jesus Christ have their names better preserved than even these worthies have, for they are written in heaven. This honor have all His saints.[155]

Chapters 22 and 23 show us that David greatly appreciated two things at the end of his life: the faithfulness of God and the devotion of his faithful servants. Let us remember that the Lord Jesus, whom David often typifies, appreciates the same.

Meditation

Soldiers of Christ, arise, and put your armor on,
Strong in the strength which God supplies through His eternal Son;
Strong in the Lord of hosts and in His mighty power,
Who in the strength of Jesus trusts is more than conqueror.

Stand then in His great might, with all His strength endued,
And take, to aid you in the fight, the panoply of God.
From strength to strength go on, wrestle and fight and pray;
Tread all the powers of darkness down and win the well-fought day.

— Charles Wesley

David Numbers Israel
2 Samuel 24

It was proper for David to specially honor those who had bravely fought with him in battle, but it was inappropriate for him to number the tribes of Israel. God had prospered Israel as He deemed appropriate – that was His business alone and a matter in which David could have no boast. Men normally count their assets to either boast in what they have or to stir up lust for what they perceive they need. Yet, at this moment, every child of God has what God wants them to have, else they would have more or less than what they presently possess. Gloating over God's blessings is not the same as resting in His sufficiency!

The following story is also recorded in 1 Chronicles 21 and likely occurred shortly after David had taken Jerusalem from the Jebusites (chp. 5), but before he erected a new tabernacle in Jerusalem and moved the Ark there (chp. 6). It is quite possible that the "again" in verse 1 relates to God's judicial three-year famine in chapter 21 (relating to Saul's slaughter of the Gibeonites). If so, the events in this chapter would fall on the heels of the three-year famine and would have occurred in the first half of David's reign.

The tenor of the passage also affirms this supposition, as the most advantageous opportunity to arouse David's pride would have been when his kingdom was approaching its apex, not after he had learned the immense consequences of personal sin and had been humbled by repeated revolts. If these assumptions are correct, David would have been in his forties, not his late sixties, when the events of this chapter unfolded. The numbering of Israel then would have occurred just a few years before David's sin with Bathsheba.

David Numbers Israel (vv. 1-9)

In verse 1 we learn that God's anger was aroused against His people, but no particular offense is mentioned. Given the rapid expansion of David's kingdom, they may have been glorying in their king or in their progress. Regardless of what the sin was, the Lord sought a means of reacquainting His people with His awesome, holy character and so instigated a situation which predetermined that David would number Israel and Judah.

Alfred Barnes notes that the Hebrew text literally reads, "For one moved David against them."[156] The "one" is not identified, but would be someone who opposed the interests of David and Israel, and would urge the king to number the people. James informs us that God entices no one to sin, for that would be against His character (Jas. 1:13). Rather, God permits the devil (who is more than happy to tempt men to sin against God) to do so, in order that God's sovereign purposes may be accomplished.

With this understanding and the information found elsewhere in Scripture, William MacDonald explains what occurred:

> We learn from 1 Chronicles 21:1 that it was Satan who moved David to take a census of Israel and Judah. Satan *precipitated* it, David *performed* it (because of the pride in his heart), and God *permitted* it. The Septuagint rendering of verse 1 reads "and Satan moved David" rather than "and He moved David."[157]

David ordered Joab to conduct a nationwide census, but Joab rebuffed the idea: *"Now may the Lord your God add to the people a hundred times more than there are, and may the eyes of my lord the king see it. But why does my lord the king desire this thing?"* (v. 3). For a carnal man, Joab's insight into the offense of numbering Israel is remarkable; in fact, this is one of the wisest statements of Joab recorded in Scripture. He understood that since David gave no explanation for numbering Israel the command was motivated by pride and vanity and would have dire consequences.

In the Ancient Near East, a census was often a precursor to war, so perhaps David had intentions of expanding his empire beyond God's designs. Or the king may have been tempted to trust in the numbers of his soldiers instead of the Lord for Israel's security. No matter what David's specific wrong motive was, Joab knew that all the soldiers on the planet could not offset God's fury.

Nevertheless, David would not heed Joab's or his captain's objections in the matter and they departed to perform the census (v. 4).

Moses numbered the men twenty years old and upwards after the Exodus in order to validate the number of souls to be ransomed; each man paid a half shekel of silver to the Levitical treasury to affirm their redemption (Ex. 30:12, 38:26). A second numbering occurred in Numbers 1 to determine the number of men able to go to war. Just before entering Canaan thirty-nine years later, Moses again numbered the people in order to determine tribal allotments of land in Canaan (Num. 26). Each of these historical censuses were commanded by the Lord for specific purposes, but there was no such command or need for a census in David's time. The ransom money had already been paid, the army was established, and the land allotments had been received.

It took Joab and his captains nine months and twenty days to number all the Jews from Dan to Beersheba in Canaan and those residing in the Transjordan (vv. 5-8). Joab began in the Transjordan and then moved counterclockwise through Canaan, stopping at each town to register the inhabitants. Joab returned to Jerusalem and gave the tally to David: *"there were in Israel eight hundred thousand valiant men who drew the sword, and the men of Judah were five hundred thousand men"* (v. 9).

The numbers here are approximations rather than exact figures. In 1 Chronicles 21 the tally for Judah is more precisely stated at 470,000, but Israel's total of 1.1 million is well above the figure of 800,000 in this chapter. The discrepancy is explained if David's standing army of 288,000 men (1 Chron. 27:1-15) is added to the 800,000 men associated with Israel. In other words, because those in David's standing army had already been numbered off, they did not need to be counted again, and since David already knew their number, Joab did not include them in the 1 Samuel 24 tally.

The Judgment on David's Sin (vv. 10-17)

As soon as David heard the number, his conscience condemned him and he called upon the Lord, *"I have sinned greatly in what I have done; but now, I pray, O Lord, take away the iniquity of Your servant, for I have done very foolishly"* (v. 10). The Lord responded to David's prayer of confession by sending the prophet Gad to him the next morning with a message (v. 11). Gad presented the Lord's determination on the matter to the king. David was to choose one of three punishments: seven years of famine, three month's oppression by Israel's enemies, or three days of pestilence (vv. 12-13).

David was in great distress – as Israel's king, he understood that his sin would have grave consequences for the entire Jewish nation. Having already experienced God's abundant mercy, David chose the pestilence under the hand of God, rather than to suffer by the hand of man (i.e., his enemies). The Lord then sent a plague throughout Israel. It apparently began in the outskirts of Israel and then moved towards Jerusalem and resulted in seventy thousand deaths (v. 15). This is the most destructive plague ever recorded in Scripture against Israel. During Korah's rebellion against Moses' leadership and God's ordained priesthood, 14,400 died (Num. 16:49). At Baal Peor, 24,000 died by pestilence because of idolatry (Num. 25:9). Whatever the unnamed sin was that had angered the Lord, we gain a sense that it was horrendous.

God's judgment from our standpoint seems extreme – seventy thousand deaths because of the king's pride? But, let us remember that David is Israel's king, and that God absolutely hates pride (Prov. 6:17) and that a proud king stimulates the same in those he rules over. The stubborn attitude in question was also deeply ingrained in David, for at any time in nine months he could have stopped the census, but he did not. Additionally, we must remember that the larger emphasis at this juncture was God's anger already kindled against Israel (v. 1). So, although it was David's sin that opened the floodgates of wrath, the people as a whole had fully contributed to the deluge.

Just as the destroying angel was preparing to raze Jerusalem, the Lord commanded the angel, *"It is enough; now restrain your hand"* (v. 16). This pause in judgment would permit the opportunity for human intercession and the intervention of divine mercy. The angel, with sword still unsheathed, then took up a position over Jerusalem above the threshing floor of Araunah the Jebusite. This was Mount Moriah, the historical site where Abraham was set to offer Isaac a millennium earlier (Gen. 22:2).

After seeing the angel, David pleaded with the Lord, *"Surely I have sinned, and I have done wickedly; but these sheep, what have they done? Let Your hand, I pray, be against me and against my father's house"* (v. 17). David knew his God to be characterized by mercy as well as justice, and therefore he was wise to put his trust in the Lord and then to intercede for the people, even if it meant his own demise.

God appreciated David's comprehension of His character and his desire to mediate on behalf of others. In response, the Lord sent the prophet Gad to inform David of the appropriate means of atoning for his sin.

The Altar on the Threshing Floor (vv. 18-25)

Gad immediately came to David and commanded him to erect an altar to the Lord at a precise location – the threshing floor of Araunah the Jebusite (where the Angel of the Lord was positioned; v. 18). David and four of his sons went up to the threshing floor specified, and when Araunah saw them coming, he bowed before the king and inquired why he had come (vv. 19-20). David responded, *"To buy the threshing floor from you, to build an altar to the Lord, that the plague may be withdrawn from the people"* (v. 21).

Hearing what was at stake, Araunah immediately offered to give his threshing floor to David, including oxen for sacrifice, and even the threshing implements and oxen yokes as wood for a fire (v. 22). The threshing implements probably included one or more threshing sleds which were made of wood and had iron teeth (these were dragged over the harvested sheaves of grain). We learn from 1 Chronicles 21:20 that David, his sons, and Araunah (also called Ornan) did see the angel there and were exceedingly afraid.

The angel's presence with a drawn sword no doubt further compelled Araunah to want to help David in any way he could to end the plague, even if it meant giving the king everything he had (v. 23). However, the king rejected Araunah's kind offer, for the atoning sacrifice must be David's, not Araunah's. David knew that a sacrifice was not truly a sacrifice unless it cost the offerer something: *"No, but I will surely buy it from you for a price; nor will I offer burnt offerings to the Lord my God with that which costs me nothing"* (v. 24). So, David bought the threshing floor, the implements, and the oxen for fifty shekels of silver.

The king then built an altar and presented burnt offerings and peace offerings on it as commanded by the Lord. The parallel account in 1 Chronicles 21 records what happened after David called on the name of the Lord:

David built there an altar to the Lord, and offered burnt offerings and peace offerings, and called on the Lord; and He answered him from heaven by fire on the altar of burnt offering. So the Lord commanded the angel and he returned his sword to its sheath (1 Chron. 21:26-27).

God's fire meant that the Lord had accepted David's offering and heeded the prayers of His people for the land – the plague was permanently ended (v. 25). David chose to put himself in God's hand for three days and to hope in His mercy. This wonderfully typifies the three days necessary to accomplish the Lord's death, burial, and resurrection so that God could extend mercy to all who will receive His resolution of sin. Interestingly, Abraham's testing also lasted three days and then in response to Abraham's obedience, God spared Isaac from being offered on Mount Moriah (Gen. 22). Abraham's obedience proved the validity of his faith.

Apparently, David bought not only the threshing floor, oxen, and implements, but Araunah's entire property for 600 shekels of gold (1 Chron. 21:25). This would be the future site of Solomon's temple, Herod's temple, the Jewish tribulation temple, and finally the vast millennial temple which Christ will fill with His glory. In mercy, God, through the circumstances of this chapter, was marking not only the future location of His temple, but indeed the very location in which eternal propitiation for human sin would be achieved. As already typified in Isaac, Abraham's only begotten son (Heb. 11:17), God's Son, the Lord Jesus Christ, was destined to be sacrificed at this location. C. H. Mackintosh writes:

> But there was mercy in the midst of wrath. By the threshing floor of Ornan the Jebusite, the angel of the judgment sheathed his sword. *"Then the Angel of the Lord commanded Gad to say to David, that David should go up, and set up an altar unto the Lord in the threshing floor of Ornan the Jebusite."* Here then, was the place where mercy triumphed, and caused her voice to be heard above the roar of judgment. Here the blood of the victim flowed, and here the foundation of the Lord's house was laid.[158]

As the writer of Hebrews affirms, Christ is our altar, our sacrifice; only in Him can we expect to receive God's mercy and escape His wrath for sin (Heb. 10:10-13). On Araunah's (Ornan's) threshing floor God marked the exact spot on which propitiation for humanity's sin would later be achieved (1 Jn. 2:2). At Calvary, God would cause His Son, the Lord Jesus Christ, the sinless Lamb of God, to *"taste death for every man"* (Heb. 2:9). Praise the Lord for His undeserved mercy and grace found only in Christ!

Meditation

We have traced David's life and have read his final words. As a young man, David had a tender heart for God. In appreciation, the Lord drew David from the lowly occupation of tending lambs to rule over the wandering sheep of Israel. He endured years of hardship and rejection, and suffered many attempts against his life, all of which God used to enhance his character and increase his faith. In God's purposes, His anointed, the rejected and exiled king, was to have the highest station in Israel. (This wonderfully pictures Christ's own destiny.)

David had his faults and character weaknesses, but he is remembered for his tenacity in serving God and his admirable love and heartfelt praise for the Lord, as testified in so many of his psalms. As MacDonald suggests, Psalm 40 perhaps best summarizes David's life:

> *I waited patiently for the Lord;*
> *And He inclined to me,*
> *And heard my cry.*
> *He also brought me up out of a horrible pit,*
> *Out of the miry clay,*
> *And set my feet upon a rock,*
> *And established my steps.*
> *He has put a new song in my mouth –*
> *Praise to our God;*
> *Many will see it and fear,*
> *And will trust in the Lord* (Ps. 40:1-3).

Endnotes

1 T. Wilson, *What the Bible Teaches – 1 Samuel* (John Ritchie LTD, Kilmarnock, Scotland; 2015), 1 Sam. Intro.

2 J. N. Darby, *Synopsis of the Books of the Bible Vol. I – Genesis-2 Chronicles* (Stow Hill Bible and Tract Depot, Kingston on the Thames; 1949), p. 318

3 C. H. Mackintosh, *The Mackintosh Treasury* (Believers Bookshelf Inc., Beamsville, ON; 1999), p. 218

4 Peter J. Pell, Bible Class Notes – 1 Samuel (Gospel Folio Press, Grand Rapids, MI; no date), p. 11

5 John J. Stubbs, *What the Bible Teaches – Numbers* (John Ritchie LTD, Kilmarnock, Scotland; 2015), Num. 6:1

6 H. L. Rossier, *1 Samuel*, STEM Publishing; chp. 1: http://stempublishing.com/authors/rossier/1SAMUEL.html#a1

7 Albert Barnes, *Notes on the Old Testament – 1 Samuel* (Baker Book House, Grand Rapids, MI; reprinted 1851), 2:12

8 H. L. Rossier, op. cit., 1 Sam. 2

9 Samuel Ridout, *King Saul – the Man After the Flesh*, STEM Publishing: http://stempublishing.com/authors/S_Ridout/SR_Saul01.html

10 Matthew Henry, *Matthew Henry's Concise Commentary on the Whole Bible* (e-Sword, electronic version), 1 Sam. 2:11-26

11 C. Knapp, *Life and Times of Samuel the Prophet* (Loizeaux Brothers, Neptune, NJ; 1975), chp. 4

12 H. L. Rossier, op. cit., 1 Sam. 3

13 Matthew Henry, op. cit., 1 Sam. 3:11-18

14 Robert Jamieson, A. R. Fausset, and David Brown, *Jamieson, Fausset and Brown Commentary* (Electronic Database via Biblesoft; 1997), 1 Sam. 3:19

15 C. Knapp, op. cit., chp. 7

16 Peter J. Pell, op. cit., p. 42

17 William MacDonald, *Believer's Bible Commentary* (Thomas Nelson Publishers, Nashville, TN: 1989); 1 Sam. 4:1

18 C. H. Mackintosh, op. cit. , p. 222

19 Peter J. Pell, op. cit., p. 50

20 Albert Barnes, op. cit., 1 Sam. 7:1

21 Eugene H. Merrill & Dallas Theological Seminary, *The Bible Knowledge Commentary: An Exposition of the Scriptures* (Victor Books, Wheaton, IL; 1983-1985), pp. 438-439

22 Peter J. Pell, op. cit., p. 66

23 William MacDonald, op. cit., 1 Sam. 7:15-17

Endnotes

24 Josephus (*Antiq.*; 5:5:4).
25 James Vernon McGee, *Thru the Bible* Vol. 1 (Thomas Nelson Publishers, Nashville, TN; 1981), p. 215
26 C. Knapp, op. cit., chp. 8
27 Jamieson, Fausset, and Brown, op. cit., 1 Sam. 9:3
28 Samuel Ridout, op. cit., 1 Sam. 9
29 H. L. Rossier, op. cit., 1 Sam. 9
30 K. Keil and F. Delitzsch, *Keil and Delitzsch Commentary on the Old Testament: New Updated Edition* (Electronic Database via Hendrickson Publishers, Inc.; 1996), 1 Sam. 9
31 C. Knapp, op. cit., chp. 9
32 William Kelly, *Isaiah - Exposition*, Part 2, STEM Publishing; chp. 26: http://stempublishing.com/authors/kelly/1Oldtest/ISA_PT2.html#a1
33 Jamieson, Fausset, and Brown, op. cit., 1 Sam. 10:1
34 T. Wilson, op. cit., 1 Sam. 9 intro.
35 William MacDonald, op. cit., 1 Sam. 10:7-9
36 Jamieson, Fausset, and Brown, op. cit., 1 Sam. 10:8
37 Samuel Ridout, op. cit., 1 Sam. 10
38 Matthew Henry, op. cit., 1 Sam. 10:17-27
39 Matthew Henry, op. cit., 1 Sam. 12:1-5
40 C. Knapp, op. cit., chp. 12
41 H. L. Rossier, op. cit., 1 Sam. 13
42 William MacDonald, op. cit., 1 Sam. 13:2-5
43 William MacDonald, op. cit., 1 Sam. 13:10-14
44 J. N. Darby, op. cit., 1 Sam. 14
45 Essence of the Rock (May 18, 2014); website: http://christinaboerma.blogspot.com/2014/05/ [last accessed June 25, 2018], figure was modified
46 Matthew Henry, op. cit., 1 Sam. 14:16-23
47 Albert Barnes, op. cit., 1 Sam. 14:39
48 Matthew Henry, op. cit., 1 Sam. 15:10-23
49 T. Wilson, op. cit., 1 Sam. 15:14
50 C. H. Mackintosh, op. cit. , p. 227
51 C. Knapp, op. cit., chp. 14
52 H. L. Rossier, op. cit., 1 Sam. 15
53 C. H. Mackintosh, op. cit. , p. 226
54 Samuel Ridout, op. cit., 1 Sam. 15
55 William MacDonald, op. cit., 1 Sam. 15:13-35
56 C. H. Mackintosh, op. cit. , p. 228
57 J. N. Darby, op. cit., pp. 334-335
58 C. H. Mackintosh, op. cit. , p. 228
59 J. A. Motyer, op. cit., p. 121
60 William MacDonald, op. cit., 1 Sam. 16:14-23
61 Matthew Henry, op. cit., 1 Sam. 16:14-23
62 C. H. Mackintosh, op. cit., p. 236

[63] C. H. Mackintosh, op. cit., p. 239
[64] Peter J. Pell, op. cit., p. 167
[65] Matthew Henry, op. cit., 1 Sam. 18:12-30
[66] Samuel Ridout, op. cit., 1 Sam. 18
[67] Albert Barnes, op. cit., 1 Sam. 18:26
[68] H. L. Rossier, op. cit., 1 Sam. 19
[69] Peter J. Pell, op. cit., p. 175
[70] T. Wilson, op. cit., 1 Sam. 19:22
[71] Peter J. Pell, op. cit., p. 185
[72] Jamieson, Fausset, and Brown, op. cit., 1 Sam. 21:1
[73] Albert Barnes, op. cit., 1 Sam. 21:9
[74] Peter J. Pell, op. cit., pp. 190-191
[75] J. N. Darby, op. cit., pp. 340
[76] C. and A. De Rothschild, *The History and Literature of the Israelites* (Spottiswoode and Co., London, 2nd ed.; 1871), p. 360
[77] T. Wilson, op. cit., 1 Sam. 21:10-15
[78] H. L. Rossier, op. cit., 1 Sam. 21
[79] T. Wilson, op. cit., 1 Sam. 22:1-5
[80] William MacDonald, op. cit., 1 Sam. 22:20-23
[81] Samuel Ridout, op. cit., 1 Sam. 23
[82] Matthew Henry, op. cit., 1 Sam. 23:14-18
[83] C. H. Mackintosh, op. cit. , p. 245
[84] Peter J. Pell, op. cit., p. 210
[85] T. Wilson, op. cit., 1 Sam. 24:16-22
[86] Josephus (*Antiq.*; 5:5:4)
[87] C. H. Mackintosh, op. cit. , p. 247
[88] Matthew Henry, op. cit., 1 Sam. 25:32-35
[89] J. N. Darby, op. cit., p. 343
[90] Albert Barnes, op. cit., 1 Sam. 25:43
[91] Jamieson, Fausset, and Brown, op. cit., 1 Sam. 26:20
[92] Peter J. Pell, op. cit., p. 241
[93] C. H. Mackintosh, op. cit. , p. 254
[94] J. N. Darby, op. cit., p. 345
[95] Edward Dennett, Exodus, STEM Publishing; Ex. 22: http://stempublishing.com/authors/dennett/EXODUS1.html
[96] William MacDonald, op. cit., 1 Sam. 28:9-10
[97] Samuel Ridout, op. cit., 1 Sam. 28
[98] H. L. Rossier, op. cit., 1 Sam. 28
[99] Jamieson, Fausset, and Brown, op. cit., 1 Sam. 28:19
[100] K. Keil and F. Delitzsch, op. cit. 1 Sam. 29:1-5
[101] Elizabeth Fletcher, *The Witch of Endor, Saul's Medium* (2006) Website: http://www.womeninthebible.net/women-bible-old-new-testaments/witch-of-endor/ [Last accessed on June 19, 2018]
[102] H. L. Rossier, op. cit., 1 Sam. 29
[103] Samuel Ridout, op. cit., 1 Sam. 29

[104] J. N. Darby, op. cit., p. 346

[105] Matthew Henry, op. cit., 1 Sam. 30:7-20

[106] Peter J. Pell, op. cit., p. 258

[107] C. H. Mackintosh, op. cit. , p. 258

[108] Adam Clarke, Adam Clarke's Commentary, Electronic Database. Copyright (c) 1997 by Biblesoft; 1 Sam. 31:4

[109] H. L. Rossier, op. cit., 1 Sam. 31

[110] H. L. Rossier, *2 Samuel*, STEM Publishing; chp. 1: http://stempublishing.com/authors/rossier/2SAMUEL.html#a1

[111] Matthew Henry, op. cit., 2 Sam 2:25-32

[112] T. Wilson, *What the Bible Teaches – 2 Samuel* (John Ritchie LTD, Kilmarnock, Scotland; 2015), 2 Sam. 2

[113] H. L. Rossier, op. cit., 2 Sam. 2

[114] T. Wilson, op. cit., 2 Sam. 3:22-30

[115] Albert Barnes, op. cit., 2 Sam. 4:2

[116] Jamieson, Fausset, and Brown, op. cit., 2 Sam. 5:9

[117] Adam Clarke, *Adam Clarke's Commentary* (Electronic Database; 1996 by Biblesoft); 2 Sam. 5:21

[118] Albert Barnes, op. cit., 2 Sam. 6:3

[119] T. Wilson, op. cit., 2 Sam. 6:1-10

[120] H. L. Rossier, op. cit., 2 Sam. 6

[121] C. H. Mackintosh, op. cit. , p. 264

[122] Matthew Henry, op. cit., 2 Sam. 7:4-17

[123] C. H. Mackintosh, op. cit. , p. 269

[124] H. L. Rossier, op. cit., 2 Sam. 7

[125] C. H. Mackintosh, op. cit. , p. 271

[126] Albert Barnes, op. cit., 2 Sam. 8:2

[127] Eugene H. Merrill, op. cit. p. 465

[128] H. L. Rossier, op. cit., 2 Sam. 8

[129] T. Wilson, op. cit., 2 Sam. 9:12-13

[130] Albert Barnes, op. cit., 2 Sam. 10:4

[131] Aharoni, Avi-Yonah, Rainey, and Safrai, *The MacMillan Bible Atlas;* 3rd Edition (MacMillan by Carta; 1993), p. 78.

[132] J. N. Darby, op. cit., p. 363

[133] C. H. Mackintosh, op. cit. , p. 273

[134] Matthew Henry, op. cit., 2 Sam. 11:1-5

[135] Matthew Henry, op. cit., 2 Sam. 12:1-14

[136] H. A. Ironside, *An Ironside Expository Commentary: Ezekiel*, op. cit., p. 116

[137] William MacDonald, op. cit., 2 Sam. 12:15-23

[138] H. L. Rossier, op. cit., 2 Sam. 12

[139] T. Wilson, op. cit., 2 Sam. 14:1-23

[140] H. L. Rossier, op. cit., 2 Sam. 15

[141] Adam Clarke, op. cit., 2 Sam. 15:14

[142] Albert Barnes, op. cit., 2 Sam. 16:21

[143] Matthew Henry, op. cit., 2 Sam. 18:9-18

144 Josephus (*Antiq.*; vii. 10, 3)
145 Jamieson, Fausset, and Brown, op. cit., 2 Sam. 19:24
146 T. Wilson, op. cit., 2 Sam. 19:40-43
147 H. A. Ironside, *Proverbs* (Loizeaux Brothers, Neptune, NJ; 1995), p. 104
148 J. N. Darby, op. cit., p. 367
149 Matthew Henry, op. cit., 2 Sam. 21:15-22
150 H. L. Rossier, op. cit., 2 Sam. 22
151 C. H. Mackintosh, op. cit. , pp. 282-283
152 David Smithers, *The Intercessors of the Hebrides Revival*
     Website: http://www.evanwiggs.com/revival/history/hebpray.html [Last accessed
     on August 22, 2018]
153 Blaikie William, quoted by William MacDonald, op. cit., 2 Sam. 23:13-17
154 William MacDonald, op. cit., 2 Sam. 23:24-39
155 Matthew Henry, op. cit., 2 Sam. 23:8-39
156 Albert Barnes, op. cit., 2 Sam. 24:1
157 William MacDonald, op. cit., 2 Sam. 24:1
158 C. H. Mackintosh, op. cit. , p. 270

www.ingramcontent.com/pod-product-compliance
Lightning Source LLC
Chambersburg PA
CBHW060239100426
42742CB00011B/1585